They've Been
Down So Long…

They've Been Down So Long…

Michael E. Tolle

ISBN: 1514322013
ISBN-13: 978-1514322017

DEDICATION

This work is dedicated to the memory
of Alan "Felix" Shafer, 1951–2014

ACKNOWLEDGMENTS

I owe my largest debt, as always, to the staff of the historical societies and libraries that I visited during my research. These include, but are not limited to, the Chester County Historical Society, the Historical Society of Montgomery County, the Phoenixville Area Historical Society, the Spring-Ford Area Historical Society, and the Pottstown Historical Society. My collective thanks to them all.

I owe special thanks to Walter Greason, PhD, professor of history at Monmouth University, who served as a beta reader—and gave me higher marks than I thought I deserved. The Pottstown segments were read by Evan Brandt of the *Pottstown Mercury*, who alerted me to typos that would have rendered several statements incorrect.

Max Gordon (max@mizmaxgordon.com) is again my editor and book/cover designer; I recommend her to aspiring writers.

Finally, I must acknowledge the contributions made by those for whom this book was written and to whom the second half is dedicated: the urban activists in my eight subject towns and, by extension, in other towns just like them. They create the reality upon which I comment in this work's second half and draw upon in reaching my conclusions in this half.

CONTENTS

"LOCAL HISTORY 101"

They've Been Down So Long... can be read independently, as a self-contained work. It was designed, however, as a companion for the second half of this book, *Getting Up's Still on Their Minds*. Together the two constitute a conceptual unity, reinforcing each other in the learning experience. While it is not necessary, I recommend that you first read the Introduction to the other half to better understand how I intend the two halves of this book to complement each other. I also encourage you to go back and forth between the two as you read, as each develops themes of the other.

Urban History in Support of Urban Activism

Soul singer Bobby Womack's 1972 release "Across 110th Street," contains a line that became rather famous: "I been down so long, getting up didn't cross my mind." That lyric most probably—and the thought behind it most certainly—is much older, for it states a stark truth that is about as old as the human condition itself. This form of acceptance may even apply to entire communities, as some critics would have it.

That sentiment does not apply to the eight towns that are the subject of this book. There are residents in all eight who do not accept their fate, and who are actively striving to make the future better than the recent past. They constitute a minority in each town, to be sure, but change always originates with a minority, and change is what these people seek. This work was designed to aid them and, by extension, others in similar situations.

I am a historian, but this is not a book solely concerned with the past. My intent is to examine the past specifically as a way to improve both the present and the future. This work examines the eight towns along the lower Schuylkill River between the cities of Reading and Philadelphia. All are classic American riverside mill towns, places that have experienced in full the calamities that overtook all such towns in the decades after the Second World War. Only one of the eight has begun a community revival, but it is an outlier. Two are being transformed—taken over, actually—by the coincidence of their location. They are experiencing economic revival, but at a high cost to their traditional sense of community. The other five remain in the stagnation that began to envelop them over fifty years ago.

As a historian, I am particularly interested in why these towns' current paths have diverged after following the same historical arc for centuries. As a citizen, I am determined to put my findings to work improving those towns that remain in stagnation, and to aid those rapidly changing towns retain their community focus and pride.

The most significant fact about the history of all eight towns on the lower Schuylkill River is that, despite their variation in physical and population size (from a mere thirteen hundred inhabitants to thirty-four thousand inhabitants), their commonalities are considerably greater than their differences. All eight came into being for the same combination of reasons. All assumed the same basic layout, with the industrial, commercial, and residential sectors within walking distance from one another. All became active and prosperous after railroad lines connected them to the wider world. All became known best for their production of iron and steel, and for products made from both. All had industries that were largely manned by new immigrants that arrived in the Schuylkill Valley from the mid-nineteenth century until the onset of World War I. All eight towns grew and prospered from the nineteenth century through the first half of the twentieth century—and then all eight fell on hard times, as their industries disappeared, their commercial sectors collapsed, and many old-time residents, followed by their adult children, took advantage of the post–World War II housing boom and moved to the new automobile suburbs.

Somewhere around 1980, all eight towns reached their nadir. Then things began to change, and their historical arcs began to diverge.

This work is structured along what I consider the three fundamental realities of life along the lower Schuylkill River. This work is divided into three chronological chapters. The first chapter, "Up to the Second World War," begins by identifying and describing the three fundamental realities common to all eight towns, followed by a brief history of each of the eight towns that touches on how each community grew, as viewed through the lens of those realities.

The second chapter, "From 1945 to 1980," covers the period after the Second World War, a time that marks the first significant turning point for all eight river towns. Before World War II, the economic and social condition of all eight had risen steadily—each in its own way, subject to the economic effects of periodic hard times, but with the same overall arc upward. That began to change shortly after World War II, and the period until at least 1980 was marked by the economic and commercial collapse of the very strengths that had built each town in the first place. The second chapter follows the same structure as the first: its first half identifies how the three realities underwent their own fundamental changes during the twentieth century; its second half makes less of a distinction among the histories of each town, and focuses more on the common distress caused by these changes.

The third chapter, "After 1980," is the shortest but arguably the most important. Through the first two periods covered, the historical arcs of all eight towns remained roughly the same. At some point around 1980, they began to diverge. That date is not absolute, but it works well; its importance lies not in what happened *during* that year, but because of what took place in the years that followed, as the historical arcs branched into three broad paths. That divergence, and the differing rates of progress of each of the eight Schuylkill River towns, has only accelerated since then.

The history of post-1980 chapter is, of course, still being written in the Schuylkill Valley (as it is everywhere), and thus the focus of the third chapter is questions and hypotheses, not conclusions. The chapter first discusses the differing fates of the eight towns, and concludes with look at the *new* fundamental realities, along with some observations on how best the towns on the river can properly exploit these changed realities to improve their individual futures.

Important Things to Keep in Mind

1. This is a thematic work. In this work, I identify three fundamental realities that have shaped the eight towns on the lower Schuylkill River, lenses through which their common histories can be views. I discuss the past, present, and future of each town within these three themes, and include those events most relevant to those realities:

what people and industries drew from and dumped into the Schuylkill (and the consequences of this); the importance of bridges; and the people of those communities, as viewed through their ethnic churches and volunteer fire departments. I have included almost no politics and precious few names other than those of people who inspired each town. I conclude by discussing the opportunities—and the obstacles—these changed realities present to the river towns.

2. This is an introductory work. This is a portrait rendered in broad strokes and primary colors. When a portrait is rendered thusly, patterns are easy to discern. As the finer strokes and shades are added, the differences become more obvious, but the pattern never disappears. Differences among the eight towns exist, but they exist within the same pattern. That so many differences can exist merely demonstrates the validity of the pattern. This work focuses on those patterns, not on the individual towns themselves.

I would be pleased if my work inspires local historians to examine their towns' pasts in light of the themes and patterns I offer. But should someone be so disturbed as to write his or her work to disprove one or more of my theses, I would be more than pleased; I would be honored. A historian can ask for no higher praise than to inspire revision.

3. This is a supportive work. This book was written to provide broad guidance to urban activists in the eight towns of the study, and perhaps even to those elsewhere, in similar communities in similar circumstances. It does not so much try to explain what happened as *why*, because not just the results but also the sources of that why are still very much with us. Both the elected leaders and the urban activists of each town must absorb this central lesson of history— *things change*—together with an understanding of just what has changed and how it has done so, if they are to direct their efforts in profitable directions. They must understand a changing reality to properly confront the challenges those changes present while taking advantage of the opportunities they also offer. The past is merely prologue: it does not determine the future; it merely sets the stage. When the props on that stage have changed, the actors must adapt, and not just with dialogue.

A Note about Geography

My previous work focused on just one river town, Norristown. In that book, I could employ the terms "south bank" and "north bank" to the river. As this work deals with a substantial length of a twisty river, using all four compass directions before "bank" would lead only to confusion. This work has, therefore, adopted the following convention: employing the direction of river flow,[1] locations are identified as being either on the left bank or the right bank. Pottstown, Royersford, Norristown, and Conshohocken are on the left bank; Phoenixville, Spring City, Bridgeport, and West Conshohocken are on the right bank. Six of the towns are located in Montgomery County, and two in Chester County. As they all share the reality of the river, they are treated as a group, without regard to larger political subdivisions.

---

1. With respect to the map on the cover, the Schuylkill River flows from Reading toward Philadelphia.

CHAPTER ONE

UP TO THE SECOND WORLD WAR

This chapter, after describing the three fundamental realities common to all eight towns, provides a much-abridged history of each, touching on events and trends relating to those three realities and the role they played in the founding and evolution of the eight towns.

Three fundamental realities have always governed life along the lower Schuylkill River, determining where towns would be established, populating those towns, and connecting them to a growing industrial civilization. Their manifestations changed frequently, and until after World War II, those changes benefited each of the river towns. That is the story of this chapter.

The first fundamental reality is the river itself—the basic reason why people settled nearby in the first place and the reality that literally nourished those who followed. The second fundamental reality is transportation, which has always been, is now, and always shall be the most important reality within which the Schuylkill River towns exist. The third fundamental reality is people: who came, when they came, where they came from, and where they settled. The history of the eight river towns reflects the waves of immigrants who arrived, settled, and then received the next wave.

The interaction of these three fundamental realities produced an era of overall growth for the eight towns on the lower Schuylkill River from their founding to the middle of the twentieth century. It was uneven growth, to be sure, and always subject to the vagaries of the national economy, but overall the trend was upward. That would change dramatically in the two decades after the end of the Second World War, and few regions of the United States would suffer as fully as those very same towns.

The River

First, there was the river. Even by the time the first Native Americans first beheld it, back in the dim recesses of time, the Schuylkill River had already flowed along its course for millennia. As a greater torrent, it had etched its winding path into the land, wearing down the rock and soil to create a valley. In this way, the river actually made its greatest contribution a great many millennia ago by carving out its adjacent floodplain. By the time humans first glimpsed the river, it had reached its more-or-less stable state. That stability, and the useful land along the river's banks, was what attracted settlement.

The first humans to set eyes on the Schuylkill, the Lenape Indians, found the river unspoiled; they used it as a food source and occasionally for transportation. Their needs were few and simple, and the river could supply the most important ones. They collected the wild grains from the river's floodplain, consumed its water, and caught the fish that swam in it. A few paddled their canoes along it. The river was a part of their environment, and their largely hunter-gatherer lifestyle fit comfortably within the river's ecological balance, a balance that had existed long before the first humans' incursion.

Then the Europeans arrived. They were different. They were not nomadic—at least most of them. They came, and they stayed. They felt no compulsion to conform to the environment; they were more than willing to force it to conform to their purposes. Almost immediately after the Europeans settled in, they began to physically alter the river to suit their steadily increasing demands, exploiting it for causes other than sustenance and personal transportation. They were the first people to view its natural course as inadequate, and the first to try and "improve" its fundamental reality. For over two hundred years, the Schuylkill's shallowness and changeability bedeviled the Europeans and their American descendants and their attempts to render it into a major transportation corridor. Although they largely abandoned those efforts, they continued to exploit the river without regard to its future, and they came perilously close to destroying it.

The Schuylkill River is fed by a multitude of creeks of varying size that collectively drain what constitutes its watershed. These creeks were of great importance to the arriving Europeans for two reasons. First, they sustained agriculture along their lengths; the earliest European settlers established farms along these creeks, drawing on the water for their livestock, crops, and themselves. Second, and more important for the growth along the riverside, some of the creeks provided power.

The Europeans' earliest use of the river's floodplain was for agriculture, but that was eclipsed as a new kind of settler began to gather at specific locations along it, people essential in an agricultural world: those who did not farm, but who provided services the farm families needed. These people carved, forged, assembled, and repaired the wood and metal implements farmers needed to produce their crops and to deliver a portion of them to market.

This was the era before the Industrial Revolution, when manufacturing was a small but important endeavor usually performed by individuals or, more correctly, families. These manufacturers needed sources of power more reliable than muscle or animal power, and the creeks provided this, as creeks always have, the world over. This made the creeks that feed the river the area's primary locations for the primitive manufacturing efforts of the day.

The most important characteristic was a creek's rate of flow. Many of the creeks that empty into the Schuylkill, and even some of the runs (which, by definition, lack a year-round flow), could power the early mills, although field works—usually in the form of an artificial channel or race—were often required. Some creeks widened at their juncture with the river, and thus many early water-powered sites were initially located some distance from the Schuylkill itself, at a point where the creek's rate of flow was greater. The Manatawny Creek is an example. Independent manufactures evolved into industries established on the banks of the creeks and the river where they could take advantage of the free source of power. French Creek offered another variation: its sizeable floodplain in the stretch just before it enters the Schuylkill River was large enough to accommodate a sizeable iron industry, which spawned Phoenixville.

By contrast, Perkiomen Creek divides and meets the Schuylkill along flat land, spreading into a slowly flowing delta. Such was the fertility of the area that it very early on earned the nickname "Fatlands," a Biblical reference to the Nile delta. The area could not, however, power more than the small mills of the time. Thus, no substantial settlement took place there.

There were a great many creeks up and down the river, and all with sufficient flow were utilized in the era of local manufactures. Only a few, however, spawned towns. There was another required factor, and it points to the true significance of the Schuylkill River to its inhabitants for most of their history.

One of the least understood realities about settlements near rivers is that the most important locations have always been those where crossings were possible. For the most people within its watershed, the Schuylkill River was not a travel boon but a barrier. Great stretches of fertile and inviting land lined both banks, clearly visible to each other and yet rendered alternately inaccessible by the river between. The Schuylkill's great variability actually favored these early attempts earn a living from it. Between stretches where the river runs deep are those where it does not—locations that are shallow enough for people, horses, oxen, and wagons to cross with less fear of being swept away. These fording spots made the Schuylkill less of a barrier to communication and trade. The Native Americans had long ago located the river's best fords, the shallowest points, and the arriving Europeans took note.

Only those creeks that were of sufficient size to provide power and were located near shallow sections of the river attracted settlements, and the shallowness of the river was the more important part of the equation. These were the locations where small manufacturing overlapped with other regional specialists, not nearly so ubiquitous but equally necessary: those who aided people in crossing the river. This was the settlements' initial function, but as the numbers of people who needed to cross steadily grew, the services they offered expanded to provide food, drink, and even lodging for the traveling farmers during their journeys.

Even the best fording locations still presented considerable difficulty in crossing, and the early methods of assistance in crossing were haphazard, but the steady stream of traders and travelers encouraged the establishment of local services nearby. These were the first steps toward trade and commerce in the area. Royersford and Spring City developed at either side of a ford, as did Conshohocken and West Conshohocken. Norristown was doubly blessed, with two employable creek mouths in close proximity to a ford, the one named not for individual nearby landowners, but for an entire group of settlers, Swedes Ford. Bridgeport grew up on the other side of this ford.

Each of the Schuylkill River towns was at or near a fording location, but the fords quickly became inadequate as the region's population increased. This led to plans for bridges to allow dry crossings. The importance of bridges, both their construction and their maintenance, can be seen clearly in the histories of each town.

The very first use of the Schuylkill River by humans had been as a source of drinking water. Sources of drinkable water grew steadily in importance as the area became settled. Each town dug wells to the best of its ability, and the use of some town wells continued into the twentieth century. These soon became inadequate as sole sources—a fact that the civic leaders of the larger towns began to comprehend by the mid-nineteenth century.

As the eight locations evolved into urban areas, their rising populations soon required more water than local wells and springs could provide. Only the Schuylkill itself could deliver the necessary volume of water, and each evolving town along the river began to tap into it. They soon discovered that they would have to purify the water first, because each of the towns had been polluting the very river that drew them there. As the separate communities began to take shape along the river, waste disposal joined drinking water as a primary use for the Schuylkill. The contradiction between those two uses was only slowly recognized, and even slower in being resolved. Industry brought jobs, population, and prosperity to the river towns, but it rendered the Schuylkill into something very different from what it had been for eons. It became an "industrial river," which is essentially a euphemism for sewer.

As the problem became more and more obvious, the river towns began to take action, largely in order of their population size. Each focused on its water supply long before its waste output. Norristown began in 1847 to draw water from the Schuylkill for municipal use, but by the 1870s, river contamination had reached the point where the borough needed to lay a new main. The problem continued to get worse, and in 1901, Norristown became the first river town to build a water filtration plant.

The initial water systems built in Norristown, and then Pottstown, were the work of private companies. The smaller towns could not afford to even plan a municipal water filtration system, let alone build one; they contracted with private firms for their water supply. In future decades, the private companies would both expand and consolidate into a utility system, continuing all the time to draw water from the Schuylkill, and having to do more and more to render it drinkable.

The other equally ancient use of the river was for waste disposal. When the population was still small, this was not an issue, but the huge increase in the number of people living along the river—and their grouping close together in towns—increasingly delivered multisensory evidence of a problem. The problem had two sources: people and industry. Individuals and families dumped their waste into existing small waterways and, later, gutters made especially for that purpose. To address—superficially, at least—some of the obvious issues of having open sewers crisscrossing the area, many of these waste-removal gutters were covered over, but they were rarely constructed as part of a larger plan, and there was little, if any, record of what had been done. Future generations of both politicians and engineers would be forced to grapple with this problem, over and over again.

Regardless of efforts to conceal waste during its journey, its destination was always the same: the river. The towns along the Schuylkill River would, during their days of prosperity and expansion, continue to deposit their bodily and food wastes directly into the river, and would do so until literally forced to cease.

Industry brought with it new forms of waste dumped into the Schuylkill. Before too long, industrial waste proved to be both more plentiful and considerably more noxious than even human waste. It was, collectively, the byproducts of the industrial processes inside the buildings that came to dominate the riverside.

Some community support could be found for at least *hiding* the flow of human waste until it got to the river, despite the vexing question of how to pay for doing so, but pressure to treat industrial waste was close to nonexistent. Each river town benefited immensely from the industry within its boundaries or just outside them. The residents of each town, and their governmental representatives in particular, recognized from the start how important industry was to the fortunes of their communities. In each town, the representatives of the biggest industries held considerable sway.

But there was a more fundamental, ideological reason why industrial pollution was tolerated for so long. The financial, political, and social dominance of industry in the river valley rested on a series of assumptions about private property and the role of government in the era of laissez-faire capitalism. In adherence to that doctrine, local government officials wished to placed few if any obstacles in the way of private industry, despite accumulating evidence of the environmental and social harm that often resulted. The general population apparently supported this approach, and continued to do so for decades. Accordingly, the inflow of industrial waste into the river continued largely unabated until well into the twentieth century.

Given the dominant ethos of the time, it was left to each river town deal with the fundamental contradiction that arises from using the same source for both drinking water and waste disposal. Each tried, within its particular financial and ideological constraints, to treat this portion of the waste problem as they were treating its collection—slowly, incompletely, and intermittently. The Pennsylvania legislature passed an act in 1913 "to preserve the purity of the waters of the state for the protection of public health and property," but enforcement proved notably lacking, as did funding. This ensured that municipal sewage systems would emerge piece by piece, with solutions always lagging behind evidence of the problem itself. While collecting sewage and directing it into the river lessened the problems of individual towns, it merely sent the problems downriver.

Sewage was not the biggest threat to the river, however. An irony of Schuylkill Valley history is that the element that did the most damage to the river is the very one most responsible for the growth and development of its towns and industries: anthracite coal. The chief culprit in the gradual deterioration of the Schuylkill was "culm," the silt-like debris formed during anthracite coal production. As the coal industry expanded its output, it likewise expanded its output of culm. The coal companies simply dumped this refuse into the local streams and the river itself. The culm, washed downriver by rain and the periodic river floods, began to clog the canal sections and accumulate at the foot of each dam. The river began to silt up, and its already variable depths became shallower, which in turn increased the severity of floods. There was so much culm sent down the Schuylkill that deposits of it were soon noticeable as far downriver as Philadelphia. By 1945, culm deposits were reported in the Delaware River, both below and above its junction with the Schuylkill. This would be the target of the first major attempt at amelioration, but not until after the end of the Second World War.

Pollution also foiled early commercial attempts to provide recreation along the river. These efforts, begun in the mid-nineteenth century, were intended to exploit a new phenomenon that prosperity and the Industrial Revolution brought to the nation, including the residents of the Schuylkill Valley. Today we refer to it as "leisure time." For time first time, too, it was not just the very rich who found themselves with at least come disposable income—money left after paying for life's necessities.

Leisure time and spending money spurred the development of recreational areas, including along the river. Private use of the river for short pleasure journeys was nothing new, of course, but now entrepreneurs saw the profit potential in providing this seemingly large market with various means to enjoy the river, individually, as couples, and in groups. The pools above the old dams were the most suitable locations. Norristown's Barbadoes Island, just above the dam, offered boat rentals, outing and picnics. Until just after the turn of the century, steamboats carried day travelers and picnickers to the island, as well as to Phoenixville, from a dock in Norristown. This service did not last, however. By the early decades of the twentieth century, the atrocious condition of the river caused organized recreation usage to dwindle to almost nothing. Large-scale recreational use of the Schuylkill would not return until after the Second World War.

The first European settlers encountered the Schuylkill River in its original, pristine condition, flowing as it had for millennia, and hosting an abundance of water creatures and wildlife. By the end of the nineteenth century, their descendants had all but destroyed it. Its employment for waste disposal had killed its aquatic life, and the river itself was clogged with coal culm and the noxious waste of many other industries. This deplorable condition continued through the

Second World War, although concerned activists had gotten some laws passed and made plans to deal with the long-obvious problem. Funding from the New Deal's Works Progress Administration (and "cease and desist" orders from the Commonwealth of Pennsylvania) began to reverse some of them damage, addressing the water quality issues that afflicted the river. Some municipalities along the river made small improvements as they were forced to deal with their contributions to the river's condition. Still, no effective, comprehensive action occurred until after the Depression and the Second World War, with plans deferred as with so many other dreams and hopes. After the war, the work of cleansing the region's historical backbone finally began in earnest. These efforts would transform the nature of the river, steadily rendering it once again suitable for human use.

Transportation

The basic transportation needs of early Americans helped to determine which settlements on the river would remain and grow into towns. The evolution of each town was due to successive transportation innovations, each serving to better connect the towns to sources of raw materials for their growing industries and markets for their manufactured goods. From the time of their foundings to the present, the economic and social history of the Schuylkill River towns has always been based on their relationship to the dominant mode of transportation of the times: first, the river and its fords, the early trails; then the rough roads; then the addition of the canals, dams, and locks of the Schuylkill Navigation System; then the railroads; and, most recently, the highways. Each town's connections to other towns nourished its continued, if uneven, growth and development.

Transportation among the river towns assumed successive forms during their history, but the layout and density of each town were the result of the oldest form of transportation: walking. The central organizational force shaping the river towns was that initially, and for a very long time, almost everyone in town had to walk to work, to shop, to attend school, and to worship. As a result, a standard pattern emerged in the Schuylkill River towns. The industries existed along the floodplain, all connected by the railroad. Housing for the workers was built as close as was practical to the industrial sector, with each dwelling as close as possible to the next. The few shops meshed into a commercial sector, which was adjacent to both the industrial and the compact residential neighborhoods.

In the early days of each town, leaders built their residences near to both their businesses and their employees, because the laid-out and structured portions of each town were compact. As each town's industrial and commercial sectors expanded, so did the areas subject to the increasing heat, dirt, and noise, not to mention the presence of a large number of people. Thus, as each town's settled area expanded, it developed a clear residential demarcation of wealth. Only the very poor—the day laborers, migrants, the infirm, and bums—lived along the river. Industry, the railroad, and the lack of sewage treatment combined to make every town's riverfront into a scene out of Dante's *Inferno*. They were crowded, hot, filthy, smelly, and, above all, noisy, as the forges and hammers provided the constant backbeat.

The core of each town became increasingly unacceptable to subsequent generations of the wealthier residents, industrial and commercial leaders began building their increasingly ornate mansions farther away from the sources of their wealth. Those residents who were neither the highest nor the lowest on the social scale filled in the areas between the two extremes, moving into or building new residences that were as far away from the stinking, noisy riverside as their financial condition would allow. The brief flowering of light rail brought this pattern to its ultimate stage, as it allowed the developing middle class to physically separate itself from those who worked with their hands by the hour. As each of the eight river towns except Pottstown is located on one or more hills that rise up from the floodplain, elevation joined distance in this demarcation of status.

Most people walked within each town, and many had no choice but to walk between towns, too. Anyone who wanted to carry a load of any size over longer distances needed at least a horse or a mule, and preferably a wagon to pull. Wagons required roads, at least rudimentary ones. The Lenape had carved out many trails across the region, just as they had identified the Schuylkill's fordable locations, and these became the foundation of the network of roads that the European immigrants gradually developed in the Delaware Valley.

While the Europeans' desire for cleared, direct roads was much greater than that of the Lenape, their means to do so were not greatly superior; the first roads were not so much built as simply worn down. This lack of both planning and engineering, together with the highly variable weather of southeastern Pennsylvania, frequently rendered the early American roads impassable even in the warm months, and almost constantly so during the winter.

Nevertheless, these primitive, execrable tracks were all that existed, and thus they were of considerable importance for the movement of both people and goods, although largely for short distances. After the colonies gained independence, the burden of road construction and maintenance legally fell on the local people, and they generally lacked both the expertise and the substantial financing required. Communities often used work gangs for local road development and repairs largely. Untrained, unequipped, and unmotivated, these road gangs accomplished little of substance.

The main roads fared better. A handful of heavily traveled roads connected Philadelphia to other important cities, spreading out in a fan shape, from north to south. One, heading northwest from Philadelphia, became known as the "Ridge Road." Actually a collection of separately constructed segments, Ridge Road largely followed the high ground along the left bank of the river. Its route along the ridge of the Schuylkill Valley meant it passed through or near the population nodules on the left bank. Ridge Road gradually reached as far as Pottstown (where it was called the "Great Road") and eventually extended to Reading. By the time of the Revolution, you could travel from Philadelphia to Reading by stagecoach in a single, if very long, day—provided the weather and everything else cooperated.

From the late eighteenth century through the first third of the nineteenth century, the settled areas of America experienced what is known as the "First Turnpike Era." This period was characterized by the establishment of private companies that received charters from the state to construct and maintain a stretch of road. The roads took many forms, according to the local prevailing conditions, but the first turnpikes were the first engineered roads in the United States. The turnpike companies earned back their investment and construction costs by charging people to use the road. Passage at a toll station would be blocked by a long pole (called a "pike" after the weapon it resembled) extended horizontally across the road. When the toll was paid, toll operator turned the pike aside to allow vehicle entrance. The Lancaster Turnpike Company, organized in 1792, built Pennsylvania's first such road, which extended west from Philadelphia. By 1830, two hundred twenty private turnpike companies had received state charters, but Pennsylvania's record of achievement in actually constructing new roads during this period was decidedly mixed, for reasons usually having to do with insufficient capital and underestimated expenses. Several roads were never even begun, and many more were never completed, as bankruptcies often overtook the chartered companies.

Even those private turnpikes that endured for a while were never more than slightly profitable. The American public appears to have been grudgingly receptive toward these roads at first, given the horrific nature of the available alternatives. It did not take long, however, for the annoyances and shortcomings of the turnpikes to give them bad local reputations and gradually turn general public sentiment against the companies as monopolies unacceptable in a free society. By the second half of the century, emphasis had shifted to "freeing" these private roads, a process made arduous and expensive by the favoritism US laws demonstrate toward private property in a market economy.

Regardless of the type of road, all of them sooner or later had to cross a creek, and some had to cross the Schuylkill River. Thus, the early bridges across both were also built by private companies hoping to make a profit. The early bridges were built invariably of wood, and their survival rate during floods was low. Then there was the problem of fire, which frequently destroyed bridges across the Schuylkill well into the twentieth century. In terms of profit, frequent replacement meant that the bridge companies tended to fare little better than the turnpike companies. Pressure to "free" local bridges was characteristic of every river town, too; while a turnpike in or near a town was an annoyance, local residents simply hated paying to cross a bridge, and would invent many ways to avoid doing so. By the beginning of the Second World War, every private bridge on the lower Schuylkill River had either been freed or torn down.

Residents of southeastern Pennsylvania from the time of William Penn knew that the Schuylkill River could be used for transportation, but only in small craft and then only in one direction. The river in its natural state was unsuitable for anything more than light and periodic transportation of either people or products.

There were several reasons for this. In some places, the river was too shallow or too strewn with rocks. During the summer, its flow could lessen until its deeper pools became close to stagnant. During the winter, ice often made it impassible for extended periods of time. Rain could rapidly turn the usually placid river into a torrent, which time and again would sweep away the fish weirs, docks, and a succession of wooden bridges. From the colonial period to the early nineteenth century, crude wooden rafts were the dominant means of shipping goods downriver to Philadelphia. This was a one-way trip; at their destination, the rafts would be broken up and sold for firewood. Anyone desiring to return upriver had to walk or take a stagecoach. Much talk was expended about the need to "improve" the Schuylkill River, but for a considerable time, it was nothing more than talk. It took a defining event for the future of the Schuylkill valley itself to actually produce a real attempt to harness its river.

That event was the discovery in 1790 of anthracite coal in the Pottsville area, northwest of Philadelphia. By that time, America's once-abundant forests were already being cut farther and farther back from its populated areas, making firewood another product that needed to be shipped from increasing distances, which made it steadily more expensive. The discovery of hard coal, with its ability to generate a greater amount of heat, proved to be the answer, initially for the Philadelphia area, and quickly elsewhere. The young nation's first anthracite-powered forge was established along the Schuylkill in 1795, and by 1810, small coal-burning stoves were gaining popularity as a means for heating houses.

The lure of profit brought about an intense focus on the question of how to get the coal from its source to its biggest market, Philadelphia. Such roads as existed were thoroughly inadequate to ship even the small volume of coal that was initially mined. For larger amounts, the Schuylkill seemed the only alternative. Much engineering talent, labor, and finance was expended between the late eighteenth and the mid-nineteenth century on projects aimed at making the Schuylkill navigable between the coalfields and Philadelphia. These projects always seemed to underestimate the obstacles to be overcome and the cost of doing so. The result, partially successful at best, was the Schuylkill Navigation System (SNS), initially chartered in 1815.

The SNS was not just a canal, but a combination of technologies adapted to the specific conditions of the river between the project's two ends. When finished, its 108-mile length contained sixty-two miles of canals and forty-six miles of slack-water pools created by dams at several points along the river. The slack-water pools were navigable by small boats. Each dam had a lock to raise and lower the water level to allow boats to pass upriver or downriver. Where geography rendered this impractical, sections of canal were built. Horses or mules pulled the canal boats at a sedate pace. Custom-designed boats with greater cargo capacity replaced the disposable rafts that had navigated the untamed river, and for the first time, travel upriver was possible.

The SNS is considered to have formally opened in 1824, although by that time the geography and weather-related difficulties that afflict any manufactured waterway had already demonstrated that work on it would never actually cease. The system never lived up to even the modest predictions for its success. The combination of river geography, Pennsylvania's highly variable weather, and inadequate financing bedeviled the SNS for its entire life. Constant maintenance ate into company revenues, and the entire canal had to shut down over the winter. Floods caused the greatest and most frequent damage.

The SNS was never more than marginally profitable, and by 1860, its decline had become irreversible. The entire route was leased to the Reading Railroad in 1870. The Reading used those few sections that could be included in its system, and let the remainder deteriorate. Unmaintained and collecting silt, the system began to close down, section-by-section, beginning at its upper reaches. Coal transport on the SNS ceased shortly after the beginning of the twentieth century.

The ultimate fate of the SNS was determined by the Pennsylvania legislature just before the outbreak of World War II, but the work necessary to rescue the clogged and filthy river would have to wait until after the war ended. By that time, there was no question of using the river for transportation; technology had long ago passed it by. Despite nearly a century of effort expended on it, the Schuylkill River never delivered on its promise of being the transportation corridor that so many saw it as.

The SNS's contribution to the river boroughs was modest at best. Transport of products along the system did increase the population of some of the early settlement clusters. The SNS spawned some small industries on the Chester County side of Royer's Ford, causing it to take on, for a time, a more industrial look than its counterpart across the river in Montgomery County. The company built a canal section just upriver from Swede's Ford on the right bank, contributing the "port" half of the Borough of Bridgeport, but little actual prosperity.

Prosperity arrived in the Schuylkill Valley by neither road nor water but by rail. The eight towns along the lower Schuylkill River are railroad towns. The railroad brought them industry, and enabled those industries to grow beyond the imaginations of the previous age of small-scale manufacturers. The railroad brought the industries raw materials from any distance, and it shipped their finished products to markets that eventually knew no geographic boundary. It also carried the laborers needed for industrial expansion up the river, depositing groups of them near every collection of factories and mills.

The railroad also shaped the towns themselves. It allowed extensive industry to locate along the floodplains of each town, and the need of their workers to walk to them determined the rest. In every Schuylkill River town, it is easy to determine where the railroad once ran, connecting the industries to the commercial district to the residential areas. Those sectors remain visible today, despite the changes to the districts themselves.

The residents of the Schuylkill Valley were among the earliest Americans to experience this revolutionary technology. As with any new technology, steam and the railroad required decades of development, but even in its early state, the railroad quickly rendered the Schuylkill obsolete as a mode of transport. Between the 1830s and the 1880s, three railroad companies built lines connecting Philadelphia to points northwest, and all three used the Schuylkill Valley. As both railroad technology and financing improved, the tracks extended farther and farther, and connected with more and more lines.

By 1830, two of the population nodules on the Schuylkill River between Philadelphia and Reading had become towns, Norristown and Pottstown. Both experienced slow growth until the railroad reached them; Norristown's 1812 population had little more than doubled by the 1830 census, to only 1,089 residents, and Pottstown's population in that year numbered only 676. Two different railroad companies spurred their dramatic growth. In 1831, the commonwealth of Pennsylvania granted a charter to the Philadelphia, Germantown and Norristown Railroad (PG&N) to construct a railroad line to connect the first- and the last-named towns via the middle. Service between Philadelphia and Germantown began in 1832. Horses pulled the first trains. By the fall of that year, however, the first steam locomotive chugged into service on the initial stretch of the route. The PG&N proceeded up the left riverbank, reaching Norristown in 1835. It did not travel beyond that point, but continued to operate on this route for several years. The railroad ignited Norristown's expansion. The borough's population numbers quickly began to climb, and they continued to climb for the next several decades.

Despite minimum financial resources, the PG&N demonstrated the practicality of the technology and the possibility of profits. Investors noticed. A railroad with considerably greater financial backing was chartered in 1833. Known initially as the Philadelphia & Reading, its purpose was not local transportation of people and assorted freight, as had been the case with the PG&N. The Reading Railroad (as it came to be called) was formed to haul anthracite coal from mines around Pottsville, Pennsylvania, to Philadelphia.

Unlike the PG&N, which was built going upriver, the Reading was built from Pottsville downriver. It reached Pottstown in 1837, and then continued downriver before crossing to the right bank above Norristown and connecting to Bridgeport; from there, it continued down the right bank. By 1842, regular rail service had begun between Reading and Philadelphia.

The Reading had designed its line for efficient delivery of coal to Philadelphia, so it initially subcontracted the carrying of both passengers and local freight. Nevertheless, the railroad quickly proved its superiority over the SNS, despite the infant state of its technology. The downriver path of the rails initially linked both Pottstown and what would become Royersford to the city of Reading, just as the PG&N had first connected Norristown to Philadelphia. For a brief period, the two were separate lines, unlinked, but that would change.

The Reading bought the PG&N in 1870, the same year that it took control of SNS. The company incorporated the PG&N's line into its network, as it did with other local railroads it purchased. Both the PG&N and the SNS continued their formal existence as subordinate components of the Reading system.

The Reading grew into a major American corporation, but after 1846, it began to see increasing competition from another, soon-to-be mighty corporation, the Pennsylvania Railroad. Unlike the Reading, which was a precursor of today's vertically integrated corporation, focusing solely on producing and delivering a single, specific product, the Pennsylvania was a transportation company, and was not defined by the products it carried.

In the early 1880s, the Pennsylvania Railroad resolved to offer the most direct challenge possible to the Reading's dominance in the Schuylkill River Valley by building its own line not just up the river, but directly adjacent to that of the Reading. The Pennsylvania's right-of-way along many stretches was remarkably close to that of the earlier line; the two rights-of-way were often just a few feet apart. The Reading used every tactic available to slow and to disrupt the new line's construction, including paying huge sums of money to learned people to exercise the power of the law; it also paid people of considerably less learning to demonstrate their contempt for the law. Physical altercations between rival work crews were common, and the communities along the route found themselves caught up in the machinations of one or another of the antagonists.

The Pennsylvania line reached Norristown in 1884. From there, it extended upriver along the left or right bank as required. Within a few years, the rival railroads were locked in a struggle that raged the length of the river. That struggle, which continued up to the Second World War, was increasingly mitigated by government requirements until it evolved into something resembling cooperation. Ultimately, however, there was no winner in the struggle of transportation giants, only losers.

The railroad launched the growth phases of the two already-existing towns, but it literally *created* the river towns of Phoenixville, Royersford, Spring City, Bridgeport, Conshohocken, and West Conshohocken. This was not an overnight process, however.

The population nodule that became Conshohocken lies between Germantown and Norristown, and thus railroad service can be said to have begun in Conshohocken in 1835, because service to Norristown began in that year. At the time, the location was little more than a brief stop along the way. The Reading began servicing Phoenixville in 1839, but not all the way to Philadelphia; Phoenixville sought borough status ten years afterward. Bridgeport received its first rail connection from the Reading in 1843, and achieved borough status just eight years later. Although the Reading reached what eventually became West Conshohocken shortly after reaching Bridgeport, this last area lagged behind, always struggling to overcome the head start granted its neighbor across the river; West Conshohocken did not become a borough until 1874.

The railroads helped shape the river towns, generating a consistent pattern that would vary only according to the specific local terrain and the pace of population growth. Rail lines all require flat or low-grade paths; the hills and valleys of southeastern Pennsylvania provided endless obstacles, but the floodplain of the Schuylkill did not. The path of the railroad dictated the specific locations of each factory and plant, as each had to be accessible to the main line. Industry and its necessary rail sidings lined both sides of the railroad tracks within each borough. The ideal location for industry was between the railroad and the river, as that provided equal access for both supplies and waste disposal, but access to the tracks was more important.

A commercial service sector grew up just above the industrial sector of each town, often no more than a block away, astride the main street that connected the borough to the local road. As the boroughs of Norristown and Pottstown grew into the area's largest towns, their commercial sections grew into downtowns that served not only the town residents but also others throughout the region.

The commercial centers of the larger towns, those with the easiest access via local roads, light rail, and the railroads, tended to grow faster than those in other towns, and began offering a wider variety of goods and services, further encouraging growth of the downtowns. The smaller, less accessible boroughs were effectively limited to developing commercial sectors that catered mainly to locals and the few nearby farms. West Conshohocken was the most obvious example, as was Bridgeport, to a lesser degree.

The railroads seemed to bring prosperity wherever they ran, but to build one was a major effort that required enormous amounts of capital available only to increasingly larger companies. Some visionaries adapted railroad technology to suit local travel, connecting neighborhoods and entire towns with light rail—usually called trolleys or streetcars, at least on the East Coast. The components of a light rail system, from track beds to rails to vehicles, were basically smaller, lighter versions of their predecessors, built to less exacting specifications. A fundamental distinction was that trolley cars could operate independently, not just in connected trains.

Light rail in the eight river towns began as basic transportation between downtown and one or more of a town's residential neighborhoods. Trolleys began to appear in the larger boroughs in the last decade of the nineteenth century. Norristown opened the first trolley line in 1885, with horses pulling a light carriage along a loop that carried people from DeKalb Street and downtown to the wealthy residential areas north of the borough.

Horses might have sufficed for local routes, but something more powerful was required for a light rail system capable of connecting separate towns. Steam engines were much too heavy for the lightly built tracks on equally light foundations. Electricity proved to be the answer. Pottstown opened the region's first electric trolley service in 1893; Norristown electrified its system the next year. The result was a quicker, quieter, more reliable, and much more sanitary method for everyday travel. Electrical traction allowed the lines to extend into the countryside, and light rail began to connect the towns of southeastern Pennsylvania to one another. In this way, the smaller river boroughs, which could never develop such lines of their own (and, in truth, had little need to do so), at least could connect to each other, as well as to either Pottstown or Norristown. By 1895, Conshohocken was connected to Norristown. In 1898, another line connected Norristown to Collegeville, and by 1905, the line had reached Pottstown. By 1908, passengers could continue past Pottstown to Boyertown, where a different line could take them as far as Reading. Several other lines extended into the interior of the region, gradually creating a local networks and hubs, complementary to the local road network still slowly evolving.

The lines that connected the local boroughs usually operated on a combination of local roads and rights-of-way adjacent to them. Light rail could not traverse the grades of many sections of the local roads, and thus were forced to follow paths of gradual ascent. This often required quite meandering diversions from the roads. A separate right-of-way was an expensive proposition, however, and often led away from the road's nearby population, so it was avoided if possible.

The best built and longest lasting of the area's light rail efforts was the dedicated line built by the Philadelphia & Western Railroad from 69th Street in West Philadelphia to Norristown in 1912. The grade preparation, rails, and equipment were considerably above the general quality of light rail in southeastern Pennsylvania; it still operates today as part of Southeastern Pennsylvania Transportation Authority, or SEPTA. Passengers arriving in Norristown could connect with the Lehigh Valley Transit Company's Liberty Bell Route, which traveled to Allentown a rather more average path that included both dedicated rights-of-way and local streets. The name comes from widely circulated tale that the Liberty Bell was taken along this route when it was removed from Philadelphia during the Revolution to keep it out of the hands of the British. The historical accuracy of this is questionable, but it proved to be an effective marketing tool.

A local light rail line offered the emerging middle class of each town the opportunity to live farther away from the crowded, noisy downtown and in a quieter setting, and these people were the financial basis for the rails' existence. The trolley lines profited from the increased ridership the region's growing prosperity delivered on a workday, but the weekends presented a challenge until several of the local trolley companies in southeastern Pennsylvania hit on a method of increasing weekend ridership: they developed local amusement parks next to the trolley lines. The large numbers of lesser-paid workers might not have been able to afford a daily trolley ride to and from work, but all but the poorest people could save up enough to take the family for a ride during their brief time off on weekends, particularly when the destination was someplace so very different from where they lived and worked. Such amusement parks became popular in the early twentieth century, and of those that sprung up in southeastern Pennsylvania, most were built by light rail companies.

Both Norristown and Pottstown, and their downtowns in particular, benefited greatly from trolley lines. The local roads had always led to both regional commercial centers; now, so did many trolleys, further benefiting both. Main Street, Norristown, had been the dominant shopping location for central Montgomery County since 1850. The trolleys delivered even more customers to its downtown, and sometimes to the very door of well-placed stores. Yost's, long Montgomery County's premier dry goods store, advertised its location at the intersection of Main and DeKalb Streets, the epicenter of downtown Norristown, by proclaiming that "500 Trolley Cars stop at Yost's Corner for passengers and exchange with all communicating lines."[2] Pottstown's location in a different regional market area led its local trolleys to meet on High Street in a very similar manner, and among the stores there was another Yost's.

Despite amusement parks and other marketing efforts, the heyday of light rail was brief. From the advent of electricity in Pottstown and Norristown in 1893, the area network quickly expanded, but the region's last new trolley line was built in 1915. The first companies were too lightly capitalized, and had seriously underestimated the construction challenges they faced, even when they could use existing roads. Then there was the southeastern Pennsylvania weather, whose extremes provided many problems for the lightly constructed tracks and equipment. The result was a history of company failures and incomplete successes, punctuated by buyouts and mergers. The strongest survived and the weak perished, culling the field through the second decade of the twentieth century. By the early 1930s,

---

2. Michael E. Tolle, *What Killed Downtown? Norristown, Pennsylvania, from Main Malls* (North Charleston, SC: CreateSpace, 2012), 28.

southeastern Pennsylvania's regional trolley network became one of the first systemic victims of the internal combustion engine. By the middle of the decade, every local trolley line except those belonging to the P&W/Lehigh Valley companies had converted to using buses, sometimes switching overnight.

The light rail lines varied greatly in quality of grading and comfort, and their availability during the winter was always uncertain. Yet, they did stitch together a surprisingly intricate network in southeastern Pennsylvania. A region that had always been characterized by the isolation of most of its population managed, in a reasonably short time, to find itself well connected, allowing its population an unprecedented ability to travel and intermingle, requiring travel times not greatly different that those of today between the same locations.

At the beginning of the twentieth century, another—and considerably more significant—technology began to make a tentative but obvious appearance on the area's roads, such as they were: automobiles. At first a toy of the rich (and a positive boon to local doctors), cars soon became numerous, particularly after Henry Ford's adoption of the assembly line in 1916.

Slowly, haltingly, and most reluctantly, the federal government, the commonwealth of Pennsylvania, its counties, and even the townships found themselves forced to address, again, the problem of local roads. They began a process of extension and improvement, but results always lagged considerably behind the increase in the number of cars. By the early 1920s, the automobile had fundamentally altered Americans' view of who belonged on urban public streets, and was putting relentless and rising pressure on local roads.

This new mode of transportation flowered after the Second World War. For the river towns, however, this was technological change produced far different results those that preceded it. Until approximately the middle of the twentieth century, the evolution of transportation modes worked first to form and then to nourish the towns of the Schuylkill Valley. That nourishing effect ended with the shift from the railroad to the automobile.

The reason is simple: all previous modes of transport—river, canal, and railroad—had placed the river towns directly athwart their routes. Proximity to both resources and markets far away via these routes brought growth and progress. The automobile's initial spur to local road building added to the benefit. The roads that had always led to the larger boroughs and their commercial centers were improved, and travel from a greater distance to even the smaller boroughs became easier. That was true up through the Second World War. The real change would come after, as foretold in 1940 by the Pennsylvania Turnpike. The new limited access highways would *bypass* the river towns, not *connect* them.

Even more significant than the change in external connections, however, was the automobile's effect within each of the river towns themselves. The transition from a population that walked to one that drove presented each with an unsolvable transportation crisis. That story will be told in the next chapter.

People

The third fundamental reality of life along the Schuylkill River is the waves of people who came to and settled in the towns along it. The towns along the lower Schuylkill River are microcosms of the history of immigration to and migration within the United States. Each river town was built on a foundation of both. Like the rest of the nation, each has suffered recurrent appearances of racism, discrimination, and nativism.

The first fundamental change in the population, of course, came with the displacement of the indigenous people. The area that is today known as Pennsylvania had been continuously inhabited by Paleo-Indians for at least the previous nineteen thousand years.[3] The people encountered by the first white explorers and settlers were primarily the Lenape ("Delaware"), along with members of the Erie, Iroquois, Shawnee, and Susquehannock nations. First came the Swedes, Finns, and Dutch, followed by the Welsh, English, Germans, and Irish, and then, around the time of the First World War, the Poles, Lithuanians, Russians, Ukrainians, Slovaks, Serbs, and Italians.

One of the defining characteristics of Englishman William Penn's colony from the very beginning was its welcoming attitude toward

---

3. Kurt W. Carr and James M. Adovasio, eds., *Ice Age Peoples of Pennsylvania* (Harrisburg: Historical and Museum Commission, 2002).

THEY'VE BEEN DOWN SO LONG...

new European settlers, even those who came from different countries. The result was a far more heterogeneous population than was the norm elsewhere in the colonies, but the first Europeans to inhabit Penn's land can still be grouped as coming from either northern or western Europe.

English Quakers formed the early elite and set the example of at least welcoming other people, even if they were reluctant to grant them social position or political power. Groups of Welsh, Swedes, and Germans dispersed into different areas of southeastern Pennsylvania. Groups of Swedes, many already resident in the area, accepted land grants from Penn, moving into an area south of Swedes Ford, and even farther upriver, to its intersection with the Manatawny Creek. Many Germans moved up the Schuylkill Valley and settled in the far northwest of what is now Montgomery County, making a lasting imprint on Pottstown and the area around it. The Germans largely managed to preserve their cultural separateness long after the others who arrived around the same time. Well into the twentieth century, it was not unusual to hear German spoken in the rural areas around Pottstown.

The Industrial Revolution brought the first "different" people to the Schuylkill Valley, most via its vanguard, the steam engine. This first large group of post-Independence immigrants traveled from Ireland, fleeing famine and oppression. They arrived at a fortuitous time, as the brand-new railroads needed workers who were willing to perform hard labor under dangerous conditions for little pay. Compared to their situation in Ireland, this sounded attractive. The Irish came up the Schuylkill Valley with the railroads, and some of them stopped along the way, settling down and becoming residents of the developing river communities.

The Irish were the largest ethnic group to arrive in the Schuylkill Valley during the period around the Civil War, but they were by no means the only group. Many Germans traveled to America at that time, too, and some found their way to the Schuylkill area. Unlike the Irish, whose relationship with agriculture had ended catastrophically in their native land, many of the Germans emigrating in the 1800s wanted to continue farming; they had moved to America to seek the land they could not have inherited at home, and were happy to put the Pennsylvania lands to the agricultural purpose.

When they arrived in America (not just in Pennsylvania), the Irish immigrants, especially the Catholic ones, were met with religious and ethnic discrimination directed at them by the "natives" who were already resident in the areas. The Irish Catholics were mocked, considered subhuman by many, and given only the most degrading, lowest paid jobs—if they were hired at all. The new arrivals were not at all surprised, having experienced similar friction with England back home.

Nevertheless, the Irish, by their persistence and their very numbers, gradually rose from society's mudsill to positions of authority in the emerging communities along the Schuylkill. By the last decade of the nineteenth century, the Irish had finally established generational stability and gained some influence, although the area's Protestant majority comprised the elite in place and largely in control.

Then there began to arrive the largest wave of voluntary immigrants in American history. Although the Protestant descendants of the North and West European settlers had looked on the Irish Catholics as outsiders and inferiors, their perceived differences were minor compared to those of these new arrivals. Overall, the newcomers were a polyglot bunch from Eastern and Southern Europe, and just as the Irish had stood out for both their differences and their sheer numbers, so did the arrivals in this much larger influx, whose significant numbers provided sufficient labor for even the fast-expanding industries in the river boroughs. Pottstown joined the industrial movement in a big way during this wave, as industry replaced trade as the primary source of employment.

The greatest number within this wave came from Italy. The Italians settled into communities along the Schuylkill, especially Norristown, where they came to comprise almost the entire population of that town's East End. Bridgeport and Conshohocken also developed two of the larger Italian communities. The Italians began as the lowest of the low (excluding black people, of course; more on that later), but by the mid-twentieth century, their descendants would be among the area's business and political elite.

The term "Eastern European" covers any number of people, and even a rudimentary coverage of its many ethnic groups represented in the Schuylkill Valley is beyond the scope of this work. These people provided much of the labor for the valley's factories, and they settled in several locations during the immigration wave that lasted until the First World War. They were often mislabeled by the immigration authorities, who were in substantial ignorance of the complex web of ethnicities in the empires of Austria-Hungary and Russia, the vast area that was the source of many of the newcomers. Therefore, the official intake statistics may be suspect, but no such confusion existed on the part of the immigrants themselves; as each attained sufficient numbers in a specific borough, they set about doing what their predecessors had done: building religious communities centered on churches appealing to their own ethnicity.

A small number of the Eastern and Southern European immigrants in that wave were Jewish, although they weren't the first of their faith in the area. Jewish immigrants had arrived not long after the first Europeans, but most had settled in Philadelphia and remained a marginal presence in the countryside. In many of their homelands, they had been for centuries prevented from owning land (the source of wealth and prestige in pre-industrial Europe), so few of the early Jewish arrivals chose to become farmers in America. Those who established themselves in the river boroughs mainly did what their ancestors had done elsewhere for centuries, engaging in commerce. As the numbers of Jews were few in any location, far fewer synagogues than churches were built.

New people who came to the population centers along the river did what so many other people did in every other place as they settled: they brought their religion with them, and planted it in their new land. Once a sufficient number of people with a particular religious affiliation and similar ethnicity were concentrated in an area, they began plans to build a place of worship. This tradition allows much of the ethnic history of the river towns to be told through the congregations that appeared in each, and by the dates of their establishment. The church histories illustrate the timeline of who came and when, and aid in understanding the differences that came to exist among the eight boroughs.

This tradition of establishing a church as an ethnic cultural center was followed in each of the eight Schuylkill River towns. Over time, the immigration waves would both populate and informally but effectively subdivide the larger boroughs. The nature of those divisions would differ—strikingly so between the boroughs with the largest populations, Norristown and Pottstown. Italians dominated the Norristown mix, to the veritable exclusion of other ethnicities, and this effectively divided the borough between those who were Italian and those who were not. By contrast, ethnic diversity proportionate to its population became the hallmark of Phoenixville—and, eventually, Pottstown, although its location as the farthest of the eight towns upriver from Philadelphia postponed its conversion from a strictly Protestant enclave until well after the other seven towns had diversified. Two towns with far smaller populations—Conshohocken and Bridgeport—also evidence this ethnic subdivision quite clearly. Conshohocken established three ethnic Catholic churches; Bridgeport, with half the population, established four. The three smallest towns—Royersford, Spring City, and West Conshohocken—had little ethnic diversity, a fact reflected by their small number of churches.

The result of all of this was that each river town became identified with a particular mix of early immigrant settlers, mostly Protestants or Catholics. The mix differed from the multiethnic Pottstown and Phoenixville to the Italian-dominated Norristown to Royersford and Spring City, which maintained Protestant dominance, even near-exclusivity.

World War I brought large-scale immigration virtually to halt, and the postwar recession gave rise to fears about new immigrants taking away "American" jobs. Congress responded in stages. The first major component was the Immigration Act of 1924, which established quotas, initially 2 percent of the ethnic population already in the country in 1890 (although that changed later). The object was to stem the flow of people from the southern and eastern parts of Europe peoples—Jews not least among them—and to calm fears that the "original American stock" from northern and western Europe would soon be outnumbered by "aliens." (The restrictions on Chinese and Japanese immigrants were more onerous, but lie outside this story).

This attempt to establish and stabilize a "national profile" lasted until 1952, when new legislation revised the entire approach.

The long-term result was that the immigration laws all but shut off the successive waves of immigrants that had populated the river towns. Immigrants continued to arrive in small numbers, but the intent of the act was fulfilled; no substantial numbers of any "new" ethnic group settled in the river towns until the very end of the twentieth century. The process of immigration meant that along with the change in the physical appearance of an urban area itself—the gradual substitution of closely packed homes fronting delineated streets for both forest and field—the people in the steadily growing river towns were becoming increasingly different from their rural neighbors. Each town, regardless of its particular mix, became distinct in both ethnicities and religions from the surrounding rural countryside.

The multiethnic and multidenominational nature of the growing towns set them apart from the countryside, but it also divided each against itself. Ethnic divisions penetrated every aspect of the towns, from their social events to the makeup of their volunteer fire companies. Most important—and the most damaging—was the continued importance of ethnicity and religion in determining town leadership, and thus its policies. Although the political battles played out formally along conventional political lines, the real battles pitted ethnicities against one another. Each subcommunity was ideal for such policies. For most of a town's residents, the core of their existence was their church, which was not just a place of worship but also the center of much of their social lives. Exploiting the memories of their ancestors and maintaining the mutual distrust among ethnic groups proved to be good politics.

The result was a gradual ossification of ethnic/religious relationships within each river community. Residents continued to identify themselves largely by their ethnic/religious heritage, and willingly separated themselves—religiously, socially, and even physically—to the maximum extent possible in small towns—from those who did not share their heritage. This last generation to emigrate freely into the United States became the newest wave of Americans who, in that oft-repeated irony of history, came to view any *new* immigrants to their communities as undesirables—foreigners with odd clothes, strange languages, and alien customs—who will accept even the most menial positions for pay, thus "stealing" the locals' jobs.

Each new influx of people aroused the ire of "natives"—anyone who had emigrated earlier—but none so much as those in the "Great Migration" of African Americans. In the first waves of this interstate migration, from about 1910–1930, mostly rural African Americans headed north to find work in the cities and to escape the Jim Crow environment of the South. After the Depression and the Second World War, the second interstate migration, from about 1941–1970, saw a shift of African Americans moving from one northern city or state to another in search of better-paying and often more highly skilled work.

The Great Migrations of African Americans largely affected the cities, but many workers migrated to smaller towns with thriving industries, and this included the Schuylkill River towns. Compared with the previous population waves, their numbers were smaller and their distribution among the river towns was more uneven. Their arrival greatly complicated the already-existing ethnic divisions within each town, adding racial discrimination to the mix of cancers that was eating away the social structure. Previous prejudices based on country of origin or religious affiliation were relatively tame compared with the aggressive bigotry faced by people of color. Racism proved to be a stronger, more resilient force than even nativism in the Schuylkill Valley, as it would across the United States of America.

To discuss the arrival of African Americans after that of European immigrants does some violence to local history. African Americans were present in southeastern Pennsylvania from the earliest years, primarily as slaves, but with some later as free property holders. The vast majority of Africans were transported to plantations in the South, but slaves, including Africans, lived throughout the colonies, and then the states.

Pennsylvania was one of the first states to act against slavery, passing the Gradual Abolition Act in 1780. A multigenerational process was required, but slavery had ceased to exist in the state by the Civil War. Long after slavery disappeared, however, African Americans remained a people apart (and below) in the communities of the Schuylkill Valley, as they did virtually everywhere else. Their numbers increased very slowly up until the Civil War, and remained very small until close to the end of the nineteenth century. Most of these African Americans, with few positive experiences with agricultural life in the United States, and virtually no chance of purchasing land once they arrived north, settled primarily in the established communities surrounding the Philadelphia area and the city itself, where they could find employment as domestics or laborers. Very few dispersed as agricultural workers to the local farms.

Cheltenham Township, adjacent to Philadelphia, had perhaps the best known of the Philadelphia area's early black communities, thanks in large part to the nearby home of Lucretia Mott, a Quaker antislavery crusader, and to the establishment during the Civil War of Camp William Penn, used to train African American volunteers for the army.

The first wave of the Great Migration of African Americans began in the Schuylkill Valley a decade into the twentieth century. In 1910, there were eight million African Americans in the United States, and seven million of them lived in the South; by 1930, 1.5 million African Americans had migrated north. The economic circumstances and oppression from which they fled made even the persecution of the Tsar's Jewish peasants in the Pale seem mild by comparison, although that point of similarity went largely unnoticed by Caucasian Americans. The promise of a free existence and self-determination drew many, despite the dangers that lay along their journey north and the uncertainty they faced when they arrived.

With the outbreak of war in Europe in 1914, northern industries, increasingly in need of labor, began to actively recruit African Americans, sending sent agents into the South to make recruitment pitches. The railroads were among the leading industries in this effort: the Illinois Central line to Chicago was often the first stage of the journey and, for some, the last. Others dispersed to other urban areas in the industrial north, especially New York. The Pennsylvania Railroad carried thousands of African Americans east, most to Pittsburgh. By 1930, Philadelphia's African American population had

almost tripled, and a number of the optimistic migrants continued up
the Schuylkill, in the old tradition, and settled in the river towns.

Within the Schuylkill Valley, the greatest percentage of and actual
numbers of African Americans settled in Norristown, with a lesser
number in Pottstown, for the usual reasons—employment opportunities (however limited and low paying) and an already-established
group of others like themselves. The African American population
did not make more than modest inroads in the smaller boroughs
along the river.

The onset of World War II created an even greater shortage of
labor than had World War I, as many more men were sent overseas
during the second war. Once again, African Americans (and women,
too, this time) gained access to jobs that had previously been denied
them. With the renewed promise of jobs, the Great Migration's
second wave began. Industries again actively recruited African
Americans, urging them to migrate from the South to the North.

This influx of African Americans into southeastern Pennsylvania
after the Second World War received a decidedly negative response
by the area's white residents. African Americans became one of the
subcommunities into which the larger towns were divided, and the
group with the least influence on the local political or social scene.

The most recent "newcomers," the ethnic minorities from Eastern
and Southern Europe, continued the American tradition of discrimi-
nating against new arrivals. They hired the African Americans for
only the lowest-paid, dirtiest, and most dangerous jobs—if they hired
them at all. They largely denied to African Americans the acceptance
and inclusion that they themselves had so fervently sought and only
eventually achieved. This intolerance and bigotry had enormous
consequences, evident in local history since the Second World War
and to this day.

American fears about the nation's "porous borders" sparked immigration legislation that had a decidedly negative effect on the river
towns. The result was social stagnation, accompanied by an increasing rigidity of opinion among valley residents with respect to race
and ethnicity. This took some time to surface, but when it did, this
bigotry undergirded the depressive effect of the massive, interactive

social changes sweeping over the American industrial and social landscape, including the towns of the Schuylkill River.

Eight Variations

Seven of the eight towns in the lower Schuylkill River Valley became independent municipalities when the prominent leaders of each concluded that their immediate area had become fundamentally different from the surrounding countryside, and took legal steps to establish local self-government. Norristown was established by an act of the state legislature as a county seat. The countryside around these locations was farmland, occupied by a few people, spread over a large area, and practicing family agriculture in relative isolation, much in the way that it always had been, everywhere. The land was divided into contiguous townships, but government structure at that level was almost nonexistent, with administrative power concentrated at the county level.

A few locales, however, did not follow the agricultural pattern about them. Those along the Schuylkill at creek outlets suitable for mills and at fords in the river did not grow things—they rendered things into usable products, or they forged the simple implements that everyone else needed. They serviced the travelers using the nearby fords, providing everything from help during the actual crossing to food and accommodations to prepare them for the next step in the journey.

As the local populations grew, so did the number of items and services offered at these locations. People who made their living by their labor alone needed to purchase the rudimentary necessities of life, food foremost among them. This led to the establishment of the first local stores near the mills and river fords, along with blacksmiths and then other craftspeople as needed.

As this process continued, these locales became steadily differentiated from the surrounding agricultural countryside. The increasing number of residents produced a pressing need for services as fundamental as water or as exclusive as streets, both of which were necessary for communal growth and expansion. When concentrations of people found that they could obtain neither financing nor support from the surrounding townships for their area's specialized, local needs, they concluded that they needed to establish separate, self-governing entities.

An introductory history of the Schuylkill River towns from the origins of each to the Second World War follows. Their stories are offered in the order of their incorporations, except for the two pairings of towns whose histories are so linked that they must be told together: Royersford with Spring City and Conshohocken with West Conshohocken. The brief histories of each town speak directly to the three themes of this work.

Norristown

Area: 3.5 sq. mi.

Year of Incorporation: 1812

The municipality of Norristown lies on the left bank of the Schuylkill River, directly opposite Bridgeport and upriver from Conshohocken. The local geography at this point features a substantial floodplain along the river's bank, then an abrupt rise in the form of three hills, split by the two watercourses. Most of Norristown's history was spent as a borough, but it substituted a home-rule charter for the state borough code in 1986, and revised it in 2004. Thus, Norristown is a municipality, while the other seven towns on the lower Schuylkill River remain boroughs. It is only the third-largest town in area on the lower Schuylkill, but has always possessed the largest population, and for some time, the largest of any town in Montgomery County.

Norristown was the first of the river towns. As the county seat, it always possessed a claim to prominence that the other river towns lacked. Like the other towns, it developed an industrial foundation, but unlike them, it was never dominated by one industry. Commerce constituted a third leg of the town's prosperity; only Pottstown and, to a lesser extent, Phoenixville, ever developed anything close in size and regional influence. From its origins as the "Town of Norris" in 1784, Norristown's historical arc set the pattern for the other communities that would form along the lower Schuylkill River. Until the Second World War, that arc was upward.

Norristown is unique among the Schuylkill River towns in that it came into existence through a decision by the state government, but the origins of its early population are the same as for every other

Schuylkill River town. The existence of Swedes Ford (further discussed below, as part of Bridgeport) was significant, as it offered one of the best locations for crossing the Schuylkill River. Just upriver on the left bank was Stony Creek, whose size and flow velocity made it suitable for mills and foundries. The land between Stony Creek and Swedes Ford became the core of the future community, but the area itself was initially agricultural and very sparsely populated.

When the new county of Montgomery was carved out of the western portions of Philadelphia County in 1784, a plot on the hillside above the river in Norriton Township between Stony Creek and Swedes Ford was specified as the location for the buildings required by a new county seat, namely a courthouse and a jail. There was no one living on the lot at the time, and how many lived nearby is in dispute, although the number was certainly very low.

The location of the new county seat was the result of the site's owner, the University of Pennsylvania, making a bid to curry political favor with the Pennsylvania legislature. The university was engaged in a very public legal dispute with its predecessor, the Academy and Charitable School in the Province of Pennsylvania, which had been disestablished during the Revolution for alleged insufficient patriotism. Sentiment had begun to change, and the trustees of the new University of Pennsylvania were alarmed. To improve their standing with the legislature, they offered a portion of their land in Norriton Township to the new county, as a "gift."

The university also hoped to add financial to political gain. It platted a town layout surrounding its gifted site, anticipating a profit from the sale of lots.[4] This original "Town of Norris" (named after Isaac Norris, who had owned the property over fifty years earlier), comprised twenty-eight acres. The university's hopes for financial profit did not materialize. Sales of lots in the new town were sluggish, and remained so for some years.

The population of the area had not greatly risen by 1812, when an act of the Pennsylvania legislature bestowed borough status on a designated 520-acre area to be called Norristown, all of it taken from the surrounding Norriton Township. The new borough contained an estimated five hundred people and one hundred dwellings. It was

---

4. Tolle, *What Killed Downtown?*

only at this point that the boundary of Norristown actually reached the left bank of the Schuylkill.

The transportation routes in existence when Montgomery County was created played an important part in why that particular piece of property was selected as the new county seat. In fact, the great difficulty in traveling between the western reaches of what was then Philadelphia County to the city of Philadelphia had been the primary motive for carving out a new county. The Pennsylvania legislature selected an open field to be the seat of Montgomery County, but the location of that open field justified that choice.

The lot was near the Schuylkill River, but the river was not a major transportation route—hardly even a minor one. The Montgomery County's founding document specified a site near "the canoeable part of the Schuylkill," but the use of "canoeable" demonstrates the limit of possible load carrying on the river. The selected site sat at the intersection of two roads, both barely cleared tracks, alternately dusty, muddy, and frozen with the change of seasons, but the best the area had to offer. The better of these two roads was known locally as the "Road to Egypt," named for its destination—the fertile "Fatlands" where the Perkiomen Creek enters the Schuylkill. The Road to Egypt was a component of the Ridge Road (discussed earlier) that broadly followed the ridge along the river's left bank. The south and east boundaries of the new country tract lay along these two roads, and the intersection of what evolved into Ridge Pike and Swede Street became the core of Norristown.

Norristown led the way in encountering and attempting to deal with the several common problems that came from building a town along a river. Foremost among these challenges was crossing the river itself. The first bridge over the Schuylkill was built in 1829 at the foot of DeKalb Street, upriver from the old Swedes Ford location. It was a covered, wooden bridge, built by a private company that charged a toll for its use. The bridge connected Norristown with the area across the river that would become Bridgeport. It also served the so-called State Road that was the sole north-south connection west of Philadelphia. This led to the intersection of Ridge Pike and DeKalb Street becoming the industrial and economic core of Norristown.

The bridge was "freed" in 1885, and became the property of the county. It was destroyed by fire in 1924, and replaced with a concrete bridge. A second bridge was built downriver at Swedes Ford in 1848 for the Reading and Philadelphia Railroad, although walkers and wagons could use it also—again, for a fee. That bridge also burned down in 1924, just after the DeKalb Street Bridge, which created a major crisis for both Norristown and Bridgeport. The Ford Street Bridge was rebuilt, but it was allowed to deteriorate until it was finally torn down in 1939 and never replaced.

The Schuylkill Navigation System was the first "new" means of transportation to become available to Norristown. The SNS itself did not contribute substantially to the growth of any river community, but it contributed perhaps the *least* to Norristown. The community's civic leaders did not want a canal built along their bank, and forced the SNS to build along the river's right bank, instead; that location on the river later become Bridgeport.

The SNS was never very successful, but a by-product of its construction certainly was: the company built a dam across the river just up from Stony Creek, with a lock to lift and lower the canal boats. The dam created a slack-water pool, making the Schuylkill navigable to the next dam and lock, upriver at Betzwood. The dam's much-greater importance lay in the fact that when a portion of this pooled water was directed down a channel, turning a wheel as it went, it created mechanical energy. That source of power was both of a greater magnitude and reliability than that offered by the creeks, even when altered with sluices and channels. Thus, the construction of the Norristown Dam launched Norristown as an industrial site.

Norristown possesses a substantial floodplain. This swath of land eventually hosted many of the area's mills and factories, but those would be the result of the railroad, not the SNS. The railroad brought about Norristown's transformation from the era of manufactures to the era of industry. The railroad's dominance into the twentieth century also shaped the growth of Norristown, as it did all eight Schuylkill River towns.

The Philadelphia, Germantown and Norristown Railroad (PG&N) was the first to arrive, in 1835. The first tracks entered Norristown along what was, on paper at least, a public street. The industrial sector would arise along this floodplain, between the railroad tracks that delivered its raw materials and the river. A spur line was built up Stony Creek for a short distance. The line was extended later, eventually opening a connection to the north as far as Allentown.

Norristown became a stop on both the Reading Railroad, which took control of the PG&N in 1870, and on the Pennsylvania Railroad's Schuylkill Branch line along the Schuylkill, in 1884. These two competing railroads, whose tracks ran up the left bank of the river in close proximity to each other, ensured that Norristown possessed frequent and swift connections to Philadelphia. So reliable and so quick was the journey that by the turn of the twentieth century, Norristown was marketing itself as a suburb of Philadelphia, seeking to attract city residents who were in search of a country refuge from which they could commute into the city for work. For Norristown residents, the railroad made it easy to travel to the big city for shopping or entertainment.

Through a combination of local roads and both heavy and light rail, Norristown eventually came to possess the region's most complete transportation connections. This interconnectedness fueled its growth in population, industry, and commerce. After the Second World War, as the most significant of those transportation connections—the rails—declined, so did Norristown itself.

Norristown was built on an industrial core, as were all the river boroughs, but it never hosted the heaviest industries—such as the manufacture of iron and steel—nor was it ever dependent on any one industry, let alone a single company. Norristown produced a remarkable variety of products, often from as little as one factory per product line.

Norristown's first true industry was textiles. Both spinning and weaving plants became prominent sights abutting the Schuylkill by the middle of the nineteenth century. Two of these factories were clumped together at the foot of Swede Street. Their cramped location along the river was necessary since both continued to use mechanical power from the dam to operate their machines. Globe Knitting Mills, which produced hosiery, had its own source of power, and was located on East Main Street.

By the time of its centennial in 1912, Norristown could boast of a great many different small-to-medium-size companies producing a diverse array of products, from machine tools to beer. While economic hard times periodically hit Norristown, as they did the entire nation in the heyday of laissez-faire capitalism, the overall trend was always upward. Even the Great Depression was more of a pause than a retreat. Norristown passed through it relatively well; no Norristown banks failed.

During this extensive period, there was a constant turnover of individual firms, of course, for a variety of specific reasons, and even entire industries, for larger reasons that had nothing to do with Norristown at all. Textiles continued to comprise a significant part of Norristown's industrial base at the opening of the twentieth century, but one by one, the textile mills closed down, as the technology changed and companies sought less expensive, more compliant labor in the south states. The Second World War postponed Norristown's decline, and temporarily reversed it, but by 1950, virtually all of the once-vibrant textile industry there had disappeared.

By the end of the Second World War, however, more than Norristown's textile industry was in trouble. Large industries had come into being all around Norristown, in response to the war-generated demand for a wide variety and high volume of goods. To meet this demand, industries largely adopted the more efficient single-story production plant design. There was no room in Norristown for such buildings, so local capital investment began to migrate to the suburbs, often simply abandoning the old, multistory buildings next to the river. Virtual repetitions of this process took place in the other Schuylkill River towns in the decades that followed.

The railroad, together with the inclines of the Schuylkill Valley, combined to shape Norristown first, setting the pattern for each of the other seven towns that would follow. That pattern would vary only according to the specific geography of each town's location. Norristown also pioneered the changes that population growth and industrial expansion forced on each of the other river towns.

When incorporated as a borough in 1812, Norristown encompassed 520 acres. The borough expanded its borders only once, in 1853, but that single expansion raised its footprint to 2,265 acres. It grew in three directions (the Schuylkill River remained its southern boundary), but the most significant element was the addition of land on a third hill, to the west of Stony Creek. This new acquisition was effectively cut off from the remainder of the borough by both Stony Creek and the railroad.

Norristown's geographic expansion came in response to population growth. That densely located, increasing population required the same basic services as any urban area. The most important one was water, to both supply the population and to fight the fires that were commonplace in any location that contained heavy industry. What goes in must come out, and thus the issue of waste disposal steadily rose in local importance. The Schuylkill River was the source for the needed water, but it was also the destination of both industrial and population wastes.

Norristown was the first river town to confront that contradiction. In 1847, it built a reservoir, and pumped water from the Schuylkill was available (for a portion of the borough). As the river grew increasingly polluted, the water company was forced to take a series of remedial actions that every other such company along the Schuylkill would end up repeating for the same reasons. First, in 1875, they moved the inlet pipe to the deeper southern channel of the river. In 1879, they abandoned the old, polluted reservoir and built a much larger one. The town added a filtration plant in 1901. That would not be the last step the borough would be required to take.

Norristown was also the first of the eight river towns to organize what was perhaps the most needed service, firefighting. They first tried in 1813, just a year after Norristown achieved borough status, but that early effort failed. In 1848, however, the community successfully established its first two volunteer firefighting companies, the Norristown Hose Company and the Montgomery Fire Company. The Humane Fire Company followed in 1852, and the Fairmont Fire Company followed in 1863. The borough's expansion on its western hill required a new company, the Hancock Chemical Engine Company, organized in 1895.

Volunteer fire companies had a geographic basis. In Norristown, geography reflected ethnicity—and so did its fire companies, to the point where the different companies painted their engines different colors to signify their volunteers' ethnicity. In the beginning, Norristown's fire companies competed more than they cooperated, though this improved in the twentieth century. Eventually competition was limited largely to the periodic parades, which were among the most prominent in the community during a time much given to parading.

Norristown also pioneered other technological advances in the Schuylkill Valley, with the first gas works in 1852 and gas street lighting in 1884. The latter was largely replaced by electricity from a municipal generating plant in 1897. The firms that pioneered gas and electricity in Norristown would undergo numerous changes until both services were consolidated throughout the region, and the river towns were all eventually absorbed into the same interconnected utility system.

Norristown's growth over the generations demonstrated how distance both from the riverbank and above the industrial floodplain became a measure of both wealth and status of its residents—another common characteristic among the eight towns on the lower Schuylkill River. Only the poorest, lowest-class people lived next to the river, which was dirty and foul smelling from human and industrial waste. An intermediate ridge one block above the floodplain but below the actual valley ridge became the route of Main Street, and of subsequent commercial construction. All eight of the river tows located their prime commercial streets just one block from the initial industrial sector, for obvious reasons: people had to walk to work and to shop. The first generation of Norristown's industrial elite built their mansions along that street, but later generations of industrialists and commercial leaders felt compelled to move farther up the hillside, then north to the generally flat plain above, building their impressive mansions along DeKalb Street. The expanding population followed behind them, as their incomes would allow.

Hotels were an early component of Norristown's developing commercial sector, as the borough was well placed between the cities of Philadelphia and Reading. Norristown's quick railroad connections largely served to undermine those hotels, however, in contrast to such establishment's continued prosperity in other river towns. Norristown's hotels largely deteriorated into the twentieth century, until the borough built a modern one (for the 1920s) in its downtown.

The Valley Forge Hotel was a private corporation, but its stockholders and officers were from Norristown, and the hotel was conceived as community project. Despite this, the Valley Forge Hotel was never a financial success.

Downtown Norristown grew along Main Street, between Stony Creek and Saw Mill Run. Additional stores appeared on intersecting streets, but only those close to Main Street. The exception was DeKalb Street, the route of regional travelers after the opening of the State Road and the DeKalb Street Bridge. Its intersection with Main Street formed the core of Norristown's commercial sector.

Norristown's population allowed it to develop the classic American downtown to a greater extent than any other town in Montgomery County. Some of its stores belonged to larger regional or national chains, but most were proprietor-owned; some even owned the building itself. Imposing structures of stone and marble dotted downtown, but most buildings were of brick, and of two or three stories. Retail businesses occupied the ground floors; the second or third floors sometimes hosted financial firms, but Main Street always contained a large number of apartment dwellers, too. This set the pattern for all subsequent commercial streets in the river towns, in materials, layout, and businesses.

As business practices in America standardized, and some companies expanded to become first regional and then national names, downtown Norristown's stores reflected this transition. Typical five-and-dime stores like as F. W. Woolworth, W. T. Grant, and S. S. Kresge appeared on Main Street in Norristown, as they did on Main Streets across the nation. Sears, Roebuck and Company opened a store on Main Street in 1933. Yet, the anchors of downtown Norristown remained stores with a local origin, ones that had established deep roots. Yost's was the first, but during the twentieth century, Chatlin's and Block's were among the many added to the list.

Norristown was the only Schuylkill River town whose combination of geography and population produced a second downtown. Since the 1853 borough expansion included land west of Stony Creek that was largely cut off by the creek and the railroad tracks, a secondary commercial area slowly developed on four blocks of West Marshall Street. This stretch eventually filled with banks, department stores, and even a movie theater, but each of those institutions, as well as every business along West Marshall Street, was long constrained by being located just a few blocks from the county's largest commercial area. In one of the ironies of local history, however, this subordinate location would survive, unlike much of the downtown, and in the 1980s, West Marshall Street began to revive as a commercial center.

The light rail evolution in southeastern Pennsylvania began early in Norristown. In 1884, horse-drawn railcars began service in Norristown along what would become known as the "DeKalb Street Loop." Electricity provided the infant transportation industry with the ability to service longer distances, and after 1893, a web of light rail and trolley lines grew in the area, largely centered in or passing through Norristown. Served by both the major railroad lines and other, less substantial trolleys serving the region, Norristown secured its central place within the rail networks of southeastern Pennsylvania. By the 1930s, however, automobiles and then buses had largely ended the brief and not-altogether-successful period of light rail in southeastern Pennsylvania, and were in the process of doing the same to their heavier progenitors. Of all the trolley lines that once entered Norristown, only the P&W line to West Philadelphia survived. By the end of the Second World War, both the Reading and the Pennsylvania lines were in trouble. For the railroads, things would only get worse.

Protestants from northern or western Europe were the earliest residents of southeastern Pennsylvania, and thus of the locations that would become the Schuylkill River towns, including Norristown. The majority came from the British Isles, although Swedes settled in just across the river, and German farms dotted the countryside. In 1784, when the university-granted land became the seat of the new county of Montgomery, the area population was so small that it had no church. Residents were forced to travel to other communities around them. When Norristown became a borough in 1812, it still had no church, largely because it had only marginally more residents than it had twenty-eight years earlier. The first church was St. John's Episcopal, in 1813. A succession of churches followed, with their Presbyterian, Methodist, Baptist, and Lutheran orientations testifying to the early dominance of Northern European settlers.

Population growth continued to be slow; it took two decades for the 1812 population to double; by the 1830 census it had reached 1,089.

Then the railroad arrived. The railroad quite clearly stimulated the real growth of Norristown. A mere five years after its arrival, the 1840 census recorded another doubling of the borough's population, this time to 2,937. It doubled again in the next decade, to 6,024. The borough's population continued to boom, reaching 22,265 in 1900. The first wave of immigrants to arrive in Norristown brought the Irish Catholics. As the first non-Protestants of any numbers to settle in the area, these Irish immigrants felt the effects of a combined religious/ethnic discrimination by the already-resident Protestants. Banding together for self-support, the Irish community in the Norristown area grew sufficiently that they were able to establish the borough's first Catholic Church, St. Patrick's, by 1836.

The new immigration wave at the end of the nineteenth century saw Norristown begin to demonstrate its particular variation on the ethnic settlement process. Norristown absorbed a substantial number of immigrants from Southern Europe—especially Italy—but very few from Eastern Europe. Norristown never achieved the wide diversity characteristic of Pottstown, Phoenixville, Conshohocken, or even of Bridgeport, its much smaller neighbor just across the river.

The arriving Italians tended to settle together with others from their particular part of Italy. An overwhelming percentage (perhaps as much as 95 percent) of the Italians who settled within the limits of Norristown Borough not only came from Sicily but from the same village there, Sciacca, on the southern part of the island.

The newly arriving Italians, although Catholic, were not welcomed at St. Patrick's, and the Irish heaped upon the new arrivals the very same forms of discrimination that their ancestors had suffered under. Predictably, once the Italian Catholics were numerous enough, they founded their own parish, Holy Saviour, in 1903. Although located in the east end, Holy Saviour was not a completely territorial parish; it welcomed Italians regardless of location. The church would become the backbone of Norristown's Italian community.

The Irish and Italians not only worshipped the same God in different churches, they also lived in the same town in different neighborhoods. A cabal of property owners, bankers, and real estate agents effectively herded the newcomers into an ethnic enclave in one end of the borough. The East End was then the poorest and least developed. In time, this ghettoization became practically an unwritten law.

Some turn-of-the-century immigrants to the Schuylkill Valley who shared Eastern European origins were distinguished by their Jewish religion. Only a very few Jews settled in Norristown, but they still would come to represent the largest Jewish community along the river. The area's first congregation, Tiferes Israel, was organized in the late nineteenth century.

Norristown's population grew to include more African Americans than any of the other river towns and the largest of any borough in Montgomery County. Unlike the other successively marginalized groups, African Americans were not directed toward any particular neighborhood; their population tended to be dispersed. Eventually, however, an increasingly homogeneous community formed north of the town's center. As the most recent wave of newcomers, African Americans found that most of the jobs available to them were those at the lowest level, both in dignity and pay. When African Americans did rise to the level of middle class in spite of the obstacles thrown in their way, they found that their progress was celebrated only within their own community. As had other new arrivals, African-Americans established their own churches once it became clear that white Christians did not welcome blacks in their churches. Norristown's first two black congregations, both African Methodist Episcopal (AME), were founded in 1849 and 1853. Racial discrimination in religion lasted well into the twentieth century; a separate Episcopal church for African Americans was established in 1930, and there were three Baptist churches for African Americans.

By 1910, Norristown's African American population numbered 1,015, or one-sixth of all the African Americans in Montgomery County at the time. Many were factory workers; in fact, their numbers on the line increased before and especially during the Second World War as white workers were drafted into the armed services.

As the United States entered the Second World War, Norristown's population, according to the census of 1940, was 38,181. Although still not diverse, it did possess the largest number of both Italians and African Americans of any town on the lower Schuylkill River. That may be one reason why it was also the most internally divided. The historic policy of directing Italians toward one part of the town paid political dividends for the Italians after 1930, but African Americans remained virtually unrepresented in local government. Although no one could have known it, the 1940 census number was very close to Norristown's all-time high.

Pottstown

Area: 4.8 sq. mi.

Year of Incorporation: 1815

Pottstown lies along the left bank of the Schuylkill River in the northwest corner of Montgomery County, fifteen miles southeast of the city of Reading. It is the largest in area of the eight towns discussed here, and the second-most populous after Norristown. It is also the only one of the eight towns that does not occupy one or more hillsides, but rather spreads over much flatter land, part of the fertile valley along Manatawny Creek. This made the locale an early center for market activity for the earliest settlers, and later allowed the borough's industries and population to spread out farther than is the norm downriver. This lack of elevation, however, would also subject Pottstown to the worst of each of the floods that periodically ravaged the Schuylkill Valley.

Two of the eight Schuylkill River towns between Philadelphia and Reading are named after people (Royersford doesn't count, since it was named after a ford that was named after people). Norristown was named after Isaac Norris, who had nothing to do with the township's founding, and whose descendants were never active in town affairs. The name Potts, however, has everything to do with the borough that bears the name.

Pottstown's distance from Philadelphia was particularly significant in the area's early years, when transportation was rudimentary and travel arduous. The town owes its early existence to the need of area farmers for a central location where they could both sell their surplus produce and purchase life's necessities.

From the earliest days, however, there were reports of mineral deposits in the area, including iron ore, lime, and a black, rocklike substance that burned longer and hotter than the softer varieties of coal. Much of Pottstown's early history can be traced to two people who responded to these rumors. One was Thomas Rutter, a Quaker, blacksmith, preacher, and prominent member of the Germantown community (not yet part of Philadelphia) during the early eighteenth century. Rutter, intrigued by tales of mineral wealth up the Schuylkill, purchased land along the Manatawny Creek. By 1717, Rutter had relocated to his new lands and begun to manufacture iron. He built his first forge on the Manatawny, about three miles from the river.

The second was Thomas Potts, a Welsh immigrant who moved to the area about 1716. Potts became first manager of Thomas Rutter's forge, Colebrookdale, and later his business partner. In subsequent years, through marriage and stock purchases, Potts became owner of the works, including what is believed to be Pennsylvania's first blast furnace. It was a small endeavor, and the Potts iron forge spent its early years as a supplier of implements to local buyers.

John Potts, son of Thomas Potts, was the individual who conceived of establishing a town at this location along the Schuylkill, and took the first steps to bring it into existence. He bought 995 acres at the confluence of the Manatawny and the Schuylkill in 1751, and in the next year began to build a mansion he called "Pottsgrove," which still stands; Montgomery County operates it today as a historic house museum.

Potts laid out a town nearby in 1761, which he also called "Pottsgrove." He platted a grid pattern, starting with a primary street running parallel to the river. What he named "High Street" met the road from Philadelphia, known locally as the "Great Road," although it was anything but. High Street was crisscrossed at right angles by other streets in a conventional grid pattern. He initially divided the area into sixty-eight lots, each sixty by one hundred feet, fronting on High Street. The principal intersecting street, which connected to the river, he named Hanover Street. The intersection of High Street and Hanover Street has always been the core of Pottstown.

Pottsgrove's growth was at first quite slow. When John Potts died in 1768, his nascent town contained only twelve to sixteen houses. By 1770, only twenty-seven of the lots were owned or rented, and only a few houses had been built. The village of Pottsgrove was incorporated as a borough and renamed Pottstown in 1815—the second borough in Montgomery County, coming just three years after Norristown. By that year, the Pottstown comprised forty homes, two churches, three inns, a small log school, a few stores, and some basic industries, such as a gristmill, tannery, and a hat factory—and, of course, more than one iron works. Growth continued to be slow after incorporation; the 1830 census recorded Pottstown's population at 676, and only 721 in 1840. After 1840, the railroad changed the borough's pace of growth.

The new village's location in the northwest corner of Montgomery County made it a local marketing center, but the journey to Philadelphia was still a long one. Pottsgrove/Pottstown's development was thus delayed, compared to the towns downriver, which were more accessible to Pennsylvania's largest city. The area's first true transportation connection came when a stagecoach line began to run between Reading and Philadelphia in 1781.

As the Great Road provided Pottstown with its most useful connections up and downriver, its leaders' first concern was to build a bridge to it across Manatawny Creek. The town's first bridge was the second stone bridge built along the Great Road; the first one spanned Perkiomen Creek downriver. Pottstown's bridge was freed in 1811, and replaced by a new bridge in 1909.

Spanning Manatawny Creek was important, but as with all of the eight river towns, the construction of a bridge across the Schuylkill River—and its maintenance in the face of fire and flood—would be a central concern for the entirety of Pottstown's existence. The foot of Hanover Street at the river saw much of this activity. The first wooden bridge over the Schuylkill, which opened in 1821, was swept away in the 1850 flood. The replacement bridge was five feet higher, but its height did not help; it succumbed to fire in 1884. The third bridge, built of iron, proved much more long-lasting, but like its predecessors, it was a toll bridge, and was not freed until 1890. The current Hanover Street Bridge opened to traffic in 1974.

In 1867, the Madison Bridge Company provided the eastern part of town with a second bridge over the Schuylkill River, downriver from Hanover Street. Opened in 1868, it was originally known as the Madison Ford Bridge. Although built of wood, it managed to survive until it was heavily damaged by the flood of 1942; it was replaced by a steel structure known as the Keim Street Bridge. It later closed, and has yet to be replaced.

Early roads and bridges made life easier, but it was the railroad that truly launched Pottstown's growth and development. This herald of the Industrial Revolution arrived in Pottstown in 1837, in the form of the Philadelphia and Reading (P&R) Railroad, a company organized for the sole purpose of transporting the increasingly valuable anthracite coal from Pennsylvania's mineral-rich regions to Philadelphia. Work on the rail line began in Reading and proceeded southeast, and Pottstown lay directly in its path. The line between Reading and Pottstown opened in 1838, and it was formally opened all the way to Philadelphia in December of 1839. By January 1842, trains were running all the way between Philadelphia and Pottsville, the location of most coal mined during that period.

During the 1840s, as the Reading prospered and grew, the company built machine shops in Pottstown to repair its locomotives. This spawned a new local industry whose product greatly helped both the railroads and the bridge makers: iron. Once it realized how much iron it needed for its bridges, the P&R started its own iron works. It began producing iron bridges at its Pottstown works, which was later organized as a separate company, the Philadelphia Bridge Works.

The backbone of Pottstown's growth was industry, and the major component of that industry was metals, first iron and then steel. The history of iron and steel production in the Pottstown area is itself long and complicated, with a succession of foundings, mergers, and acquisitions that eventually resulted in an industrial giant, Bethlehem Steel, owning and controlling most of them. Only a brief outline is possible here.

In 1846, Henry and David Potts Jr., the family's sixth generation, established the first iron works actually located inside the borough limits. The name of the works changed several times, with the Potts family selling its interest in 1916, thus ending a connection to metal production in Pottstown that had lasted almost two hundred years.

The rolling mill that would become the nucleus of the first Pottstown Iron Company was built in 1863. Additional metal production and fabricating firms were established in the borough, the most prominent being the Warwick Furnace in 1875, the Ellis and Lessig

Works after 1880, and Sotter Brothers Inc. in 1879. What followed was a succession of openings, expansions, failures, and consolidations. During this process, Pottstown's production capacity increased dramatically, with the greatest period of expansion in the early decades of the twentieth century, as shop after shop began producing raw steel or steel products.

In 1900, the McClintic-Marshall Company of Pittsburgh purchased the Philadelphia Bridge Company. In 1928, the same firm bought the adjacent Pottstown Iron Company works and continued to expand both its output and product lines. In 1931, its extensive works were purchased by the Bethlehem Steel Corporation. The plants continued to operate under the McClintic-Marshall name until 1936, when they were consolidated as the Fabricated Steel Construction Division of Bethlehem Steel. By that time, it encompassed ninety-two acres, with almost thirty of them under one roof.

The Depression hurt Pottstown's metals industry badly, so when plans for the Golden Gate Bridge in San Francisco finally became a reality, Pottstown's hopes soared. The McClintic-Marshall Company submitted a bid for its steel towers and superstructure. That contract meant jobs for about a thousand workers in those lean times; that would be a huge boost for the local economy—not to mention the workers themselves. There was great joy when McClintic-Marshall announced it had won the bid; the contract was signed in January 1933. The firm wasted no time, and shipped its first steel—for one of the bridge piers—by the end of February. The Pottstown works fabricated slightly less than half of the steel for that portion of the overall project, with the remainder produced at other Bethlehem Steel locations.

Pottstown steel became part of several famous bridges, including San Francisco's contemporary but lesser-known span, the Bay Bridge to Oakland. Other famous structures included the Chesapeake Bay Bridge and the George Washington Bridge, as well as an infamous bridge in the state of Washington: "Galloping Gertie," the Tacoma Narrows Bridge. (That is the bridge caught on film as it gyrated and then collapsed in high winds just four months after opening; the fault was in the design, not the steel.) These destinations won the headlines, but Pottstown steel was also used for smaller bridges such as those along the Pennsylvania and New Jersey Turnpikes, as well as thousands of other projects, from buildings to dry docks.

The Bethlehem Steel works served as the anchor of a steadily expanding industrial manufacturing sector in Pottstown, as other firms set up shop. A number of independent companies were established in Pottstown and prospered or failed, as their individual histories played out. Most of these produced implements of iron or steel, from bicycles to vehicles to aircraft engines. The bicycle was the transportation craze of the late 1890s, and inspired Pottstown's Light Cycle Company, whose exact date of founding remains uncertain. Pottstown also produced a luxury automobile, the Chadwick, between 1905 and 1916—the early, heady days of the American automotive industry. The Jacobs Aircraft Engine Company produced engines for light planes. In 1932, the firm purchased a portion of the old Chadwick production plant and began to sell its engines in several countries. The Second World War greatly increased the demand for this engine—and many other locally made products, stressing to the limit virtually all of Pottstown's industries. The Pottstown Bethlehem Steel works resounded with noise and smoke on a three-shift basis.

A later-arriving but longer-lasting product than Chadwick was the Firestone Tire plant, although the company was not native to Pottstown. The Firestone plant survived the Depression and prospered during the war years and for some years afterward, but the equipment and techniques that had sufficed during the early years and the years of high demand were hopelessly outdated by the end of the war.

Metal fabrication was always Pottstown's dominant industry, but as in the other river towns, textiles also became a substantial presence. There were several knitting mills, along with firms producing silk products, underwear, hosiery, and dresses. During the Depression, the textile factories operated at a higher level than other industries, providing steady work for many.

Although Pottstown became locally known for iron and steel, another all-American story about pies and pluck describes a long-lasting employer and a national connection. Amanda W. Smith, born in Pottstown in 1860, loved to bake pies. Mrs. Smith's pies were so popular that Robert, the youngest of her nine sons, dropped out of Penn State University and began to sell his mother's pies on the road out of his car. A small store opened in Pottstown in 1923, and in 1925, Mrs. Smith's Homemade Pies was incorporated. Before long, Mrs. Smith's bakeries opened in other Pennsylvania cities, and the product line expanded. The company prospered through the end of World War II, though it was sold off to Kellogg in 1976. The Pottstown pie factory closed in 1998.

Pottstown tended to lag behind the downriver towns in attracting immigrants, largely because of its distance from Philadelphia and the existence of established immigrant communities along that distance. Growth really began after 1840, thanks to the Reading Railroad, but Pottstown retained its homogenous makeup for the next few decades. By 1880, however, Pottstown was booming, with industry expanding and immigrants arriving in much greater numbers, eager to work. Between 1880 and 1890, Pottstown experienced the largest population growth of any Schuylkill River town during any decade, growing from 5,305 to 13,285. The population remained largely stable during the final decade of the nineteenth century, but began a steady rise after 1900, growing by about two thousand people a year through 1930. Slow growth during the 1930s produced a 1940 population of 20,194, but the number continued to grow during the war.

Pottstown greatly expanded its original borders in 1885, incorporating the population growth that had spread outside the original town. Other, smaller expansions took place piecemeal well into the twentieth century. In this manner, Pottstown became the largest of eight towns in total area.

In the other river towns, the wealthy built homes in the hills. Pottstown has no hills. Its early generations of elite built their mansions close to what was still a relatively small downtown, but later generations removed themselves a greater distance from the source of their wealth, the better to avoid the noise and smell of the river.

As if in compensation for its early lack of diversity, Pottstown eventually developed one of the most clearly defined and identifiable immigrant residential areas of the river towns, known as the South End. Anyone who lived within an area that ran from High Street to the river, and from Hanover Street to Washington Street, was a "Southie." That patch was also the home of much of Pottstown's heavy industry—the "wrong side of the tracks" in every sense. The

Reading line and its spurs ran right through it. The factories and the trains combined to make the area smoky, noisy, foul smelling, and shabby. Ethnic prejudice and nativism forced the new immigrants into tiny, ill-maintained housing, with few, if any, public services. The population in 1910 was 15,599, of which 1,119 (7 percent) were newly arrived immigrants, and most of them lived within this area. The census revealed the South End to be literally packed with people; there were many more boarders than registered homeowners.

Expanding Pottstown's municipal boundaries was easy compared with dealing with the demands of a greatly increased number of people within those expanded boundaries. Municipal organization took place on a spasmodic basis (typical of every river town), but always lagged behind the need. When its boom decade opened in 1880, Pottstown men could join any number of fraternal clubs (the Masons had been the first to organize, in 1851), but not the police department, because none existed. The borough began to budget for police protection in 1883, and by 1887, they had a police department consisting of a chief and four patrolmen in place, but the borough's population more than doubled during that time, with the inevitable results on paydays. Newspaper accounts of the period frequently publicized alcohol-fueled disputes, followed by calls for a greater police presence.

As the population increased, so did the need for other services in the increasingly urban environment. As with every town along the river, the most pressing need was for water, both for human consumption and, of course, to fight fires. For the former, the original Pottstown Gas and Water Company, chartered in 1864, built a facility to pump water from the Schuylkill River to a reservoir. By 1870, at least part of the town had a water supply, but people soon began to realize that pumping water from the Schuylkill only spread the wastes it contained. In 1885, the pumping facilities were moved outside the borough, to Stowe. Despite local resistance for cost reasons, the town later built an additional reservoir and processing facilities.

Several major fires had already ravaged the town by the time Pottstown established its first volunteer fire companies. In January 1871, once water was readily available for fighting fires, the borough incorporated the Philadelphia Steam Fire Engine Company No. 1, followed by the Good Will Fire Company No. 1 later same year. The borough was able to purchase many needed items for its fledgling units from Philadelphia when the city switched from a volunteer to a paid fire department, leaving a surplus of equipment. Pottstown's Empire Hook & Ladder Co. No. 1 was the next to form, in November 1876. The North End Fire Company No. 1 was the last, in June 1955.

When it came to disposing of the wastes produced by use of that water, Pottstown did what virtually every other municipality along the river also did; it directed its sewage into local streams and runs. Sewage runoff systems were the responsibility of local builders, not the borough, and the systems multiplied, all dumping raw sewage into local creeks and runs. As Pottstown grew, the runoff lines were covered over and their exact locations, unrecorded, eventually faded from memory. Pottstown built a system of sewer lines, but these also dumped raw sewage directly into the river. They did not build a sewage treatment plant until 1931, when they were able to defray the costs using the same targeted federal assistance employed by other Schuylkill River towns.

Gas lighting became available in 1856, and High Street was lit by arc lamps until 1889, when they were replaced by electric lamps. The region's various utility companies were organizing, merging, and expanding, and gradually Pottstown's local community services became part of larger electric, gas, and sewage networks.

The area around Pottstown remained largely rural and agricultural, but did grow in population. Where once farm people had traveled to Pottstown to sell, they now traveled there to buy as well. By 1880, the borough's swelling population had created a demand for a large and convenient commercial sector. In 1900, Pottstown had four variety stores and eight dry goods stores, and the number continued to grow. As more immigrant newcomers poured in, more stores opened to take advantage of both their greater numbers and varying tastes.

Downtown Pottstown grew large enough to attract not just the five-and-dime national retailers, but also larger and more respected ones such as Sears, Roebuck and Company. In this period of expansion and fierce retail competition, however, Pottstown's biggest—and most popular—stores were always those of local origin; these had appeared first, and they had established local reputations by the time the national chains arrived. The first major store was Bunting's, which opened in 1850. The company initially both made and sold hats, before expanding into general merchandise. By the end of the nineteenth century, men and women in search of clothing could choose from several stores, the most prominent being Ellis Mills (Pottstown's first true department store, which opened in 1898) and Weitzenkorn's, both on High Street. Other major stores came to include Van Buskirk and Brother, and Mosheim's. The borough's first large shoe store was Block's, which opened in 1884. Businesses would come and go in the way of retail everywhere, but these stores earned a place in the memory of Pottstown residents for generations.

By 1930, almost one-quarter of Montgomery County's population of 265,804 lived one of in three locations: Norristown, Pottstown, or Conshohocken. These three towns combined also comprised almost 40 percent of the county's retail stores. Pottstown was second only to Norristown, and its commercial center reflected the fact that it was far more than a Main Street for borough shoppers. *Boyd's Pottstown Directory: 1930–31* identified Pottstown as the center of a regional trading area serving perhaps ninety thousand people within a radius of some twelve miles.

The Depression brought hard times to High Street. The factories between it and the river lost orders, and their workers—even those that still had jobs—had to economize even further. The contraction of Pottstown's industrial workforce was reflected in the receipts of the stores along its commercial downtown. McClintic-Marshall Company's big steel contract somewhat stabilized things after 1933. The growth of Pottstown's textile industry during the Depression also helped mitigate the commercial crisis somewhat, and the best-known commercial names survived. The tradition of strong local businesses was carried on in its banking community; no Pottstown bank failed during the Depression. High Street's commercial crisis began to abate along with its industrial crisis in the late 1930s, as a wary United States began to rearm.

Pottstown was a late starter in the light rail era at the end of the nineteenth century. The delay meant that its first trolley lines were electrified from the start. Two lines were built. The first, the Potts-town Passenger Railway, opened in 1893, and ran along High Street from one end of the borough to the other. The second, the Ringing Rocks Railroad, opened in 1896. The two lines met at the intersection of High and Hanover Streets, the very center of town, and both lines gradually linked with others, so that by the end of World War I, people could traverse the entire area between Philadelphia, Reading, and Allentown via trolley lines.

As did so many other trolley lines, both companies developed their own amusement parks to attract ridership on the weekend days, when it was normally the slowest. The Pottstown Passenger Railway built Sanatoga Park, while the Ringing Rocks Railroad built a park named after itself. Both offered entertainment and recreational activities, but their real lure was their sylvan settings, which offered their customers a pleasant place to go during their limited leisure time—someplace as unlike their dirty and noisy weekday environments as possible.

The good times did not last. As happened throughout southeastern Pennsylvania, the convenience of automobiles and buses destroyed Pottstown's trolley lines. The trolley companies began to decline and discontinue service after the mid-1920s. The last trolley traversed High Street in September 1936.

The people who populated Pottstown shared the general ethnic history of those in the other seven river towns, albeit with a greater German influence. Its distance from Philadelphia filtered out many of the early and mid-nineteenth century immigrants, who settled elsewhere before they reached Pottstown, delaying the fundamental shift in demographics that waves of immigration effected on all but the smallest of the river towns. Thus, the descendants of Pottstown's original European settlers remained dominant for much longer, ensuring that the borough would retain its more German-influenced culture for a long time.

The ethnic distribution of the area's early settlers is reflected in the founding and growth of Pottstown's churches. The Society of Friends (Quakers) built the first house of worship on land donated by John Potts, but never became numerous or dominant in local affairs. By the end of the eighteenth century, the German Protestant presence in the Pottstown area was reflected by the existence of two Lutheran Churches; the English- and German-speaking congregations split. By

1850, other Christian denominations—Baptist, Episcopal, Methodist, and Presbyterian—had gained sufficient numbers of adherents to establish churches. The Irish immigration surge of the nineteenth century was comparatively slight in Pottstown, but still sufficient to increase the population enough for an Irish Catholic church to be established in 1856.

A much larger number of the industrial immigrants at the turn of the nineteenth and twentieth centuries made their way to Pottstown, and during that time the borough began to assume the ethnic and religious diversity characteristic of the larger towns downriver. These new immigrants were a polyglot lot, from diverse locations. They added several new ethnicities and religious denominations to the borough's population. A small Slavic church was established in 1901, a Polish church in 1924, and a Greek church (Catholic, not Eastern Rite) some years later. A small Russian Orthodox Church was built in 1928. The first Jewish congregation was established in 1889, with a second one following in 1892.

African Americans were among the area's first residents, although documentation is scarce and questionable. They were almost certainly servants of (if not slaves to) a few of the wealthiest locals. As was the case in Norristown, little official record of any African American community was kept. There is a record of a collective 1812 purchase of property by area African American residents to establish a church, but there is no record of when the church actually built, just a report that it burned in the 1870s. Ample documentation exists, however, for the Bethel African Methodist Episcopal Church, which was organized in 1871 and survives to this day. The slow growth of the borough's African American population did not change until into the twentieth century, when Pottstown's industries and the labor shortages of both world wars combined to stimulate it. Pottstown would become home to the second-largest number of African Americans among the eight towns on the lower Schuylkill, but both the numbers and the percentage of the total population were a distant second to those of Norristown.

The 1940 census reported Pottstown's population as 20,194. The residents were predominately white but ethnically subdivided. Like Phoenixville, Pottstown's population grew substantially in the period immediately following the Second World War. Unlike Phoenixville, however, Pottstown's growth spurt would end. Good years still lay ahead, but they would not last long.

Phoenixville

Area: 3.6 sq. mi.

Year of Incorporation: 1849

Phoenixville lies on the right bank of the Schuylkill River where it joins French Creek, in Chester County and just downriver from Spring City. The borough's basic layout varies somewhat from the standard pattern of Schuylkill River towns in that its grid sits at a right angle to the river rather than parallel to it. The reason is simple. The Schuylkill's right bank had no appreciable floodplain to attract early industries, but French Creek did offer a substantial floodplain in the stretch just before it empties into the river. The Phoenix Iron Works (later, Phoenix Steel Works) set up shop on the French Creek floodplain, and the basic layout of Phoenixville extends from there. The main line of the Reading Railroad ran along the right bank of the Schuylkill, with spur lines threading into the valley to the iron works, and these spurs served as main lines in the Phoenixville variation of the basic layout. The borough's main commercial street, Bridge Street, runs to the bridge over the Schuylkill, but as is typical of the river towns, Bridge Street is also the first main street a block removed from industrial sector, which in this case fronts on French Creek.

Rendering ore into iron and steel (and machining both into industrial products) was a common among the Schuylkill River towns, but Phoenixville was not just a mill town but also a company town. The various evolutions of the Phoenix Iron Company into the borough's biggest employer, taxpayer, benefactor, and landlord would determine the borough's evolution in the most intimate way. This relationship produced growth, prosperity, and a national reputation, at least up until about two decades after the Second World War. It also produced a history of community unity that has lasted even longer.

Phoenixville grew out of the Manavon Tract, about a thousand acres on both banks of French Creek where it meets the Schuylkill. An earlier grant, the Pickering Tract, lay to the south, with a third, smaller tract, the Buckley Tract, between them. The site's first settler,

Francis Buckwalter, purchased 650 acres in 1720; his descendants remained active in the area. Settlement began in earnest in 1731 when Moses Coates purchased 150 acres, and then persuaded his friend James Starr to move to the area. Starr's gristmill was the first use of French Creek for power, and his house at 10 Main Street is the oldest in the borough.

By the time of the American Revolution, the area's population numbered about 450. During the Philadelphia phase of the war, many units marched through the Phoenixville area, and engaged in small skirmishes; the borough was barely five miles upriver from General George Washington and the Continental Army's 1777–78 winter encampment at Valley Forge.

By 1840, the village that would become Phoenixville still had only about eight hundred residents. Population grew with increased iron production, and by 1846, the population had doubled to over sixteen hundred people. Efforts to incorporate the area into a borough began in 1847. While the village's population largely supported the effort, the firm of Reeves, Buck and Company (the future Phoenix Iron Company) was strongly opposed, fearing greater taxes without any benefit. Thus, a bill to incorporate Phoenixville died in the state legislature in 1848, despite support from Isaac Pennypacker, the speaker of the legislature and a nearby resident.

Undaunted, its supporters tried again the next year, and this time were successful. On March 6, 1849, the state legislature passed an act transforming Phoenixville into a self-governing entity. The 1850 census records reported that 2,670 people lived in the new borough—considerably more than the five hundred or so residents of the other river communities at the times of their incorporations (West Conshohocken alone excepted).

Like all the developing river locations, the area needed a bridge across the river. Phoenixville had one in place by the time of its incorporation, a covered wooden bridge begun in 1844 and completed the following year. As with so many other wooden bridges over the lower Schuylkill, however, a successor span burned down in 1912. Phoenixville installed a temporary replacement while constructing a new concrete bridge, which finally opened in 1917 and lasted until

1997. The new borough also benefited from a bridge built by Chester County in 1847 that spanned French Creek.

As with all the river towns, it was the railroad that brought the world to Phoenixville in the form of people, and sent Phoenixville to the world in the form of products. And, as with all of the river towns except Norristown and Conshohocken, the Reading Railroad was the initial line. In 1835, the Reading began constructing the Black Rock Tunnel at the north end of town. The tunnel was one of the major engineering efforts in the early age of rail, requiring several years and hundreds of laborers to complete. The laborers who came to work on the tunnel—largely Irish immigrants—lived in tiny, temporary huts nearby. The money they spent provided some small prosperity to the community. They were a hard-working lot, but prone to drunkenness and violence in their off hours. They were also migrants, which meant that most followed the railroad, although enough stayed that there was soon a significant Irish population in the area.

Laborers completed the tunnel in 1837, and in 1839 the first trains passed through Phoenixville. The Reading threaded lower French Creek with spur lines, adding locomotive smoke to the factory smoke that already threatened to obscure the Phoenixville sky. Perched above it all on the Schuylkill's right bank was the Reading Terminal, between the river and Main Street.

The Reading enjoyed a monopoly of rail freight up and down the Schuylkill until 1884, when the Pennsylvania Railroad began construction of its Schuylkill branch line. The Pennsylvania ran its line on the left bank of the river, but entered Phoenixville by crossing a bridge from the Montgomery County side. It also built a substantial terminal, but one not as centrally located as that of the Reading. This branch line was no more financially successful than the rest of the Pennsylvania's Schuylkill Valley efforts.

The railroad made Phoenixville an excellent location for industry, connecting it to the anthracite mines and other raw materials to the northwest, and to Philadelphia in the southeast, which provided a gateway into the wider world for the finished products. The Reading would ultimately ship a large variety of products from Phoenixville to a great many locations, but the bulk of those products would always be of iron or steel, and they would come from the one company that would come to define Phoenixville.

As with much of American industry in the early phases of the Industrial Revolution, the production of iron in Phoenixville was undertaken by a bewildering procession of individuals, partnerships, and corporations, as the combination of a new technology and a raw nation with few financial structures produced rapid turnover of ownership and management. The story of what would eventually become the Phoenix Steel Company is twisty and complicated in the matter of ownership, but even a sparse outline demonstrates how central it became to the town.

In 1790, Benjamin Longstreth established the first iron works in the Phoenixville area in 1790—and the first nail factory in the United States—the French Creek Nail Works. It struggled until 1813, when Lewis Wernwag, the most famous bridge builder of his time, took over the works and renamed it the Phoenix Iron Works. Legend says that Wernwag looked into his furnace, visualized the heated iron as a phoenix arising from the ashes, and so named his company. This tale has long ago become the conventional wisdom, although actual evidence is lacking.

Wernwag, while capable and energetic, proved to be a poor financial manager, and his firm and its buildings came under the control of George and Jonah Thompson in 1821. Nails continued to be the company's main product, and output grew steadily. By the 1820s, the Phoenix Iron Works was producing forty tons of nails per week and was, at midcentury, the largest such producer in the United States. Still, the Thompsons were forced to transfer the firm to local competitors who also owned the nearby Cumberland Works. Via withdrawals and deaths, the property came under the control of Joseph Whitaker. He proved to be a better businessman than his predecessors, and expanded nail production. In 1828, the works became part of the firm of Reeves & Whitaker. Whitaker departed the iron works in 1846, and built himself a splendid house across the river. He called the mansion Mont Clare, which would become the name of the area itself. Reeves & Whitaker became Reeves, Buck and Company, which was then incorporated as the Phoenix Iron Company in 1855.

By the 1840s, the Phoenixville works was experiencing a critical shortage of wood for its blast furnaces. When the works were built, the region had still been thickly forested. Increasing demand had made locally forested stove wood scarce, and thus wood had to be transported from steadily farther away, driving up production costs. The company had begun using anthracite coal to produce steam by about 1825, and in 1840, the local works built and began to operate America's first blast furnace fed by anthracite coal. The fire it produced was much hotter, and an abundant supply of coal was readily available via the Reading Railroad.

In 1846, the works opened a rolling mill to produce a critical product: iron rails to carry the rapidly improving steam engines and railcars. Rails continued to be a large portion of the firm's production through the Civil War. Despite occasional slow periods, it steadily expanded, with iron rails and bar iron as its primary products. Then the company bought a small, local firm that built bridges. That savvy purchase paid dividends after the Civil War, but it was the war itself that first brought the Phoenix Iron Company—and Phoenixville—to national attention. When the Civil War broke out, the standard artillery guns of the time were muzzle-loaded, and either smoothbore or rifled. A popular rifled cannon used on both sides was the Parrott Rifle, named after its inventor, Robert Parrott. It had a nasty safety reputation, and was generally unpopular. John Griffen, a designer at the Phoenix works, produced a cannon with better rifling, the "3-inch Ordnance Rifle," known locally as the "Griffen Gun." Both Federal and Confederate artillery used the much-sought-after weapon (the Confederate forces looted them from the Federals). The Phoenix Iron Company produced over a thousand Griffen guns during the war, and surviving cannons, stamped PIC, are on proud display in Civil War battlefields from Gettysburg to Stones River.

With the close of the Civil War, the Phoenix Iron Company began to design and build iron columns, beams, and girders to meet the growing market of the railroads for trestles and bridges. Its most famous product was a lightweight, latticework column, patented in 1862 by Samuel Reeves. The "Phoenix Column," instead of being cast as one piece as was then common, was assembled from between four and eight semicircular wrought-iron segments riveted together. The resulting columns possessed greater support strength at a fraction of the weight of cast iron columns. Phoenix Columns were used in the construction of many viaducts, elevated lines, and other structures built during this period, including the staircase and elevator shafts of the Washington Monument.

Phoenix Columns turned out to be excellent for building bridges. The structural flexibility they offered proved to be ideal for the many locations across the country that required small to medium bridges for both rails and roads. Heretofore, all bridges of any size had had to be custom designed, which substantially increased their construction price. The Phoenix Column allowed basic designs to be easily and cheaply adapted.

The success of this new product led to the organization of the subsidiary company of Clarke, Reeves & Company (later the Phoenix Bridge Company) to design and build complete bridges. Iron bridges, an enormous advance over flammable wooden ones, proved popular; the company built more than forty-two hundred bridges across the country, and many have been preserved under the National Register of Historic Places. During the latter half of the nineteenth century, these bridges made the Phoenix Iron Company's national reputation. Interest in the new construction technique led streams of visitors to the plant, many of them researching bridge designs for their communities. In 1871, the company built a functional "sample bridge" across French Creek at the foot of the iron works to showcase its patented Phoenix Columns. Although it was regularly used by a small engine pulling small railroad cars, the bridge's primary benefit was as a powerful advertisement for potential buyers.

During its peak years, the Phoenix Bridge Company consumed some 20 to 40 percent of its parent firm's iron output. By 1900, however, heavier loads on bridges had led to new technologies, and the firm's fortunes began to suffer. In addition to bridges, the firm occasionally bid on—and sometimes won—contracts to build very large structures. Most of these were successful, but during the last decade of the nineteenth century, several widely publicized failures of Phoenix structures hurt its reputation, including the 1907 collapse of a bridge over the St. Lawrence River that killed seventy-five workers. Nevertheless, it was changes in technology in the twentieth century—

primarily the increasing use of concrete in bridge construction—that truly led to the bridge company's decline. Both world wars provided temporary respites, as the company fabricated items for the government's wartime shipbuilding programs. The Phoenix Bridge Company lasted until after the Second World War, but only as a shell of its former self. It closed in 1962.

Meanwhile, the parent firm, the Phoenix Iron Company, was by 1881 the largest mill in the United States, employing fifteen hundred people. Bridges were its most famous product, but the bulk of the firm's wrought iron production was beams, joists, and columns for buildings, ships, and other construction projects. In 1882, the firm built its landmark Foundry Building, a huge, beautifully designed structure of dark red sandstone quarried from the north side of French Creek. The cupolas atop the building were designed to let in as much light as possible, but they helped the building earn admirers for its architecture even when it was in full production.

The rapid pace of technological change meant that after 1890, the company's basic products continued as before, but they were increasingly produced from steel instead of iron. Steel was the metal that dominated the twentieth-century products of the company, which (after several near-failures and reorganizations) became the Phoenix Steel Corporation in 1960. In 1919, an off year in an otherwise peak period (World War I had just ended and the federal government was canceling previously contracted projects), the Phoenix Iron Company employed 1,207 people.

Though iron and steel dominated Phoenixville's industries, they were not the only products made in the thriving borough. In 1867, the Phoenix Iron Company helped organize the Phoenixville Pottery, Kaolin and Fire Brick Company to produce firebricks needed for the ovens of its works. The company gradually expanded its line in several ways, most notably to produce a fine pottery called "Etruscan majolica," which won prizes during the 1880s. An 1890 fire devastated the works, which never recovered. It closed in 1901. The national craze for such pottery died out, but its subsequent lack of production has today made "majolica" pottery, including that from Phoenixville, a popular collector's item.

Textiles were the second-most common industry in the Schuylkill River towns, including Phoenixville. The Eagle Silk Mill manufactured silk ribbon in many varieties and colors. The company lasted until imports of silk from Japan became increasingly difficult when relations between the two countries deteriorated in the 1930s. The Byrne Knitting Mill was the largest of the several in Phoenixville, and a major employer of women. Around the turn of the century, the borough also boasted the substantial firm of Parsons & Baker, which was by 1910 the largest producer of women's underwear in the country, while producing corset laces as a sideline product. The firm lasted until the mid-1950s, by which time the Schuylkill Valley textile industry had largely decamped for the American South.

Industry, nourished by the railroad, attracted new residents to Phoenixville. The 1850 census listed the new borough's population at 2,667. That came close to doubling within a decade; the 1860 census reported 4,886 inhabitants. The borough's post–Civil War population rose by varying numbers, finally exceeding 10,000 by 1910, making Phoenixville the third town on the lower Schuylkill River to reach this milestone, after Norristown and Pottstown.

As the town grew with the Phoenix Iron Company and other businesses, so did the need for support and services. As in the other seven river towns, residential and commercial expansion was piecemeal, with individual landowners dividing properties into subdivisions and selling the lots individually. The Phoenix Iron Company led the way, purchasing land along French Creek to build small, spare housing for its workers. The company eventually owned almost all the land along both banks of French Creek close to the river, using it for production, storage, or residences. It also purchased plots along Bridge Street, where it constructed some of the buildings that made Phoenixville locally famous.

Other enterprising individuals bet on the increase of the iron company's workforce. Slowly the borough began to take on an urban feel on the north and south sides of French Creek. As was the pattern in all seven Schuylkill River towns with hills, the wealthiest residents purchased or built their houses farther away from the river and up the hill. The local elite built on the highest ground above Main Street.

Residences built by local figures, including two built for John Griffen, began to decorate the town. Some of these remain.

Water from springs and pumps was adequate while the population was rising slowly, but more rapid growth thanks to the rise of the Phoenix Iron Company precipitated the need for action on a municipal scale. As with the other river towns, much time elapsed between recognition of the need for such action and the action itself. The first municipal water to be made available—and then only to a portion of the borough—was not in service until after 1873. Extensions of this effort would be halting and slow, and it would be many years before water was available throughout the entire town.

Like the other river towns, Phoenixville began by pumping water directly from the Schuylkill through its slowly growing system. As elsewhere, this led to calls for a purification system, and issues of cost similarly delayed Phoenixville's efforts. It was not until 1913 that Phoenixville judged the quality of the unfiltered water bad enough to justify constructing its first processing plant.

By the 1930s, the combination of a severely polluted river and continued growth along its banks led the state to begin a serious push to mandate municipal sewage collection and processing plants. At that time, of the towns downriver from Reading, only Pottstown had such a system, and it processed only about one-third of the borough's sewage. Royersford and Spring City still dumped their sewage directly into the river. Below Phoenixville, only Norristown had installed a sewage plant. All of the river towns found themselves increasingly in the crosshairs of federal and state regulators—Phoenixville included.

In 1928, the state of Pennsylvania filed suit against the borough for polluting French Creek, and requested amelioration, while reminding its elected council members that substantial fines could be levied for noncompliance. A formal order to cease polluting the creek followed in 1929. The borough appealed, and the dispute simmered for years. In 1935, the state ordered Phoenixville to cease dumping wastewater in the Schuylkill River, and followed with a lawsuit to collect the fines overdue since 1929. Phoenixville protested, pointing out that in such hard economic times, construction of a sewage plant was financially impossible. The state continued to press for system upgrades.

Fortunately for the river towns, while the state applied the stick, the federal government followed up with the carrot: in 1937, the Works Progress Administration (WPA) offered a grant to Phoenixville that would cover about 45 percent of the expected cost of constructing both sanitary sewers and a sewage plant. Under intense pressure, the Phoenixville Borough Council finally voted to build the required system. The processing plant was ready by 1939, although at first it and its supply lines served only a portion of the borough.

Phoenixville was no exception to the frequency of foundry and factory fires, and, as with the other river town, the formation of a fire company was an early priority. In 1849, the community made an informal attempt to organize a firefighting unit, generally referred as the No. 1 Company, after the Phoenix Iron Company donated an ancient piece of hand-powered equipment. The lack of a borough water supply, along with the old pump's age—it was built in 1738— made the gesture largely symbolic.

The borough's first true volunteer fire company was the Phoenix Hose, Hook & Ladder Company, chartered in April 1874, one year after the installation of the borough's first water system. A second company, the Friendship Fire Company, was organized in 1904 to service the borough's north end, followed by the West End Fire Company in 1906. As with each of the Schuylkill River towns, Phoenixville's volunteer fire companies provided the cornerstones of the community's social life.

During the late nineteenth and early twentieth centuries, Phoe- nixville grew to be one of the larger towns on the lower Schuylkill River, although it never approached the population numbers of Norristown or Pottstown. This spurred the growth of its commercial sector. Given Phoenixville's right-angle twist on the pattern, the industrial floodplain was on French Creek, making Bridge Street the borough's commercial backbone, a function it continues to serve to this day. Its core intersection was with Main Street, with additional stores and services located a short distance from Bridge Street on adjoining streets. At this main intersection sat the borough's primary banking and lending institutions, the Phoenixville Trust Company and the Farmers and Mechanics National Bank. By the latter decades of the nineteenth century, Phoenixville could boast, arguably, of having the largest commercial sector of any town in Chester County save West Chester, the county seat.

Even during the colonial and Federal periods, the area that would become Phoenixville was well traveled. Thanks to its location along the main road between Philadelphia and both Reading and Lancaster, it became a popular stopover and connection point between them or to local destinations like Yellow Springs. As a consequence, hotels feature heavily in its history. Norristown and Pottstown also had downtown hotels central to their commercial sectors, but both of those towns eventually tore down their famous hotels. By contrast, Phoenixville maintained its traditional hotels, thanks in part to the Phoenix Iron Company's sponsorship and to the railroads, which made the last decade of the nineteenth century and the first of the twentieth golden years for ornate local hotels. The Phoenix Hotel was the borough's best known, but the Hotel Chester best symbolizes this tradition: it was built in 1894 on the site of a previous hotel, and the building itself survives to this day.

Phoenixville had a total of four theaters built for live performances, at least initially, during its glory years, which largely overlapped the golden age of such theaters. The best known of these was the Colonial Theatre, which opened in 1902. Though remodeled several times and utterly changed in appearance, it has not only survived, but its role in the filming of a B movie in the 1950s (*The Blob*) later blossomed into Phoenixville's signature cultural event.

The era of the five-and-dime stores flourished in Phoenixville, as it did in the other large river towns. The F. W. Woolworth store, located at Bridge and Main, was the largest and most patronized, with its lunch counter the scene of countless get-togethers. Again, though, it was the local businesses, some lasting through generations, that formed the core of the borough's commercial sector: Keinard Brothers, the drugstores of Dancy and Dorman, and the Deininger and Kremer jewelry stores thrived during the boom years of the early twentieth century. The businesses eventually closed, but a remarkable number of the buildings they inhabited were saved, unlike in Norristown or Conshohocken.

The trolley era came to Phoenixville when the Montgomery and Chester Electric Railway opened in 1898. At first, it provided only limited service within the borough, but eventually it connected the borough to Spring City, upriver. The second trolley line to begin service was the Phoenixville, Valley Forge and Strafford Electric Railway in 1910, whose line eventually extended to Valley Forge, but never did reach Strafford.

While it was now possible for Phoenixville residents seeking recreation to take the trolley to Valley Forge, which had become a significant tourist attraction, most of them chose to spend their brief leisure time, usually on Sundays, closer to home. The Montgomery and Chester followed the lead of several other regional trolley companies and purchased land adjacent to its line about two miles southwest of Spring City. There it built the Bonnie Brae Amusement Park, which became famous for its carousel and, like the others, prospered as long as the trolley lines did. As with each of the other river towns, however, the trolley era in Phoenixville was brief. Automobiles and buses had begun to supplant the trolley companies by the 1920s, and this in turn steadily reduced expenditures on their amusement parks. The Montgomery and Chester Railway sold the park grounds in 1926 and went out of business shortly thereafter. The rails that carried the trolleys down Bridge Street were torn up and removed.

As was typical of the entire southeastern Pennsylvania area, the first settlers in the Phoenixville area were Protestants, with Episcopalians, Mennonites, and Quakers the most numerous among them. As the numbers of each increased, they began to organize their worship services. The early-to-mid-nineteenth-century's "Great Revival" that was sweeping the country brought an influx of Methodists to the area, as well as Baptists and Presbyterians. By the early nineteenth century, Phoenixville had plenty of Protestant residents of northern European descent, and a wide variety of churches. That Protestant domination gradually lessened with the successive waves of immigrants. The newcomers built four Catholic churches in the borough, each for a specific ethnic group. The Irish established the borough's first Catholic Church, St. Ann's (built with a substantial contribution from the Byrne family from its knitting mill profits). This was followed by St. Mary's, built by the Italian Catholics, and the most architecturally notable, St. Michael's, built by the Eastern Rite congregation.

Shortly after organizing their churches, each of the new ethnic groups also formed clubs to promote self-help and citizenship. The Polish-American Citizens Club organized in 1921, followed by the Hungarian-American Club, the Slovak American Citizens Club, and the St. Michael's Athletic Club, all in the 1920s. By the time the US Congress formally choked off the flow of immigrants in the 1920s, the people of Phoenixville had become one of the most diverse of any of the towns along the Schuylkill River.

Phoenixville's population growth during the twentieth century demonstrated neither great spurts nor precipitous declines. Growth almost stagnated between 1910 and 1920, then rose substantially during the 1920s, and then largely stagnated again during the 1930s, although the net population rose slightly. Overall, the borough's population has risen steadily, and has not demonstrated a net decline for any decade of its history. On the eve of the Second World War, Phoenixville claimed 12,282 residents. Each of them had benefited from the borough's close relationship with the Phoenix Steel Corporation, as had their ancestors for longer than anyone could remember. Phoenixville was always a company town, and the company had been good to it. But the times were about to turn against the Phoenix Steel Corporation, and Phoenixville would come to experience the downside of that close relationship.

Conshohocken

Area: 1.0 sq. mi.

Year of Incorporation: 1850

West Conshohocken

Area: .94 sq. mi.

Year of Incorporation: 1874

Conshohocken and West Conshohocken are just downriver from Norristown and Bridgeport, on the left and right banks, respectively, of the Schuylkill River. They are the last two independent municipalities on the lower Schuylkill before Philadelphia. One the left bank of the river, Conshohocken sits on a moderate to steep hillside divided by small watercourses. The land after that largely flattens out. The right bank is more rugged, with no dominant hillside, and contains creeks, valleys, hills, and ridges extending to the west. West Conshohocken clings to the first few of these hills along this bank. At the base of both is the floodplain of the Schuylkill, home of the earliest settlers and the site for their future industries.

The histories of Conshohocken and West Conshohocken must be told together. The towns began at opposite sides of the same ford, and they have been linked ever since. In 1920, the *Conshohocken Register* (a booklet, not a newspaper) observed that for West Conshohocken, "The social and industrial life of the borough is so closely associated with its sister borough across the river that the two towns form practically one community."[5] This is how I will treat them here.

The two towns demonstrate the left-bank dominance that is characteristic of the lower Schuylkill River towns. Conshohocken became a borough almost a quarter of a century before its neighbor across the river, and its dominance extended through every aspect of their coexistence, including size, population, products, and diversity.

As with the other six towns, the history of both Conshohockens dates back to William Penn, who purchased a large amount of land in the area through two treaties with the Lenape people, in 1683 and 1685. Although the Lenape did not understand the European concept of land ownership and thus may not have realized what they were signing away, Penn's respect for and willingness to negotiate with the indigenous people still distinguished him from most of the founders of the American colonies, who mostly just claimed ownership.

Penn gifted his lands to his family, immigrant groups (including the Swedes who settled just upriver), and individuals. The relevant gift for a study of the Conshohockens was the one Penn made to John Matson. That grant included a portion of land along the Schuylkill's right bank that extended from Lower Merion Township to about the location of present-day Bridgeport. Matson's son Peter built a house in 1747 along the riverbank near a shallow section, and the Matsons did what they could to fill in the shallow area with rocks, making a fording location that was passable—at least most of the time. This came to be called "Matson's Ford." The road leading to each side of the ford slowly grew into a major transportation artery. It ran along the boundary lines between two townships on each side, earning the name Township Line Road on both sides of the ford.

---

5. *Conshohocken Register: Useful Information about Conshohocken, West Conshohocken and Their Officials, Churches, Organizations, Business Institutions, Etc.* (Conshohocken, PA: Recorder Publishing Company, 1920), 72.

Matson's Ford's moment in the historical limelight came during the American Revolution. After the Battle of Whitemarsh ended on December 8, 1777, the Continental Army retreated down Township Line Road on the left bank and attempted to cross the Schuylkill to the right bank, employing a line of wagons tied together in the river as a bridge. Once a portion of the army was across, however, they discovered a superior British force near Gulph Mills. After a hasty retreat back across the river, they destroyed the wagon bridge behind them, and then marched upriver and crossed at Swedes Ford on their way to the winter encampment at Valley Forge. Six months later, the war returned to the Conshohocken area. The Marquis de Lafayette, the French aristocrat who crossed the Atlantic to volunteer his services to the revolutionary cause, had ventured toward the British lines northwest of Philadelphia, only to find himself and his small force in considerable jeopardy from British units that nearly surrounded them. Their only choice was retreat, and Lafayette's retreat led him and his army down the same road to the river that General Washington's army had initially followed the previous winter. Lafayette also crossed at Matson's Ford, but they made it to safety, although a brief skirmish did take place on the Conshohocken side.

By the time it became a borough, Conshohocken had assumed physical characteristics different from those of agricultural countryside, but still barely those of a town. Its growth before 1835 had been slow. In 1833, what people were then calling Conshohocken had just one store, one tavern, a gristmill, and six dwellings. This made it quite like many locations along the river at this time, but Conshohocken also possessed both a limekiln and a rolling mill. The kiln was opened to process limestone, and James Wood's company, which owned the rolling mill, used the resulting lime. That company would turn out to be the major benefit bestowed on Conshohocken by the Schuylkill Navigation System.

The Conshohockens owe their origins to a crossing of the Schuylkill River and their growth to the railroads. Yet Conshohocken—and by extension, West Conshohocken—may owe the most of any of the eight river town to the SNS, however indirectly. The SNS built one of its canal/lock sections on the left bank of the river. After 1824, mules hauling barges became a common sight, although most simply passed through the area on their journeys between Philadelphia and the lands upriver. In early 1831, James Wood and his son Alan were searching the lower Schuylkill Valley for a place to locate an iron mill. They decided that Conshohocken was that place, as the canal at that point could both supply power to the mill through a diversion sluice and allow them to easily ship the mill's output. They leased land from the SNS and obtained the right to use its water. The Wood surname became central to Conshohocken history, which the SNS never did. By 1833, the little village of Conshohocken, even with just six houses, could legitimately claim the beginnings of an industry.

In May 1850, Conshohocken became Montgomery County's third borough, after Norristown and Pottstown. The process began in 1848 when five men were selected to apply for a charter of incorporation. The identity of three of the men suggests the themes that led to the creation of Conshohocken and that resonated through its history: Isaac Jones, the president of the Matson Ford Bridge Company; James Wells, the owner of the local hotel/train depot; and James Wood, the ironmaster and rolling mill owner. As legend has it, the five men met in Norristown to select a name for their proposed borough. They narrowed the list down to three, wrote them on paper, and then placed the names in a hat. "Conshohocken" was the name drawn. The land for the new borough came in equal parts from the townships of Plymouth and Whitemarsh, on both sides of Township Line Road, which became Fayette Street in the new borough. The residents of Conshohocken at the time of its incorporation numbered 727. James Wood's son John became the borough's first burgess.

West Conshohocken did not become a borough until 1874. Its territory of .94 square miles was taken from Upper and Lower Merion Townships, on both sides of Township Line Road. Conshohocken's earlier start gave it an insurmountable lead over its younger neighbor. West Conshohocken would never grow to more than a quarter of Conshohocken's population, and its portion of the local industries was lower still. The ford and a railroad brought West Conshohocken into existence, but the sway exerted by its neighbor across the Schuylkill always ensured that West Conshohocken remained both smaller and subordinate.

The history of bridges built across Matson's Ford to connect the Conshohockens is considerably less dramatic than that of those bridges built upriver between Norristown and Bridgeport, Mont Clare and Phoenixville, and Royersford and Spring City. None burnt down, and there were no collapses during construction. The bridges in the Conshohockens did, however, suffer from the same flooding issues as those in the other towns. A flood in 1839 washed away the first bridge, a covered wooden one that had opened in 1833. A new wooden bridge had reopened by late 1840, only to be washed away by the great 1850 flood. Yet another wooden one was built to replace it.

Iron replaced wood for the next bridge, at least for the supporting structure; the roadway was still paved with wood planks. This bridge, which opened in 1872, was considerably safer, but like its wooden predecessors, it spanned only the river itself, terminating at the heart of both boroughs' industrial sections, short of the railroad tracks on both banks. Travelers were thus required to navigate railroad grade crossings on both sides, as well as a second, much smaller bridge on the West Conshohocken side to cross the SNS. Originally, all these bridges were owned by the Matsonford Bridge Company and its successive incarnations, and all were toll bridges. Then, in 1886, Montgomery County purchased the company, thus "freeing" the bridge. By the early 1900s, the main bridge had deteriorated to such an extent that it was closed and a temporary wooden bridge built to carry traffic while a new concrete bridge was built. The concrete bridge opened in 1921, and was not replaced until 1987.

Conshohocken was the first of the eight river towns to experience the railroad revolution. The Philadelphia, Germantown & Norristown Railroad (PG&N) pioneered one of America's very early lines up the left bank of the Schuylkill, passing through what would become Conshohocken. Service between Philadelphia and Norristown began in 1835, with the Conshohocken area a stop along the way. The success of this small, seminal effort spurred the creation of a much larger corporation, the Philadelphia & Reading Railroad (later the Reading Railroad). The Reading built its line from the Pennsylvania coal fields down the Schuylkill Valley's right bank, with service to what would become West Conshohocken beginning in 1839. This did not give the residents of the right bank nearly as significant a boost as

Conshohocken had Local passengers in the Schuylkill Valley were hardly considered and never accommodated. Local industry found the Reading much more receptive, but the connection to West Conshohocken was never large or significant.

All three of Conshohocken's transportation connections—local roads to the bridge, the SNS, and the new railroad—were established by 1835, and the area began to transform. The rail presence encouraged manufacturers to locate there and to expand, and the trains brought the workers to the mills and factories. The Reading's late-nineteenth-century competition, the Pennsylvania Railroad, built its line up the Schuylkill directly adjacent to that of the Reading, opening its Conshohocken station in 1883. The building still stands, at the foot of Harry Street, but it is the old PG&N/Reading line that survived, as a regional commuter line.

Thanks to these transportation connections, both banks of the river developed industries. By the time of Conshohocken's first application for borough status in 1848, it had already become the center of a manufacturing area. Much of this industry focused on iron and later steel. As in the other Schuylkill Valley towns, industry also included products made from both iron and steel, plus glass and textiles. Foundries and factories established along the riverbanks in the Matson's Ford area on the left bank were always greater in number and size than those on the right bank. The 1920 *Conshohocken Register* listed thirty-two industrial sites on the Conshohocken side, but only four in West Conshohocken.

The largest and best known of the area's industries rose from the decision of James and Alan Wood to locate their iron mill in the area. Wood was a country blacksmith's son who first began working with iron in 1792. His initial establishment in 1832 became the Schuylkill Iron Works, and subsequent companies producing iron or its products often included the name "Wood."

James's son John assumed control of the new borough's politics, but it was another son, Alan, who in 1885 founded the company with which Conshohocken would be most closely associated. He and Lewis Lukens, whose descendants also figured prominently in the local iron and steel industries, founded the Alan Wood Company. This grew to be the most prominent business not just in the borough, but in the immediate area. It survived the hard times that dogged the 1870s, and afterward entered a new era of growth and profit. It incorporated as the Alan Wood Steel Company in 1885, and became the Alan Wood Iron and Steel Company in 1901, incorporating the former Schuylkill Iron Works. The company built a new plant on a former farm at Ivy Rock, just upriver from Conshohocken, producing its first steel in 1903. By 1920, the company's output represented 8 percent of the US steelmaking capacity. The Wood family sold its controlling interest during the Depression, but bought it back in 1945. The company thrived during the Second World War.

The name "Lee" is also closely linked to Conshohocken. J. Ellwood Lee opened his first business in 1883, in the attic of his Conshohocken home, producing surgical dressings on his mother's sewing machine, which he had adapted for the purpose. He prospered, gradually expanded his product line, and then made a fortune from his invention of an orthopedic splint. The firm became a national leader in surgical appliances. Lee's need for glass vials in his business led him to hire glassblowers, some of whom later struck out on their own, founding Conshohocken's glass industry. By the early twentieth century, the J. Ellwood Lee Company occupied some five acres of floor space and employed about five hundred people.

Lee became intrigued early on by the promise of the automobile, and in 1910, he built an automobile tire factory in Spring Mill, just downriver from Conshohocken, calling it the Lee Rubber & Tire Company. His timing was good, as Henry Ford's assembly line would soon begin making the automobile a must-have proposition. The firm incorporated in 1915. It prospered, taking over other companies and managing to weather the frequent ups and downs of rubber production, changes in tire technology, and the vicissitudes of international trade. The firm's initial approach to tire manufacture had to be restructured in the 1930s when the low-pressure, "balloon" tire became standard, but soon rearmament orders began to pour in, and the Lee Rubber & Tire Company prospered during the war.

Other companies popped up during Conshohocken's industrial era. Some were branches, like the Adam Scheidt Brewing Company, whose main plant was in Norristown, but most were small, independent companies. Standing out from the long list is the Quaker

Chemical Company, which processed oil for specialty industrial uses from 1917 to the present, and both the Hale Fire Pump Company and C&D Batteries, two companies that would also survive.

West Conshohocken's industries never approached either the number or the size of their counterparts across the river. Local creek beds evolved into small industrial sites (like the wonderfully named Balligomingo Creek), but the river floodplain housed the largest factories. Textiles led the way; two of these small factories supplied the US Army with uniform blouses from the Civil War to the Second World War. Other products included paper, stone from the local quarry (once in great demand), and carpet.

A ford—and even more, a bridge—bestows benefits at both ends, but rarely in equal proportion, given the other factors affecting local development. It was those other factors, and not the bridge, that would combine to produce the considerable disparity between the Conshohockens. It is one of the minor ironies of local history that West Conshohocken, which has always had the smallest population of the eight Schuylkill River towns, happened to have the second-largest number of residents when it became a borough in 1874, below that only of Phoenixville. The exact number is uncertain, but by the 1880 census, West Conshohocken listed 1,462 residents.

By that date, however, Conshohocken across the river had already been a borough for twenty-four years, and its population numbered 4,561. It had already established its local dominance in population, commerce, and industry, and that gap would only widen in the ensuing decades. Conshohocken's population increased at a higher rate every decade until 1930, while West Conshohocken's population was the first of the towns along the lower Schuylkill to reach its historic peak (2,579) in the same year. By 1940, Conshohocken's population had suffered a miniscule drop of thirty-nine people since 1930, but that rose again (briefly) after the Second World War.

Both Conshohockens followed the typical Schuylkill River layout, with their industries occupying the floodplain, their commercial sectors within walking distance of the least-expensive housing, and their other residences rising up the hillside or, in West Conshohocken's case, the hillsides plural, according to the wealth of their owners. Expansion to the east and west brought Conshohocken to its full size, and people gradually made Conshohocken's hillside one of the most densely populated along the river. Although only slightly larger (by .6 of a square mile), Conshohocken's population exceeded that of its neighbor across the river by a factor of at least four during the years prior to World War II. As with elsewhere on the river, the mansions of Conshohocken's industrialists also moved uphill from those of the first generation, who had built theirs in the heart of the considerably smaller town. No mansion of equal size or fame was ever built in West Conshohocken.

Both Conshohockens established companies to pump their water from the Schuylkill River, and both encountered the same problems as the other river boroughs, in the same order. They first drew water from the river and built reservoirs, and then realized that they had to filter the increasingly polluted Schuylkill water. The industries of both boroughs dumped their wastes directly into the river. Domestic sewage went from gutters to underground pipes, in the usual haphazard and largely unrecorded manner, then directly into the river. By the 1920s, the dire condition of the river—downriver from the thriving industries of Norristown, Bridgeport, Phoenixville, Royersford, Spring City, and Pottstown—was pungently obvious. Human and industrial waste, not to mention waste from factories in Reading and even farther upriver, along with the coal culm that so greatly contributed to the problem, had rendered the river extraordinarily polluted.

Both Conshohockens found that their remediation efforts always lagged behind the growth of their communities and the resulting demand for water. The usual legal disputes between the boroughs and officials of both the state and federal governments dragged on, greatly exacerbated by the Depression, which left the Conshohockens jointly ill-prepared to undertake such a major expense. Nevertheless, in 1935 the state ordered Conshohocken to cease dumping sewage into the Schuylkill River. With no alternative, the borough began building a sewage treatment plant in 1937. They also installed sewer mains and laterals throughout the borough to connect every building in town— except, initially, Borough Hall itself, in one of the more embarrassing gaffes in local engineering history.

Conshohocken's initial attempt at electric lighting produced an equally embarrassing episode. Illuminating gas had become available from a local plant after 1875, but less than a decade later, the arrival of electricity promised a safer, better-lit borough. The Conshohocken Electric Light and Power Company built a small generating plant in 1888 to illuminate street lamps on Fayette Street. Inexplicably, given the late date, the electrical generator was powered by water diverted from the canal, and the flow proved to be horribly inadequate. Once the water-driven wheel was replaced by a stationary steam engine, the system worked much better. Both the initial electric company and the borough's first gas company were later subsumed into the regional power networks in southeastern Pennsylvania.

Conshohocken's commercial downtown spread out from its core, a T intersection of Elm Street (parallel to the river) and Fayette Street (ascending the hillside). Early businesses servicing the town were, in typical river-town fashion, located along the first street parallel to and up from the river, which in Conshohocken's case was Washington Street. The railroad built its line along Washington Street, however, causing Conshohocken's river-parallel commercial sector to develop on Elm Street, one block up. With the borough's population expansion, the commercial sector also began to climb the hill, extending up Fayette Street. As Conshohocken's commercial downtown became fully established, Fayette Street became the backbone street.

As with the commercial sector of every river town, the majority of its customers always reached it by walking. Still, Conshohocken's boom times were largely congruent with those of the trolley, followed by the developmental phase of the automobile (pre–World War II), as were those of each river town. For Conshohocken, located so close to and with excellent connections to Norristown, this was a mixed blessing. While first the trolley and then the automobile expedited family journeys, both also allowed Conshohocken residents to shop in the larger urban centers, which in Montgomery County meant Norristown. Thus, no truly regional retail commercial firms were ever established in Conshohocken, although national names of the five-and-dime variety, like the ubiquitous F. W. Woolworth, were staples downtown. Conshohocken's commercial sector was thus even more dominated by locally owned businesses than Norristown or Pottstown, which both had true regional downtowns. Conshohocken's commercial marketing area extended beyond its boundaries, but not to any great distance, likely due to its proximity to Norristown.

If proximity to Norristown inhibited Conshohocken's commercial growth, then proximity to Conshohocken kept an even tighter lid on commercial growth in West Conshohocken, whose merchants always existed under the constraints of what was available across the river, particularly after the Matsonford Bridge was freed. Another factor was the respective populations of each borough; as late as 1900, West Conshohocken's population remained at fewer than a thousand people. Such a number, plus Conshohocken's presence just across the river, limited West Conshohocken's commercial sector to only those firms providing the basic, day-to-day items and services. In its early years, these were largely stores providing lumber, coal, horse-related services, and merchandise. When automobiles became popular, grocery stores and drug stores moved in, along with automobile-oriented businesses like gas stations and mechanics.

In considerable contrast, Conshohocken's population had reached 10,815 by 1930, and its commercial sector boasted 230 retail stores within the borough limits, as well as seventeen hotels. The commercial sector suffered severely during the Depression (one Conshohocken bank failed), but recovered to even greater heights thanks to war-related demands for steel, rubber tires, and surgical supplies.

The brief trolley era encompassed Conshohocken, but never West Conshohocken. In 1893, the Conshohocken Street Railway Company opened a line that connected to both Norristown and Plymouth Meeting. Originally constructed only to 12th Street, tracks on Fayette Street followed, carrying people south to the heart of the borough. When the regional light rail system reached its apogee in the first decade of the twentieth century, Conshohocken was a component, albeit a minor one. Residents could reach just about any other location between Philadelphia and Reading by making connections among the several local lines. Trolleys ceased serving Conshohocken in 1933, and were immediately replaced by buses running essentially the same routes.

As with William Penn's lands elsewhere, the initial settlers of the area were a mix of northern and western European immigrants, all of them Protestant. Swedish immigrants settled on the right bank just upriver, lending their name to the fording location. The first Irish arrived to work on the Schuylkill Navigation System, and more came to work on the railroad, and that timing allowed the Irish to be both immigrants and among the original residents of the new borough of Conshohocken; of the 727 people living in Conshohocken when it incorporated, 658 had come from Ireland.

The Irish played a major role in Conshohocken's history, and in 1900, they were still the largest of the borough's ethnic groups. That began to change as immigrants from southern and eastern Europe began to arrive in the last decade of the nineteenth century—first the Poles and then the Italians. For several decades, a substantial portion of Conshohocken's population—perhaps as much as 75 percent—was be foreign-born.

The borough's immigrants each brought their religions with them, and, as with all the Schuylkill River towns, the ethnic waves of the Conshohockens can be charted by when their various churches were established. The Conshohocken Presbyterian Church was built in 1847, and the Methodist Episcopal Church in 1854. The Irish Catholics built a church in 1851, and this was joined by Catholic Churches for Polish residents in 1905 and Italian residents in 1912. There was also the Calvary Protestant Episcopal Church, built in 1859, the First Baptist Church, built in 1871, St. John's African Methodist Episcopal Church, built in 1881, and St. Mark's Lutheran church. By 1920, the borough had nine churches serving eight denominations. West Conshohocken's population never grew enough to support the same degree of diversity. The Holiness Christian Church was the first to appear, in 1888. The Irish also built a Catholic Church, St. Gertrude's, in 1888. The borough also had the Free Baptist Church, built in 1895, and the Balligomingo Baptist Church, organized in 1840 but built in 1907. No other ethnic Catholic Churches were ever established.

Conshohocken's slight decline between the 1930 census and the 1940 tally of 10,776—thirty-nine fewer people—can easily be seen as a result of the Depression. Like all the river towns except Pottstown (and, to a lesser extent, Phoenixville), Conshohocken saw a near-stasis in its population between 1940 and 1950, but its 1950 population of 10,922 was the highest the borough ever attained. Sadly,

Conshohocken's good times after the Second World War would be brief indeed.

West Conshohocken was the only town of the eight river towns whose population peaked before the Second World War. Its population loss of 115 people over the next decade, while by no means large, was almost three times that of its neighbor across the river. Its population gain during the 1940s was just eighteen people. Such small changes were characteristic of West Conshohocken's history, but the minute gain of the 1940s would not make up the loss of the previous decade, and it would be the borough's last net gain. The trend would be all downhill from that point on.

Bridgeport

Area: .66 sq. mi.

Year of Incorporation: 1851

Bridgeport perches on a hillside above a floodplain on the right bank of the Schuylkill River, opposite Norristown and upriver from West Conshohocken. The river does not mark the county lines just upriver, so Bridgeport, despite being a right-bank town, sits in Montgomery County. The floodplain of the Schuylkill is substantial at that point, so Bridgeport eventually had both a canal and a railroad, although the combination never gave the borough anything close to the benefits those transportation modes gave Conshohocken, or even anything close to the benefits that the railroad alone gave Norristown.

Six of the towns discussed here are paired on opposite banks of the Schuylkill River—the legacy of prime fording locations. In two of these three pairings, the town on the river's left bank grew to dominate its pair on the right bank. While the Conshohockens demonstrate this, the stunting effect is best demonstrated in Bridgeport. Norristown's earlier establishment, its position as the county seat, and its size combined to limit Bridgeport's industrial, commercial, and political aspirations in the period before the Second World War. Having a thriving neighbor made Bridgeport into a quiet, unassuming, modestly sized and locally oriented community whose residents worked in equally modest-sized industries along the river floodplain, and who walked across the river to Norristown to purchase just about everything more than their daily necessities. Bridgeport grew, and a commercial sector sufficient for the population did arise, but Bridgeport would always exist in the shadow of its larger neighbor.

Bridgeport can trace its roots to a Schuylkill ford that bore the name of a people, not an individual. A group of Swedes purchased land along the right bank of the Schuylkill from Welsh settlers who had, in turn, purchased land from Letitia Penn, William Penn's daughter, to whom the Proprietor had originally gifted it. The Swedes moved up the Schuylkill in 1712 and settled in an area whose subsequent names would continue to reflect their nationality. The northernmost landowner among this group was Mats Holstein; his land included much of what would be Bridgeport, but his real contribution was to establish a ford at that location by stretching a rope across the river from his house to the opposite bank. He later added a small boat to aid in the crossing. The ford was well used, but unlike Matson and Royer, Holstein's name was never associated with the crossing; it was always known as "Swedes Ford" (the apostrophe, if it every actually existed, disappeared quickly).

Swedes Ford, like Matson's Ford downriver, earned a place in history during the American Revolution. In 1777, after the disheartening loss at the Battle of Brandywine in September, the ragged Continental Army was forced to retreat. It began a withdrawal that would not end until it had established its winter encampment at Valley Forge. On the last stage of the journey, Washington's army crossed the Schuylkill at Swedes Ford by pushing wagons into the river, linking them together and laying a path of planks and fence rails across them. With the crossing accomplished, a scouting party of British troops that had observed the maneuver returned to the relative warmth of Philadelphia, while the Continental Army pushed on to Gulph Mills and, eventually, Valley Forge.

Little happened in the wake of the Revolution in the area. Swedes Ford met a modest but necessary transportation need, Holstein built a tavern on the right bank, and another enterprising individual built one on the other side. Those taverns, and on-call repair services from a blacksmith as needed, were the only exceptions to the farm life that developed on both banks of the river in that early period. As elsewhere, significant transformations followed the changes in transportation. For Bridgeport, there would be three of these in the nineteenth century: the Schuylkill Navigation System, a bridge across the river, and, in particular, the railroad.

At the borough's boundary, a road sign (which begins by noting that Norristown is just one mile away) identifies Bridgeport as having been "named on account of port and building of bridge. Founded 1829." This properly celebrates Bridgeport's two earliest transportation influences. The bridge was still under construction in 1829, but placing "bridge" before "port" accurately reflects their respective influence. The combination began the process of transforming the rural village into an urban borough; as with every other river town, the railroad would speed that process significantly.

The Schuylkill Navigation System provided the first step in the transformation. Elisha Evans, who owned an inn on the Norristown bank of the river, also owned considerable land along the right bank. In 1816, the nascent borough of Norristown refused to allow the SNS to build a canal section the left bank of the river, so Evans offered his land on the right bank. Both Elisha and his son Cadwallader shared the role of founders of Bridgeport.

The canal stimulated some local manufacturing but little settlement, as its pace was slow, and it shut down entirely over the winter. It brought no more prosperity to the area than it had to Spring City or Phoenixville upriver. What the SNS *did* do was effectively determine the east and west boundaries of the future borough of Bridgeport, according to the wording of the original charter.

The SNS was functioning by 1824. The next major step in Bridgeport's evolution into a town was the construction of its first bridge over the Schuylkill in 1830. The wooden bridge was built to align with DeKalb Street in Norristown, upriver from Swedes Ford. It could accommodate carts and people, for a fee. Vehicles paid according to weight and size, but walkers were charged a penny. Anyone who purchased a roll of a hundred tickets paid fifty cents, thus halving the price. The bridge company soon regretted its policy that walking across the bridge was free for anyone headed to church, as there were soon increasingly large numbers of men going to church on weekdays. Their complaints ended when the DeKalb Street Bridge was freed in 1884. The road to the new bridge was called DeKalb Street in Bridgeport as well, and called the "State Road" to the south. This quickly caused the focus of Bridgeport's existence to shift from Swedes Ford to DeKalb Street, where it would remain.

Bridgeport got a second bridge over the Schuylkill in the area of Swedes Ford in 1848, terminating at Ford Streets in both Bridgeport and Norristown. This bridge was built primarily for the Chester Valley Railroad, and thus had tracks, although pedestrians and vehicles could also cross, for a fee. The railroad line was unprofitable, and the bridge fell into disrepair. The Reading Company purchased it in 1872, but it burned substantially in 1883. The railroad sold it to the Federal Bridge Company, which rebuilt it and named it the "Ford Street Bridge." In the absence of any substantial train traffic, the company made it more accessible to foot and automobile traffic. The Ford Street Bridge continued to charge for crossings, and was known to generations of residents in both Bridgeport and Norristown as the "penny bridge" until it was condemned and torn down in 1939. It was not replaced. The road to and from the original Swedes Ford continued to exist, and became Swedesford Road south of Bridgeport, but it always carried just local traffic.

As a town that depended heavily on its bridge connections across the Schuylkill, Bridgeport suffered greatly in 1924. On April 14, the ancient, wooden, covered bridge at DeKalb Street burned. Fewer than two months later, on June 11, the not-so-ancient Ford Street Bridge also burned. The latter was partially repaired, with planks across the foundation, and although that restored foot traffic, vehicles could not cross. The loss of both bridges within three months severed all road connections between the Norristown and Bridgeport, leaving only the P&W trolley bridge between them. This was inconvenience to both boroughs, but Bridgeport needed Norristown more than Norristown needed Bridgeport. The two boroughs engaged in a joint effort to erect a new, modern bridge, and the concrete DeKalb Street Bridge opened in November 1925.

A bridge was an absolute necessity for any growth to take place, but the real stimulus to Bridgeport came in 1839, when the Reading Railroad first ran trains between its home city and Philadelphia along its new tracks on the river's right bank. The trains carried primarily coal, and the Reading gave little attention to passengers along this line. Still, it was enough to kill off what little stagecoach and canal

passenger traffic remained. Bridgeport was little more than a whistle-
stop on the line, a circumstance that changed somewhat after local
industries began to locate there. Passenger service on the Reading's
line through Bridgeport continued until the 1930s, when it fell victim
to cutbacks during the Depression.

Bridgeport was incorporated as a borough on February 27, 1851,
taking land from Upper Merion Township. Its population of 572,
according to the 1850 census, was only slightly more than Norristown
had when it had become a borough thirty-eight years earlier.

Bridgeport never produced iron or steel, and no industry comparable in size to the larger ones in Pottstown, Phoenixville, or Conshohocken was ever established there. Only in textiles did Bridgeport
produce a name recognizable outside the town limits. Like Norristown, which also never enticed any of the major smokestack industries, Bridgeport developed a diverse industrial sector of small to
midsize firms. Its history is replete with the comings and goings of
such manufacturing firms, from brick kilns to makers of bonnets and
straw hats, textiles, paper, and even kerosene. One of the textile mills
after the Civil War even produced substantial quantities of a new
product known as "jeans."

Textile firms existed in Bridgeport, as in every other river town,
but they could not compete in scale with what existed across the river.
In fact, Bridgeport's largest textile plant during the early decades of
the twentieth century belonged to the Norristown firm of Rambo &
Regar, and closed by 1930. Another, Energetic Worsted Company,
lasted until after the Second World War. Aside from textiles, however, Bridgeport's industrial history is peppered with many names that
became better known after the war, like Tose, Inc., a trucking firm
that originated in Bridgeport; after several changes and mergers (and
well after World War II), the surname became quite familiar outside
the area in 1949 when Leonard Tose, the founder's son, purchased
the Philadelphia Eagles professional football franchise.

Bridgeport's most important product during its prosperous years
was wool. The largest and best known of Bridgeport's wool companies originated in 1846 when English immigrant James Lees opened a
water-powered spinning mill in the area. After that burned down in
1864, Lees relocated to another burnt-out mill, and began once more.

His company, originally called Minerva Mills, managed a steady, if unspectacular, success. The mill at first produced yarn varieties, and sold much of its product to carpet manufacturers. By the time of Lees's death in 1887, he and his sons had built a company with six plant locations and several hundred employees. In 1928, the firm purchased two carpet manufacturing companies, and from that point on focused solely on producing carpet, earning its place in local history as Lees Carpet Mill. Lees was Bridgeport's largest employer for over a century. The company began its move to the South in the 1930s, and although it retained its administrative headquarters in Bridgeport, actual carpet production there did not long survive the Second World War.

At least some of Bridgeport's industrial growth can be attributed to positive action by its borough council; in 1900, the council voted to lure businesses by offering a ten-year tax exemption to any industry that located in Bridgeport, as long as it did not conflict with existing industries. The results were positive; in the decades of the twentieth century leading up to World War II, Bridgeport had a reputation for being a town where anyone could find a job. At the onset of that war, the borough's industrial workforce numbered about four thousand. The community's boast was that people who worked in Bridgeport outnumbered those who lived there. Within a decade after the end of the Second World War, that boast would begin to ring hollow.

Bridgeport never grew beyond its original boundaries, and remained deeply in Norristown's shadow for the period of its entire existence up through the Second World War. This proximity had several effects on Bridgeport's development, none of them good. The most baleful of these effects was on those institutions fundamental to vital communities, such as volunteer fire departments, local newspapers, and centers for community culture and entertainment. Additionally, since Bridgeport residents had easy access to the county's largest shopping location just across the river, its own attempts to develop a strong commercial sector were always at a disadvantage. For virtually all of the nineteenth century, the lack of any means to preserve food in the average home made shopping a daily requirement. The reality of bridge tolls encouraged the purveyors of day-to-day items to establish businesses on the Bridgeport side of the river.

However, when the DeKalb Street Bridge was freed in 1884, even the poorest of Bridgeport's citizens could access downtown Norristown without much difficulty.

Local stores that stocked the most common items survived, but no stores with regional aspirations could survive in Bridgeport. Mom-and-pop stores came to comprise the majority of the shops in the borough's commercial sector, just as small firms came to comprise the vast majority of the businesses in its industrial sector. Similar stores of similar size dominated each of the river towns in sheer numbers, and only the larger towns produced the famous local commercial names. Bridgeport falls into the category of those that didn't, along with Royersford, Spring City, and West Conshohocken.

As in the other river towns, Bridgeport's commercial sector developed along the road to the river crossing (in this case, DeKalb Street) and along a street parallel to the river (in this case, Fourth Street). Businesses that did not front directly on either of these streets were usually no more than a block away. Since DeKalb Street was part of the State Road, and later US Route 202, through traffic made this a significant commercial location. Businesses attuned to servicing those travelers, beginning with blacksmiths and wheelwrights, and later shifting to automobile parts stores and service stations, were established uphill at the borough line.

Still, as the population of Bridgeport grew, a wider variety of businesses and retail stores moved in, although some were branches of Norristown-based stores, such as Daub Hardware. One long-lasting exception was the I. F. March and Sons Company, although its moves would reflect the difference between the two boroughs; the company began in Bridgeport, but later shifted its larger retail operations to Norristown and retained just a manufacturing plant in Bridgeport.

Bridgeport's two long-lasting banks began at the intersection of Fourth and DeKalb Streets, the Bridgeport Federal Savings and Loan Association in 1878, and the Bridgeport National Bank in 1928. Both serviced the population and the regular needs of the business community, and continued to do so for years under a frequently changing array of names. All major business and banking affairs, however, took place across the river, as did virtually all legal work.

Bridgeport, and in particular its industrial sector, suffered its share of the bane of nineteenth-century existence: fire. The borough's slow growth greatly delayed its firefighting capabilities. For its first forty years of existence, Bridgeport was forced to depend on Norristown fire companies to deal with any conflagrations on its side of the river. Norristown companies begrudgingly took responsibility, with the various fire companies taking turns to respond or, as was occasionally alleged, fail to respond. The Lees Carpet Mill was a frequent site for fires. Without any municipal firefighting capability, the company was eventually forced to purchase its own hand-operated pump.

A major reason for the delay in forming a local volunteer fire company was the lack of a municipal water supply. Bridgeport depended on privately owned wells until quite late in the century. In 1886, it began laying the first pipes for a water system to serve at least the industrial floodplain, but a period of frequent and devastating fires demonstrated the need for both a more comprehensive water supply and a volunteer fire company. By 1889, Bridgeport had extended its the water system to include fire hydrants, and built a reservoir on high ground. In 1891, the community established the Bridgeport Fire Company No. 1, but it was some years before the firehouse had enough equipment to be as effective in action as it was during parades. Still, the borough's growth led to a second company, the Goodwill Fire Company, being formed in 1915, although it, too, required some years to achieve practicality. Both fire companies became centers of Bridgeport's locally oriented social life, as firehouses did in every river town.

The first street lighting was by gas lamps, but in 1889, the borough received its first electric lamps, supplied by the Norristown Electric Company. The borough never developed its own utility for either electricity or gas. Bridgeport also never established a local newspaper that survived for any length of time. One attempt by a Bridgeport resident to establish a newspaper helps illustrate the relationship between the two boroughs during that period. In 1881, one of Bridgeport's leading citizens, Captain William Rennyson, joined the large number of local people angry that the DeKalb Street Bridge still charged a toll to cross. He was unable to convince the *Norristown Register* to support the cause, so he established his own newspaper that supported freeing the bridge. He wrote, edited, and printed his paper, which he called the *Norristown Daily Times*, in Norristown.

Competition from Norristown was one reason that Bridgeport's culture became so community-oriented. Only one movie theater, the Broadway, was ever established in Bridgeport. The Broadway began by offering live performances on stage, as did every borough theater, before adjusting to accommodate the silver screen. In contrast, Norristown had five movie theaters in the first half of the twentieth century, and that competition just across the now-free bridge worked against the Broadway, which barely survived the Second World War.

Bridgeport partook, in a small way, in the era of light rail from the 1880s through the early twentieth century. The Norristown Passenger Railway Company laid tracks down DeKalb Street, and in 1887 extended the route across the bridge into Bridgeport. The trolley crossed the Reading Railroad tracks (without any assistance from the Reading Company, as was typical of the heavy-and-light-rail right-of-way disputes of the time), and eventually on to Lees Carpet Mill. The early trolleys were horse-drawn, but in 1893, the Citizens Passenger Railway completed an electrified line through the borough. As with all but one of the region's trolley companies in the 1930s, Bridgeport saw its limited trolley service replaced—in this case, more than replaced—by buses in 1933.

A second light rail line left a more lasting legacy, and it is still running. In 1912, the Philadelphia and Western Railway Company (P&W) opened a line that still runs from 69th Street in West Philadelphia to Norristown and across the Schuylkill River, casting a daily shadow on portions of the borough.

Bridgeport's population experienced a near doubling in the first decade of existence after the railroad's arrival, as had the other boroughs along the river, except for West Conshohocken, the last to incorporate. Bridgeport's population growth thereafter was slow and steady, never exceeding a thousand new residents per decade.

The religious inclinations of the people who first populated what would become Bridgeport were typical of the first European settlers in the other seven river towns. Bridgeport's first church was Baptist, completed in 1850. In 1875, enough of the members of Norristown's Second Presbyterian Church actually lived in Bridgeport that they could build their own church, the Bridgeport Presbyterian Church. The waves of immigration that altered the demographics of the other river towns did the same in Bridgeport. The Irish were the first to arrive, initially to work on the SNS and later to work on the railroad, and thus were present at the time of its incorporation. Nevertheless, the borough's slow population growth meant that for several decades, Irish Catholics had to attend St. Patrick's Church in Norristown. It wasn't until 1892 that the Irish built their own church in Bridgeport, St. Augustine's.

By that time, the more ethnically diverse industrial immigrants had begun arriving. Italians were the early major component of this movement. (In fact, Italians eventually became the largest ethnic group in Bridgeport, after the war.) The newcomers were, of course, no more welcome at the Irish Catholic church, St. Augustine's, than they were at St. Patrick's in Norristown. The much more numerous Italians in Norristown, however, had established their own church, Holy Saviour, and Bridgeport's Italians were welcomed there. As their numbers increased, they began to meet in a room in Bridgeport rented from an Italian landlord. They founded their own congregation in 1924, and began to erect a church by 1926, Our Lady of Mount Carmel. The year of its founding also marked the first year of what would become perhaps Bridgeport's signature event, the Grande Festa Italiana, better known as "The Feast." Our Lady of Mount Carmel Church has hosted the festival from the beginning, and it grew into a sizeable event and remained so through the end of the Second World War, and afterward.

The two largest groups after the Italians to settle in Bridgeport came from Ukraine and Slovakia. Their numbers were considerably smaller (about four hundred of each), but upon arrival, they found themselves tossed into and further complicating the ethnic mix in the borough. "Mix" is most likely the wrong word, however, as neither the Ukrainians nor the Slovaks were welcomed by the Irish nor by the Italians, and the newcomers demonstrated no great desire to worship with those groups or with each other. The Ukrainians organized their own congregation in 1924 and the Slovaks in 1926, and built their churches somewhat later.

After the turn of the twentieth century, the diverse flood of immigrants continued to produce Catholic Churches, including Sacred Heart Church in 1907, and Our Mother of Sorrows, whose official opening in March 1929 proved to be ill timed. The former, however, was not in Bridgeport but in Swedesburg, its neighbor to the east.

Like the other river towns, Bridgeport divided itself into ethnic and religious subcommunities that centered on its churches. Bridgeport was the smallest of the eight river towns to achieve such diversity; West Conshohocken, Royersford, and Spring City never did. This was a great stimulus to the local focus so characteristic of Bridgeport, but in the period up to the Second World War, the result was also a community subdivided within itself by ethnicity, although to a lesser extent than Norristown.

In 1940, Bridgeport became the second of the eight towns to reach its peak population, 5,904 people. That this represented a substantial gain from the borough's 1930 population of 5,195 was a positive sign, but there would be no others. The war brought the mix of economic good and personal sorrow to Bridgeport, as it did to each river town. The economic good lasted but a few years, and Bridgeport soon joined the other towns along the lower Schuylkill in an economic and demographic free fall.

Spring City   Royersford
Area: .8 sq. mi.   *Area: .86 sq. mi.*

Year of Incorporation: 1867   *Year of Incorporation: 1879*

The boroughs of Royersford and Spring City are located directly opposite one another on the left and right banks respectively of the Schuylkill River, below Pottstown and just above Phoenixville. They are referred to as "the twin boroughs," as they are almost the same size, they both sit on steep hillsides, and they have close to the same number of residents. They are thus the only paired towns that do not demonstrate a left-bank dominance over their history. Spring City is also the only right bank borough paired by a fording location to incorporate before its left-bank partner.

Their history demonstrates several linkages—so many that the story of both towns must be told together. Both Royersford and Spring City grew up at the same river ford location; repeated attempts to replace the ford with a bridge dominated the affairs of both, as did the connection between them once a lasting bridge was built. The arrival of the railroads spurred the growth of each and their adoption of borough status. The railroad caused their physical layouts to be near mirror images of each other, and smaller versions of the standard Schuylkill River layout. The population trends of both are very similar, and they jointly experienced the same basic historical trajectory as the other six towns in this study, including their most recent years. Major events such as floods and fires required cooperation between the two boroughs, and provided a repetitive lesson in the importance of across-the-river ties.

Their specific differences have little to do with the major difference between them, which is that they reside in different counties. The Schuylkill River is the county line along the stretch where they lie, placing Royersford in Montgomery County and Spring City in Chester County. The fundamental ties between them have always been stronger than that political divide. Even the current school district they share crosses county lines, one of the very few in Pennsylvania to do so. They even share a common historical society.

The real differences the twin boroughs have exhibited during their history derive in large part from the evolution of their connections to transportation, from the Schuylkill Navigation System to the railroads to, more recently, a limited-access highway. The boroughs of Royersford and Spring City grew at a ford of the Schuylkill River. In the early nineteenth century, the land by the ford on both banks of the Schuylkill River was divided into four farms, two on each riverbank. Two brothers, David and Benjamin Royer, farmed adjoining properties on the right bank, while Fred Berkstrasser and Samuel Custer operated adjoining farms on the left bank. Both pairs of farms were separated by a public road that descended to the fording location; the two roads met at a shallow spot in the river. The Royer brothers' name became associated with the ford and to the eventual borough across the river from their farms, but the land they owned would actually become part of Spring City.

Not all fording locations are created equal, and the one associated with the Royer brothers was more difficult to cross than some, even when the river was at its usual flow. To keep those crossing from being swept downriver, the brothers stretched a substantial rope across the river at the point near the juncture of their farms to the left bank, and secured each end to trees. They threaded the rope through an iron ring that could slide along the entire length, from bank to bank, and used as a primitive safety line. Those crossing could tie a rope from the ring to themselves, their animals, or their carriages, and be guided across the river. A local history notes that a crossing via this system this was often a risky endeavor. A small boat was later added to aid in some of these short journeys.

The initial histories of both boroughs demonstrate how little benefit the SNS generated for the river communities, and how the creation of the twin boroughs had everything to do with the railroad. The SNS had begun to operate there by 1818, although it was not officially finished until 1824. The initial growth of the still-unincorporated area on the right bank was largely due to the arrival of the SNS; the first small industries located there, while the left bank remained agricultural, and was thus even more sparsely populated except near the ford itself. There were no mills on the left bank. Until the railroad arrived, that area saw less activity than its counterpart across the river.

The early connection via the SNS gave the residents of the right bank a head start, even if it did prove to be only temporary. The small community that grew up on the right bank was called "Pumptown" for the number of small, freshwater springs in the area, and the centrally located pump, although the appellation was unpopular with the residents themselves.

Pumptown never accumulated sufficient numbers from the SNS's proximity to seek borough status, but it did gain sufficient stimulus, oddly enough, from the construction of the Reading Railroad across the river. The all-important bridge connection across the Schuylkill nourished both locations, and was the agent that delivered borough status to both sides of the river.

The residents of Pumptown were interested in building a bridge to replace the unreliable ford, and once they learned that the Reading Railroad's route would be on the other side of the river, that interest achieved a new urgency. They formed a committee, which petitioned the legislature for permission to form a bridge company. The legislature granted a charter in 1839, and the new company set to work, buying land from both Custer and Berkstrasser for the bridge's left bank abutments. On September 7, 1840, the first bridge—built of wood—opened, charging tolls for the crossing.

This first all-weather connection between the two small communities spurred further development. In 1843, James Rogers built a small foundry on the river's right bank to cast iron stoves, the first such effort in an area that would soon be known for its stoves and stove accessories. This gradually evolved into the Spring City Stove Works, the most famous of Spring City's industries. Frederick Yost, another early business pioneer, constructed a gristmill at the foot of the bridge, and he also sold lime, lumber, and coal. Together, Rogers and Yost were the prime movers in the effort to convert their nascent community into a borough. They succeeded in 1867, when the area centered on the former Royer property was chartered as the Borough of Springville. In 1872, while preparing to open their first post office, the residents discovered that Pennsylvania already had a Springville. Following a town meeting, the borough adopted the name "Spring City," which it has retained ever since.

The longer-established and more-populated Chester County side, Springville, may have incorporated first, but the railroad stimulated considerable economic and population growth on both banks. In fact, the still-unincorporated community on the left bank of Royer's Ford was already becoming statistically dominant, thanks to the railroad. The Philadelphia and Reading Railroad was scheduled to arrive in the area in 1839. Its specific route along the left bank was announced in advance, which led to serious local competition. Since the announced route would run right past the lands of both Berkstrasser and Custer, each realized the profit to be made by becoming the new railroad's stopping point, and both made plans accordingly. By the time the railroad arrived, the two existing structures in the area—the homes of Berkstrasser and Custer respectively—had been joined by two others, each built as a tavern and hotel, located close to one another on the adjoining properties of both. As it turned out, Berkstrasser's hotel became the first station, with tickets for the railroad sold at the bar. A later owner opened a store at the rear of the hotel. This first store in the area also served as the first post office. The Reading Railroad formalized the name of this small stop, initially terming it "Royer's

Ford." The apostrophe would later be discarded and the name run together as it is today.

A bridge across the river connected the two communities by 1840, but for the next fifty years, both locations were challenged in their attempts to maintain that connection by floods, fires, and construction calamities. After the Schuylkill's massive 1850 flood destroyed the first bridge at Royer's Ford (and many others between Reading and Philadelphia), the communities built another bridge, but not without difficulty. The first contractor selected to build it, along with a few of the town fathers, were testing the new bridge in the most elementary manner—they were collectively walking across—when it gave way. Everyone survived, but the contractor departed shortly afterward under cover of darkness. The next bridge was stronger, but also built of wood. It was destroyed in 1884 by a fire that originated in an old factory building on the Spring City side. The construction of an iron bridge shortly afterward ended the string of disasters. The nearby Phoenixville Bridge Company forged its components, and the bridge opened in 1887. A small ferry was procured to transport people and items across the river for the three years required to build the bridge. While inconvenient, it did spare the residents of both boroughs from having to return to the days of fording the river. The new bridge served without major incident until a concrete bridge replaced it in 1922.

By the time the iron bridge was being constructed, a reliable span was an absolute necessity, as the left bank above the ford, largely woodland and small farm fields before 1839, was in the middle of a major transformation. The initial manufacturing success with iron stoves and grates on the Chester County side had spurred similar efforts across the river in Montgomery County. These companies produced similar products, and soon surpassed those in Spring City in both size and variety, largely because of their immediate proximity to the Reading Railroad.

Industry in Royersford and Spring City soon expanded to other small iron- or steel-related fabrication works, glass manufacture, and hosiery mills. The Royersford Iron Foundry Company was the area's first such concern, opening in 1865. A year later, the company sold some of its buildings to a new firm that would become one of the foundations of Royersford's prosperity: Francis, Buckwalter and Company. It grew, becoming the Buckwalter Stove Company in 1888 and eventually Continental Stove Works. Additional stove manufacturers and other small industries set up shop on both sides of the river, transforming both boroughs into small industrial centers. Glass manufacturing joined the mix in 1886, and by the last decade of the nineteenth century, several other industries familiar to the Schuylkill Valley—bricks, iron and steel fittings, machine tools, and hosiery—had appeared. As with the other river towns, metal products tended to dominate, but for the period up until the 1930s, textiles were of major importance. In 1919, Spring City's second- and third-largest employers were the Schuylkill Valley Mills, which employed 420 people, and the Century Knitting Company, which had a payroll of 313. The largest of them all was emblematic of how little difference the bank of the river (and thus the county) actually made: this was the Spring City Knitting Company, which became Royersford's largest employer with around one thousand workers.

All of this depended on the railroad, which expanded its local facilities with the growth of local industrial products; freight cars loaded with the products of both boroughs were attached to incoming freight trains, and transported to distant destinations. Railroad-inspired growth led Royersford to incorporate, and it received its charter on June 14, 1879—the last of the eight towns along the lower Schuylkill River to do so. The new borough, carved from the southeastern corner of Limerick Township, then had a population estimated at five hundred people. As one of their first acts, its civic leaders immediately renamed their borough's roads: the road leading to the ford was named Main Street; the road that ran parallel to the river was initially named High Street, and later renamed Second Avenue. Main and High Streets would become, respectively, the backbones of the borough's commercial district and its industrial sector. In Spring City, growth and development delivered the opposite result: its more narrow floodplain led the town's commercial sector to grow along the road that paralleled the river, Main Street.

Shortly after Royersford's incorporation, the Reading Railroad began to feel the first direct challenge to its transportation monopoly along the Schuylkill Valley when the Pennsylvania Railroad decided to built its own line in the valley and compete directly for the transportation of products. The Pennsylvania Railroad's direct challenge to the Reading's lines was fought on both sides of the Schuylkill Valley. The Reading's earlier purchase of the PG&N had given it tracks on both banks of the river, and the Pennsylvania subsequently concluded that a reasonably efficient route along the valley required it to cross the meandering Schuylkill at various points.

Thus it was that, while the Pennsylvania built its main line in the Royersford/Spring City area along the right bank—the first train through Spring City ran in September 1884—it also wanted to serve the Royersford side. In 1892, the Pennsylvania built a bridge to carry a spur across the river into Royersford along River Street (later First Avenue), and applied for permission to lay its track. This new line would run directly alongside the existing Reading tracks, as both would serve the same industrial locations. The Reading fought this vigorously in court, but in the evening of June 14, the Royersford Borough Council finally signed the ordinance allowing the Pennsylvania to construct its parallel track. Managers of the Pennsylvania's local work gangs fully expected that the next day's efforts and those that followed would feature harassment by Reading workers, and they planned accordingly: while waiting for the formal approval, they collected all the rails, ties, spikes, and other necessary materials and hid them, nearby but accessible. That night, as soon as the ordinance was signed, they quietly moved in a small army of laborers and set to work. By dawn, when Reading employees gathered for the expected confrontation, the track had already been spiked into place.

The 1880 census put Royersford's population at 558 residents. At 1,112, Spring City possessed almost twice that number, and could claim to be the more significant of the two boroughs for a while longer. Royersford had no jail when it became a borough, and had to pay Spring City a dollar a head to lock up Royersford miscreants until a local jail was built in 1884.

The 1890 census reflected a change in the relationship between the twin boroughs: although Spring City's population had increased to 1,797, Royersford had exploded, and its population now numbered 1,815. Royersford already had three banks and a savings and loan association. That statistical trend would continue, eventually placing

Royersford above Spring City in virtually every category, although the difference would never amount to much. Both underwent slow population growth, with some periodic dips. In 1940, Royersford's population of 3,605 only slightly exceeded Spring City's 3,022.

Both Royersford and Spring City remained small enough that each could continue to depend on wells for drinking water long after larger boroughs had begun to tap the Schuylkill. The Home Water Company was organized in 1889 to serve both boroughs; it initially drew from local wells, but by 1893, the company had to build a new plant to draw water from the river. By that time, however, the lessons of similar projects both up and downriver had been learned, and the new plant filtered its water from the very start.

For towns as small as Royersford and Spring City, the lack of tax receipts meant that both water and waste treatment plants had to wait until government funding became available during the Depression. Spring City's sewer system, including a treatment plant, was first built under WPA program, with the agency supplying 45 percent of the cost. Construction began in 1937, and the system began operating the next year. Royersford's sewer collection system was completed in 1938, also with WPA funding. Before the completion of its treatment plant, the stench in Royersford would get so bad that fire companies had to be called to flush the streets.

The industries of Spring City and Royersford were small by comparison to other river towns, but their furnaces and stoves were as hot as any. Thus, both boroughs suffered from the biggest threat to any industrial town during the nineteenth and early twentieth centuries: fire. This was a primary concern to both boroughs from their inception, but their small and slowly growing populations delayed the organization of fire companies. An 1881 blaze demonstrated both the danger of fire and the need for community cooperation. In the early hours of July 5, a fire began in a warehouse of the Shantz and Keeley Foundry in Spring City. Once roused, local residents did their best, but Spring City had not installed any water mains, and its springs and hand wells were inadequate to fight the blaze. There was ample water available from the river, but there was no means to raise it from the river and deliver it to the fire. The town appealed to Phoenixville, Pottstown, and even Norristown for help. All three sent contingents, which arrived in Spring City by noon via the railroad and remained on site through July 6. Local residents did what they could, wetting down carpets and blankets and spreading them over the roofs of their houses, remaining aloft to soak them with buckets of water brought by friends and family. The fire leveled almost the entire foundry and damaged a large inventory of stoves, but the rest of the borough, including the all-important bridge, was saved.

This disaster led to the founding of Spring City's Liberty Steam Engine Company in 1882. A fire in Royersford, although not as large, led to its first fire company being organized in 1883, although it was unable to purchase its first piece of equipment until 1895. A second company—the Friendship Hook, Ladder and Hose Company—was organized in 1897, but it was unable to purchase its first piece of equipment until 1906. Organizing fire companies was one indication that both boroughs were settling into life as urban centers, however small. Their fire companies followed the area's pattern of becoming focal points for the community.

Each of the twin boroughs established a small commercial sector, no larger than it needed to service its small local populations plus people in the nearby countryside. Main Street was the home for the retail stores of both boroughs, but Royersford's Main Street ran from 2nd Street up the hillside, while Spring City's Main Street paralleled the river. Small, owner-proprietor stores filled both streets. None of the national chains, except for the usual five-and-dimes, had stores in either city, nor did any local shops grow to the size or popularity of the larger stores in Pottstown or Phoenixville. The boroughs' tightly knit communities, however, were highly loyal to their local stores, allowing the Main Street retail tradition to continue until after the Second World War.

Spring City had one significant organization that Royersford did not: the Pennhurst State School and Hospital, which opened in 1908, eventually housing some three thousand patients. This was a state institution for the mentally ill, as defined during that time, and as the population grew, so did its aspect as a separate community. It was largely self-contained, providing recreation and work for its residents in addition to living quarters. The complex overlooked the river in one of its most scenic locations, but remained isolated and largely overlooked by Spring City residents.

No trolleys ever connected to Royersford, although lines did pass north of the borough on their way to Norristown and Pottstown. Across the river, the Montgomery and Chester Electric Railway opened service between Phoenixville and Spring City on July 5, 1899. As did other trolley companies, it sought supplement its profits by boosting weekend usage, building the Bonnie Brae Amusement Park; and, as with all but one regional trolley line, it fell victim to the bus and the automobile.

By the beginning of the twentieth century, both boroughs had settled into an established pattern, each developing a small version of the classic Schuylkill River Valley town layout. Their industries were located along the river's floodplain, adjacent to the railroad, along with the lowest-quality housing. The commercial sectors were located within the respective four-block Main Streets. The people worked in their industries, shopped along their commercial streets, and lived in homes up both hillsides according to their incomes, as in the other Schuylkill River towns; the greater a household's wealth, the farther up the hill and away from the river it was likely to be.

The ethnic and racial backgrounds of these people, however, differed substantially from those of the other six towns in this study. The ethnic and religious mix of the twin boroughs remained closer to colonial times, with far less diversity than graced the other six towns. Even after the successive waves of immigrants bestowed their benefits on most of the Schuylkill River towns, the twin boroughs were even more homogeneous than the equally small borough of West Conshohocken. Both Spring City and Royersford remained overwhelmingly Protestant. In 1910, as the industrial immigrants were flooding the eastern half of the United States, only 1 percent of the population of the twin boroughs was foreign born—a remarkable contrast with the other six river towns. For example, Conshohocken's foreign-born population during that period approached 75 percent.

The first building in the twin boroughs constructed specifically for religious services was the Union Meeting House in Spring City, in 1851. A Methodist congregation bought the building in 1855, making it the first active church in the borough. Lutherans had opened a church in a vacant school building by 1870, just outside the borough. Baptists built Royersford's first church in 1879; Methodists built another shortly thereafter. Others followed, all of them Protestant. In testimony to Spring City's dominance at this time, several Royersford churches began as offshoots from its twin: for example, the United Methodist Church of Royersford first organized in 1882 as the "daughter" of the Spring City Methodist Church.

Immigrant Catholics did arrive, but not in the numbers sufficient to replicate the ethnic neighborhoods that were springing up in the other river towns. Catholic worship first appeared in Spring City in 1891, at a private house. By 1892, St. Joseph's Parish of Spring City was sufficiently organized to sponsor the Sacred Heart Church of Royersford, that borough's first Catholic place of worship.

More workers were needed to staff the mills and factories, however, and some immigrants did flow into and settle in the two communities. Most were laborers, but the artisans of the Royersford Glass Works were an exception. The company recruited skilled glassblowers from Belgium, and even constructed a number of houses along a street for them that became known as "Belgium Row." Their daily work was humdrum, producing standard bottles over and over again, so the company allowed them to use the pieces of glass that were left over at the end of the working day to make whatever their imagination inspired; the Spring-Ford Historical Society has a collection of these pieces on display, testimony to the glassblowers' art.

The small waves of European immigrants were tolerated, barely, but African Americans continued to be unwelcome, and—by custom, at least—excluded. Before the Second World War, neither borough had more than a few African American residents. The Great Migration from the south to the industrial cities in the north was well under way after World War I, and while some African Americans found their way to the Schuylkill Valley, both Royersford and Spring City largely resisted the influx. The residents of the twin boroughs largely continued to be "white, Protestant, and proud of it."[6]

Aside from a lack of racial and ethnic diversity, the twin boroughs both grew to be miniature versions of towns up and downriver. They

6. Personal communication by the president of the Spring Ford Area Historical Society, Bill Brunner, to the author.

were intensely local communities. This was an age of club member-ship, and the residents of both boroughs organized volunteer and civic organizations, as well as a plethora of the lodges and societies that were popular at the time. In towns the size of the twin boroughs, the old cliché that "everybody knew everybody" came close to being true. The outside world existed, but the focus of each borough and its population extended little farther than the other side of the bridge. Their newspaper symbolized this connection. The *Twin-Boro Weekly Advertiser* was founded in 1890 by locals for their neighbors. It was a family affair, passed down from parent to child, and gained such a large local advertising base that it was distributed free.

The Depression was the first significant and lasting interruption in the steadily growing prosperity of the twin boroughs. Royersford celebrated its fiftieth anniversary in June 1929; shortly afterward, the stock market crash inaugurated an era that would never be as golden as the previous one—for the twin boroughs or for the other industrial communities along the river.

The Depression taught both boroughs that even locally focused communities were not immune to events and changes far beyond their borders. The orders for their factories' products began to slow, and local companies had to deal with the ripple effects of industrial contraction. The Depression doomed many of the small firms in each borough, but others survived. One of Royersford's three banks failed, and officials later faced over three hundred counts of embezzlement, an event that revealed the downside to a community's local focus; its depositors, all local residents, lost heavily.

The first census after the end of the Depression showed the first decline in Royersford's population since it had become a borough, although by only 114 people; its 1940 population was 3,605. By that date, Spring City's population had increased by fifty-nine people to 3,022. Such small changes for each decade had characterized the population levels of both boroughs since the first decade of each, but the overall trend had been up.

Postwar Optimism

By 1940, the threat of American involvement in the wars of Europe and Asia, still separate at that point, had restored industrial activity in each of the river boroughs, although by little compared with what would soon follow. When the nation plunged into war again, this time on two fronts, the residents of the Schuylkill River boroughs went through much of what they had gone through just over twenty years earlier, but for a longer time, with more restrictions.

Whether white or black, rich and poor, male or female, native or immigrant, and regardless of ethnicity or religion, the people of the Schuylkill River towns endured the Second World War, working long hours, contributing to war-related activities, and supporting the many soldiers and medical personnel overseas. The residents of each town coped dutifully with the deprivations, the rationing, the travel restrictions, and the constant concern over the fate of loved ones. What social life they had usually centered on their ethnically homogenous churches, along with patriotic rallies and events. The recent past had been unpleasant, and the present was even more so, so the hopes of the people centered on the future.

When the final peace was announced in August 1945, the residents of all eight river towns—all ethnicities, races, and denominations—celebrated spontaneously, as did people across America, from small towns to large cities. They had survived the Depression and war, and hopes were high.

All knew that the future was uncertain one, for their local industries had been strained to the maximum for the war efforts and now faced an inevitable letdown when the government orders ceased. Women and African Americans hired during the war knew their jobs were in jeopardy from both declining orders and the returning veterans. Still, the feeling was one of optimism across the spectrum.

Perhaps the most optimistic in each of the eight communities were the Main Street merchants. They had largely survived lean times, when few customers could be found for their goods, and they had survived the war, when few goods could be found for their customers. Surely, after the switchover from production for war to production for peace, the good times would be back again? The merchants knew that pent-up demand was a reality, and expected that their time in the sun was again approaching.

The merchants' confidence was not misplaced, although they may have been even more hopeful than the average citizen. At the end of the war, though, everyone optimistic, and few envisioned a future that was anything less than good—a just reward for all they had been through. They were right: prosperity did return. Tragically, it lasted only a brief time.

CHAPTER TWO

AFTER THE SECOND WORLD WAR

Changing Realities

By the end of the Second World War, unprecedented changes to all three of the fundamental realities that had undergirded the history of the Schuylkill Valley were already well under way. Their respective processes had been retarded by the war, but the period between 1945 and about 1980 saw a greatly increased pace of change in both the river and in transportation. A cleaner river improved both the health and lifestyles of all, but that positive effect drowned in the combination of a fundamental change in transportation and the decline of industry. The reality of the people had already changed; the arrival of immigrants had slowed to a trickle decades earlier. Together, the changes devastated the river towns, ending the steadily upward arc that their histories had shared. A period of decline had set in by the mid-to-late 1960s, and all eight towns on the lower Schuylkill River suffered severely, all for the same combination of reasons.

Beginning shortly after the war's end (although planned *before* the war), the Schuylkill River was subjected to systematic cleaning. These efforts made great progress in reducing the effects of so much raw residential and industrial waste having been dumped directly into the river. The state made the single-biggest contribution by removing the accumulated culm along the entire length of the river. The federal government continued to pressure the individual towns to clean up their sewage disposal systems. Much of the progress in reducing the amount of new industrial waste, however, came from a most unwelcome source: the closing of the factories and mills that had contributed so much pollution to the river during their prosperous years. For the river towns, this catastrophe more than negated the positive effects of river improvement.

And then there were the effects of the big change in transportation. This change and these effects were not unique to the Schuylkill River Valley, of course; they were national in scope. The shift from external to internal combustion engines had begun in the early twentieth century, but the growth in popularity of the automobile had been slowed by both the Depression and the war efforts. From the outset of the postwar period, however, the shift was nearly wholesale and immediate, achieving close to universal acceptance.

The transportation revolution had both external and internal effects on all eight towns, and both effects were bad. Externally, the shift destroyed the rail connections that connected Schuylkill Valley residents with the rest of the country and replaced them with a new network of roads that largely bypassed the river towns. Internally, each town was suddenly faced with the challenge of trying to integrate the profusion of personal vehicle traffic into a fixed urban grid.

The reality of people had already changed earlier. After the end of the Second World War, the results of that change—ethnicity-based divisions, and often outright animosity, within each town—crippled the efforts of each borough to deal with the changes and challenges brought on by the shift away from rail to road. Not least of these changes was that individual transportation simply made it easier for people to leave for the new suburbs—themselves a creation of the automobile—than to remain in a congested downtown and work on difficult problems alongside people their parents had been able to avoid. During the four postwar decades, factory closings and the increasing prevalence of the automobile demonstrated a continuation of another of the area's traditions: just as each town had grown and prospered together, so did they decline together.

The enormous effects of two entirely external factors during this period must also be acknowledged and factored into any history of what happened, and what didn't. Only at the very beginning of their existence could the Schuylkill River towns have claimed to live in a small, local world. By the end of the Second World War, that had clearly ceased to be the case.

The federal government made decisions just before and just after the end of World War II that enabled the phenomenon of suburbanization, which wreaked catastrophe on the nation's urban areas. The government's subsequent embrace of the Interstate Highway System further tore at the already-delicate fabric of race relations. As the deplorable results of these well-intentioned policies became obvious, the federal government undertook another round of actions designed to deal with the problems their immediate postwar decisions had created, and by 1980, housing assistance programs and urban renewal had made their appearance in the river towns, with decidedly mixed results. The situation would only become more controversial in the decades that followed.

Tectonic events on the international scene also caused national distress in the United States during this time, and these affected the towns on the Schuylkill River. The United States lost its dominant position in heavy, "smokestack" industries, most notably in steel production. The timing of that decline in supremacy could not have been worse for the eight towns. It removed their traditional industrial economic base at precisely the same time that the transportation revolution choked and devastated their commercial sectors—and at the same time that the government-enacted policies and veterans' benefits were encouraging people to move to the suburbs.

As the changing realities of life along the river combined and interacted with those on both a national and an international scale, the result was a perfect storm of troubles for each of the towns on the lower Schuylkill River. What followed was a downhill slide for all—a decline that had not ended by 1980.

The River

By 1945, the Schuylkill River was in dire straits. It was clogged with industrial wastes, sewage, and coal culm, all of which had virtually destroyed its aquatic life. The river smelled in hot weather and periods of low flow—times that often coincided, of course—and anyone brave enough to swim in the water emerged coated with a black, grimy film.

The problem of unhealthy input into the river had been apparent for decades. Laws existed, but enforcement continued to lag in a laissez-faire economy. The Second World War actually worsened the river's condition, but that was seen as just another necessary wartime sacrifice. Once the war ended, however, the consensus for action had already assembled the necessary political support and funding to begin addressing a problem as old as the river towns themselves.

The Pennsylvania legislature was poised to begin a top-to-bottom cleanup of the Schuylkill's most pressing problem, the culm from anthracite coal that by then had clogged virtually every foot of the usable river, and portions of the Delaware River as well. The Pennsylvania legislature authorized the Schuylkill River Desilting Project in June 1945. A contract followed two years later, and work on the massive effort began. River silt was dredged and collected, mostly from the major collection points—the dams and locks. By the time the project concluded in 1951, thirty million cubic yards of sludge had been pumped into twenty-six temporary impounding basins and left there to dry. The culm was then shipped to various locations, including Philadelphia International Airport. Much of the dewatered culm was processed through recovery plants back into a product that would burn, and then shipped to factories. The project removed most of what remained of the Schuylkill Navigation System, except for a few locks. Some dams were removed, including the Pawling Dam below the Perkiomen Reservoir and Catfish Dam, above Norristown.[7] The Norristown Dam not only survived but also has since been rebuilt.

The Schuylkill River Desilting Project was a major step forward in removing a major pollutant, but four centuries of disregard for the river would not be so easily cleansed away. Fortunately, in the 1960s, the pendulum of public opinion had begun its swing toward a greater sense of environmental awareness. The original Pennsylvania Clean Streams Act had been passed in 1937; the postwar period saw the act amended in 1945, 1950, 1965, 1970, and 1976. The Pennsylvania Department of Environmental Resources came into being to enforce this progressive tightening of pollution control efforts. Its efforts received a boost with the passage of the Federal Clean Water Act, and the Scenic Rivers Act in 1972 allowed the commonwealth to extend special protections to its rivers. In 1978, the Schuylkill was designated as Pennsylvania's first "Scenic River."

A steady stream of antipollution mandates, coupled with more available funding, upgraded the sanitary and sewage systems that served the river towns. Government regulations and requirements for treating sewage expanded both in scope and in the amount of

---

7. Catfish Dam was not actually removed, just knocked down. Its remains lurk today just below the water level in the extended Norristown Pool, awaiting unwary boaters.

processing required. The sewage collection systems of each borough were duly extended, a process that included locating and connecting many of the heretofore hidden, independent lines into a rationalized system to be funneled into treatment plants.

Proper treatment of the collected sewage proceeded at a much slower rate. In what was bad financial timing, the government mandates during this period that required increasing local expenditures coincided with the collapse of the revenue structure of each town, in proportion to the loss of its industries. The river towns found themselves forced to curtail even the most basic services, and they often placed sewage treatment low on the priority list. This brought from Harrisburg a new onslaught of orders to improve performance, and temporary discharge waivers when improvement lagged.

The steady improvement in river quality did bring about a return of organized recreational use of the Schuylkill, which had been all but abandoned by the beginning of the twentieth century. A pioneer in this was the Port Indian Civic & Boating Association, which began to host hydroplane races and a ski show in the 1950s on the pool above the Norristown dam, using the proceeds to fund community improvements. Upriver in Mont Clare, a remnant of the Schuylkill Navigation System was renovated, making it the only operable lock (although it only opens once a year).

During the 1950s, the Pennsylvania also undertook major studies and remedial action directed at the age-old problem of floods—efforts that are, in fact, ongoing. Floods in the Schuylkill River Valley most often occur in the spring, a part of the established regional weather pattern that is broadly predictable. A few, however, had reached such heights as to be remembered over the generations. The most memorable ones were initially identified by the year they struck—each river town has memories of the flood of 1933, for example—until their identification as parts of specific, named storms became commonplace.

The differing local geographies of each river town, as well as the specific dynamics of any major storm, have caused the successive floods to vary in intensity and in the extent of damage along the lower Schuylkill. Pottstown, with the flattest topography, has tended to suffer the deepest water spread over the greatest area. Still, the record amply demonstrates that floods can wreak havoc in any and every river town.

The years since 1945 have demonstrated another issue with the river—one shared with rivers in other populated areas across the nation. Due largely to changes in the landscape in the valley overall (for example, more impenetrable surface area thanks to more roads, parking lots, and construction), the river has flooded more frequently and with more destructive results. Statistical evidence clearly demonstrates that floods along the lower Schuylkill have increased both in occurrence and severity since the Second World War. Only one prewar flood, that of 1933, still ranks among the top ten crests along the lower Schuylkill as measured by the National Weather Service hydrological gauges at Pottstown and Norristown.

Local results are more variable. The 1933 flood ranks third in Norristown, but only fifth in Pottstown. Four of Pottstown's twenty-seven highest flood crests took place before 1945 (a 1902 flood still occupies second place). Five occurred between 1945 and 1980, and nineteen between 1980 and 2014. Only one of Norristown's nineteen highest floods, the one in 1933, occurred before 1945. Four occurred between 1945 and 1980, with the remaining fifteen all taking place between 1980 and 2014.

The reason for this trend is well understood: steady development of the countryside within the Schuylkill watershed has produced an equally steady increase in the amount of runoff—that is, the portion of each rainfall that the land cannot absorb. This excess makes its way into creeks and streams and then into the river itself. After the Second World War, as the countryside adjacent to the Schuylkill began to host the new automobile suburbs, the amount of rainfall that could be absorbed decreased with every square foot of ground covered with roofs, concrete, or asphalt. Various projects have been undertaken to deal with this problem, from the small local sources of periodic distress such as Saw Mill Run in Norristown to large, multiuse dams, such as the Blue Marsh Dam built in 1978 northwest of Reading, for which flood control was a major component of the design. The record of historic crests suggests that to date, the work undertaken by the public sector to control floods has not only lagged behind the work undertaken by the private sector to make them worse, but that the gap between the two has increased.

All trends notwithstanding, each town along the Schuylkill, regardless of its local topography, shares the same date for the highest recorded flood: June 1972, following the double passage over central Pennsylvania of Tropical Storm Agnes. What had been a hurricane had been downgraded by the time it reached the state, but the storm's erratic route produced repetitive rainfall in the state's middle and eastern areas. The resulting flood sent the Susquehanna River flowing into much of Pennsylvania's state capital, Harrisburg, and the smaller Schuylkill River flowing into the towns along its banks. Each of the eight boroughs suffered damage as the water inundated the industrial riverbanks of every town and at least a portion of every downtown.

Pottstown suffered the worst. The water from Tropical Storm Agnes crested at seventeen feet above flood stage. Businesses along High Street, the core of the borough's commercial center, were inundated with several feet of water, and at least three thousand people had to be evacuated (by contrast, "only" five hundred people had to be evacuated from Bridgeport). Virtually every sewage treatment plant along the river flooded, which contaminated the water supplies. The water level fell quickly after the storm moved on, leaving behind an odiferous mud; many private and small-company oil tanks had been breached, in addition to the sewage treatment plants.

The Agnes-spawned flood did not destroy any of the bridges connecting the river towns, a testament to the strength of concrete and steel. It did render each bridge inaccessible for a period, of course. Graphic evidence of the river's unprecedented height remained visible for months, with dried and hardened debris clinging to bridge abutments. Floods high enough to cause concern have arrived since, with increasing frequency, but Agnes remains the standard by which each is judged.

By the 1980s, the quality of the Schuylkill River was much improved, although much remained to be done. The desilting project had removed the culm, and the boroughs were making progress in upgrading their municipal sewage collection and treatment facilities. Of course, the volume of *new* industrial waste had also declined precipitately. A systematic program of watershed improvements, including dam construction, had even begun to address the long-standing problem of periodic flooding. Aquatic life was coming back, and recreation that involved actual prolonged contact with the river was considerably safer. By 1980, it was clear that this positive trend would likely continue. This was welcome news to every town, but by then, each was mired in its own sea of troubles, and largely unable to take advantage of this fundamental improvement.

Transportation

The shift from rail to road began early in the twentieth century, but its full effects were delayed by the wars. After the end of the Second World War, the automobile was the newly dominant mode of travel. This victory came at the expense of the nation's railroads, which spelled disaster for the eight river towns. While the railroad dominated, the boroughs prospered. The eclipse of the railroads led to the decline of the river towns, just as its rise had led to their growth. The railroad towns across the nation suffered a similar fate.

The change to private transportation by automobile, and the building of entirely new roads to accommodate the huge number of personal and commercial vehicles, had two broad effects on the river towns, and both were bad. First, it severed the favorable connections each river town had had with the wider worlds of commerce and business. At the same time, it demonstrated that their tightly packed urban grids could not accommodate the number of vehicles each required to sustain profitable businesses. Each town faced a two-sided problem: traffic congestion and parking. The combination of each town's isolation within the new network and the inability of each to accommodate to the new vehicles within it would prove unsolvable.

That isolation only grew as the towns confronted the newest challenge to their traditional marketing dominance: at the intersections of the larger roads, both old and new, there began to appear evidence of the growing popularity of the newest concept in retail marketing—shopping designed around the automobile. These plazas, strip malls, shopping centers, and other precursors to the malls presented the classic downtowns with a level of competition they could not match.

The decline of the railroad lasted for over half a century. The railroads were clearly in decline by the 1930s, but the Second World War had raised rail traffic to all-time highs. The surge was deceptive, as the increased traffic was not predictive of any postwar peacetime reality, especially as it had not been accompanied by increased maintenance or capital investments. The nation's railroads emerged from the war overused and worn out. The heretofore mighty railroad companies, themselves grappling with their own change from steam to diesel power, heavily regulated into maintaining unprofitable lines, and restricted by labor contracts, proved unequal to the challenge posed by smaller diesel engines in steadily larger trucks.

Passenger traffic had never provided substantial profit for either the Reading or the Pennsylvania's Schuylkill Valley lines, and had often meant operating at a loss. Passenger trains made the headlines, and their schedules affected a great many people, but it was freight that paid the way. As the river industries began their decline, the freight trains ran less and less frequently, and the high overhead costs typical of any railroad led the budget cutters of both the Reading and the Pennsylvania to the same conclusion: passenger train schedules had to be reduced, or even eliminated.

The crisis forced the two railroads, despite their long history of antagonism, to coordinate their policies toward the public, and more importantly, to the Federal Interstate Commerce Commission. As early as the 1930s, the two lines began to coordinate their schedules in the Schuylkill Valley. During the 1950s, they made joint requests to cut service, raise rates, or both. These measures were not sufficient; the Pennsylvania ended service west of Norristown in the 1950s, then between Norristown and Philadelphia (actually Manayunk) in 1960.

The collapse of private service lines into and out of Philadelphia led to their takeover by an oversight agency that was provided with government subsidies to cover the expected operating losses. In 1964, the newly created Southeastern Pennsylvania Transportation Authority (SEPTA) began operations, having integrated the remnants of several existing lines. In this manner, the Reading line up to Norristown (the track of the original PG&N) survived as a commuter line, becoming a regional rail transit link to Philadelphia, at least for Norristown and Conshohocken. Portions of the Pennsylvania along the Schuylkill's right bank also survived, becoming part of the government-sponsored and -funded Consolidated Rail Corporation

(Conrail) after 1976. A few sections of other lines continued a limited existence under private ownership.

One of the consequences of the long period of local rail dominance had been that the maintenance of local roads had not kept up with their increasing use. The owners of automobiles and trucks, together with manufacturers of oil, gasoline, rubber, concrete, and asphalt, began demanding more attention to and expenditure on roads, at the local and the national level. The result up through the Second World War was a bevy of erratic, piecemeal, and largely uncoordinated efforts to improve existing roads and build new ones. A succession of acts by both the federal and the state governments strove to keep up with the mushrooming sales of motor vehicles, but failed. Planning was, for a long time, rarely considered, and construction and maintenance have always lagged behind the public's road use.

The years between the World Wars had given the nation's engineers and planners a glimpse of the future promised by the automobile, and it was a sobering experience. The public's fascination with cars, even during the Depression, suggested just how inadequate the nation's local road systems were. This warned of a crisis looming when prosperity returned and many people began to buy automobiles. Greater effort and expense, at all levels of government, would be required to upgrade the nation's local roads, which would bear the initial impact of the postwar automobile boom.

Some planners, however, concluded that a policy of upgrading and expanding the existing road network was doomed; a great many of these roads were of ancient lineage, their paths tortuous, dating from the days when neither technology nor finance were sufficient to do much more than hug the existing landscape. Most had also long ago distributed population along them; to reroute or even widen many would not only be horrendously expensive but often impractical. An entirely new approach to designing American's roads was needed. Fortunately, an example of such one new approach already existed, and it was the model on which the future of American road construction would be based: the Pennsylvania Turnpike.

The Depression—or rather, efforts to survive it—had left America with many legacies, economic, psychological, and physical. One of these last was the Pennsylvania Turnpike. Its construction had been inspired by the desire to improve on the tortuous journey endured by anyone who traveled the length of the Commonwealth of Pennsylvania—a slow, seemingly endless trek up and down several ridges, one after another. These had required even the railroad, the first technology to enable east to west travel, to follow a circuitous route.

In the years before World War II, Pennsylvania had begun working toward a solution to this long-standing issue. The key to that answer already existed...sort of. The cutthroat competition among railroads in the late nineteenth century had left a scar in Pennsylvania in the form of a long-abandoned and only partially completed right-of-way across much of the commonwealth. That was all that remained of the South Pennsylvania Railroad, a relic of "robber baron" capitalism, and the product of the mighty New York Central Railroad and its multistate rivalry with the Pennsylvania Railroad. The uncompleted route's attraction was that it had not done as its predecessors had and skirted the several ridges in its path but had tunneled right through. The tunnels still remained—unfinished, much returned to nature, and inadequate, but the heavy work had already been done. They existed.

Today, with Interstate highways crisscrossing the continent, it is difficult to envision just what a risk people believed building the Pennsylvania Turnpike to be. Even with federal financing, the project still presented a considerable financial risk to its investors. To allay concerns, the turnpike was created as a toll road, akin to those built during America's "first turnpike era," but for the semiofficial nature of its constructing authority.

When the Pennsylvania Turnpike opened on October 1, 1940, residents quickly showed their approval by using it in even greater numbers than its advocates had dared hope. Even as war loomed and projects were put on back burners, Pennsylvania formally committed to extending the turnpike after the war ended. Private use of the road was largely replaced by military use during the war, and the military found the turnpike to be useful indeed.

The Pennsylvania Turnpike was a true turning point for road design, with its wide concrete lanes, median barrier, gentle curves, and grade separations at intersections built high enough to accommodate trucks. Its major significance, however, was that it represented a 180-degree change in the concept of what roads were for and where they should be located. The turnpike was not designed to accommodate local, place-to-place traffic. The emphasis was on the whole, not the part, and every part was designed and built to expedite traffic across long distances. This reversal of purpose established the pattern for the vast majority of road construction in the decades after the Second World War.

Other states followed Pennsylvania's lead, adopting the turnpike's standards, and soon a limited network of such roads spread across the northeastern United States. These were considerable undertakings, but even they were soon dwarfed by an even grander scheme, the turnpike-inspired Interstate Highway System. This extension of limited-access highways across the entire country seriously affected our major cities, and a multitude of minor ones. The system's design called for new roads to direct traffic to and from the big cities, but not its many smaller ones. While some cities and towns were faced with the challenge of dealing with an exponential growth in traffic, others faced the opposite problem: those bypassed were now isolated.

The results of these new roads for the eight Schuylkill River towns varied considerably. The Conshohockens benefited from one of the first new highways in the region, the Schuylkill Expressway, which had an exit in West Conshohocken. Norristown chose in 1950 to reject a proposed turnpike exit at its east end, and thereby lost an opportunity to rewrite its postwar history. The towns upriver had to wait until quite late in the new road-building phase, but with the eventual completion of US Route 422, Pottstown and Royersford finally saw some of the hoped-for benefits. Nevertheless, much of the growth from that actually occurred outside the boroughs' boundaries and along the new road's route.

But by the time the new roads reached—or bypassed—the nation's towns and cities, each was already undergoing an internal crisis brought on by the same source: the overwhelming popularity of the automobile. The problem was, and still is, actually a simple one: not enough space. Automobiles required much more space to transport the same number of people than did trolleys (not to mention walking), but that space could not be found in any town built around the standard urban grid. Every urban area established in the horse-and-buggy era was physically inadequate for people now driving into, within, and out of its municipal limits. The river towns are excellent examples of this.

Each town quickly discovered that the roads that people had used to get to the town itself were no longer adequate to transport the number of people each downtown needed for the area to remain profitable. As workers and shoppers began to transport themselves around in steel cocoons of substantial dimensions, the laws of physics weighed ever more heavily. More and more space was required to accommodate fewer and fewer people. The roads were upgraded, of course, frequently. It was never enough, and traffic congestion, a problem known previously only in the bigger cities, became a problem for every older American town.

The timing of this crisis could not have been worse. The river towns were reeling from factory closings, which meant hugely reduced receipts for the towns' commercial sector. Job losses hurt the towns' commercial sectors the most, but most of the towns had depended on shoppers from at least their immediate areas, and in some cases, from much farther away. Thus, it was the towns with the largest commercial sectors that first felt the pinch. Norristown and Pottstown, the two largest along the lower Schuylkill, were experiencing the phenomenon of the "traffic jam" by the late 1940s. Eventually, even access to the commercial sectors in such small towns as Spring City and Royersford became difficult at the busiest times of the day.

Then there was the new and vexing problem of parking. Street parking increased traffic congestion by reducing the available lanes, and the relationship between the two became a continuous source of contention for the municipal councils. Each town had been largely built out, so creating off-street parking meant tearing down existing buildings. In the early decades, such efforts were resisted. As the downtown shopping sectors continued to suffer, desperation eased those restraints, but by then it was too late. Each town tried everything its leaders could agree on, but nothing was enough. People who wanted to shop in town had to drive into the congested downtowns and circle the block looking for parking. When they were done, they had to exit on those same crowded streets. This quickly discouraged people who lived elsewhere but who had always shopped downtown.

It also began to affect even the traditional downtowns' most reliable shoppers, those who resided in town. Their ancestors either walked or took public transportation, but the automobile enabled them to travel farther afield to avoid parking issues. This was the death knell for the old, traditional downtowns.

The residents of the towns could shop elsewhere, because "elsewhere" not only existed, it was thriving. The automobile-sponsored migration to the new suburbs had quickly brought about a fundamental reversal in the historic marketing patterns in southeastern Pennsylvania. Each of the river downtowns had always possessed a local monopoly on products and services within a marketing area proportionate to the town's population and its location vis-à-vis other towns along the river. The result had been a development of regional marketing areas of different sizes, all operating under differing constraints, but with the downtowns of each river town benefiting from a monopoly position within its own area.

The automobile and exploding regional population changed all that after the Second World War. The area's population exploded, and the vast majority of new residents settled in the suburbs, often some distance from the downtown commercial sectors. Retailers saw this new market developing, and realized that locations outside the traditional towns but near these burgeoning residential developments could effectively intercept automobile shoppers in their own neighborhoods, luring them in with the promise of eliminating the time and hassle involved trying to park and shop downtown.

The roads in southeastern Pennsylvania began to sprout commercial centers at their intersections. The new shopping centers were not only closer to people's home, but they also offered new stores, fresh marketing concepts, a wider variety of goods, and most of all, *free, ample parking.* This last was the killer, because downtown parking efforts, from meters to garages, required the customer to pay to park. No so for the shopping centers and then the malls, as the cost of parking was built into the pricing. Out of sight, out of mind.

The downtown areas of the eight towns suffered first under this multifaceted pressure from the automobile, but soon the residential areas in town were found to be equally inadequate. Most of the original housing in each town had been built for its workers. The plots were small, and built close to the factories and commercial sectors. The houses were likewise small and minimally appointed. The size of the houses and the lots grew proportionately with the distance from downtown. Automobile ownership proceeded largely in the opposite direction, as those who could afford the nicer homes away from the noise and grime of the factories were also the first who could afford automobiles. Gradually, even people with only modest incomes could afford cars, or were forced to borrow to buy one so they could get to their new jobs outside the downtown. The old narrow housing lots could not accommodate an automobile parked in front of each. Many households had two cars, as even those without jobs often wanted their own cars to use while the breadwinners were away at work. The collapse of the old commercial downtowns largely solved their parking problems, but parking problems in the residential areas of the river towns is remains an issue to this day.

It is important to understand that all of this happened *before* the arrival of the malls. The new shopping centers in the suburbs had already begun to eat away at the traditional commercial dominance of the region's downtowns by the time the Pennsylvania Turnpike arrived at the bucolic farmland of King of Prussia. Once the turnpike had linked to the Schuylkill Expressway coming out of Philadelphia, the local stage was set for the revolution in marketing that the spread of limited-access highways offered. The King of Prussia Plaza, later the King of Prussia Mall, would become both the first and the largest of these new retail meccas, capable of drawing on a marketing area larger than any local merchant had ever before conceived. These benefited from the marketing revolution begun by the suburban plazas spawned by the automobile suburbs, but by the time the malls arrived, the old downtowns along the Schuylkill River were already dying; the malls only served to greatly accelerate the pace.

The process was well under way by 1950, and in the next three decades, it both spread and intensified. As early as the 1960s, and certainly by the early 1970s, the once-prosperous towns of the Schuylkill Valley found themselves in a downward spiral. The closure of their industrial sectors was at the heart of the problem, but the change from rails to roads drastically reduced their ability to respond effectively. Their downtowns, once choked with shoppers, were now choked only with cars, and then only during rush hour, as people tried to get someplace else. Those who remained living in town found themselves increasingly forced to get jobs out of town, and to buy cars to get to those jobs, joining those trying to get someplace else.

The wave of industry and commercial business closures ran its course, and at least left space available for whatever would replace them, but the traffic and parking issues in residential areas only grew. The problem of the fundamental incompatibility between the urban grid and the automobile remains, and will haunt all future attempts to find those replacements.

People

The first paragraph of *The History of Bridgeport*, a pamphlet published in 1951 to celebrate the borough's centennial, identified it as being "in no hurry to do anything—especially anything which threatens its present equilibrium."[8] By that date, the word "equilibrium" could have been applied to all eight river towns. The residents of the river towns had grown accustomed to the condition, which was at least preferable to depression or war. But by the end of the same decade, every river town had begun to realize that its version of equilibrium was slipping away—not in favor of growth, but toward decline.

Industrial decline and the emergence of the automobile suburbs are well understood as causes, but there was a deeper reason underlying the decline of the Schuylkill River towns, one that has gone largely unappreciated. Throughout the Schuylkill River Valley towns, the growth always returned, even after hard times, thanks to the periodic arrivals of new residents—immigrants looking to make their way in a new land. But the people had ceased to arrive.

This component of that sad time is a history not of what happened, but of what *didn't* happen. But what didn't happen helps to explain what did. Equilibrium was, in truth, something no river town had ever experienced for very long. Their histories had instead been ones of growth and improvement, sometimes for brief and intense periods, and sometimes for longer and steadier periods. Those histories had also been stressful ones, because growth was generally spurred by

8. Edward Pinkowski, *History of Bridgeport, PA* (1951), 3.

waves of new arrivals—strange new people with different accents, different traditions, different faiths. However, growth had ended with the Depression, before being artificially stimulated by war. Peacetime economic growth was expected to return soon, but the arrival of new people from other countries was not, with good reason; the tap had been shut off for over thirty years.

The First World War halted the immigrant influx, and afterward, the federal government began to structure immigration laws with two goals: to restrict the number of immigrants allowed in, and to ensure that those who did enter did not disrupt the existing representation of ethnicities among the general population. In other words, during that period of conservative reaction, the country made an attempt to prevent the influx of any *truly* new immigrant nationalities. This idea received broad popular support, but it proved to be most unfortunate for many towns, including those on the lower Schuylkill.

Few, if any, of the river towns' residents understood the connection between immigration and community growth. The contribution of new arrivals to the communities had not always been immediately apparent, as few were able to share their unique knowledge or skills with the communities in which they settled. They were, however, willing to work at the lowest levels for the least money, if that was required—as it usually was—to get ahead. Every one of them brought with them a desire to improve the lives of their loved ones, even if that meant spending their own working lives in those lowest jobs.

This process of periodic influx was not without strife, as each successive wave encountered and had to surmount the prejudice and suspicion of those who had arrived before them. Often they were reviled for their very willingness to do the jobs that earlier immigrants had once been forced to accept so *they* could get ahead. But although first-generation immigrants were often forced to remain in those jobs, many of their children, and even more of their children's children, contributed greatly to the community. These were the people who populated the Schuylkill River towns after the war.

This change caused by the end of immigration was the first of the changes in the fundamental realities to negatively affect the Schuylkill Valley towns. It was not all about numbers, but also about newness. The noticeable result in the numbers was a steep decline in new residents, but its real significance was the equally steep decline in the influx of energy, ideas, and goals that the new residents had brought with them. The periodic arrival of newness that had regenerated and revitalized the populations of the Schuylkill Valley ended when Congress enacted its new immigration policies.

Shutting off the flow of immigrants to the Schuylkill Valley had another consequence evidenced by public records. Ending the waves of immigrants contributed to community stagnation and ethnic hardening within the communities. The immigrants in the final big wave before the new immigration policies settled into the river towns but continued the ethnic separation that had characterized earlier arrivals. This seems somewhat paradoxical, given that at the same time they were in the process of becoming American citizens, and pledging a single national allegiance. Be that as it may, records from the river towns offer evidence that the members of the ethnic and religious groupings continued to resist local assimilation, remaining focused on their churches and associating for the most part only with other like themselves. They also extended the ethnic and religious differences among themselves into the municipal political sphere.

The official program for Bridgeport's 1951 centennial celebration contained an editorial statement that painted a picture of these now-entrenched differences:

> "The intermingling of people of widely varied cultural and religious backgrounds has not altogether been smooth. One strand frequently sows its dislike of another. Certain elements in the community want to favor people of their extraction in public office. As a result of this racial prejudice, little cliques form in many organizations and do everything to discourage other people from taking part in them.... This is not an Italian town. This is Bridgeport. The celebration of Bridgeport's 100th anniversary shows that it took people from many lands to build the borough. Let not a few try to turn it into sinkhole of bigotry and racial prejudice."

The picture was much the same across the river in Norristown, which had the largest concentration of Italians. The immigrant mix in Pottstown, Phoenixville, and Conshohocken was different within each, with no dominant ethnicity among the immigrants, and the political affairs of each town reflected the local situation accordingly. The populations of Royersford, Spring City, and West Conshohocken were much smaller as well as less diverse, but even there ethnicity continued to exert its pull.

In other words, that sacrosanct American principle of the "melting pot" proved to be a myth. The river towns remained subdivided into ethnic enclaves, socially and often geographically; they continued to cling to their own, and to view all others with suspicion.

While the various European ethnicities sparred with one another, they did join in one common opinion and effort: to keep as many African Americans as possible from moving into "their" communities. After the Second World War, African Americans were the only population group of any size in the Schuylkill Valley still looking for political power proportionate to their numbers. They did not constitute more than a fragment of the population in the smaller towns. Only Norristown and, to a decreasing extent, Pottstown and Phoenixville, possessed sufficient numbers to perhaps make a difference, but this was still the era of black disenfranchisement, as unofficial as it usually was in the North.

The continuing and often contentious divisions are clear evidence of the community stagnation and ethnic hardening that afflicted the eight towns after immigration restrictions. They are also one reason why the river towns—the larger towns in particular—proved so inadequate in their responses to the challenges they faced after the 1950s. A unified response requires a unified community, and as equilibrium slipped away, the lack of community unity became increasingly obvious.

Later in this chapter, I will discuss the census numbers for each Schuylkill River town during the postwar period. Those numbers point to decline, but they also disguise the true nature of the population shifts during the period. The census provides a *net* number; that is a combination of gains and losses, and does not reveal *who* is leaving or moving in. Thus, the net numbers do not tell the real story, and in some cases serve to mask it. The underlying reality for the Schuylkill River towns was one of both departure and replacement. Its significance lay in the net loss of value, both financial and human, that characterized this two-way movement from the late 1950s to 1980 and beyond.

The story of postwar departure followed by partial replacement has been told from many perspectives. Most of these fail to present the true significance of what happened, free of ethnic, racial, or religious filters. The significance of the postwar exchange through population departure and replacement is that those who departed the river towns were largely replaced by people with fewer skills and less wealth.

The communities' most prominent citizens were often those who exited first, many before the Second World War. Some continued to own and operate businesses in the river towns, but they largely ceased to *live* there. Many of the well-off residents, most of them related to the earliest immigrants, the Protestants, exited during this phase. The older families who had shunned and rebuffed newcomers now found themselves surrounded by people of different ethnicities, and the new people were beginning to usurp the incumbents' political, economic, and social power. The evidence is there in something as simple and yet tangible as congregation numbers: each town's Protestant congregations declined during this time; many of the old Protestant churches were the first to close down as their congregations relocated to the suburbs, where they built new churches.

After the exodus of the old guard, whose long-time presence had contributed so heavily to the communities, came the middle class. Government financial incentives financed their exit with the GI Bill and incentives offered to the builders of new suburban communities. Those who could afford to leave—a financial target that steadily dropped—gave up their rentals and bought inexpensive first homes, or sold their old houses and bought bigger, more expensive ones outside of town. Not surprisingly, people with less wealth (and in greater need of services) moved into the houses the new suburbanites no longer wanted.

This net negative exchange became a continual downward spiral, the exact course and dates of which differ for each of the Schuylkill River towns in relation to their individual economic collapses. The decline in perceived property values allowed residents of less net worth to move in, further spreading and speeding the process. By 1980, the movement to the suburbs had spent its initial force, but continued to drain urban residents in the coming decades.

In the context of the enormous changes that took place within each of the eight Schuylkill River towns between 1945 and 1980, the makeup of ethnicities and races changed very little. The smallest towns remained close to lily white; Caucasians comprised at least 98 percent of the populations of Royersford, Spring City, and West Conshohocken, about 96 percent of the population of Bridgeport, and about 93 percent of the population of Conshohocken. Even in Pottstown and Phoenixville, with their legacy of minority hiring in the mills, whites still accounted for approximately 85 percent of the population. Norristown actually extended its position as the primary home for the area's African Americans, but whites still represented at 75 percent of its people.

What had changed were the towns themselves, and the attitude of the people who now lived there. The optimism that had characterized the immediate postwar period had disappeared, along with the jobs and the businesses. The new residents brought with them less wealth; with fewer highly paid skills, they had less leisure time to invest in local community involvement, and their chilly reception by the towns likely inspired little interest in participation and "community spirit." From 1945 to 1980, the path was all downhill. By the later date, each town on the lower Schuylkill River would have been glad to see again a period of "equilibrium" like that of the 1950s. But none did.

All Downhill

The postwar period in the lower Schuylkill Valley began with high promise and even higher hopes, but within thirty years, everything changed for the worse, or so it seemed. The census numbers show the decade-by-decade shift from equilibrium to decline, but to a lesser degree than they might, for reasons that will be more fully discussed later. At the conclusion of World War II, each river town saw an initial, and brief, return to something like the way things had been before, a period that lasted perhaps through the 1950s. The sixties were the decade during which things began to change, and by the 1970s, each of the eight towns was in free fall. Each saw both its industrial and commercial sectors all but disappear, and its wealthiest and most influential residents leave town, followed by a substantial portion of its middle class, particularly the young.

It did not take long for the catastrophic effects of the US government's post–World War II policies to become apparent in America's urban areas. The Housing Act of 1949, which had introduced some of those policies, was amended in 1954, adding provisions largely designed to counteract the effects of its initial passage. This period introduced the phrase "urban renewal" into the public lexicon, although federal funding for similar projects had been one of the original components of the act.

Each town on the lower Schuylkill River took advantage of one or more of the programs that fell under the rubric of urban renewal. Pottstown took the early lead, employing government-assisted urban renewal programs several times, although Spring City was the first to convert old factories into new residences. But two towns—Royersford and Conshohocken—availed themselves of urban renewal programs that almost completely removed and replaced their core downtowns. I discuss the process and results of those efforts below.

A coincidental data collection date for *Montgomery County: The Second Hundred Years*[9] meant that a written summary of community attitudes in 1980 is available for six of the eight towns in this study. I have added the two Chester County river towns, despite the lack of a formal written summary by a resident historian, since up until that date, Phoenixville and Spring City largely continued the common experiences that had been their histories. However, the tectonic post–World War II changes in the reality of the river valley had, by 1980, gutted each of the eight towns so thoroughly that the commonalities they had shared and that created their common natures—industrial employment, a downtown to walk to, and ethnically organized and church-based subcommunities—were ceasing to be major factors. This would mean the end of their longtime common historical arc, a fact that would be clearly demonstrated in the decades after 1980.

Deceptive Numbers

An almost-wholesale population decline took place among the eight Schuylkill River towns between 1950 and 1980. In 1950, they collec-

---

9. Jean Barth Toll and Michael J. Schwager, eds., *Montgomery County: The Second Hundred Years* (Norristown, PA: Montgomery County Federation of Historical Societies, 1983).

tively housed 99,998 people; by 1980, that number had dropped to 94,044, a net loss of just under 6 percent. That net-loss figure ignores individual population trends, however, thus masking how unsettling the period actually was for the eight river towns.

Two towns had already seen their populations peak before the war, West Conshohocken in 1930 and Bridgeport in 1940. During the war, every town except Norristown and Bridgeport gained population, in varying numbers. (West Conshohocken had already declined more than its wartime gain.) Norristown's population drop was negligible. Only Bridgeport continued its decline. Each town then enjoyed what everyone believed was the dawning of a new prosperity, which the 1950 census seemed to confirm. Sadly, the period that followed soon dashed those hopes.

Between 1950 and 1980, four of the eight river towns—Pottstown, Royersford, Spring City, and Phoenixville—gained population. The increases for the first three were minimal; Pottstown gained 140 people, Royersford gained 381, and Spring City gained 131. It is here that Phoenixville begins its breakaway from the common historical arc; its population increase over the whole period was 1,233 people, or almost 10 percent.

The declining populations of the other four towns more than outweighed those gains. Norristown alone lost 3,442 people, more than the collective gains of the four that improved. Conshohocken lost 2,447 people, and Bridgeport lost almost a thousand. West Conshohocken lost just under a thousand people, or almost 40 percent of its population; in addition to the broad industrial collapse then under way, West Conshohocken lost substantial territory, and inhabitants, to the Interstate Highway System. It was the only one of the eight boroughs to suffer from the Interstate in this very direct way.

The fifties brought the last period of broadly distributed growth; of the eight river towns, only Spring City lost population, and that was minimal. In contrast, Pottstown added about 2,500 people; it reached its all-time high of 26,144 in 1960. Norristown also reached its all-time high in 1960 at 38,925.

The sixties were a much more equivocal decade; the eight towns demonstrated a net population gain, but of less than four hundred people. Four towns gained people, and four lost people. Phoenixville posted the greatest gain, of just over a thousand, while Pottstown lost the most—also just over a thousand. Bridgeport briefly broke from its steady decline and actually posted a net gain, although one of fewer than three hundred people. Royersford and Spring City had modest gains, while Norristown and both Conshohockens had modest losses, in proportion to their relative sizes. Then the dam broke.

The decade between 1970 and 1980 presents eight pictures ranging from decline to collapse. Combined, the eight river towns lost more than ten thousand residents. Seven of the river towns showed net population losses. Phoenixville lost about 4 percent and Spring City about 5 percent. Faring still worse, Norristown lost almost 10 percent of its population, Pottstown about 15 percent, and Conshohocken almost 17 percent. These are sad numbers, but Bridgeport and West Conshohocken suffered the worst during the 1970s; each posted population losses of almost 31 percent. Royersford was the only town to grow. It gained eight people.

Viewed in isolation, these numbers indicate declines that went from modest to precipitate over the period, with the 1970s clearly being the worst. They make a clear case that the river towns were declining as a group, even Phoenixville, by that decade. The numbers, however, only begin to tell the story; they need to be understood within a wider context to properly appreciate their significance.

The core of that context is the unprecedented population growth in southeastern Pennsylvania during that period, and the fact that this population explosion almost completely avoided the river towns. Within thirty years, the Schuylkill Valley towns that had historically been among the major population centers in two counties found themselves quite literally on the sidelines, as both people and wealth deserted the river valley and its railroad network to settle on the high ground along the new highways.

The population increase in the counties surrounding Philadelphia after the Second World War deserves the term "explosion." In 1950, the population of Montgomery County stood at 353,068; by 1980, it had risen to 643,621. The more rural Chester County had 159,141 residents in 1950. It joined the population explosion later, but by 1980, its population had reached 316,660. This was no temporary blip. The upward population trend in both counties continued.

However, the new residents were not settling in the existing river towns but elsewhere in the counties. In 1950, the six river towns in Montgomery County—Pottstown, Royersford, Norristown, Bridgeport, Conshohocken, and West Conshohocken—together totaled 83,808 residents, or almost 24 percent of the population of Montgomery County at that time. During the next thirty years, the six towns recorded a net loss of 7,318 people, or just under 9 percent—but the population of Montgomery County almost doubled. Thus, the six towns went from almost a quarter of the county's population in 1950 to less than 12 percent in 1980.

The story was much the same in Chester County, even though its two river towns—Spring City and Phoenixville—both gained population during the next thirty years. In 1950, the 16,190 residents of Phoenixville and Spring City combined represented just under 10 percent of Chester County's population of 159,141. During the next thirty years, Phoenixville added 1,233 residents, while Spring City gained 131, bringing its collective population total to 17,554 by 1980. During that same period, however, Chester County's population came close to doubling. Thus, the two towns that in 1950 housed about 10 percent of Chester County's residents housed only 6 percent in 1980. During those three decades, the towns were not only losing their current residents, but also being avoided by the huge numbers of new arrivals in the region. The established people, and most of the wealth, were leaving the towns and moving out to the suburbs.

Industrial Collapse

The greatest blow to the Schuylkill River towns during this period was the huge loss of jobs as the traditional smokestack industries began to close. Different industries closed their plants for different reasons, but underlying everything was the widespread collapse of the American steel industry, an event that, together with the near collapse of the closely related automotive industry, largely transformed America's Industrial Belt into its Rust Belt.

The mills and factories of the Schuylkill Valley were just minor players in the nation's widespread tragedy, but they were—and had always been—the backbone of local industry and thus of local prosperity for the eight towns. From the first forge in 1752 until after the Second World War, metals—iron, steel, and products made from both—had been the most important component of industry in the Schuylkill Valley. The Schuylkill Valley towns rose to prosperity with the metals industry…and followed it into decline.

At the end of the Second World War, the industries in the Schuylkill River Valley found themselves in a situation similar to that of their old allies, the railroads. The plants were old, they had been run at peak capacity during the war with little emphasis on maintenance, and they needed modernization in their basic layouts and processes if they were going to compete with other countries. At first, it seemed that might happen. American heavy industry experienced a grace period after the war. Even after the readjustment from military production was complete, the companies continued to fill national and worldwide orders while its international competitors rebuilt their war-shattered industrial plants.

The eight towns received some benefit from this very temporary condition. In 1957, Bethlehem Steel Corporation employed 165,000 people nationwide, its post–World War II high. Its Pottstown works covered approximately ninety-two acres, with three fabricating shops, buildings for storing equipment, and shops for machining, forge-and-bending, carpentry, templates, and welded joists. The Pottstown works produced 17,500 tons of fabricated steel work, and its payroll averaged about eighteen hundred workers. The company's bridge-building tradition continued as the plant fabricated steel for the Walt Whitman Bridge in Philadelphia, the Chesapeake Bay Bridge–Tunnel in Virginia, and both the Throgs Neck Bridge and the Verrazano-Narrows Bridge in New York. Pottstown also benefited from a 1945 decision by the Firestone Rubber Company to move into a tire plant built with government money in nearby Lower Pottsgrove Township during the war. The first tires appeared that same year and, by 1951, the company had produced over twenty-one million tires. Its annual payroll of $27 million dollars pumped a yearly average of $7.2 million dollars into the borough's commercial community.

In the 1950s, Conshohocken had about five thousand people working in the steel and iron industries. The Alan Wood Steel Company was the county's largest employer, with thirty-one hundred workers. The old Schuylkill Iron Works plant in the borough closed in 1953, severing Conshohocken's last physical connection with steel production, but the company retained its close Conshohocken connection.

During the 1960s, basic heavy-industry products from foreign competitors began to arrive on American shores, at equal quality and at lower prices than US firms could match. In 1965, the United States imported ten million tons of foreign steel, the first time this had occurred since the original rise of the industry in America. By the end of the decade, Alan Wood Steel, once the county's largest employer, had reduced its employees to about seven hundred. Management filed a petition for bankruptcy in the summer of 1977, and what had been the county's largest employer closed. The Pottstown plant of Bethlehem Steel started to contract in 1975. The last "heat" of steel at the Phoenix Steel Company at took place in November 1976, although the combination of layoffs and wage/benefit reductions agreed to by its unions at least helped postpone the inevitable.

From then on, there were waves of layoffs. The actual date of a company's formal demise meant little since by the time its doors were padlocked shut, it would have long since shed all but its most essential personnel. By 1980, the former Bethlehem Steel grounds held only a few small, unrelated companies. The company did not declare bankruptcy until 2001, after an unsuccessful merger, but the damage to Pottstown was done long before then.

The loss of the steel mills and fabricating plants was the most damaging blow, but ferrous metals was not the first industry to leave. By the time the foreign competition was just beginning to affect the river towns, the centuries-old Schuylkill River textile industry had all but vanished. Yet foreign competition had nothing to do with it: the local textile industry did not fall victim to product competition from abroad, but from the American South, where the factories had moved in search of a cheaper—and more compliant—labor force.

This trend was, to an extent, delayed and disguised by the war, as even old operations like the Tyson Shirt Factory in Norristown went to three shifts to meet the demand for military blouses. The war's end saw the end of the huge orders, and by 1950, the most of the textile plants in the Schuylkill Valley had closed. The few that still operated did not last much longer. The largest of them all, the Spring City Knitting Company, which once employed a thousand people, closed in 1981, letting go its last 145 workers. The Gruber Knitting Mill continued to operate, and in 1976, the company (no longer controlled by the Gruber family) was Royersford's largest operating textile company. Not for long, however; Gruber shut down all borough operations by 1987.

The 1950s was the beginning of the end for Bridgeport's long-time industry, Lees Carpets. The firm moved to Virginia, Georgia, and North Carolina, and closed its factories in the borough in 1956. Burlington Industries Inc. purchased the firm in 1960, and then moved all its administrative personnel to Valley Forge Industrial Park in King of Prussia in 1968, thus ending Bridgeport's long association with its largest industrial employer.

The loss of names like Bethlehem, Phoenix, and Alan Wood Steel; Firestone and Lee Tires; and Lees Carpets won the biggest headlines, but there were multiple losses up and down the river of smaller firms that counted for a great deal in the smaller boroughs of West Conshohocken, Bridgeport, Royersford, and Spring City, as well as in Norristown, which had never possessed a large, dominant industry.

The exodus was steady, and it began early. Bridgeport lost the Summerill Tubing Company to Pittsburgh in 1946. R. S. Newbold & Son Company, Norristown's largest metal fabricator, which had built machines and boilers since just after the Civil War, ceased business in the 1950s. Other long-standing Norristown businesses to close by the early 1980s were Scheidt's Brewery (more recently named Schmidt's), the W. K. Gresh cigar factory, and two textile plants, the Wildman Manufacturing Company and the Tyson Shirt Company.

Amid collapse, the more common forms of business failures tend to be overlooked. During this period, many factories closed for one or more common reasons, including bad management and product obsolescence. The Conshohocken area's second-biggest company is an example of both. While the Alan Wood Steel Company was the area's largest employer, the Lee Tire & Rubber Company became one of southeastern Pennsylvania's best-known firms during the 1960s. The reason was the Schuylkill Expressway. Once it opened along its full length in 1960, every weekday morning, thousands of cars and trucks drove around the crest of a bluff on the right bank of the river opposite the factory. Management placed large letters spelling out

"LEE TIRE" along the roofline to attract the attention of drivers, and it worked. Drive-time radio treated a generation of commuters to warnings about sun glare on the "Lee Tire curve." The experience lasted longer than the company, because the beginning of Lee Tire's regional fame coincided with the beginning of its decline. A group of corporate raiders gained control of the company's stock in 1962, and proceeded to milk its assets. Little but inventory remained when the Goodyear Tire and Rubber Company of Akron, Ohio, purchased the company in 1965. A period of revival began, but Goodyear's national reach spelled trouble for what was by this time a small manufacturing firm. In 1978, when radial tires became popular, Lee Tire decided to close the Conshohocken plant rather than retool.

No large company survived the devastation, and many smaller companies fell as well, but there were a few survivors. Pottstown and Bridgeport made the greatest attempts to retain industry, creating industrial parks and offering tax incentives for firms to relocate there. Since the firms they sought were small, the parks attained some success. Unfortunately, most of the new manufacturing firms that moved into southeastern Pennsylvania chose suburban locations that were more suited to their single-floor production techniques and offered quicker access to main roads for the transporting products.

Whatever the size of the plant, its closing hurt the towns in several ways. The loss of jobs removed some of the population, of course, but the greatest impact was economic, as the ripples from the industrial and commercial collapses combined to form a sea of red ink drowning each town in varying ways of bad. Individual closures of factories and stores hurt those affected directly—owners, employees, landlords, customers, vendors—but cumulatively, they also undermined the municipal governments of each river town as the tax bases melted away at the very time Americans were becoming more demanding of government services at all levels.

This reversal in prosperity powered the general downward population drift of the Schuylkill River towns during this period, but the net population numbers demonstrate less of a decline than these substantial job losses might have otherwise produced. One reason was the widespread nature of the industrial decline itself. The loss of industries from the region in the decades after the 1960s was part of a trend affecting towns and cities nationwide. The people laid off from jobs in these industries could not simply migrate elsewhere for similar work; there was none to be had. Those who could leave did, but the older workers, who had already spent most of their lives in the mills that stretched between the Bethlehem Steel works in Pottstown to the Alan Wood plant near Conshohocken, had little choice. They largely remained in their homes, helping to maintain their community's population totals but adding to the unemployment rolls. They spent less at the downtown stores, and thus contributed in a small way to the second great collapse within each river town during this period—that of their downtowns.

The Death of Downtown

Phoenixville celebrated its centennial year, 1949, with the appropriate festivities, including the obligatory parade. During this year of celebrating the past, one of most central components of that past, the landmark Phoenix Hotel, fell to the wrecking ball, ending its half-century existence at Bridge and Main Streets. It was replaced by a W. T. Grant department store, but that did not survive nearly as long; it was torn down just a few years later for a parking lot. That sequence of events serves as a metaphor for every one of the downtowns along the lower Schuylkill River after the Second World War. Community landmarks of long standing disappeared, and few were replaced. By 1980, each of the river towns had been hollowed out, with residential areas surrounding the barren remains of what had once been vibrant commercial sectors.

The commercial downtowns of the eight towns suffered an even higher casualty rate than their industrial sectors during the same period, at least in raw numbers. The downtowns suffered an overwhelming departure of retail and service businesses. Once the cores of prospering, self-contained communities, the downtown commercial sectors were no longer shopping destinations by the 1960s.

No one had seen that coming. At war's end, each town had looked forward to the return of good times. Political and business leaders in the towns had expected their postwar world to stay more or less the same as it always had. Their towns had prospered under the old ways, and all were confident of their return, invigorated by the shedding of depression and war. They were wrong. The old ways were not going to return.

The largest of the Schuylkill River downtowns, which had been the most dependent on sheer volume of sales from a wide area, were the most affected. Norristown's Main Street–centered retail community, which had served central Montgomery County, suffered the most, not just in numbers but also in the physical loss of downtown buildings. Between 1950 and 1975, the six-block core of Main Street lost 65 percent of its for-profit businesses.[10] A few were repurposed, but many were simply abandoned, as no buyer could be found, and subsequently came down, either by contract or by suspicious fire. The smaller West Marshall Street shopping area also suffered, but was at least spared the wholesale destruction of its old buildings.

Pottstown, which had traditionally served as the commercial center for not only the northwest corner of Montgomery County but also much of northern Chester County and southern Berks County, suffered proportionally, although it retained more of its downtown buildings than did Norristown. Several of Pottstown's most significant buildings along High Street fell to the wrecking ball, and many abandoned buildings were torn down.

The arc of Phoenixville's downtown followed the general pattern, but with its individual fortunes more tied to one company than any other town on the lower Schuylkill, its timing was more individual timing. It also managed to keep many of its old downtown buildings.

Conshohocken, Royersford, and, to a lesser extent, Pottstown, signed up for a federal government program that promised to rebuild and revitalize their deteriorated commercial sectors. Conshohocken sacrificed nearly the entire core of its old downtown, and Royersford something close to it, for the sake of government-subsidized urban renewal. Pottstown participated, too, but in a smaller and more piecemeal fashion, with more of a focus on its industrial areas.

The destruction of each old downtown was supposed to have been followed by the rise of a new one, according to the promises of developers, investors, the government, and community leaders. By 1980, however, those promises had not been fulfilled. The fate of urban renewal in each of the three towns technically still hung in the

---

10. Tolle. *What Killed Downtown?*. 236.

balance. The destruction half of the project had occurred, but the lack of replacement buildings suggested that the urban renewal movement had failed, as it had nationwide.

Urban Renewal?

The elected leaders of each community responded in different ways to the hollowing out of their downtowns. Their stories are complex and unique, but in each location, struggle broke out between two basic groups, the progressives and the traditionalists. Both groups were aware of the steadily deteriorating financial conditions of their towns and the eroding tax bases. The split came over whether to take advantage of the programs offered to municipalities by the federal government. The "progressives" were willing to explore the funding sources offered by the federal government if it would improve their towns, even if doing so meant a radical departure from American laissez-faire ideology. The "traditionalists" were more inclined to let the economy sort things out, without the towns becoming beholden to Washington. The disagreement tended to center on the issue of government oversight—that is, how much they should and would let the federal government dictate how they spent the funds on local urban renewal efforts.

The American attachment to local government supremacy was strong, but the underlying disagreement was even more fundamental: whether future economic growth—who would be able to do what and where—would be planned. In the Adam Smith free-market tradition, economic planning was anathema; the "hidden hand" was believed to deliver the best of all possible worlds. The struggle went on longer than it should have in some communities, particularly Norristown, but the traditionalists eventually found themselves overwhelmed by the scope of the collapse all about them.

One by one, each river community began to at least try to structure itself in a manner that the federal government would consider acceptable. The first step toward obtaining those federal dollars was to establish the requisite subordinate agencies. This meant primarily forming a municipal-level planning commission, but it also included such fundamentals as establishing zoning ordinances. Montgomery County established a planning commission in 1950, and then joined the Southeastern Pennsylvania Regional Planning Commission in 1952. That was replaced by the even-more-encompassing Delaware Valley Regional Planning Commission in 1965.

Some municipalities were quick to join the movement, while others held back. Norristown voted to establish a planning commission in 1961, then killed it in 1972. Conshohocken established a borough planning commission in 1959, although not without controversy, and adopted its first zoning ordinance and first subdivision ordinance in 1965. One by one, the other towns followed suit. Even Norristown reconstituted its planning commission. West Conshohocken finally established zoning ordinances in 1976, making it the last political entity in Montgomery County to do so.

Once the municipal planning commissions had been established, the next step was for them to fulfill their function and plan for the future of their respective communities. The expertise—as well as the funding—for such projects could not be found on the municipal level, so each planning commission established a relationship with the county's planning commission to produce plans that were formally joint reports. These were, in each case, overwhelmingly the work of the county commission's staff. Some of them focused on downtowns (the "central business area"), while others offered a look at the entire community. Comprehensive plans were prepared for each river town, and presented to the local governments with appropriate ceremony. They were formally accepted by each borough, even Norristown, but a plan means nothing without implementation, and those efforts invariably fell short of what had been proposed.

What followed differed in each town, but they all eventually took advantage of federal funding, accepting the concomitant loss of oversight. The process has not ended, and an accounting of all such projects is beyond the scope of this work. I will discuss the three largest projects of this era, however, with a focus on the two towns that gambled heavily on programs for the total rebuilding of their deteriorated downtowns.

Pottstown was the first river town to buy into the program, and did so several times, in a sequence of projects. These specific programs combined to remove both abandoned industrial sites and some commercial and residential buildings in the downtown area. Industrial renewal focused on clearing out old structures and constructing the "industrial highway" that paralleled the river, and was intended to service the new industries Pottstown hoped to attract. This was not just a program of destruction; it also enabled some old factories to move to better locations within the borough. This was more effective at helping Pottstown than the residential and commercial projects. In 1980, much was still in flux, as the borough was still negotiating with potential developers for its most recent project. On balance, urban renewal posted its best record in Pottstown, although the future demonstrated that enthusiasm for occupying the cleared areas was less than had been anticipated.

Royersford bet heavily on urban renewal, too, and it would be the most disappointed. It was the first river town to take a comprehensive approach to removal and replacement. By 1980, it was obvious that its urban renewal had failed. Expectations had been very different in 1966, when Royersford considered how to implement the downtown portion of the comprehensive plan that had been prepared for it. The original plan called for the removal of forty-four buildings, including ten businesses. The borough's council voted to draw up a formal proposal to HUD that increased the scale of the project. The number of buildings to be demolished grew to sixty, and included some of the finest examples of local architecture. They were to be replaced with a shopping center with stores facing a parking lot on the block south of Main Street, anchored by a large food store and a department store. The last examples of both had left Royersford by that time.

As was standard for such comprehensive projects, there were two phases: demolition and development. Federal funding made it all possible, or so it seemed. Royersford was to pay one-eighth of the cost of the demolition work before turning the site over to a developer. A four-month wait time was expected for federal approval, and the target completion date for the demolition phase was in March 1970. An additional $1.1 million low-cost housing project for the elderly was included in the development plan. The Royersford Development Corporation would be the developer, contracting with demolition and construction firms.

The plan was not formally approved until May 1967, and the funding was not available until May 1969. Further roadblocks followed. In

January 1969, the borough's mayor wrote a letter to county officials complaining that the project was at a standstill, and had been for some time. The uncertainty around the project's future had led affected landlords to cease maintenance on the properties within the area, which was rapidly becoming a slum.

Demolition did not begin until 1976, and endless delays in actually receiving the promised HUD funding seriously affected the initial development. The delays cost the Royersford project its expected anchor store, an A&P supermarket, which Limerick Township lured away. The Montgomery County Redevelopment Authority took over the project, writing another comprehensive plan, but still nothing happened. In 1979, HUD finally gave up and transferred ownership of the entire block of land back to the borough. From then on, lots were sold to individual purchasers. On the positive side, the elderly housing project did finally open as the Golden Age Manor in 1971.

Urban renewal in Royersford just seemed to fizzle out. The grand dreams were never realized, and those buildings that were constructed were of secondary quality and design. Worse, they remained largely empty. They did not stimulate any new construction, and the cleared site remains partially vacant to this day. In the final analysis, urban renewal failed in Royersford.

Conshohocken also took a comprehensive approach, and, as with Royersford, its urban renewal plans focused on its downtown area. Conshohocken's project was several times larger than Royersford's, and it began later. The original plan was a product of a 1966 County Redevelopment Authority study. It proposed to create a new, multipurpose downtown, encompassing everything from residential, retail, and office space to a hotel complex. The Conshohocken council adopted a plan in 1971 and submitted it to HUD. Three years of negotiations followed. Finally, in 1974, HUD accepted a modified plan to purchase and clear twenty-five acres at the core of the old downtown. Conshohocken was the last of the three Schuylkill Valley towns to subject itself to urban renewal; in fact, its program was the last one contracted for in the entire country.

Fifty-five businesses and more than six hundred residents had to be relocated before demolition could begin. By the time the removal phase was finally completed in 1981, more than 248 buildings were gone. What had been downtown Conshohocken was now empty lots surrounded by protective fencing. Only three buildings survived, including the Washington Hose and Steam Fire Engine Company No. 1 (the "Washies"), which was protected by its historical status, and the old Pennsylvania Railroad Station.

While the removal phase progressed apace, planning for the replacement phase struggled. In 1979, the Redevelopment Authority adopted a plan for a portion of the downtown that had been cleared, and then contracted with a developer. In 1980, when interest rates were sky high, the original developer was unable to secure financing and withdrew from the project. As 1980 drew to a close, the success or failure of urban renewal in Conshohocken remained uncertain.

Appearances can be deceiving, and in 1980, Conshohocken appeared to be even worse off than Royersford. In reality, its future was brighter. The reason was the pending approval of one of the final phases of the Mid-County Expressway, known locally as the "Blue Route," one of the most-disputed and most-delayed roads in the history of the Interstate Highway System. Developers knew that once the new highway was completed, the Conshohockens would sit at the intersection of two major limited-access highways. They had studied the King of Prussia experience, and realized what could follow.

The differing futures of the Schuylkill Valley's three urban renewal projects after 1980 would demonstrate beyond a doubt that while money can buy expertise, and that expertise can produce impressive plans, actual results can vary significantly. In these cases, the results depended almost entirely on factors external to the program itself. Urban renewal in Royersford remained a failure, but that would not deter borough officials from attempting later versions. Urban renewal in Pottstown sputtered and died out, with decidedly mixed results. Only Conshohocken would see its downtown born again, but urban renewal and similar programs would have very little to do with it.

1980: An Assessment

To produce *Montgomery County: The Second Hundred Years* in time for the anniversary year of 1984, the board overseeing the book asked contributors to submit the town histories by 1980. Thus, the descriptions of the municipalities have a "1980 View" that summarizes the

status of each community at the turn of that decade. All six of the
river towns in Montgomery County complied, giving us an insight
into the conditions of each town as seen through the eyes of a
resident versed in local history. While these historical snapshots are
an entirely coincidental contribution to this study, the then-current
views about conditions in 1980 illustrate the psychological state of
their residents at the time. They all tell virtually the same story.

Two of the river towns in this study, Phoenixville and Spring City,
are located in Chester County, and therefore no such convenient
1980 summaries for them exist. At the introductory level toward
which this work is aimed, that is no problem for Spring City, as what
can be applied in general to Royersford can be applied to its twin
across the river up to that time. Phoenixville's general outlook at the
time can be inferred from other sources; although it is a larger town,
and its situation and mood more complex, the status of its namesake
employment giant did not differ greatly from that of those in Pottstown or Conshohocken. At this introductory level, Phoenixville by
1980 remained a variant of the general pattern then prevalent
throughout the Schuylkill Valley.

What makes the summaries useful to this study is that they provide
evidence that the common historical arc of the river towns continued
in bad times as it had in good times. What followed shortly, however,
would *not* be common. This provides the initial evidence that 1980 is
an adequate date to mark a turning point in the collective history of
the eight Schuylkill River towns. It serves this function not for
anything that specifically happened in that year, but because that is a
convenient round-number-year around which significant events did
take place. These events would—for the first time—send the eight
river towns along differing paths.

It is strikingly obvious that in 1980, the eight towns of the lower
Schuylkill River shared a common concern: uncertainty about the
future. The Norristown chapter in *The Second Hundred Years* began
the "1980 View" segment by saying, "The state of the borough in 1980
was not a matter of general agreement." It then enumerated an array
of problems sufficient to suggest that there was a general agreement
after all, at least that things were not good. What followed was a
litany of problems Norristown shared with its fellow river towns,

along with a list of those particular to Norristown, which the writer largely attributed to the town's status as the county seat: "Being a county seat, the borough was especially attractive to those seeking public aid from the borough and county, and from the state, federal, and private agencies locally represented." The inclination to blame the poor for the area's problem, as well as the growing need for and significance of government welfare programs, had already taken root in Norristown, and it would continue to grow.

Pottstown's chronicler for *The Second Hundred Years* got right to the point on the subject of Pottstown in 1980, declaring "The Prospects for Pottstown are not bright." The borough's population had dropped to just slightly above what it had been in 1950, and many of those residents who remained, the author observed, did so because they had no prospect of employment elsewhere. The unemployment rate in the borough ranged between 12 and 14 percent. The Pottstown section closed with a statement of hope for the future, based on the expected 1983 completion of the long-desired highway connection to the Schuylkill Expressway, now termed the "Pottstown Expressway." This would, the chronicler claimed, "open Pottstown to Philadelphia markets and make Pottstown an attractive commercial and industrial site."[11] The highway would open—in 1985—but its benefit to Pottstown would be questionable, to say the least.

Conshohocken's contributor to *The Second Hundred Years* also got to the point quickly, opening with the statement that "Conshohocken is no longer a mill town but a residential area with a wide main street."[12] The author had good reason to make such a statement. A community that had always prided itself on its strong work ethic, Conshohocken had lost about forty-five hundred jobs in the previous five years. The twenty-five core acres of its once-thriving downtown lay behind fences, shorn of all but three of its buildings.

As befitted an even smaller community, West Conshohocken's 1980 summation for *The Second Hundred Years* was even more brief. It recognized that the old mills had gone, but indicated that some residents held out hope for local industry since some new, small firms were moving in. But the stark reality of West Conshohocken in

---

11. Toll and Schwager, *The Second Hundred Years*, 548.

12. Ibid., 144.

1980 could not be avoided: "It has no sewers, no doctor, no lawyer, and no pharmacist. Although the borough has been devastated by the coming of the Schuylkill Expressway and the Blue Route—it lost commercial enterprises, 125 houses, and the taxes they paid—the residents seem content in their small, friendly community."

When it came to offering a 1980 perspective, Bridgeport's contributor to *The Second Hundred Years* emphasized how much had been lost, even including a list of the most recent departures. The extent of the borough's uncertainty about its future can be judged by that fact that the writer saw "some merit" in the idea that Bridgeport should shed its independent status and become part of Upper Merion. By 1980, however, there was virtually no chance of that happening. Upper Merion was prosperous and growing, with a tax rate that was the envy of every township and municipality for miles around. Bridgeport no longer possessed a sufficient tax base for the township that almost surrounded it to even consider the idea.

The chronicler of Royersford in 1980 joined the general lament that all the industries that had once characterized the borough had departed. Adding to the woe was the fact that four additional companies in the borough had announced plans to either close or relocate, taking another two hundred jobs with them. With little opportunity for work within the borough, most of the residents of Royersford in 1980 worked in other towns or suburbs. The residents were growing older, as the young left in search of opportunity, and such housing as had been built in recent years had been apartments. Only a small number of new people were migrating into the borough. The business district still lay empty, as urban renewal had not proved to be the answer. As a final gesture, the writer repeated the hope that the "Pottstown Expressway" might be the borough's salvation.

Just across the river, Spring City's industries were all but gone. It, too, was losing its younger residents. The borough's population had declined only slightly, and continued to be as white as its twin across the river. Its postwar highpoint had been due to the commercial effect of the nearby Philco Inc. plant, and that had closed. The local government had seen no compelling reason to undertake anything like Royersford had, and Royersford's experience strongly suggested that they should not do so in the future. Its small downtown had fallen victim to a strip shopping center inside borough limits that, although small, offered parking spots.

Inferring Phoenixville's condition and attitude requires caution, for, as a much larger town, it possessed greater complexity than its upriver neighbor. Yet, its traditional reliance on the metals industry put it squarely in the quandary of the other river towns. The difference lay in the relationship between the borough and its one overwhelmingly important economic contributor. Phoenixville was a company town, and the relationship between Phoenix Steel and the town had been much more cordial and more mutually beneficial than other company towns had experienced. Thus, the arc of the company's final years was reflected by its namesake neighbor. The Phoenix Steel plant would not close until 1983 (a small portion would continue beyond that), but its course had been downhill: in 1976, it had ceased to produce new steel; by 1980, its payroll had already shrunk a great deal. Nevertheless, the willingness of the union to accept layoffs and reductions in wages and benefits to save the situation had been greater than that of Bethlehem Steel. Still, by 1980, Phoenixville, as with each of the other river towns, was being forced to consider a future without the most important part of what had been its past.

By 1980, much remained uncertain for the Schuylkill River towns. Each was caught in the trap of declining value as long-time residents, businesses, and industries closed down or moved elsewhere. Each labored under the strain of high unemployment and declining revenue at precisely the time when fresh capital was needed to implement the hopeful municipal plans. Each plan ostensibly pointed out the way back to prosperity; unfortunately, they each pointed in different directions. As each river town took stock of its situation in 1980, all agreed that the past had gone, but all were equally unsure as to what the future held.

Historians who seek to comprehend the deeper and broader sweep of events must be wary of offering hasty conclusions. Historical analysis grows more difficult—and more critical—the closer the subjects are to the present. The history of the Schuylkill River towns since 1980 calls for such care. Still, the activists of each town simply *must* understand this recent period if they are to effectively pursue a better urban environment. That is because the period after 1980 presents a sea change in the collective history of these eight Schuylkill River towns. It was only after around this convenient round-number year that the congruence of the river towns' historical arcs began to break down. This process produced the first dramatic differences between both the physical conditions and psychological attitudes among the eight towns in their entire existence. In the decades that followed, those differences have only been reinforced, widening the gap among the recent histories of each town.

This chapter begins with a brief summary of the recent histories of each town in relation to this work's three themes, and then follows an analysis of the current state of those three fundamental realities. They are the old realities, but so different now as to be new realities. Anyone interested in improving the urban environments of the river towns *must* understand these new conditions, and then apply that understanding to their hopes and plans for their towns. Huge challenges face each town, but with each challenge comes opportunity, if the reality of the challenge is understood.

The sections that follow should be understood as theses, not conclusions. The events upon which they are based are of too recent origin to allow for proper historical analysis, yet the activists of each river town cannot wait for a more nuanced interpretation. I believe that the points I make below are firmly grounded in the changing historical realities, and offer solid guidelines for how future attempts at community revival should be undertaken.

At this time, the most recent verifiable data for any analysis comes from the 2010 census. Real estate–oriented online sources purport to update some of that data. I have selected one online source for additional numbers concerning all eight towns, and employed it exclusively to avoid even subconsciously massaging the numbers. However, readers are advised to keep in mind the underlying uncertainty about the accuracy of any number after the 2010 census.

Different Paths

Even a cursory reading of the last thirty years of history in the Schuylkill Valley reveals that the eight towns have, for the first time, finally diverged along different historical arcs. The path of each is an individual one, but the emerging differences among the Schuylkill River towns suggest a grouping into three broadly drawn categories: stagnation, revival, and takeover.

I judge five towns—Pottstown, Royersford, Spring City, Norristown, and Bridgeport—to be in stagnation, a term I apply largely but not entirely for economic reasons. An examination of the boroughs' individual conditions demonstrates significant differences in how each earned its placement in this category. I categorize the stagnation of Royersford and Spring City as quaint, that of Norristown and Pottstown as disturbing, and that of Bridgeport as subordinate.

Residents' self-perception plays a significant part of this judgment about the five towns in economic stagnation, and is the basis for their subgrouping. The internal perception in the boroughs of Pottstown, Norristown, and Bridgeport stems largely from the more substantial population shift in race and ethnicity that has taken place in these three towns. Royersford and Spring City are much less affected by that, and are more self-satisfied with their increasing orientation as small bedroom communities.

Phoenixville, alone among the eight river towns, can be said to be undergoing a revival, a term that, while based on the town's improving economic condition, applies even more to its psychological condition or its self-view. The two are interlinked, because what has taken place—reinvention is a much better word than revival—is internally generated. This locally oriented interaction of people and capital makes Phoenixville unique among the eight river towns.

Both Conshohockens are also being reinvented, but in a process I consider to be a takeover, as the efforts are not internally generated, as they are in Phoenixville. The Conshohockens are undergoing the best times of any of the river towns—if you count only money. Their reinvention is being forced on them. They are being taken over. That, and the resulting lack of a psychological consensus regarding their future, makes all the difference.

Stagnation

Pottstown

Taking the pulse of an entire town is a risky endeavor, but any observer of Pottstown in the second decade of the new millennium would be struck by how the self-image of its residents seems to be lower than that of any other town on the lower Schuylkill River, Norristown included. Part of that conclusion would be based on the often-vocalized belief that Pottstown is in the process of becoming "another Norristown." That belief stems from a combination of perceived causes, but is grounded in the population replacement Pottstown has seen in recent decades.

By 1980, Pottstown's population had already plunged by almost 15 percent from its all-time high of 26,144, to 22,729. The decline continued through the 1990 census, and then the number remained virtually unchanged for the next decade. The 2010 census showed a modest increase of some five hundred people, but the overall number of 22,377 is still below that for 1980, which was itself near the bottom of a greater plunge.

The changes in Pottstown's demographics must be understood within this context of shrinkage. That shrinkage amplifies the locally perceived process of "population debasement." Caucasians remain the dominant majority, at 72 percent of the population, but that represents a decline from the 87 percent figure in 1980; they are a smaller percentage of a smaller population. On the opposite side, the nonwhite presence has increased overall from 13 percent in 1980 to 19.5 percent in 2010; they are a larger percentage of a smaller population. The African American presence has increased the most in raw numbers, rising to 19.5 percent, but combined with the increase in the number of Latino residents from negligible in 1980 to 5.6 percent in 2010, they deliver a substantial message of a changing town.

The same old ethnic biases and nativism are at the root of the white population's sense that things are changing for the worse in Potts-town, but this is further amplified by the racial prejudice that causes many to cling to negative preconceptions. In this narrow worldview, the nonwhites are flooding Pottstown to game the system for cheap housing and endless welfare benefits. In a more open worldview, the latest wave of newcomers—the most-grievously disenfranchised groups—is being systematically segregated into specific neighbor-hoods and towns, to the detriment of all.

It is true that Pottstown possesses the largest number of public housing complexes in Montgomery County, but all of those were constructed before 1980; they have merely been maintained since that time. However, the real hot-button issue in Pottstown is usually referred to, quite disdainfully, as "Section 8," whether it concerns the Housing Choice Voucher Program or not.

Pottstown is the county's eleventh-most populous town, comprising 2.8 percent of the county's population, yet it provides 17 percent of the county's housing choice vouchers. While Pottstown provides 452 such vouchers, the total number in the nine municipalities with populations greater than Pottstown's (excluding Norristown) is 323. In other words, all nine of the larger cities combined provide 71 percent of what the borough of Pottstown provides all by itself.

Despite this, Pottstown's percentage of rental housing was pegged in 2012 at 44 percent. This is high, but the borough's rate is still among the lowest of the towns along the lower Schuylkill, tied with prosperous Phoenixville and higher only than Royersford and Spring City among the towns in stagnation. The coincidence of Pottstown and Phoenixville having the same percentage of rentals suggests that further research is needed on this complex subject.

Self-perceptions aside, Pottstown's root problem today is the same one that has always plagued it, and that was recognized by its civic leaders from the beginning. The borough's location in the extreme northwestern corner of Montgomery County means that it has little in common with the more influential towns in the southern and eastern portions of the county to which it is legally tied. Pottstown always has been, and remains, not just closer but better connected to lower Berks County and upper Chester County than to its home county. The era of the railroad and the trolley disguised the problem by providing frequent, reliable transportation to lower Montgomery County and Philadelphia, as well as farther up the Schuylkill, to Reading and beyond, and even east as far as Allentown. However, the automobile reversed that. The lower portion of Montgomery County hosted the new Interstate highways, and through them generated the greatest increase in both population and invested wealth. Pottstown could not participate in this boon, because by that time, the new road network had effectively isolated it. Pottstown is still difficult to reach from prosperous lower Montgomery County, and its road connections to Reading and beyond connect it to cities that are doing nowhere near as well as those to the southeast.

Pottstown had been eager to gain a connection to the new limited-access highway system in southeastern Pennsylvania, ever since the Schuylkill Expressway first made its appearance in King of Prussia in 1950. Several decades passed while local officials discussed the possibility of extending the highway. That never happened, but a new, modern highway did gradually appear, opening in segments and completed by the mid-1980s. Pottstown was the last connection along US Route 422. The delay served only to worsen the borough's decline, and finally connecting Pottstown to a big, modern road was like connecting a stream to a mighty river: it sped up the departure of the borough's remaining wealth toward the highway-inspired development appearing at every entrance/exit along the route between King of Prussia and Pottstown. That heretofore-underdeveloped area was the *real* beneficiary of the new highway.

Area shoppers today still drive to the malls and the new shopping centers, just as they were already doing by 1980. Downtown Pottstown has experienced no commercial revival, although at least it has also avoided wholesale destruction of its old commercial district along High Street. Individual buildings have been removed, leaving a gap-toothed appearance, but a majority of the older commercial buildings still stand. Commercial use of several has changed; both a church and a mosque currently inhabit buildings on High Street, and others have been transformed into residences. One of the town's major stores, Weitzenkorn's, at 145 East High Street, has managed to survive since 1864. Few other stores of any size have survived. The

Steel River Playhouse, a community theater, is a popular new addition that harkens back to the old days.

Pottstown's attempts to retain a manufacturing sector have had some success, but no large industries have relocated there. The last survivor among the borough's once well-known firms, Mrs. Smith's Pies, participated in one of the early urban renewal projects, occupying a new building built for the firm, but the company has since been sold; its new ownership relocated the factory, and nothing like it has appeared in its place. The industrial park created with federal urban renewal funds still exists along a portion of the borough's old waterfront, and houses several small businesses. A portion of the industrial area upriver from the Hanover Street Bridge, adjacent to the remaining tracks of what was once the Reading Railroad, has become the site of Montgomery County Community College's West Campus, and may grow to include other educational institutions. This, and the popularity of the Schuylkill River Trail, offers perhaps the most positive of any near-future contributions. The future of Pottstown is as uncertain today as it was in 1980.

Norristown

By 1980, the postwar population explosion had transformed Montgomery County into the richest county in Pennsylvania. That process would continue in the succeeding decades, but it would not affect the county seat, at least not positively. By 1980, Norristown had lost both its manufacturing base and its status as the commercial shopping mecca for central Montgomery County. Between 1980 and 2010, Norristown continued its economic stagnation. No new industrial or commercial businesses of any size came to the borough during this period. Norristown's psychological view of itself deteriorated, and today many residents believe that Norristown remains in continued decline. The root of that belief lies in the singular pattern of population replacement since 1980.

People have been replaced, but Norristown's most iconic buildings have simply been abandoned and sold. In 1980, *The Second Hundred Years* listed the borough's "principal claims to fame [as] the Court House, the county offices, and One Montgomery Plaza at Swede and Airy Streets; Montgomery Hospital at Fornance and Powell; Sacred

Heart Hospital at Fornance and DeKalb; and Norristown State Hospital at Stanbridge and Sterigere." As of 2012, the courthouse and the county offices were little changed. In the years since 1980, however, One Montgomery Plaza has been revealed to be a seriously flawed structure, with an uncertain future. Both Montgomery Hospital and Sacred Heart Hospital have closed. Sacred Heart has been repurposed, but Montgomery Hospital was torn down. The process of "deinstitutionalization" has also meant the gradual emptying out of Norristown State Hospital. The extensive grounds remain, but most buildings are no longer used, making the hospital but a shadow of it former self, both in number of occupants and economic contribution to the community.

Downtown also remains but a shadow of what it once was. It is ragged and largely unused. Main Street remains sadly empty of buildings, not to mention businesses. Even Swede Street, known as "lawyers' row" for so many years, has declined. Since the digital revolution has removed many of the reasons for people to come to Norristown to transact routine legal business, as well as for law firms to be located close to the courthouse, they are now largely gone. Little more than a block to the north of the courthouse lies Norristown's most depressed sector, a collection of tawdry buildings and residents with seemingly little to do.

The Montgomery County commissioners have not been disposed to lend a helping hand, arguing that they cannot favor one municipality over another in the expenditure of funds. In response, Norristown's municipal government has undertaken a more activist stance, making several attempts at beautification to tempt new businesses into the downtown. Beautiful bricked intersections, lamps, sidewalk benches, and the like put a good face on things, but the small service businesses lured to town have largely come and gone. A grandiose dream of transforming the defunct Logan Square Shopping Center into a motion picture theater failed in spectacular fashion, adding only debt to the already-strapped town.

Projects to improve Norristown's road and rail connections have been perhaps the most positive steps for the town's future. A new SEPTA Transportation Center that connects regional rail, the trolley to 69th Street, and local bus routes, and that also provides ample vehicle parking, has transformed a formerly shabby sector of town. A new road connection to the turnpike from Plymouth Township is also under construction, in hopes of rectifying Norristown's historic disconnect from the new local roads built since World War II.

The previous statement about the lack of commercial activity requires a coda. The general conclusion is true for Main Street and the traditional downtown, but not for the smaller stretch of West Marshall Street not far away. That shopping sector has been reborn. New businesses have opened, including restaurants that are giving Norristown the positive culinary reputation that it has always lacked. The reason for all this introduces the most significant change in recent Norristown history, a demographic change: the arrival of Latinos, mostly Mexicans, in large numbers.

Norristown's population peaked at 38,925 with the 1960 census. The 1970 census reported a small population drop, but by 1980, the decline had become a free fall that continued through 1990; Norristown lost almost three thousand residents per decade, and its 1990 population of 30,749 was its lowest number since the 1920 census. A slight rebound was evident by 2000, and a larger one during the next decade, but the 2010 census listed Norristown's population at 34,324, still lower than in 1930.

In 1980, the population had been 76 percent white. In the next three decades, Norristown followed a singular path of population replacement, a shift unlike that of any other river town. By 2010, the census recorded a remarkable fact: Caucasians had ceased to be the majority of the population. The 2010 census also revealed another aspect to Norristown's population shift unique among the eight river towns, which is that its residents were almost evenly distributed between three population groups: 41 percent Caucasian, 36 percent African American, and 28 percent Latino. Most of the new residents had moved into apartments, not homes. Norristown has the highest percentage of rental properties of any town on the lower Schuylkill. A majority of the population, 52 percent, rents rather than owns.

In March 1995, the latest of several suspicious fires that had gutted the old downtown over the previous decades destroyed a portion of the town's core intersection at Main and DeKalb Streets. A March 14 article on the website *Philly.com* discussed the fire, and Norristown's overall decline: "Norristown is the poorest city in Pennsylvania's richest county. It is home to one in six families living below the poverty line in Montgomery County, and the 3.5-square-mile borough [sic] houses more government-subsidized housing than the rest of the county combined." Things had gotten so bad that the article concluded with the question, "Is Norristown worth saving?"

Sometime around 1995, the decades-long population decline in Norristown ended. Slowly, the trend began to reverse. It is a sad truth that when people begin to think of a town as inferior—especially to the point of questioning its very existence—housing values drop. The houses themselves do not change, only people's perceptions of them. "Desirability" drives housing prices. When word gets around that such-and-such a place is cheaper to live, the people who have been struggling to live elsewhere move in.

As these undesirable areas are financially depressed for a reason— no commercial or industrial activity means no good jobs—these same people continue to struggle. Norristown still has a staggering number of people who need subsidized housing; that has not changed much since the *Philly.com* article in 1995. Norristown in 2012 was the county's fourth-most-populous municipality, housing 4.3 percent of the total county population, yet it still provided almost 43 percent of the county's housing choice vouchers. The three towns with larger populations—Lower Merion, Abington, and Cheltenham—together provided 227 housing vouchers, barely 20 percent of the number in Norristown alone. Norristown's percentage of the county's vouchers may have dropped slightly since 1995, but the increase in its population means that there are more voucher holders in the town than there were. Norristown's 1,115 housing vouchers represent almost 16 percent of the city's total occupied rental units. Such a number produces a doubly bad result: far too many low-quality residences, and rents artificially inflated by the HUD-determined formula that the Montgomery County Housing Authority must follow. Similar statistics for Pottstown are a primary reason some residents fear that it is becoming "another Norristown."[13]

---

13. For an explanation of how HUD and the county housing authorities artificially drive up area rents, see "Housing Choice Vouchers: It's Not *All* About the Beniamins," in *Getting Up's Still on Their Minds*, the second half of this book.

Between 1980 and 2014, Norristown, with its population increasingly divided by race and ethnicity, has endured economic stagnation and political turmoil, including the removal of a mayor for corruption. There is no easy solution anywhere on the horizon, and even the difficult (read: expensive) possibilities are limited.

Bridgeport

In the decades following 1980, Bridgeport's stagnation mirrored Norristown's, psychologically and economically. Both had fallen victim to largely the same forces, losing both industry and commerce. Bridgeport's commercial collapse had been nowhere near as large as Norristown's, but it was just as total. The same ethnic mix of people had long inhabited both towns, with Italians dominating, although far fewer African Americans had moved to Bridgeport than to Norristown. Bridgeport traditionally suffered from its proximity to the larger, healthier town across the river, but after 1980, Bridgeport's decline was increasingly less related to Norristown's presence and increasingly more a result of other causal factors. Neither of the financially distressed towns has been able to budget for major changes, but Bridgeport's tax base has suffered perhaps the greater hit. Both towns have stagnated, and the changes both have experienced have had external causes, both good and bad.

As with Norristown, Bridgeport recorded a net population decrease in the decades since 1980. Bridgeport's population bottomed out in 1990, and has since begun to rise slowly, but its 2010 population of 4,554 was still some three hundred people below that of 1980. Like Norristown, Bridgeport has undergone population replacement, as evidenced by the change in its places of worship. Since 1980, Bridgeport has seen its churches close, one after another. By the time this book goes to print in 2015, the final two Catholic churches will have shut down, leaving Bridgeport Catholics without a local place of worship for the first time since 1892. The departure of the ethnic base of each doomed them all.

The period since 1980 has seen the borough's social fabric being just as depleted, but less replaced than has been happening across the river. In 1980, the borough's population of 4,843 was 98 percent Caucasian; by 2010, that figure was 80 percent. Of the eight towns in this study, only Norristown has seen a larger percentage drop among its white residents. African Americans have increased their percentage, but the significant change has been the rise in the Latino population, which constitutes almost 13 percent of the borough's numbers, by far the second-highest on the lower Schuylkill, and yet another spillover from Norristown. Older, more established residents view this influx of Latinos as suspect, and issues of immigration status cloud the developing relationship between the town's long-time and more recent residents.

The borough's longer-time residents have been steadily departing. Statistics do not differentiate among housing owners, but since a full 50 percent of Bridgetown's housing units are inhabited by renters, it seems highly probable that the families departing are not selling their homes but renting them to the new arrivals. The shift in ownership from residents to absentee landlords, a phenomenon known to be prevalent in Norristown, is less well documented in Bridgeport.

Bridgeport's connections to the new road network in southeastern Pennsylvania have not improved. Although it lies but a short distance from the Interstate intersection at King of Prussia, development along DeKalb Pike (US Route 202) between the two has rendered the journey lengthy, and largely unnecessary anyway, except to initiate travel to somewhere else.

The remains of the old Southeastern Pennsylvania rail network extend out of Philadelphia, and connections between its lines outside of the city itself are few. A still-active railroad runs along the right bank of the Schuylkill and thus through Bridgeport, but its trains carry only freight and do not stop. In recent decades, they have done little for the borough except to cut it off from access to its riverfront.

Bridgeport has one unique transportation asset: the SEPTA rail line between 69th Street in West Philadelphia and Norristown. Originally the Philadelphia & Western, the line has always stopped in Bridgeport, and continues to do so. Its terminus in Norristown, the hugely upgraded Norristown Transportation Center, connects the remaining regional rail line to downtown Philadelphia. This convenience to transportation is one of the few spillovers from Norristown that has actually benefited Bridgeport. If SEPTA can develop a true regional transportation network around the Norristown Transportation Center—and particularly if this includes rail access to the King of Prussia Mall—Bridgeport could once again find itself building its future on its transportation connections.

A small portion of the old industrial area along the river remains active. In this period after industrial collapse, only Bridgeport joined Pottstown in a municipal effort to retain an industrial presence along the river, continuing the municipal tradition of offering tax breaks to newly locating companies. The result has been a modest success, although a 2001 fire demonstrated that some of the concerns facing industrialists in the late nineteenth century continued to persist even into the dawn of the twenty-first; Bridgeport had to once again call upon local fire companies for assistance, even beyond Norristown.

While Norristown's commercial downtown had always severely limited the growth of a strong commercial sector in Bridgetown, when Norristown's downtown collapsed between 1950 and 1975, its demise did not benefit Bridgeport, whose much smaller sector also declined—almost to the point of disappearance. An overview of subsequent years reveals that Bridgeport merely saw one dominant commercial neighbor replaced by another; the new, automobile-oriented shopping facilities at King of Prussia rapidly drew shoppers away from downtown Norristown, leaving it in ruins—and it took Bridgeport's commercial sector along with it. US Route 202 has long since ceased to be a major regional north-south route, and the Dannehower Bridge allows drivers to bypass Bridgeport entirely. Few enterprises of any size can survive on local patronage alone.

Industry may continue to provide some support, and planned improvements in the transportation infrastructure hold some promise, but Bridgeport's future, as viewed from 2015, is as uncertain as it appeared in 1980.

The Twin Boroughs: Spring City and Royersford

In 1980, the nickname of the "twin boroughs" remained relevant, despite Royersford having established a relatively substantial lead in population (about a thousand more residents) over Spring City. Both boroughs had lost almost all of their industries, as well as their small commercial sectors, and stood an equal chance of regaining both: zero. Both towns needed to reinvent themselves. Since that time, little has changed; the reinvention has yet to occur.

After the first decade of the twenty-first century, Royersford and Spring City remain twins, for their differences remain slight. Royersford has shown a small population growth and more civic efforts than its twin, but can overall be said to remain in stagnation. For Spring City, the term "stasis" is more accurate.

In the thirty-year period following 1980, Royersford added 509 residents, while Spring City lost sixty-six. Neither saw any major demographic changes in its population, although both added Latino residents. The percentage of whites dropped in both towns. In 1980, Caucasians constituted almost 99 percent of the residents in both towns. By 2010, that number had dropped to just below 90 percent. African Americans constitute only 5 percent of Royersford's and 3 percent of Spring City's population. Latinos, the newest demographic, now represent 4.2 percent of Royersford's population and 3.4 percent of Spring City's. Almost half of the new residents live in rental housing, much of it still owned by the long-time residents who left each town. Rental units make up 48 percent of Royersford's housing, and 49 percent of Spring City's.

Both boroughs remain in the economic doldrums. Only a few, insignificant businesses still operate out of their old downtowns. The mini-mall at the foot of the bridge in Spring City, as well as the Lakeview Shopping Center adjacent to Royersford, has usurped the function of downtown shopping. Royersford did manage to retain a one substantial retail business, LeBow Furniture, a family-owned downtown fixture since the 1940s, but even that closed in 2014. Substantial development, both residential and commercial, has taken place in nearby Limerick Township, the result of US Route 422 passing through previously undeveloped areas. These will probably serve to keep any major store out of Royersford's downtown, as its residents have only a somewhat longer drive to the growing commercial presence just outside Royersford's borough limits.

Heavy industry has virtually disappeared from both boroughs. The few industries that remain contribute neither noise nor smoke, which has allowed the twin boroughs to settle in as quiet, peaceful residential towns. Spring City's greater inertia and its surviving downtown combine to render the borough positively quaint. The same could be said for Royersford had a previous generation not ripped out the core of its downtown. On the other hand, Royersford has taken a decided lead in converting its old industrial sites for housing and recreation.

There is a difference in tempo between the two boroughs, but it is slight. Spring City appears to first-time visitors as a town suspended in time. The time in which it seems frozen is better than bad, and worse than good. It is, however, that sense of timelessness (some might say "paralysis") that leaves the biggest impression. Spring City's population has changed the least of the eight towns, with a net loss of just under 2 percent, as have its demographics.

Its former industries are almost silent, but several structures remain, including the two buildings of the old Flag Factory, close to the center of Spring City. Phoenix Homes (no longer the principal), used grant money to upgrade the two old buildings and convert them into Flag House, senior citizens housing, in 1990. The main mill building owned by Ira Gruber, who founded the Spring City Knitting Factory, sat empty and decrepit until HUD invested $6.1 million to reconvert the 1910 building into low-income senior citizens housing. Phoenix Homes, also the initial developer on this project, required additional money to finish, which they received from the Bard Foundation; this accounts for the name, the Bard Complex.

Spring City has more of its older buildings than does its twin, since its downtown was not removed in the name of "urban renewal." Its oldest buildings, many of them along the old Main Street commercial sector, date back to the 1840s. Only a few are still active commercial ventures, though, and none show any obvious vitality. Among the few remaining industrial sites on the street are the Spring City Electrical Manufacturing Company and the Spring City Foundry Company, both located on the site of the original stove factory; cast iron products have been made on that site since 1840, and are still made there today. The firm currently specializes in lampposts. In fact, the new ones installed in both Royersford and Spring City were made there, as were all the lampposts in all Disney park locations.

Remarkably, in the middle of all this stasis, Spring City has just accomplished something that is regrettably rare in modern-day towns: the borough now has a new library. When the town's long-time librarian passed away in 2001 without heirs, she left $500,000 to her church, and an equal amount to construct a new library. The library struggled for years to fulfill her bequest in the face of strident opposition. Some members of the borough council argued that libraries are a thing of the past in the digital era. Other opposition came, sadly, from the very church that had been granted the other $500,000. It is located next door, and its administrators argued that the new building would encroach on their space. Fortunately, Bertha Bower's wishes were respected, and the gorgeous new Spring City Library opened in September 2014. It now has a community room (sponsored by the Phoenixville Community Health Foundation) for library programs and public use, study and computer spaces, and a children's area—all at no taxpayer expense, thanks to grant funding added to the original bequest.

The day-to-day pace of Royersford is only slightly more lively greater than that of Spring City, as evidenced by its population growth, however modest it has been. Memories of its past still echo there, as freights cars still run on the local railroad network through the borough on occasion, but they are carrying goods from someplace else to someplace else, and do not stop. The source for the faint heartbeat that the borough *does* show is its connection to a newer transportation network by way of US Route 422. It does not pass through Royersford, but through adjacent Limerick Township to the east. The new limited-access highway has promoted some residential growth in the borough, but has simultaneously prevented any new commercial activity from taking root there.

The Royersford Borough Council has attempted to take advantage of this new connection to the larger transportation network to promote the borough as a desirable residential location, with mixed results. The borough's industrial sector, still occupied by abandoned buildings until after the end of the century, has been largely cleared. Upriver from the Schuylkill Bridge, very little remains of Buckwalter Stove Works. Only one building remains, preserved and repurposed with a grant. The Lewis Environmental Company owns the site now, and uses it primarily for storage. The company does have a display of stoves in the building, but no directions guiding anyone to them. Downriver from the bridge, where the borough's smaller industries were located, there is now a residential development, the "RiverWalk at Royersford," begun by Granor-Price (who has since sold it). The housing units were supposed to be for purchase, but lack of demand led to some being rented. The actual construction of the units stretched out over a decade, but is now reportedly finished. Granor-Price arranged for a mural to cover the wall of the one remaining industrial building close by. This mural should be judged as art, not history; the mural's Reading locomotive is purple, where it should have been green.

A physical memory of the old days—a Reading Railroad station—still exists. It is the one built in 1932, not the original one from 1839. The Norfolk Southern Railroad, which still runs the occasional train along the old Reading line, leased the building to developer Granor-Price for a dollar a year for twenty years. Following a grant-financed renovation, the building has been rented out. The borough built a small riverfront park along 1st Street nearby. The site was originally to be a six-floor apartment building, but when no developer could be found, the borough bought the ground and made it into a park with a walking trail and space for small outdoor concerts. The new street-lamps there and elsewhere in lower Royersford were made just across the river in Spring City.

The civic leadership of Royersford—and, to a lesser extent, Spring City—has grasped the fundamental point of any attempt at community revival: reinvention. They have recognized that their hillside towns, now bare of noise and smoke, nestle up to a river that is now scenic as well as clean. One of their best hopes will be to reinvent their relationship to that river.

Revival

Phoenixville

Phoenixville's historical arc since 1980 is unique among the eight towns on the lower Schuylkill River for its upward bend. It is the only one that has undergone, and is still experiencing, what can properly be termed a "revival," although it is also a reinvention. As with the other river towns, Phoenixville long ago lost its steel manufacturing and rendering companies, and although no major industries have replaced them, the town has transitioned from an industrial center to a desirable residential community, and one that possesses a high degree of confidence in itself and its future. What most distinguishes Phoenixville's post-1980 path is that the positive changes that have taken place have been locally generated. This contrasts in a most fundamental manner with the nature of the revival now under way in the Conshohockens, where the changes have been generated from outside the community, for reasons that are equally external.

The 1980 census recorded Phoenixville's population as 14,165. The previous decade was the worst in the borough's history, as it lost 4.4 percent of its 1970 population of 14,823. Between 1980 and 1990, the population began to rise again, and, despite a small decline (1.8 percent) between 1990 and 2000, recovered sharply during the next decade. According to the 2010 census, Phoenixville's population was 16,440, the highest it ever recorded.

In 1980, whites made up 78 percent of Phoenixville's population, and blacks less than 9 percent. In the following years, the white percentage increased, and by 2010, Caucasians counted for almost 82 percent of the population. The African American population has remained almost stable; in 2010 it accounted for 8.6 percent of the borough's total. The truly growing demographic is the Latino population. A negligible portion of the population in 1980, Latinos in 2010 accounted for 7.4 percent. By that year, the Asian population had also risen, to 3.5 percent.

The slow demise of the Phoenix Steel Company demonstrates the protracted agony felt by each of the river towns during the period when the traditional smokestack industries of the river towns slowly disappeared. All eight towns shared the pain during the late 1960s through the 1970s, suffering with every major closure. This loss was especially poignant and personal in Phoenixville, since it had always been a company town.

The final years of the Phoenix Steel Company also illustrate that the official closure date of any company in any town in the post–World War II era had little actual significance. By the time a large company formally closed its doors, its workforce would have been shrinking for years, with the biggest layoffs long since completed. This was certainly true of the Phoenix Steel Company. After the company's last heat of fresh steel in 1976, it was all downhill from there. The historic closeness between the company and the town played out its final scenes of successive layoffs and wage and benefit reductions for years after that, and these successive hits were accepted more stoically by the workers at Phoenix Steel than elsewhere. The unknown number of workers who left the premises for the last time when it finally closed was certainly a pitifully small fraction of the number who had worked there in the 1950s. The company's closing largely accounts for Phoenixville's population loss during the 1970s.

The *Phoenix Mercury* proclaimed 1983 to be the "year when hard times hit home," but hard times had been knocking on the door for some time. That year, Phoenix Steel had again reduced both wages and benefits for its remaining workers, but in vain, and the company declared bankruptcy by August. Strenuous efforts that included its purchase by an investment company prolonged its troubled existence, bringing still further retrenchment of its operations and more reductions for its employees. By the time of the firm's final closing in 1987, its remaining workers had become, in the words of the president of its steelworkers union, the "lowest paid steelworkers union in the country."[14]

Phoenix Steel left a mixed legacy in its namesake borough. The site along French Creek was dirty and polluted, and the buildings that remained after the company's closing had to be removed, a slow process. Amid the decay, however, lay an architectural gem: the company's foundry, built in 1882. A Richardson-Romanesque tour de force now listed on the National Register of Historic Places, the Foundry Building had been constructed from local sandstone and designed at a time when companies often made statements with architecture. The company had definitely made a grand statement with that building; even abandoned and strewn with trash, it still attracted attention. The Phoenixville Area Economic Development Corporation (PAEDCO) took ownership in 1998. The beautiful shell was retained, and the interior completely remodeled, although a striking wooden crane, part of the original works, was kept. The result became popular site for public and private events, and the centerpiece of Phoenixville's rebirth. A private developer acquired the site in

---

14. Rich Henson, "For Phoenixville, Steelmaking History to Close with Plant," *Philadelphia Inquirer*, February 14, 1987.

2006. Nearby is the old "sample bridge" of Phoenix columns. It still spans French Creek, but no longer carries local train cars. As many people come to view the historic structure as to cross it.

The Phoenix Company also constructed several grand buildings in town, primarily along Bridge Street. A significant number of these offices, hotels, and residences remain standing today. Buildings from other prominent Phoenixville industries also survive, most notably the headquarters for the Phoenix Pipe and Tube. Some of the impressive structures that once graced the town have been torn down, but overall, Phoenixville has the best record of all eight towns of preserving the old buildings along its main commercial street. These buildings now host trendy restaurants, boutiques, and beer gardens.

Phoenixville retains a connection to its railroad past, but only a slight one: the tracks along the river's right bank are still in use, although not by passengers, and no train stops in the borough. The old Reading Station still exists at trackside, but it houses a private firm that conducts all its business by motor vehicle.

Phoenixville was perhaps more graced than any other Schuylkill town with beautiful structures that remained after their original purpose—not to mention owners—had changed. This circumstance provided the physical lodestones to which new entrepreneurs were attracted, but that does not explain why Phoenixville seen such a rebirth, both economic and psychological. The borough's revival may have arguably begun in the 1990s; preliminary statistics seem to indicate this. But its flowering is largely a product of the twenty-first century, and thus much too recent for any true historical analysis. The following topics are offered merely as possibilities or, at best, theses, because they ultimately produce only more questions.

Phoenixville does posses the perfect name. The symbolism of something new arising from the ashes of the old is a powerful one, and the borough has exploited it to the fullest. The town once known for building iron bridges may today be best known for burning down a wooden statue. Every December, Phoenixville holds its Firebird Festival, a celebration that "welcomes the approaching winter solstice, as well as acknowledging the rebirth of the borough in recent years."[15] Phoenixville's artist community is the impetus behind and the backbone of the event, and thus the emphasis of the festival is on celebrating creativity. The event itself has grown to be something like an East Coast version of Burning Man in Nevada, minus the heat, sand, and the long drive west. The Firebird Festival has expanded in recent years to include more creative outlets (music, dance, art, storytelling, wine tasting—even a group of "medievalists" showing off their iron armor), but the climax is still the burning of the phoenix, a massive wooden bird structure that gets more complex and varied each year.

Phoenixville also has a summer festival—*Blob*fest, whose sponsors would likely dispute the Firebird Festival's claim of being Phoenixville's most famous event. In 1958, Phoenixville's Colonial Theatre was the background for a few scenes of the B movie *The Blob*. Little distinguishes it from a host of other low-budget sci-fi movies of the same era, except that its star was a then-unknown twenty-seven-year-old—Steve McQueen—playing a teenager. The movie about an oozing alien taking over a Pennsylvania town somehow became a cult favorite, and Phoenixville has taken full advantage of that remarkable fact. Each year, the borough stages a "reenactment" of the movie scene where patrons flee the Colonial Theatre in panic to escape the insatiable Blob. As with the Firebird Festival, organizers have steadily expanded on the original concept. It should be noted that no such fame has attached itself to another southeastern Pennsylvania location for that movie, the nearby municipality of Downingtown.

Although the Firebird Festival and *Blob*fest get the most attention, Phoenixville has also actively organized, pursued, and publicized numerous other public events, from 5k races to car shows. Still, in terms of urban revival, such events are only the most noticeable whitecaps of the rising sea of revival; the wave that produces them must have deeper sources.

A 2014 *Phoenixville Mercury* editorial pleaded for funding for additional police officers, and in summing up just why they were needed, chose 1991 as the beginning year for the added stress on the existing force. These included, of course, the Firebird Festival and

---

15. Virginia Lindak, "Firebird Fest Returns to Phoenixville for Its 11th Burn," *Phoenix Reporter & Item*, November 25, 2014.

*Blob*fest, but there were more substantial reasons listed. Since 1991, more than 750 new residences were constructed in various locations within the borough. Commerce had shifted westward, as the intersection of PA Route 29 (which enters Phoenixville across the river from Mont Clare as Bridge Street) with PA Route 23 to the west replaced the road's intersection of the Schuylkill River as the commercial nexus of the borough. That commerce still includes such names as Sears and K-Mart. Bridge Street to the east anchors what is now designated as the Historic Business District, largely filled with trendy eating and drinking establishments, several in famous old buildings.

The amount of development that has taken place in Phoenixville since the 1990s cannot be compared to what is happening in the Conshohockens, as measured by any physical standard, from square footage to the amount invested. This is because no major improvement in transportation has overwhelmed the Phoenixville area. The local roads have been steadily upgraded, but none are anything close to Interstate standards. They are sufficient to transport borough residents to the new highways in King of Prussia, but the borough itself is far enough away to moderate the amount of interest developers might otherwise possess. The development that has come to Phoenixville has been generated in response to the growth and economic improvement of the general area. Locals support the new commercial projects, with little contribution from outsiders arriving via Interstate highways.

Phoenixville's situation is far from ideal. Not all the borough's efforts have been successful, but even those that are bring problems with them. Several empty storefronts mar Bridge Street, and the turnover rate for the new bars/restaurants is disturbingly high. So is the problem of public intoxication on weekends. Public discourse in the borough frequently focuses on traffic jams and the lack of available parking downtown. That these are problems their neighboring towns would love to have does not diminish their importance to borough residents and visitors. The fact that the Neighborhood Watch of Phoenixville invited the Citizens Action Committee for Pottstown to brief it on the Better Landlord program that Pottstown has enacted also suggests that Phoenixville's recent history needs more nuanced study.

One caveat stands out above all: the revival of the Phoenixville is most often portrayed as "how an old town became trendy." The term is justified; in recent years, publication after publication has proclaimed Phoenixville's hip status. A 2014 blog called *Mototo* ranked the borough as the fifth most exciting place in Pennsylvania, using some interesting criteria: the blog writer extracted and totaled the number of bars, clubs, live music venues, festivals, and the like from the 2010 census; it also took into account population density, but emphasized the eighteen-to-thirty-four-year-old age demographic.

But trendiness is transitory. Today's hipsters will wake up one morning to discover that they yesterday's hippies. History suggests that Phoenixville's growth based on "excitement" will likely not continue for very long. Is the borough's more substantial development sufficient for a more balanced future?

Takeover

The Conshohockens

The history of the Conshohockens from 1980 to the present is quite distinct from that of its fellow river towns. By that date, the old industrial, railroad, and commercial sectors of every town on the lower Schuylkill had been almost eliminated, Conshohocken's among them. The last thirty years has largely seen the removal of the old industrial and commercial structures in every town, but only the Conshohockens have seen them replaced with new buildings.

Once just two of the eight Schuylkill River towns in similar distress, both the Conshohockens have, since 1980, become meccas for investment, with a steadily increasing array of new buildings, both for work and for living. This crescendo of construction has been gathering steam, and has become a substantial force during the first two decades of the twenty-first century. The number of proposals and new buildings has waxed and waned with the national economy, but as of 2015, the largest wave is under way, with the total value of development projects in the pipeline seeking approval estimated at $500 million.

There is one, and only one, reason for this construction boom: the now-completed intersection of two Interstate highways in West

Conshohocken. This has made both towns *locations*—easily accessible bedroom communities amid a region of broad prosperity. The process has, however, come close to physically destroying West Conshohocken, and is fundamentally changing Conshohocken.

Conshohocken's population in 1980 stood at 8,475. That number had been dropping since 1950, when the borough reached its all-time high of 10,922. The decline continued through the 2000 census, and then began to reverse. By 2010, Conshohocken's population had risen to 7,883, a healthy increase from its low, but still below that of 1980.

West Conshohocken's population peaked in 1930 at 2,579. That number remained virtually stagnant until 1950, and then began to decline slowly. The 2000 census recorded a small increase of just over 150 people, but by 2010 the number had begun to drop again, to 1,320. That most recent number represents the borough's lowest population since its formation in 1874.

Neither borough has seen a great change in its racial or ethnic composition. In 1980, Conshohocken's population was 93 percent white; the 2010 census puts it at 88 percent. There has been no substantial increase in the borough's African American population, but its Latino population has increased. West Conshohocken, meanwhile, had a 1980 population that was 99 percent white; by 2010 that had declined to 91 percent. As with Conshohocken, the percentage of African Americans in West Conshohocken has not increased; the percentage drop in Caucasians also appears to have been filled largely by Latinos and Asians.

The singular position of the Conshohockens as sites for new investment has generated a somewhat different situation regarding the owner/rental ratios of its inhabitants. The percentage of rental housing in both boroughs is by far the lowest of the eight towns on the lower Schuylkill: 39 percent in Conshohocken and only 29 percent across the river. Given the amount of new investment that has poured into both boroughs, these numbers should be viewed with care. The influx of investment has mostly taken the form of new, higher-income housing and new office buildings. The new arrivals did not move there for cheap housing or government benefits. A survey of real estate sites indicates that the new prosperity has likewise increased the market value of older homes, although many are being knocked down and replaced with new ones.

The intersection of two Interstate highways has been the motor of development for both the Conshohockens, but the process took a long time to take effect. The first major highway, the Schuylkill Expressway, arrived in the Conshohockens quite early. The segment from the Pennsylvania Turnpike to Conshohocken opened in 1952, and the segment from Conshohocken to Philadelphia via City Line Avenue opened in 1954. This helped, no doubt, but such incremental advances in the emerging regional transportation network were woefully insufficient to stem the tide of bad events coming from so many other directions, as the Conshohockens continued their decline and population loss.

One Interstate highway helped both boroughs stave off disaster, but little more. It was the completion of the second highway that truly began the current revival and reinvention. That Interstate construction was equally incremental and fraught with delays. The highway was enormously controversial, and dogged by lawsuits and criticism for the many years of its gestation. Its local nickname, the "Blue Route," dates back to 1958. The original completion date was to be 1964, but by that date only a stretch had actually been built, and did not connect to anything. The portion from Conshohocken north to just short of the Pennsylvania Turnpike opened in 1979, giving the Conshohockens the beginnings of a major highway intersection. That section was of questionable help, and not just to Conshohocken; for years it merely deposited northbound traffic onto overburdened local roads. The main section of the highway from Interstate 95 south of Philadelphia to Conshohocken was finally finished with the completion of the Mid-County Interchange at the turnpike. In December 1991, the new highway opened along its full length, and became a section of Interstate 476, sharing the Northeast Extension of the turnpike for its route north. The Conshohockens were now connected to the larger network, located at the nexus of a brand new transportation system that specialized in moving people and products speedily over great distances, expanding the horizons of those seeking potential markets, residents, and employees.

Those attracted to the possibilities offered up by an intersection of two major traffic routes first looked to the land immediately adjacent, in West Conshohocken. They soon realized that just across the river was a far greater opportunity, a less rugged area where the work of demolition had already been largely accomplished thanks to the half-completed urban renewal efforts: twenty-five acres of downtown Conshohocken had been razed, and there had been no new development. In 1982, Meehan-Weinmann built a forty-unit subsidized housing project called Pleasant Valley Apartments. That first success, despite being highly subsidized, was encouraging, and the Montgomery County Redevelopment Authority contracted with Meehan-Weinmann to develop the entire twenty-five-acre downtown location. While there would be continuity in the formal arrangements that would rebuild downtown Conshohocken, Pleasant Valley Apartments effectively marked the transition in Conshohocken from what was to be a project inspired and planned, and integrated by the government to a series of private development efforts inspired by profit and with no central planning. Urban renewal in Conshohocken did not so much succeed as merely provide a perfect foundation for the later success of private entrepreneurs.

Federal financing did continue to play a part, helping to produce the borough's next two construction projects. In 1984, construction began on the first office building of what was called the Pleasant Valley Business Center, the first substantial new business construction in Conshohocken in twenty years. A second building at the Center followed in 1985.

That was a promising year for the Conshohockens in other ways. A federal judge's decision gave the long-stalled Mid-County Expressway new life, allowing more substantial local development planning to commence. In addition, 1985 promised the delivery of a new version of that basic requirement for both towns: a new bridge across the Schuylkill. The new Matsonford Bridge opened in 1987, accompanied by substantial road alterations on the West Conshohocken side—a futile attempt to contend with the rapidly increasing vehicle traffic. There would be more such accommodations, but with no more success. The new highway intersection that loomed almost overhead saw to that.

Development in West Conshohocken did not begin as a government program. It began later, on a larger scale, and as a purely private project. This was the Four Falls Corporate Center, an office complex on a scenic and long-visited site. Its design explains its existence and continued success: the first four floors of the office buildings are for parking. The workers all drive to the site, some from a considerable distance.

The Four Falls Corporate Center was an imposing building on the town's outskirts, but the two that followed it fundamentally altered the core of old West Conshohocken. Two eye-catching new towers arose on each side of the new bridge: One Tower Bridge in 1988 and the Philadelphia Marriott West in 1991. By then, some $250 million had been invested around the intersection, and the influx of both money and people would not just continue, it would expand. Seven subsequent Tower Bridge projects followed, and other large condominium projects began to appear along the riverfront. Even a devastating 2008 fire that swept through five of the new residential buildings, destroying two completely, proved to be only a hiccup along the way. As of 2015, the Conshohockens are home to eighteen office buildings, two hotels, and over a thousand new residential units, most of it clustered closely along both banks of the river, and even bigger development proposals yet being considered.

The values of local property and the incomes of local residents have both risen since the intersection of two Interstates began to work its effect. The rise in property values has been spectacular; the median value of a house or a condo in both locations has more than doubled just since 2000. A 2012 online estimate pegged it at $251,658 for Conshohocken, with an even higher median value across the river, at $310,722. West Conshohocken can also claim the higher median household income—$96,454 compared to $65,521. None of the other river towns, including Phoenixville, experienced increases of such magnitude.

The intersection of two limited-access highways has already benefited the immediate area beyond previous imagination, and more is to come. Change and prosperity come at a price, however, and the nature of that price is becoming apparent in both towns. This is where the question of the *psychological* revival of the Conshohockens enters the picture. There is an obvious and growing dichotomy between what remains of "old Conshy" on the hillside and what is replacing industry and commerce in the river valley. The future relationship between the Old and the New will determine the fate of Conshohocken as a community. Can Conshohocken retain its traditional sense of community pride and, if so, what will be the source of that pride?

That question, so pressing on the river's left bank, may already be academic on the right. Whereas Conshohocken is being taken over, West Conshohocken is being obliterated. The roads and ramps have cost the borough heavily, in land, population, and, perhaps most of all, in self-perception. The acreage needed to accommodate so many automobiles, plus the necessary changes to connecting roads (including a practically new Matsonford Road) wiped out much of what had been the borough, including residences and playgrounds. The work has also divided what remains of West Conshohocken into separate sections cut off from each other by large highways and merge lanes. The cumulative effect has been to overwhelm what had once been a tiny but coherent, internally centered community, sundering it physically and rendering its traditional community centers—its churches, schools, and downtown—irrelevant, if not destroying them. The destruction of the old community has reached the point where the continued existence of the separate municipality of West Conshohocken has become a valid question. Always small and always short on resources, West Conshohocken now faces challenges that are even more massive and perhaps insurmountable. What was once a village in Upper Merion Township may eventually return to that condition, through no fault of its own.

The Conshohockens are quickly coming to inhabit a separate universe from their fellow towns upriver. New buildings are rising. Money is pouring into the community, and some of it is being applied to bring both public space and recreation to the riverfront, which had never before hosted much of either. Residents benefit from rising house values, but have to contend with an exponential increase in the number of vehicles using the borough streets. The ultimate effect of this flood of investment is as yet uncertain, but one thing is already clear: the old Conshohockens—both of them—have been irrevocably changed.

New Realities

Philosopher George Santayana wrote, "Those who cannot remember the past are condemned to repeat it." But as far as the towns in the lower Schuylkill Valley are concerned, it is those who remember and try to repeat history that are doomed. History provides almost no guide for any of the eight towns' futures. The reason is that the fundamental realities of life along the river have changed—not just a little, but a full 180 degrees during the twentieth century.

The Schuylkill is no longer what it was during the years of growth and prosperity, and that is to the good. The vastly improved water quality is the source of all that is positive in the recent history of each town. The fundamental change in transportation that characterized the twentieth century, the shift from rails to roads, locked the river towns into a transportation conundrum that each town lacks the ability to resolve on its own—that is, how to survive the transition from a population that walked around town to shop, work, go to school, and worship to one that drives away from town for all that and more.

As for the people, by the end of the twentieth century, a new wave of immigrants had begun to appear, reversing the historical reality yet again. Latinos are becoming a presence in each river town, and their arrival has already refreshed the vigor of Norristown. Since the tightened restrictions and quotas that followed the wars, however, this the first wave to have its "immigration status" routinely questioned.

The history of the towns on the lower Schuylkill River must be understood to deliver the immutable lesson of history: *things change.* It is all well and good to remember the past, but to make the future better requires understanding that simple, basic lesson. The fundamental realities of life along the Schuylkill River have changed, and their new versions offer both challenges and opportunities. If we understand the lessons and work within the new realities, there is a chance that the opportunities will outweigh the challenges. If we do not, there is no chance.

Residence and Recreation

Of the three uses each town traditionally made of the Schuylkill river—water for consumption by people and industry, transportation, and waste disposal—two remain, but in hugely altered forms. Transportation on the river ceased long ago, and will not return. The need for water remains as fundamental, but the steady upgrade of sewage treatment has changed the river well beyond the comprehension of those who built and lived in its towns during their glory years.

During those years, the eight towns on the lower Schuylkill established priorities for use of the floodplain and of the river itself. The highest priorities were those tasks that served industry and transportation. Today, industry is all but gone, and only a shard of the old rail system remains. The dramatic improvement in the quality of the river and the virtual disappearance of what used to occupy its floodplain has brought about a complete reversal of the traditional priorities for their use. Residence and recreation were always the lowest priorities for the use of the floodplain and the river itself. Today they have become the highest.

The Schuylkill River was clean and beautiful before the European immigrants began to arrive in large numbers and settled along the riverbanks. By the time photographic evidence began to be compiled, that cleanliness and beauty had been largely destroyed. The water was foul, the air was smoky, and the din was painful. For manufacturing plants and railroads, this did not matter. Neither did it matter to those few impoverished residents who squatted along the riverside.

But that was then, this is now, and things have changed. The new residences that have sprung up along the river—and the remarkable upgrades to those already in existence—demonstrate the reversal of polarity that is taking place between residential location and value. Riverfront residences have become more highly valued than those on higher ground. How valued they are depends on a site's access to transportation, particularly if the site is to house a substantial number of residences. The Conshohockens best demonstrate the total reversal, with high-density but high-ticket housing packed in along the riverfront in a borough whose strongest selling point is its access to elsewhere via the major highways. What is happening to the Conshohockens is unique among the river towns, but each now encompasses valuable—and almost vacant—riverfronts. We must take an individual look at each town to understand how residence and recreation are currently affecting them, and focus on possibilities for the future.

The old towns reflected the nature of their riverfronts, but the almost total reversal of the old realities now allows each community the opportunity to take advantage of the new interest in riverfront residences according to its individual topography. This presents a mixed bag of opportunities, with little for Pottstown or Spring City (and, technically, Phoenixville), a better future for Royersford's existing efforts, and close to a blank slate for Norristown and Bridgeport. For the Conshohockens, the pattern is already in place. For the other six towns upriver, it has yet to be established.

In Pottstown, where the floodplain is wider than average and the land adjacent does not immediately rise on one or more hills, residence along the river is more problematical than in the towns downriver. Pottstown has also placed a major emphasis on industrial revitalization along the river, and sought industries for its riverside industrial park and rearranged roadways. This has not been very productive, but Pottstown has too many other problems among the residences it already has for anyone to contemplate any new developments, whether Royersford small or Conshohocken large.

Neither Spring City nor Phoenixville has much of a floodplain. Spring City has led the way in converting old factories to new residences, but the borough's small size limits the nature of its future ambitions. Phoenixville is already well into the process of integrating what river floodplain it has, using the Schuylkill River Trail and lower French Creek. Its size and location opposite a usable section of the Schuylkill Navigation Systems and a lock make Phoenixville's riverfront more suited to recreation than for residence.

Royersford remains among the smallest of the river towns, but it is second only to the Conshohockens for the largest amount of riverfront residential development, although the distance between the two amounts is significant. Royersford's mixed record to date has more to do with fluctuations in the national economy than anything intrinsic to the borough. Its connections to US Route 422 and an improving economy will likely attract more people to what Royersford has become, a quiet, almost bucolic riverside town not too far from a major highway.

The river's new reality stands to benefit Norristown and Bridgeport the most, and offers them both the opportunity to start almost from scratch. Both have seen the old disappear (mostly), but neither has seen more than a glimpse of the new. The buildings along Norristown's once-industrial riverfront are largely gone. There is no legacy building around which to organize, and no history of non-commercial use of its floodplain. The same applies to Bridgeport, only more so. That borough's residential areas are set somewhat farther back than those in the other river towns, and the continued existence of a functioning railroad line along its floodplain imposes a physical barrier between the borough and its riverfront.

Bridgeport's continuing commitment to an industrial park along the river also limits the possible sites for new residences. Yet, Bridgeport has received a proposal from a builder that specializes in repurposing old riverside brownfields, and is responsible for some of the largest projects just downriver in the Conshohockens. The fate of this initial proposal, and whether it will be followed by others in either Bridgeport or Norristown, will be determined by two things: improved transportation connections, and whether both municipalities can develop in coordination with each other. Neither municipality possesses good road connections, although Bridgeport is technically quite close to them. The huge amount of development just next door in King of Prussia, and the resulting traffic jams, limits what at first seems like an excellent location. Norristown is currently upgrading its road connections with an eye to an eventual connection to the Pennsylvania Turnpike. This project has the potential to give Norristown the connection to the new road system that is has always lacked. An external stimulus such as a new road connection will be necessary to kick-start residential development in either town.

Such an incentive is necessary, because the two boroughs lie directly opposite one another along the river, and neither presents a scenic river view of the other to new riverside residents. It follows that each should plan its riverfront reinvention in full view of, if not actually in consultation with, the other. The scenic river view of the potential new Bridgeport residents would be Norristown, which is not at present a selling point. The same applies to any potential residential development in Norristown, of course. All it takes is the first successful one for residential developers to begin looking at both Norristown and Bridgeport afresh.

At this point, every river town save the Conshohockens can debate the issues that arise around new residences and road connections in a relaxed, academic manner, as their futures remain conceptual in this respect. For the civic leaders and residents of the Conshohockens, the question is much more immediate. The old riverfront area is developing quickly, largely with huge multiunit residential buildings. What had been effectively open space with a scenic view is rapidly becoming its own section of town where residents will receive the benefits, including the recreational ones. Whether these benefits will be accessible to other Conshohocken residents up the hill is in serious question. The roads that separate the Old from the New Conshohocken are built to transport vehicles, not to allow people to cross. Will the hillside residents actually have to drive to enjoy the new riverfront; if so, where will they park? The local roads and streets in West Conshohocken that have been upgraded to service the Intersection have also divided the borough into separate neighborhoods, cut off from one another by these changes. West Conshohocken sacrificed community to expedite transportation; Conshohocken seems poised to do the same.

The reversal of fortune for both residence and recreation along the river is not limited just to the towns. Other stretches of the floodplain have, for a long time, hosted either industry or residences, depending on their local geography. The industries are all but gone, and many of the sites now contain residences. The old residential stretches are also demonstrating a reversal of fortune. Shacks are being replaced with high-end, often custom-designed homes. This is happening all along the lower Schuylkill river, but the specific situation of each such stretch of the floodplain is ultimately subject to local topographical conditions and road connections.

The two-mile stretch of the Schuylkill's left bank from Valley Forge downriver to Indian Creek, about a mile above Norristown, is an excellent example of the increasing importance of both residence and recreation. The floodplain along this bank is initially both wide and relatively high, and was historically home to industry. Both the floodplain and the high ground immediately above are called Betzwood, after an early industrialist, but the area's most historically notable product was early silent movies, when the property was the site of the Lubin Film Studios. The studio failed, and a succession of other, less-glamorous industrial firms later occupied the site. By the 1980s, it was largely abandoned and suspect, since at least one former inhabitant had manufactured asbestos.

At about one mile downriver from the Betzwood Bridge, the floodplain begins to narrow, and the ground progressively lowers until it reaches Indian Creek. This stretch is known as Port Indian. Narrow land that floods frequently was unsuitable for industry, but marginally useful for residences. This portion of the floodplain came to be inhabited by people typical of the riverside residents during the heyday of the river towns, indigents for whom low price was worth periodic flooding. Their homes could be most charitably described as shacks, and many were only part-time residences. The stretch came to be known locally as "Dogpatch," which meant pretty much what the term means everywhere. There was no water or sewer service, and the residents depended on individual shallow wells and outhouses until well into the second half of the twentieth century.

The higher ground at Betzwood owes it resurgence to tax breaks given to those who rehab and build on old industrial sites, or brownfields, but the residences just downriver owe theirs to the Schuylkill Valley Trail. In truth, both areas owe the most to the postwar cleanup of the Schuylkill River. The water that flows past them no longer smells like an open sewer in the summer; it supports fish and other aquatic life, as well as swimming, boating, rowing, and water-skiing.

The old Lubin site, locally known as Synthane-Taylor, after its last industrial resident, was remade in one step. It is now the site of both The Lofts at Valley Forge and Riverview Landing, apartment complexes that promise both a sylvan riverside setting and quick access to a limited-access highway, the new US Route 422. As of 2015, the commissioners of West Norriton Township, which encompasses both areas, are considering a plan to add some three hundred additional residences. Valley Forge National Park is just across the river, and the Schuylkill Valley trail runs along the rear of the complex. It is close to an ideal location, as its lease rates testify. All the residences are, by federal law, built at a fixed elevation to clear the statistical "One-Hundred-Year Flood." The parking lots below, however, are not, and the upscale residents periodically learn the most fundamental lesson of the Schuylkill River: it's not *if* it will flood, it's *when* it will flood.

Downriver, the shacks in Port Indian are almost gone, and those that remain have been added to or remodeled beyond recognition. New construction is of large, year-round, showpiece homes. The Schuylkill Valley Trail now occupies the old Pennsylvania Railroad bed, making the community only a short walk or an even shorter ride from Valley Forge Park. This local feature has enabled Port Indian's development, as it provides easy access for trucks, both for maintenance and construction. Before the coming of the trail, access to Port Indian was limited to vehicles that could clear the low-arched Pennsylvania Railroad Bridge over Indian Creek (trash trucks had to ford the creek itself). That point, through which all traffic had to flow, is also the lowest point on the community's road, which presented problems whenever the river rose. Riders and walkers passing by now see Port Indian as a beautiful, peaceful, quiet, and upscale neighborhood. But it still floods.

The new structures appearing along the lower Schuylkill, whether in towns or just along the riverside, are residences. While they are all accessible by car, the prime locations are those with easy access to the major highways. However, there is a more important connection, a common thread that connects them along the river. It is a recreation-transportation hybrid, and the best thing that ever happened to Port Indian. It is doing good things for several communities up and down the river. This is the paved rail-to-trail path that began as the Philadelphia to Valley Forge Bikeway and has been extended and expanded to become the Schuylkill River Trail. It rests on one of the river's old rail track beds, but the trail itself was designed and built for recreation. The trail now stretches along the river from Philadelphia to Reading, with just two remaining gaps. Funding for these last two sections appeared to be in place as of 2015, and the final segments will connect Phoenixville to Mont Clare (this is largely a bridge modification) and across the Schuylkill to Pottstown. The completed Schuylkill River Trail will link all eight river communities to each other. Once Pottstown becomes connected, bicyclists, runners, and walkers will have a new way to access the borough, and Pottstown is counting on this to aid in its revival. The lower trail is already extensively utilized, and its completion will link each town more closely to the others, and to their common history.

Recreation has become increasingly important on the Schuylkill as well as alongside it. Now that the river is clean enough to swim in, those who live along sections of it (or are friends with those who do) enjoy it regularly. Nevertheless, outdoor activities that require an upfront investment are a risky proposition in southeast Pennsylvania. The Port Indian Regatta, one of the earliest attempts at using the Schuylkill for recreation, fell victim to the combination of sharply increasing prices for community support services and the unreliable weather. The last regatta took place in 1991.

Other private events on or near the water that do not involve engines have appeared in the years since the death of the Port Indian Regatta. Canoes were the original means of getting up and down the river, and canoes and kayaks are making a considerable comeback. Volunteer river organizations have organized the annual Schuylkill River Sojourn, a group excursion down the river that combines recreation with environmental awareness. Private boats are common in the remaining "pools" originally created by the Schuylkill Navigation System, with the Norristown Pool being the most popular.

Rowing has been a traditional sport along the lower Schuylkill, and its popularity is coming back. Both academic teams and private organizations now employ the river, with the newest setting up in the Conshohockens. The "start from scratch" principle mentioned earlier also applies to the Norristown Dragon Boat Club, which is attempting to create a recreational tradition where little existed before. This is the essence of what the new Schuylkill River offers its residents: a chance to write history anew.

Recreation may be growing, but residences will provide the physical and financial basis for riverside revival in each of the eight towns. The rate and place of construction of these residences will be a function of their accessibility to existing and new roads, but the basic reason for their existence at all is the opportunity presented by a clean and beautiful river. This is opportunity offered as challenge, but with the chance of great rewards. As with each of the basic realities of life along the lower Schuylkill River, the river's past is fixed, but its future is very much in flux.

The Transportation Conundrum

The Merriam-Webster dictionary defines *conundrum* as "an intricate and difficult problem," and "a question or a problem having only a conjectural answer." The latter definition is the appropriate one for the transportation problem each of the towns on the lower Schuylkill River faces. At the root is the fundamental incompatibility between the urban grid and the automobile. The post–World War II history of the Schuylkill River towns testifies that their urban grid layouts, the dimensions of their lots, and in particular of their streets could not accommodate enough automobiles to compete with suburban locations. Yet, despite this conclusive evidence, each river town must plan its revival around the reality that large numbers of automobiles must somehow be accommodated by that very same—and little changed—grid. The goal of each municipal government is to actually increase the problems that the fundamental incompatibility between the urban grid and the automobile is guaranteed to bring about. They have no other choice. Why? Because the transportation conundrum is a combination of very basic components: simple measurement—linear, square and, on occasion, cubic—the laws of physics, and the facts of history. None of these can be changed, and each town must confront that reality as it plans for its future.

The automobile's acceptance by just about everyone today has exactly reversed the most fundamental fact of small town life, around which each town had been laid out: the overwhelming percentage of the population walked to wherever they needed to go. They walked to work, they walked to shop, they walked to school, they walked to church, and then they walked home again. Each town's layout is testimony to that fact.

Today, almost no one walks to work. Walking and even bicycling from one place to another has become so nonstandard in modern America that it is referred to as "alternative transportation," an irony that neatly underlines the reversal. While these numbers have not been fully vetted, information culled from several sources suggests that among the towns on the lower Schuylkill, some 7.5 to 10 percent of Norristown's population allegedly walk to work, and from there the percentage drops steadily to West Conshohocken, where only 1.3 to 3 percent do so. The number who drive to shop is at least comparable, given the emptiness of the old downtown commercial sectors. The question of how residents get to church today is rather more complicated, given the pace of church closures; many people who once walked to church now have to drive to there, not because *they* have moved but because the church has.

"Alternative transportation" now includes another once-common mode of travel, the regional rail network. Small pieces of that network remain, and their use is once again growing. About 20 percent of people who work in Conshohocken arrive by train. Still, a fundamental component of the transportation conundrum is that for the vast majority of the residents of all eight towns, and for all the residents of at least four of them, there is simply no alternative to the automobile. Pottstown, Royersford, Spring City, and Phoenixville may all be included in the dreams of regional transportation planners, but no municipal council can base any actions for the foreseeable future on the timely arrival of any alternative transportation. Norristown and Conshohocken possess the best of the remaining connections, and Bridgeport's are not far behind. Residents of West Conshohocken can access the remaining commuter line by crossing the bridge, but that trip is often best accomplished in an automobile.

The transportation conundrum has several interlocking components, but its two most common manifestations are traffic congestion and a lack of parking. Although often discussed separately, the two are but halves of the same issue. Neither problem can be truly solved, and attempts at amelioration just begin with the obvious disadvantage of potentially worsening one to improve the other, and mix in additional issues after that. This conundrum exists in all urban areas, regardless of size. The large cities may possess the ability to finance larger or more innovative projects based on the improvements the promise, but even that is increasingly uncertain. The small towns along the lower Schuylkill River do not possess this ability.

The twin problems of traffic congestion and parking plague all eight river towns, but some more than others. Traffic congestion downtown is hardly an issue of the same magnitude as when each town, still thriving, first grappled with the automobile (with the growing exception of the Conshohockens), but it remains a factor critical to planning, and a highly variable one. Traffic congestion in residential areas is more often than not a spillover of rush-hour congestion on the main streets as drivers seek alternate ways to shorten an increasingly lengthy commutes. What makes this equally irksome to the affected residents is that this traffic is largely people moving *through* a town to and from other locations, not local residents trying to get to or from their homes.

Every town, however, regardless of its current level of prosperity, still has a parking problem. That issue first appeared in the downtowns, but it is the residential streets where the drama largely plays out now. The downtowns' parking problem largely disappeared when the downtowns died, but parking remains a prominent, even dominant, issue in the residential areas of all eight river towns.

As long as almost every adult resident of working age must possess an automobile, the residential parking problem will remain unsolvable. The reason is obvious: very few residential streets have sufficient parking spaces for the number of drivers that live along them. This creates obvious problems on a daily basis, but it becomes significant—even dangerous—during the winter months. First, there is the need for emergency vehicles and plows to pass through snow-narrowed streets. And second, there is increasing anecdotal evidence of "parking rage"—verbal and even physical altercations when residents claim possession of a portion of a public street on the basis of propinquity and labor spent clearing snow from it.

The transportation conundrum cannot be solved, it cannot be avoided, and each river town must deal with its own version. The five towns that remain in stagnation must all plan their recovery within these constraints. So, too, must Phoenixville, to sustain its revival. The Conshohockens, already in the throes of development, are now scrambling to impose some sort of community order on the transportation difficulties that rapid and intensive development has brought.

Because of its size, Norristown demonstrates the transportation conundrum more dramatically than the seven smaller towns, although Pottstown comes close. Downtown Norristown now has more parking spaces than customers. Traffic congestion on Main Street is almost entirely from people passing through town on their way to or from some other location. Norristown's other traditional shopping stretch, West Marshall Street, exhibits the exact opposite situation: a commercial and psychological revival. Traffic there is reminiscent of the "good old days," when cars had to circle the area looking for parking spots. The residential sections just off Marshall Street have some of the narrowest lots in town, and thus exhibit a severe version of the standard residential parking problem. The reason for this anomaly has nothing to do with transportation, and lies with the people who have come to inhabit West Marshall Street, so this will be discussed in the following people-oriented section.

A long-planned and even longer wished-for link from Norristown to the Pennsylvania Turnpike appears to be in the offing. The project, which would also help Plymouth Township, appears to be the single-greatest opportunity for a Norristown revival in the foreseeable future. Despite its apparent proximity to the new regional road network, Norristown has been largely isolated from it, with unfortunate consequences that date back more than half a century. Change will be both welcome and necessary.

Bridgeport still lies just across the DeKalb Street Bridge from Norristown, but that is no longer a determining factor with respect to commerce, although it definitely remains a factor with respect to people. Bridgeport's potential future as a bedroom community may be a benefit of spillover from the Conshohockens. As available sites there fill up, interest may well spread as far as Bridgeport, which is just a few minutes upriver by car, and on the same side of the river as the interchange. Glimmers of interest in the borough's riverside have surfaced, but if Bridgeport is to benefit from a spreading regional development, a better transportation link is needed, and that is unlikely to come from new roads. A new light rail system is in the conceptual stage, and devoutly to be wished for, but Bridgeport must continue to plan its immediate future around the automobile.

The small size and quaint hillside nature of Royersford, and even more of Spring City, appears to destine them both for bedroom community status, with little increase in their present populations. Any net increase in Royersford will likely be larger than in Spring

City, due to its easier connection to the new developments off US Route 422. That accessibility also predisposes the borough toward bedroom status, especially since it has produced considerable commercial development just beyond its borders. Royersford has a largely vacant riverfront with the beginnings of residential use. As the economy strengthens, this will be an area of potential development.

Spring City exists today as the lower Schuylkill's best example of a beautiful, quiet, bucolic river community. It even qualifies for the appellation of "quaint" due to the number of old buildings and the minimal changes to borough streets. Spring City's chance for growth probably depends more on what development takes place to the west, in Chester County, than on what is taking place across the river in Montgomery County. Extensive residential development is unlikely absent a future connection to a major road to the west, but the ability of a small town on a steep hillside to accommodate such change seems marginal. Spring City's continuing old-time appearance, and its tiny Main Street shopping stretch, where old buildings remain but are underused, seems to earmark it for boutique development.

Pottstown has always been at the "end of the road" in Philadelphia-oriented Montgomery County. When the railroad—and thus Pottstown's neighbor, Reading—prospered, that did not matter a great deal. Now it does. The center of regional prosperity has actually moved closer to Pottstown, from Philadelphia to King of Prussia, but the borough's transportation connections are much worse. With the railroad gone, road-dependent Pottstown connects more easily to the largely less-than-prosperous Berks County communities than to its own county. This is the reality, despite the completion of the new US Route 422, which actually bypasses Pottstown and thus makes it easy for travelers to do so as well. Second, and more significant, its construction opened up large swaths of undeveloped land to Pottstown's southeast. The new US Route 422 has brought much new development to that stretch, spreading out from its intersections—not to Pottstown. This, and the prospect of traveling a road rendered twice daily into an extended parking lot, makes the trip to Pottstown of questionable value for far too many.

Pottstown's internal transportation conundrum is basically the same as the other towns still in stagnation: its downtown has only rare problems with traffic congestion, and it has no parking problem. High Street is the face of stagnation, a once-jammed commercial sector now gap-toothed and starved of customers. If and when High Street begins to host a revival, however, the borough's current angle-parking rules will have to be revisited.

The intersection of High Street and Hanover Street remains the core of Pottstown. High Street's importance has diminished, but Hanover Street connects Pottstown to the new US Route 422. This connection to the new road brought about Pottstown's only attempt at repurposing the old industrial section for residences, the Hanover Square Apartments. The results have been mixed, at best. This underachieving project demonstrates that Pottstown's traditional problem—its geographic location in the northwest corner of Montgomery County—continues to bedevil it today.

Thanks to Phoenixville's community-centered revival within its traditional layout, the borough is once again facing the same traffic congestion and parking problems it faced after World War II. There has been no major change in either its internal streets or its external road connections. The latter have been substantially upgraded over the years, but no superhighway has been built nearby, and none is planned. Bridge Street downtown has reached its limit in terms of widening and lane layout. Parking—or rather the lack of it—is as much a complaint in Phoenixville today as it was during the 1960s.

Bridge Street was Phoenixville's commercial section during its best days, and its core lay at the east of town, beginning with the intersection of the railroad. But the railroad no longer stops in Phoenixville, and while one state road still passes through the borough, its main road intersections lie to the west. As a consequence, that is where commercial activity is concentrated, and without regard to municipal boundaries.

Yet while people who shop in Phoenixville today do so largely on the western side of town, those who seek entertainment gravitate to the eastern side. The old commercial stretch along Bridge Street is today the center of the borough's trendy nightspot and eatery scene. The recent revival of Bridge Street as a hip destination has greatly benefited the borough, but it is also raising concerns about parking and traffic congestion.

The current railroad does not serve Phoenixville, but the remnants of old ones allow the borough to tie together quite neatly its industrial, commercial, and transportation past into an entertainment future. Phoenixville, as of 2015, was completing its connections to the Schuylkill Valley Trail. One of them will allow walkers and bicyclists across the Schuylkill from Mont Clare (and its still-navigable stretch of the Schuylkill Navigation). This will complete an already felicitous gathering of artifacts of the borough's past. The foundry no longer renders metals. People no longer come to Phoenixville to buy bridges for their communities; now they come to see—and avail themselves of—repurposed historic structures. In this way, the old area at the core of Bridge Street demonstrates how remnants of a vanished past can support the community of the future.

The Conshohockens are in the process of discovering that even with an almost-bare downtown to work with, the best design teams money can employ, and the cooperation of municipal officials, they cannot easily address the fundamental contradiction between the urban grid and the automobile. The external transportation connections of both towns have been transformed by the two new Interstates and a reviving economy. Planners have had something close to a clean slate to work with thanks to urban renewal. Streets on the floodplain have been and are still being widened, with turn lanes and carefully timed streetlights, to move vehicles between the new buildings and the all-important intersection as efficiently as possible. It will not be enough, however, because it can't be.

New money and new buildings allow architects to deal with one of the twin problems the automobile brings with it: parking. Many of the new professional buildings come complete with multilevel garages in their lower levels. The new residences have extensive parking areas under the buildings (due to the federal and state floodplain construction laws). The old Conshohocken did not possess this luxury. That advantage is being taken to the extreme, however, and the result will be widespread traffic congestion. The new structures and their built-in garages will likely meet most of the immediate parking need, but the insertion of these vehicles onto the borough's streets is already causing problems, and much greater ones are on the horizon. Borough streets have been straightened, widened, given turning lanes, and governed by a carefully timed system of traffic lights, but there is only so much even financially well-lubricated Conshohocken can do given its old urban grid. Once the new automobiles depart their new parking garages, the town's streets will prove inadequate for the number of cars rush hour will bring to them. The legend of Conshohocken traffic jams is only beginning.

Conshohocken's otherwise welcome revival raises another issue. Most of the new construction is close to the river, as will be the new recreational opportunities; the hillsides remain largely unchanged. The threat is that the new prosperity will be reserved for those close to the riverside, and that the new roads, by expediting traffic into and out of town, will effectively divide the borough into the New and the Old. Conshohocken's automobile-based economic revival threatens to exact a heavy price from its historic sense of community.

West Conshohocken has already faced a similar challenge to its sense of community. Where the new developments are in the process of dividing Conshohocken into two, they have already divided its smaller neighbor across the river into several different parts. West Conshohocken's physical division in favor of wider roads to accommodate motor vehicles largely leaves its old core on the hills largely intact, but has sliced off other portions of the borough. The economic results are positive; homes are increasing in value, and municipal income from large corporate towers makes a substantial contribution. Still, West Conshohocken's future as a *community* is in serious doubt. The combination of its small size and the overwhelming forces arrayed against its continuation as a coherent community present perhaps the most fundamental challenge currently facing any of the eight towns on the river. Only one thing in their rapidly changing conditions is certain. After all is said and done, and all the money is spent, the future of the Conshohockens will be as subject to the realities of measurement and physics as will each of the other towns.

The transportation conundrum presents varied challenges to each of the river towns, according to the combination of its geography and transportation history. The transportation revolution of the twentieth century caused great damage to urban grids established earlier, and its most obvious manifestations remain problems in each. The lack of any new change on the horizon thus requires each town to seek a repetition of what each experienced during the second half of the century, in the hope that this time things will turn out better. That is truly a conundrum.

Inclusive Diversity

The last half of the twentieth century wrought several tragedies on the towns of the lower Schuylkill River. The greatest tragedy of all, however, arrived earlier, when World War I and then congressional action ended the waves of immigration to American shores that had characterized much of the nineteenth century. That tragedy is twofold. First is what didn't happen: the periodic infusion of "new blood," new dreams, and new energy that had revitalized each town. Second is what did happen: the ethnicities that had managed to arrive before the shut-off now called themselves "Americans," but continued to live in what were unofficially (and voluntarily) segregated, subcommunities of people of "their own kind" within each town. These internal community divisions persisted after the Second World War, and contributed to each town's inability to mount a collective response to the rapidly changing realities of the postwar world.

We can only speculate about what might have been had new immigrants continued to arrive in large numbers. Their very arrival testified to their willingness to take risks, and to their faith in the American myth. We cannot know what their willingness to work hard at the most demeaning jobs, and to build better futures for their children, would have contributed to each river town. Unknown also is the new direction each town might have been galvanized to take if inspired by the input of new ideas and fresh energy. Only one thing is certain; each town on the lower Schuylkill River lost what had periodically regenerated each, and each was the worst for it.

What did happen is in direct contravention to the myth of the American "melting pot," but the evidence is undisputable. Each ethnic community largely focused on itself, with its identity heavily centered on its church. This enduring ethnocentrism, regardless of the specific details, had a divisive and depressing effect on each town. The result in each was ossification, not melding.

Each town saw its population decline and, one by one, saw its ethnically segregated churches close. Too many people of the postwar generation left, taking their energy and vision with them. The first to leave were the Protestant denominations, those most able to afford that initial journey to the "crabgrass frontier," to employ Kenneth Jackson's famous phrase.[16] The longer presence of Catholic parishes was due to both their close ethnic identifications and the structure of the Catholic Church, but they, too, began to suffer under the steady exodus from their traditional communities. The late twentieth and early twenty-first centuries have seen the closing of many churches, to the sorrow and consternation of those would-be parishioners who remain. Their loyalty may remain undiminished, but their numbers are too low to sustain all the old ways without change.

As the twentieth century drew to a close, the reality of people began to change once more. That change was, in effect, a return to earlier years, as a new ethnicity began to arrive in the Schuylkill Valley in ever-growing numbers, and to settle into its towns: Latinos. The results have been both positive and negative, but this latest influx takes place under a cloud the previous ones did not: the issue of immigration status—their "legality." Some of the Latinos moving into the towns are legal aliens with proper documentation; some are already US citizens; and some are illegal aliens, living under the radar. The ultimate fate of individual Latinos in every river town will not be determined there, nor in the county seats, nor even in Pennsylvania, but in Washington, DC. In the meantime, what the boroughs must do is decide whether they will treat the new arrivals as an invasion or a blessing. The towns must recognize and deal with both the positive and negative attributes of this new influx.

The 2010 census provides some perspective on the numbers. In 1980, the Latino population of the towns on the lower Schuylkill River was negligible. Thirty years later, they represent a significant demographic presence in every town, and in Norristown and Bridgeport in particular.

Not surprisingly, the smallest towns show not just the smallest numbers of Latinos but the smallest percentage. The Latino population of Royersford, Spring City, and both the Conshohockens hover around 4 percent. The lowest numbers are in the latter two, illustrat-

---

16. Kenneth T. Jackson, *Crabgrass Frontier: The Suburbanization of the United States* (New York: Oxford University Press, 1985).

ing a traditional truth about new immigrant groups upon their early arrival: most arrived in poverty, and thus sought out the least expensive towns in which to settle. Both the Conshohockens have seen a substantial increase in the cost of renting and buying property, and thus offer the fewest opportunities to such new arrivals. Rising property values are also a likely reason the numbers of Latinos remains low in Phoenixville, which the 2010 census recorded as just 7.4 percent.

Pottstown's 2010 Latino population comprised only 5.6 percent of its total, despite broadly depressed housing prices in the borough. This apparent anomaly is actually quite consistent with Pottstown's immigration history; the simple fact of its distance upriver from Philadelphia seems to have caused each wave of immigrants to arrive there later and in smaller numbers. More time is needed to assess the relevance of that tradition today, as well as the future of Latino numbers in Pottstown.

Norristown sits at the other end of the scale. Its Latino population has almost tripled in the decade since the 2000 census, jumping from 10.49 percent to 28.3 percent. Some, unfortunately, have joined the community's criminal population, and this receives a disproportionate amount of negative attention. Anyone visiting Norristown and walking down Marshall Street can see that the Latinos are responsible for its economic rebirth, which stands in stark contrast to the stagnation on Main Street. Norristown's best hope for an economic and psychological revival is the influx of Latinos now under way. Bridgeport could also see a commercial resurgence fueled by its new Latino residents.

The entire Schuylkill Valley has suffered since World War I from the lack of energy the waves of immigrants always provided. New ideas, fresh perspectives, and a universal desire to thrive—these are all positives that new arrivals bring, and that should be embraced by a town caught in a downward spiral. This "newcomers' energy" was essential in creating and establishing the river towns, and it should be welcomed now as a natural source of reinvigoration.

The significance of this can already be seen in Norristown. With the declining number of Caucasians and an increasing number of African Americans, the recent influx of Latinos into Norristown has produced a unique condition among Schuylkill River towns: Norristown no longer possesses a majority group, whether of race, religion, or ethnicity.

Norristown thus has a unique opportunity to absorb and apply the lessons of history, and ensure that the errors of the past are not repeated. With no majority ethnic or racial group, and a community-wide dissatisfaction with the status quo, Norristown is ideally suited to attempt a combination of racial and ethnic reconciliation. Norristown was the first borough along the river, and, as the county seat, it remained a center of power and influence for a long time. The twenty-first century offers it the chance to lead the way once again—to be the first to build on the promise of the future by learning from the mistakes of the past. Its people need to acknowledge the often-unpleasant truths of that past, and commit themselves to not repeating them. They must jointly resolve to let go of damaging ethnocentrism, nativism, and racism that have historically divided their town. Its radically changed and providentially balanced demographic offers it a chance to lead the community to a better future for all. Setting such an example could be Norristown's greatest contribution to the twenty-first century.

The twenty-first century offers a combination of challenges and advantages to each of the eight towns along the lower Schuylkill River. A river changed for the better will benefit them all, but all must contend with the transportation conundrum. The deciding factor may well be people—as it should be. The people of the Schuylkill River came from a great many places, and with individual hopes, but they all came in search of the American Dream. Interpreted in strictly economic terms, many of them found it, only to see their children seek it elsewhere. The current residents of each of the towns still seek the economic version of the American Dream. By far the best way to help each other do so would be to acknowledge and work toward what should also be an American Dream: inclusive diversity.

Getting Up's Still on Their Minds…

Michael E. Tolle

DEDICATION

I was not able to fit onto the cover the names of all the urban activist groups among my eight subject towns, and deciding which ones to omit was difficult. That's why this work is dedicated to each and every urban activist out there, whether as part of a group or as an individual. You are why I have written this book.

CONTENTS

"LOCAL HISTORY 101"

My Purpose

This book has a simple purpose: to encourage communities to share the hard-earned lessons of their existence with others in the same locale or situation. I offer it as the initial text in a potential "college of communities." It will be an informal school, to be sure, but it will encourage communities to share accumulated knowledge of their existence, to the benefit of all. Our smaller and older urban areas in particular need to engage in such exchanges, because otherwise they exist in semi-isolation, for two reasons.

First, the extant literature on community revival focuses on large cities, with little attention paid to our smaller towns. There is little reference material available, and too much of what is out there is accessible only to academics. More significant, however, is the fact that much of this isolation results from the attitudes of the residents of these long-established communities themselves. One of the most disabling myths held by too many residents of a community is that no one can understand their situation except other members of the same community. This is not only wrong, it is decidedly counterproductive. No city, town, village, or neighborhood is unique; all can be grouped by location, function, size, and a great many other characteristics. All are shaped by their regional topography, and all are acted upon by the same broad social forces. Thus, each can learn from others, because ultimately they are all in the same boat.

My initial offering toward this community exchange of information focuses on the eight towns along the lower Schuylkill River between the cities of Reading and Philadelphia. Their history—and particularly their most recent history—demonstrates that they have much to offer each other. As a group, their similarities greatly outweigh their differences. They differ in size of land area, river frontage, and population, but are remarkably similar in structure and share a common past. For most of that past, the story told of growth and expansion; shortly after World War II, that changed. The communities then shared a common story of decline, losing their manufacturing sectors and the railroad that serviced them, and watching their traditional downtowns die.

But that unity of their historical arcs changed; sometime after 1980, they began to pursue different paths, for the first time in their history. These recently developed differences among towns that are so similar testify to their ability—and their need—to learn from each others' experiences. They have much to teach each other, and each can learn from the other.

My primary audience is the residents of these towns (as well as those who live elsewhere, but who nevertheless care about the area). My secondary audience is anyone who cares about smaller towns in America. I want to share the experiences of my region's organizations, with the goal of helping activists and would-be activists everywhere help each other. That means it's time to go back to school. Actually, by reading these words, you are already enrolled in a "course," which is why I took this approach.

My Approach

This hybrid work combines both components of what I call "Local History 101." You are all still in school, whether you know it or not. You are matriculating in the School of Hard Knocks or, as we usually refer to it, "Life." We all begin as undergraduates in this school, and most of us will never be more. With a curriculum as complex as the one each of us faces, few have time to actually think about what has happened to us with any perspective. This book provides you with that opportunity. Unlike most actual college classes, it also allows you to educate yourself at your own pace.

In the academic world, history undergraduates study who, what, where, and when; graduate students study how and why. *They've Been Down So Long.../Getting Ups Still on Their Minds* is an introduction to graduate-level local history in the School of hard Knocks. In this half of the hybrid work, I have collected from my blog[1] those posts that most directly relate to the communities along the lower Schuylkill Valley; in the other half, I have presented a thematic history of life

---

1. *The More Things Change...*: http://themorethingschange.michaeltolle.com/

along the river. Combined, the two halves of this work constitute a unity: the posts discuss current situations, while the history explains their context. I hope readers will refer between the two halves.

Of course, you never actually leave the School of Hard Knocks; only your brain can pass on to graduate school, and even then, only on occasion. Your body—and much of your current attention—remains in the undergraduate world. At the graduate level, however, the brain can learn much to benefit the body that remains in school. You can't go back and do things differently than you did earlier, but you can give yourself the opportunity to do things differently today and in the future as you continue to study Life.

Don't worry about tuition fees, by the way. Personal life lessons are generally "pay as you go," although some lessons can never be fully paid off. (Fortunately, they are investments that continue to accrue interest in your knowledge bank.) You will continue to pay your tuition until you leave the school of Life, and there is only one way to do that. Careful attendance to the class lessons—and their application within your communities—may actually lower the amount you are called upon to pay, and improve your condition in the process.

Also, there will be no tests—at least, none administered by me; you face enough tests in the School of Hard Knocks. My goal is to help you prepare for some of those. They will determine whether you pass or fail, so study hard.

I want to emphasize that despite its claims to graduate school status, this work takes a fundamentally community college approach. I have done most of my teaching in community colleges, and have come to appreciate the fundamental difference between them and four-year academic institutions and their bachelor degree programs. That difference lies in the students' motives for attending.

My community college students were not tabulae rasae—blank slates receptive to a balanced, academic rendering of history on any subject. They were in my class for the specific goal of improving their situations in life, not for the abstract pleasure of learning. They needed the credits, and my class was scheduled at a convenient time. Every student's concept of "What can I get from this class?" was both uniquely individual and very particular. This made teaching a survey course in American history—let alone one in the history of Western civilization—an intriguing question of relevance.

I view those people who read my blog and who are reading this book through this community college prism—that is, as an extension of the people I have encountered while teaching history at two Philadelphia-area community colleges. You share the general goal of improving the urban conditions you see around you, or in the town where you grew up, but you have seen so much promised and not delivered that a well-merited skepticism now greets anyone who claims to have the answers.

You are also, as my students tended to be and my blog readers are, mature adults, with lives already well under way. This is one reason for the academic self-interest I referred to above, but it also means that too many of you already "know what you know." Unfortunately, much of what you "know" about what happened to your old town is wrong, and much of that is due to your previous and continuing exposure to popular myths about recent US history.

Thus, I come to the need for some graduate study about what happened—and what is still happening—in our small communities. For that, I offer this book. The work addresses what I consider to be the three fundamental realities of life along the Schuylkill River (and, by extension, other riverside towns). There is much more to the story of each, but these subjects count the most. You can consider *Getting Up's Still on Their Minds* as the lectures and class discussion, while *They've Been Down So Long* is the assigned reading, under the same cover and at no extra charge.

The blog posts that constitute *Getting Up's Still on Their Minds* are arranged in four chapters. Chapter One provides background material for Chapter Two of *They've Been Down So Long...*, discussing the national and international reasons behind the decline of our classic old towns. The chapters that follow put a current emphasis on issues of long standing—first, those common to all, followed by posts targeted at one specific community. The work concludes with some advice to urban activists on tactics, with suggestions for those to avoid as well as those to follow. In these "lectures," I have set myself a two-sided task: to attack the myths that plague the public consciousness, and to replace them with understandings that, however simplistic, are much closer to the truth. This, and an awareness of my core audience, accounts for my often decidedly nonacademic prose. Some entries have been edited to correct typographic errors and ambiguities, but the essence of each remains faithful to the posted versions.

CHAPTER ONE
WHAT HAPPENED TO OUR CITIES AND TOWNS, AND WHY?

Chapter Two of *They've Been Down So Long...* examines the fates of my eight subject towns after the World War II. The following blog posts provide an informational background on the national—and even international—forces that combined to bring about the debacle.

1/3/14   **#1 in a Series**

Playing "Disinvestment" Against a Stacked Deck

As you greet the New Year, those of you living in our smaller urban communities could find yourselves in quite different situations. Some will wake up in growing, reviving towns that can actually lay claim to the term "community." In others, the morning will reveal a reality considerably less optimistic. This variation represents a historical sea change in urban history since the dark days of the 1970s and 1980s. Some of our towns are "coming back," but some aren't. We need to closely examine why this has come to be, and I will return to the subject. But we should begin with what they *all* had in common, the decline of their historical importance as the centers of commerce and culture, whether on a national scale or just within a locality.

Claiming when anything in history "began" is inherently risky (roots run deep, and academics just love to push the chronological envelope of causation), but I'm on reasonably safe ground when I begin the study of urban decline in the United States after the Second World War. This is an oversimplification, of course, as is every generalization about history. It was at the end of the war and afterward, however, that the major decisions were made and huge social forces began to take shape that would send our urban areas into the state we find them in today. As a further clarification, I will focus on the northeast and north central regions of our country, which endured the transformation from Industrial Heartland to Rust Belt. The basics of the urban dynamic apply in all locations, but cities possess a redundancy that requires analysis of a different order. My narrative encompasses urban areas of all sizes, but my focus is on the smaller ones.

The postwar period began with what seemed like great promise for the return of much of traditional America, now freed from the Depression and war. And so it seemed, for a while, as American downtowns did, on the whole, begin to revive. But this was deceiving, as fundamental change was already under way. By the 1950s, the economic and social clouds had begun to gather over our urban areas, and by the late 1970s, many towns were experiencing what Billy Joel meant when he sang, "Well, we're living here in Allentown, and they're tearing all the factories down."

In future posts, I will attempt to explain how things got to be the way they were for our urban areas, and in many places still are. My basic thesis is that in the immediate postwar period, a combination of forces stacked the deck against our urban areas, and then played out a cruel game of "disinvestment." None of this was intentional, and it was by no means a conspiracy, but that doesn't mitigate its disastrous effects, and should only increase our desire to better understand just what happened. Some of you are of an age to have lived through what happened when the deal went down. Many others live among its physical and social results. Yet its true causes are often misunderstood. We need to understand what happened, and, more important, *why* it happened. If we don't, we will carry self-defeating myths into our discussions of what needs to be done. Bad results are very likely to follow decisions based on myths, and it's very late in the game to continue making the same bad mistakes because we continue to believe in the same old myths.

The name of this game was *disinvestment*, and my previous post introduced you to the fact that it is not over. What takes time is explaining even a part of what the word means. In its broadest sense, it means exactly what it says: the wealth and capital (they are not the same) that had previously been concentrated in our urban areas were removed (or simply not replaced) and directed instead toward what we will broadly term "the suburbs." Among the most significant of these capital drains was that of human capital; all the rest basically followed. This depressing subject has been extensively studied; acres of forests and rivers of ink have been sacrificed to tell the story. I can only touch on a few topics, those most closely related (as causes) to the story, and must employ a host of generalizations as I do so.

So here goes.

The process went something like this: first we moved our homes out of the cities, then our workplaces and our shopping areas. Business capital followed the market, and exited the urban centers for the suburbs. Urban residences could not compete in value or attractiveness with subsidized "modern" housing in fresh, young neighborhoods. The move of people to the suburbs, powered by the automobile, allowed businesses, from manufacturing to retail, to follow the city residents in their flight to the periphery. Major firms could establish new, modern factories on previously open land; with the automobile, their workers did not need to live anywhere near their actual place of work. Retail merchants discovered that grouping of stores and services at the intersections of prominent local roads (along with ample, free parking) was the way serve the population expanding into the countryside, within a marketing area unimaginable just a generation earlier.

Notice a common factor here? The automobile. Cars existed before the war, of course, as did early shopping centers, most notably Suburban Square in Ardmore. Ardmore, however, was an already-developed "streetcar suburb," not open land in the countryside, and after the war it did not take long for the merchants of Suburban Square to realize that they had not moved far enough away; they couldn't obtain enough parking, and could only be reached by congested local roads. That congestion was the result of the Second World War's development of the internal combustion engine and the means to produce huge quantities of the items it powered.

Of course, the modern soon aged, as did the fresh and young aspect of suburban living. The neighborhood part was never achieved. It never had a chance. Building houses was profitable; building communities was not, and it was not considered. This is, however, only a peripheral part of our story; it should loom in the background as a reminder that gain is always accompanied by loss. Our focus remains reestablishing community in our smaller urban areas, the ones that existed before the suburbs.

My mantra is that understanding the past better equips you to live in the present and plan for the future, but I don't want my consistent historical focus to obscure the fact that disinvestment in urban areas is still happening today. That's why I opened this series with a post about slumlords. Although they are among the principal agents of urban disinvestment, they are so small that they often operate "under the radar," particularly when a municipality does not provide sufficient resources for code enforcement. This question of resources is another subject I shall return to, as history should always take a backseat to community activism (and provide some backseat driving).

In subsequent posts, I'll talk about who left our towns, why they left, and who replaced them, but I can't resist the opportunity to next time turn the spotlight on everyone's favorite whipping boy, the federal government. Even those of you predisposed to blame it for almost anything might be surprised on how important a part it played.

1/17/14   **#2 in a Series**
Can We Blame the Federal Government?

It is said that the road to hell is paved with good intentions. The road to the urban hell of today was not only paved with them, but good intentions were the graded rock of its foundations. There is blame to go around for what happened to our urban areas, and I will spread it, but we can begin by focusing on two decisions made by the federal government at the very end of and not long after the end of the Second World War. The government made both decisions with the best of intentions and a total unawareness of how extensively they would affect postwar America. The effects of these two decisions joined forces, and the results would be so far-reaching that we can identify them as two of the prime movers behind what was going to happen to our cities and towns.

The US government made two fundamental decisions between 1944 and 1947. One focused overseas, and one focused at home. Each was actually a number of decisions, of course, and I merely combine them, sacrificing factual minutiae for the sake of brevity.

I'll refer them as the "domestic" and the "overseas" decisions, and I'm going to take them out of chronological order. The domestic decision was made earlier, but I'm going to discuss the overseas decision first. The results of the overseas decision gathered strength outside of the United States for decades, peripheral to our story. Then those results appeared on our shores and joined with the already-under-way effects of the domestic decision; together, they ravaged our cities and towns.

The overseas decision was to help the countries devastated by the war. The immediate postwar years were bitter ones for Europe (and much of Asia as well); hunger, homelessness, and unemployment stalked the continents. The war that had raged across Europe had left more than physical desolation; its surviving—or newly reinstalled—governments were obviously inadequate to the enormous task that confronted them.

This decision to revive shattered countries and their industries did not just include our former enemies, Germany and Japan; they were its focus. We had spent the war years trying to bomb and burn their industrial capacities into rubble, including all forms of transportation, and we had largely succeeded. Once our nation's leaders were confident that the war was being won, some of them began to think about what they wanted the new peacetime world to look like. They concurred that the physical—and psychological—consequences of what they had accomplished during the war had to be corrected, but there was fundamental disagreement as to how to proceed with both Germany and Japan. An influential faction argued that both should be permanently transformed into agricultural states, forbidden any significant industry.

This is where another factor came into play, one that was crucial to the final decision.

The immediate postwar years spawned the Cold War. An enormous Soviet army sat just on the other side of a rapidly descending Iron Curtain, and the Communist victors of the war gave every indication that they wanted to extend their rule over pretty much all of Europe they didn't already occupy. A strong West Germany was the core of any alliance to resist this. Even more threatening than the Red Army, however, was the threat of a Communist revolution among the discontented masses of Western Europe, which seemed very real at the time.

America's answer to these problems was to lend money and expertise to the suffering, both allies and former foes alike, to promote economic recovery. Its most famous component was the Marshall Plan, which focused on Western Europe (the plan was offered to the Soviet bloc states, but was refused). The decision has been hailed (rightly) for the suffering it eased and the lives it saved, but our motives were not entirely altruistic. US leaders, convinced that prosperity was Communism's worst enemy, resolved to help those masses, and to fend off Communism. The answers to the Soviet army and the threat of revolution were the North Atlantic Treat Organization (NATO) and the Marshall Plan respectively, famously termed "two halves of the same walnut."

Much less well known is the decision about Japan. The early plans to radically restructure Japanese society (under the direction of Douglas

MacArthur, who would dearly have loved the opportunity to keep fighting) were changed sufficiently to give the decision the title of the Reverse Course. As with Germany in Europe, Japan was the key to Asia. These decisions to aid our recent enemies were controversial, but for reasons that were then current in people's minds—not because anyone saw what would be coming down the road two decades later.

This overseas decision led to the expenditure of a considerable amount of money in several countries, and it was remarkably successful. The Iron Curtain did not advance, and the peoples of Europe embraced consumption rather than revolution. As US foreign policies go, this was one of the winners. Make no mistake about it, however: the recovery of both Germany and Japan was due to their own efforts; they worked hard, went without, and invested surplus capital once basic consumption requirements had been met. US aid played a part, but we should keep a sense of proportion here.

One discovery by the industrialists during this transfer of capital and experience was that when you are forced to start an industry virtually from the beginning (there being precious little of the old to build on), you can employ the newest ideas about production and efficiency, unencumbered by old physical plant, old machinery, and the old way of doing things. You will also find workers grateful enough for a job that they will put little pressure on management (at least initially). Thus, our two primary World War II adversaries spent the postwar years building modern industrial plants to replace those destroyed by Allied bombs. They focused on the basics, steel among them. Once they had gained sufficient strength, they began to market worldwide. Their brand new and efficient factories could turn out products of a quality and at a price that the old, worn-out factories in places from Detroit to the Schuylkill Valley could not match.

Yes, their employees worked harder and longer for less than did our employees, and this was part of the advantage foreign steel was able to exploit, but to blame "the unions" for an industry-wide collapse is to place prejudice where knowledge should be. As further evidence, we should remember that in subsequent years, what Japan did to us, Korea in turn did to Japan, and China is doing to Korea, taking away the heavy, "smokestack" industries with new factories, lower-paid workers, and no environmental restrictions. The more things change…

All this took time. In 1960, the Volkswagen was making disturbing inroads in the domestic automobile market, but "made in Japan" was still a punch line for comedians. The change from joke to threat seemed to develop quickly after that, as imports from foreign industries rose quickly to prominence in a number of fields, steel and automobiles among them. The early Honda step-through motorcycles were precision Swiss watches compared to US (yes, and British) offerings. They were hardly worthy of the name by American standards, but they caught on, and had a Beach Boys tune celebrate them. By 1960, the health of the US steel industry was tied to that of the automobile. Everyone involved, whether in steel, automobiles, or the plethora of parts and services that automobiles require, subscribed to the same belief: "If we don't sell cars, we won't sell steel, and if we don't sell steel, there will be hell to pay." Truer words were never spoken. Japan Incorporated learned from its initial forays and began to market automobiles here. They were small and underpowered at first, but that was corrected; many more arrived on our shores and were sold. We (almost) stopped selling cars; we sold even less steel, and hell duly arrived, bill in hand.

But by the time foreign competition began to be felt, the picking clean of our urban carcasses was already well under way. We will begin discussing that subject next time, with that "domestic decision" mentioned at the beginning.

1/24/14   #3 in a Series

Blaming the Federal Government Some More

In my previous post, I briefly outlined what I termed the "overseas decision" made by the federal government after the end of World War II, and how that decision had devastating consequences for our urban areas, dependent as they were on heavy industries. Foreign competition in basic heavy industry would have wreaked essentially the same havoc on our industrial cities and towns if it had been the only challenge they had to face. As it happened, however, by the time foreign competition began to undercut our traditional industries, our urban areas were already in the grip of disinvestment, and had been for some time. The biggest blows to urban America came from the federal government's "domestic decision."

That decision was that the soldiers who had won the war deserved federal help returning to civilian life. Rather hard to fault, no? These were the people who had been wrenched from their civilian lives to fight in far-off corners of the world, and who had survived. Surely they deserved some help in establishing a normal life? Besides, the nation's leaders had a very unpleasant historical lesson to learn from, one they had not forgotten. Many of them had been the young Progressives who had seen how World War I had ended their era, and how World War II had done the same to the New Deal. They remembered how badly the US government handled the end of the first war, abruptly canceling contracts with heavily invested businesses and failing to assist the transition of the doughboys back to civilian life, to name but two examples. The young men so shabbily treated after WW I were the older, desperate men, many unemployed since the start of the Depression, who with their families descended on the nation's capital in July, 1932, in what is known to history as the Bonus March. Some twenty thousand veterans and their families set up camps along the Anacostia River. Their goal was, by today's standards, rather modest; they simply wanted an earlier redemption of certificates each veteran had been issued. On July 28, upon order of President Hoover, local units of the army under the command of General Douglas MacArthur physically drove everyone from the tent city, burning it in the process. MacArthur, disregarding an order from President Hoover to cease, employed both cavalry and tanks, the latter commanded by then-Major George Patton, to complete the rout. Four people were killed, and over a thousand wounded. That incident, and the whole ugly controversy over the treatment of our World War I veterans, was fresh in the minds of our leaders. They knew that the number of soon-to-be-veterans was exponentially larger than in 1918, making the potential problem exponentially worse. They were determined not to make the same mistake twice.

Several actions were taken to fulfill this decision, but the best-known result was the Servicemen's Readjustment Act, better known as the GI Bill. FDR signed it into law on June 22, 1944 (more than a year before the end of the war, keep in mind). The Servicemen's Readjustment Act significantly changed the course of our nation's history. The act had several provisions, such as government loans for education, that in the coming decades transformed higher education in America from an elitist privilege to every man's possibility. That alone is quite a story, but the provision most relevant to our tale was the one that guaranteed mortgages for the enormous numbers of veterans and their families seeking to settle down and establish—or resume—a peacetime routine. Veterans armed with such mortgage guarantees could obtain homes with no down payment.

Between 1947 and 1957, veterans' loans accounted for almost 50 percent of new mortgages. In all, fourteen million home loans were guaranteed by the federal government under the original bill. These were the loans that fueled the growth of the American suburbs.

The GI Bill was not the only government incentive for homeownership. The federal government was anxious to avoid a return to financial depression, and knew that the returning veterans would need jobs to avoid such a future. There was another ace to play, and the government did not hesitate to play it—the same ace that had been America's greatest contribution to winning the war. When all is said and done, the decisive Allied advantage over the Axis and Japanese forces had been the productive capacity of the United States. We could equip our own armies, supply our allies, and replace what both lost in combat; our enemies could not. We learned the principles of how to standardize design and build in huge quantities during the war, and the production capacity remained when peace arrived. The government realized that putting that productive capacity toward peacetime goals would provide jobs for the returning veterans.

The manufacturing approach that had contributed so much to the war effort was turned toward solving the housing shortage, in a manner largely determined by further actions of the government. The American Housing Act of 1949 offered builders financial incentives to build large, and they responded, producing enormous developments of single-family residences outside the cities. The housing industry, previously populated by a great many small businesses that built from one to perhaps a dozen homes at a time, became dominated by major firms that employed mass-production techniques on a large scale.

The most successful of these was William J. Levitt. He was among the first to realize the potential the GI Bill offered to those who were willing to think big. The new families crowded on the nation's campuses and in its cities pursuing their GI Bill–sponsored educations would soon become families seeking places to live, under conditions very different from what they had endured so far in their lives. With their mortgages guaranteed under the GI Bill, they would constitute an enormous market for new housing. Levitt's organization of the house-building process produced towns named after him, first on Long Island and then in New Jersey and north of Philadelphia, and inspired many imitators. Utilizing their war experience, Levitt and others applied mass-production techniques to house construction. In 1950, this mass-production approach built 1.95 million houses, and continued to produce them at the rate of over one million per year, despite a steady increase in the size and furnishings of suburban tract housing. Very few of these new homes were built in cities or towns, of course; there was no space, and mass production requires space.

By 1953, Levitt and others were building over one hundred thousand homes each month from coast to coast, while automobiles, an absolute necessity to live in those homes, were selling at the rate of half a million per month. Thus did Levitt and others, with a substantial boost from the federal government, create a new version of the American Dream, and make it accessible to anyone. They made the price so low that all you needed was a job, it seemed. And an automobile, of course. The mass-produced automobile enabled the mass-produced suburbs. Together, they symbolized America's unprecedented postwar prosperity. Together, they also produced the recurrent image of that prosperity: cars jammed together during the rush hour, entering or leaving the city. Initially, this was into the cities—where the jobs were—in the morning, and out of them in the afternoon to home. (As a historical footnote, Levitt, who had perhaps more to do with the rise of the rush hour than any other single individual, was one of those commuters, but in the opposite pattern. His office was on Long Island, but he lived in a substantial apartment in Manhattan.)

The enormous growth of the suburbs came at the expense of the cities. The GI Bill stimulated a migration of people, and a reorientation of America itself. For our cities, the outflow of people was greater than the inflow, by a substantial margin. By 1960, more people lived in suburbs than in cities. Eighteen of America's twenty-five largest cities declined in population from the end of the war to 1980. Our midsize cities and smaller urban communities broadly followed this disturbing pattern, losing more people than they gained.

That's *what* happened, but *why* did this happen? Why didn't the government-guaranteed loans that fueled the growth of the suburbs not also fuel regrowth in our cities and towns? Why, in fact, did the exact opposite happen?

Future posts will develop and explore this topic, but we must be careful; the path to understanding is strewn with both red herrings and hot-button issues, far too often in combination. For now, let's just accept that the federal government intended only good to flow from its decisions, and certainly did not plan the disinvestment of our urban areas that followed (sorry, conspiracy buffs). It laid the groundwork, but the blame for what resulted cannot really be laid at the foot of the federal government alone. We have to probe deeper, into local governments, private institutions, and, ultimately, the attitudes of the American people themselves during this period. Be warned: it is not a pretty story, but it is one that must be confronted and understood for what it was, and what it did.

2/7/14   #4 in a Series

To the "Crabgrass Frontier"

My previous post in this series concluded with an introduction to the population changes our urban areas underwent with the advent of the automobile suburbs. Between 1945 and 1980, our urban areas, large and small, suffered a general population decline. But the raw numbers tell only part of the story, and not the important part by any means. To understand what really happened, we must learn the answers two questions:

- Who left our urban areas and why?
- Who took their place, and why?

These two questions and their answers are interrelated, because they influenced each other. Let's begin with the first question, and pick up where we left off in discussing the immediate postwar period.

Last time I focused on how the federal government provided considerable financial incentives to both buyers and builders for the migration to the suburbs, for the best of reasons. But financial incentives alone cannot fully explain the national phenomenon that resulted.

The young veterans who bought those Cape Cods on a concrete slab could have purchased a home in an urban area, if enough homes had been available. Previous generations of young farm-raised men—and their families—had been doing precisely that. America's farm population had been decreasing steadily through the twentieth century prior to World War II, and the move had primarily been from rural to urban locations. Part of the reason the new veterans didn't follow this pattern was that few new homes were being built in our urban areas, given the profitability of mass-produced suburbs. So far, so good. The insufficient housing supply might explain why our towns and cities did not increase in population, but certainly not why the population declined or changed in composition. To begin to understand, we need to go back to a very different era, and suspend some of our current thinking.

Part of the reason for the first phase of this movement was psychological, and could not have been overcome by any actions of urban advocates. A social factor was at work. It's hard to quantify, but necessary to understand. It was basically a component of what was known as *pent-up demand*. People had done without for a very long time. We had won the war, and now people felt determined to live new lives, as different as possible from what they had grown up around. The overwhelming majority of the people we are discussing, whether veterans and their families or factory workers and their families, had grown up in the Depression. Whether they had lived on a farm, in a small town, a midsized borough, or a large city, that experience had quite likely not been pleasant. After a childhood of economic sacrifice followed by a war of human sacrifice, our young men came home to face…a housing shortage. Little residential construction had taken place during the Depression (and even less maintenance), and the newly returned veterans often found themselves living again with their relatives in old, shabby buildings, or with their new families in temporary prefab trailers while pursuing their government-subsidized college degrees. The experience did not dispose them toward urban living, or very close to other people.

Our urban areas never had much of a chance with these people; their memories and the times directed them to the suburbs. The vast majority had not owned a home before the war; they were first-time buyers. They moved back in with Mom and Dad or into trailers or cheap prefab quarters to get their GI Bill education benefits, and by the time they graduated, the new housing in the new suburbs had begun to be available in large numbers. So they left. Some did return, of course. Some came back to their longtime family homes and resumed their previous jobs or even their places in the family businesses. They would provide the leadership—and the followership—for our urban areas in the hard times ahead. But too many didn't want to go back, and armed with college educations and mortgage guarantees, courtesy of the federal government, they didn't have to.

But the returning veterans weren't the only ones in the first phase of this movement who were entranced by the possibility of experiencing something new, something different from how their lives had been so far.

That's part of the psychology we need to understand, and it applied to a lot of people. Life in a new community seemed attractive for many, particularly somewhat different from where they had been living. After decades of deprivation and war, the urge to do something different, go somewhere different, spanned generations and geography. Some moved to new homes. And some just hit the road, to travel…

> "See the USA in your Chevrolet,
> America's asking you to call,
> Drive the USA in your Chevrolet,
> America's the greatest land of all."[2]

Madison Avenue picked up on this mood very quickly, and proceeded to add its contribution, which was beyond substantial. Moving to the suburbs became the thing to do because, well, everyone was doing it; everybody said so. That message, in many forms, first legitimized and then popularized the move to the periphery. Sensing a mass movement, popular culture coalesced to make the move seem like a continuation of America's frontier heritage, this time to the "crabgrass frontier," in the words of historian Kenneth Jackson.[3] Pundits invoked our frontier heritage, our supposed need to keep moving in search of a better life. The frontier was a central image in the American psyche during this time; we had fallen in love with the myth of the cowboy not long after the lifestyle had disappeared, and continued to show the depth of our interest by the size of our financial commitment, from dime novels to cowboy movies. The TV era was taking shape, and cowboys would dominate its early decades. It all seemed to come together; everyone pitched in to sell the image, particularly those pitching something more physical to sell.

The reality, of course, was rather different. Forty acres and a mule had been the goal of frontier homesteaders; for this new version it was one-eighth of an acre and an automobile. That one-eighth of an acre still needed to be cultivated, but the goal was lush green grass, not a crop, and an eighth of an acre is a damn sight easier to tend than forty. On the other hand, frontier homesteaders staked out their claims on good arable land; their descendants found their land stripped of topsoil, which had been sold, and

---

2. "See the USA in Your Chevrolet," copyright © 1950, Leo Corday (ASCAP) and Leon Carr (ASCAP).

3. Kenneth T. Jackson, *Crabgrass Frontier: The Suburbanization of the United States* (New York: Oxford University Press, 1985).

of trees, because trees got in the way of mass production. Not to mention the fact that the journey to this new frontier (before the term was formally adopted by the Kennedy administration) was a daily one, which the automobile had made not only possible, but also faster and much more comfortable.

But Madison Avenue—and, indeed, American popular culture—is not about reality, but about dreams. The dream lived on, and people continued to buy into it. The result was a movement—usually in the form of families—from the cities to the new automobile suburbs. This movement took place in numbers large enough to earn the term *migration*.

The motives for this migration, and the urban population turnover it brought about, were mixed from the beginning. They also changed considerably over time. We will give that change in motive further scrutiny.

Next time: an overlooked point about *who* left on this migration and *why*.

2/28/14   #5 in a Series

It's About the Benjamins, Remember?

So far, we have identified a significant psychological motive for people to leave our urban areas after the Second World War, as well as several federally funded financial incentives that enabled them to do just that. As these two forces interacted, America began a shift to a suburban culture— first homes, then shopping centers, and then the jobs themselves.

There is a great deal to the story of how thing changed in our urban areas, and a much has been written on the subject. The vast majority of the histories that trace the rise of the suburbs at the expense of cities and towns are organized along racial and/or ethnic lines. This approach does well presenting what happened because it employs common, familiar groupings. However, it is susceptible to misuse by those who are predetermined to view race or ethnicity as *causal* factors. Such a discourse can be used (and often has been) to perpetuate division and discord.

I'll have more to say on the subjects of race and ethnicity (trust me), but I am asking you to view what happened through a different prism. I won't be avoiding race or ethnicity, but will consistently suggest a different form of analysis, one that is much better if your goal is not just to understand what happened, but *why* it happened. If you have been reading my posts, you probably already suspect how I am going to approach the subject. It's about the Benjamins, remember?

Here's some evidence to introduce my treatment of this controversial topic. In 1962, the University of Pennsylvania published in book form *The Norristown Study*, selected academic research articles combined with an editorial overview of Norristown history between 1900 and 1950. An interdisciplinary graduate school research project had blanketed the borough, researching its documents and interviewing its residents. The project produced several PhD dissertations, some of which were abstracted in the book. The project's supervisor also offered general conclusions to tie the papers of the study together. One of those conclusions was that, by 1950, virtually all of Norristown's business and social leadership had already moved out of town—so many that, as the study proclaimed, "Norristown proper lacks a resident upper class."

Two quick observations to begin the process of avoiding simplistic stereotypes: first, they did not leave for the new automobile suburbs (in 1950, Levitt's company had not yet purchased the land for its Pennsylvania Levittown). Norristown's "resident upper class" families had been the owners of the DeKalb Street mansions and the fine houses of the upper north and west ends; they were not about to move to anything new and prefabricated. Those who moved to the suburbs more than likely moved to those on the Main Line, an address much longer established and far more valuable. They also appear to have begun this move well before the Second World War.

Second, they did not leave because black people were moving into their neighborhood. Black people had lived in their neighborhood for generations, as their servants, occupying the shacks in the alleys behind their upper DeKalb and western Main Street mansions. The black people certainly hadn't bought any of the fine houses the "resident upper class" had abandoned.

This amply established fact suggests another way to view those who left the urban areas, one that gets beyond motives. To seek solely the motives for why people moved is to miss a significant point. While there are a great many different reasons why these people left, once we move beyond individual motives, we can focus on the one thing they all had in common: *they left because they could afford to.* The best off left the earliest, and for the most prestigious destinations. The loss of Norristown's "resident upper class" testifies to this. The less well off followed, for the less-expensive, Levitt-inspired suburbs, *once they could afford to*.

If that's what happened in Norristown, what about in your community? It's quite unlikely that Norristown was an isolated case, so here's a subject worth researching about *your* town. Had your town's "resident upper class" also left by 1950? Remember, we are not talking about closing their well-known businesses or even their professional offices, just about whether they had moved their residences. And 1950 is by no means a cutoff date when we are speaking of net financial loss to your town. It's a subject community historians would do well to look into.

Here's my point: if you are going to judge the effect of population exchange on an urban area, use a *financial* calculation. Establish a sliding scale. At one end, place people who contribute the most while requiring the fewest services; at the other, place those who make no contribution to the community while requiring the most services. Rank those who left and those who arrived along this scale. Did the exchange result in a net benefit or a net loss to your community? This is the truly important question. Using the example from *The Norristown Study*, the borough's "resident upper class" contributed much (including civic positions at no salary), but required few services. Those who replaced them prior to 1950 cannot possibly have ranked as high, regardless of ethnicity, race, or occupation. In other words, this exchange of net value to the community began in the negative. The ratio would only get steadily worse in the following decades, but, by 1950, the exchange would have already removed those who would have rated the highest on any scale of contributions made vs. services required. If you judge the post–World War II history of our urban communities by this scale, race and ethnicity remain informative, but cease to provide by themselves any explanation for what happened.

It's about the Benjamins; it always has been. Once we accept that people left our urban areas as soon as they could afford to, then we can apply the same analysis to those who replaced them. This will bring us up smack dab against perhaps the most pervasive—and most pernicious—myth of recent American urban history. I'll begin to tackle that whopper when this series resumes.

Do You Believe the Big Lie?

Our urban areas declined in value relative to their peripheries after the 1950s; that is beyond dispute. This process of disinvestment lasted for decades. The reasons for the collective debacle are many, and—most important of all—they interacted. We must never forget that, even as we try to isolate one of those many reasons by discussing the transfer of the resident urban population to the suburbs during this period, and those who replaced them. Still, we are early enough in the process that such a focus is reasonably accurate. Things will get more complicated later.

Last time, I offered some solid evidence that the first people to leave our towns and cities after the Second World War were the richest—those who, regardless of motive, could afford to. They had started to leave long before the federal government intervened in the postwar era. These people were followed by the less well off, who could afford to leave once they had federal mortgage financing and a federally subsidized college degree.

I suggested (okay, that's putting it politely) that we measure the movement out of our urban areas using a contributions/needs scale to compare the people who left to those who replaced them. But I spoke only of those who left. What about those who replaced them, the other half of the equation? Beginning with this question, I will try to tackle one of the most pervasive myths of our time—one that is widely held, but is totally wrong. That's why I term it the Big Lie. As long people continue to believe it, little real progress in obtaining *community* for our towns can be achieved.

I have spoken with a substantial number of people in the course of my research about the decline of our smaller urban areas in the Schuylkill Valley, amassing opinions from recorded interviews to brief conversations to offhand comments. I actually had one individual deliver to me, word for word, the classic expression of the pernicious myth that I dare to tackle:

> *"Things were okay around here until the colored started moving in."*

More recently, I received a comment on a recent post–World War II urban history post, the last portion of which I reproduce below, complete with original grammar and punctuation:

> *"i think it is amazing you don't acknowledge that poor quality immigrants ,low quality natives filled these small towns with substandard people who caused and poor living quality,causing the good people to flee"*

Ignore—for now—the obvious racism in the first and the implied racism and nativism in the second. Let's focus instead on the point they both have in common, the myth I am talking about. Both believe that it was the arrival of poor (or just "low quality"; these tend to be the same in the eyes of many) people in a town that caused the rich people to leave. This is a lie, and it offers history exactly backward: the departure of the rich allowed the poor to move in *afterward*. Poor people simply do not move into rich neighborhoods; they can't afford to. Once a neighborhood *has already begun to decline*, poorer people can move in, and, as the decline continues, so can those who are even poorer.

Once we accept that people left our urban areas as they could afford to, let's try to accept that people arrived for the same reason, and in the same progression. They couldn't even start to move in until they could afford to, and they certainly couldn't afford to while the "resident upper class" was still there. We really must bury the old lie that the rich, "valued" (white?) people left a community because the poorer minorities were moving in; the poorer minorities were able to move in only *because* the rich had already left. To accept the hoary myth of the poor driving out the rich is to reverse cause and effect. This myth has achieved both a spread and a tenacity that is quite remarkable, given that it is obvious nonsense, as anyone with common sense and experience living in the real world could readily attest.

The net exchange that began in the negative before the Second World War with the loss of the local "resident upper class" worsened as the steadily less well off could afford to leave (thanks to federal government incentives), and proceeded to do so in large numbers. The result was an urban community's progressive decline along the contributions/needs scale. The exodus of the young and recently educated robbed a community of its actual (and potential) middle class, widened the decline of property values, and greatly accelerated the downward spiral of our urban communities.

Let's be careful here, and not jump to conclusions about the complex point I am trying to make. I am chronologically still in the early phase of "suburbanization." The net value loss to our urban areas that was well under way by the end of the Second World War would continue long enough for the motives of many of those who left to undergo a significant change. This change would in turn contribute to further urban decline along the contributions/needs scale—not initially, but all too quickly afterward. People began to leave not just because they could afford to (they could have done so earlier), but because they did not like the people who were moving in, even though these people could also afford to buy the home next door. Yes, now we are talking about minorities here, primarily African Americans. Many people seem to have fixated on this, concluding erroneously that what was actually the middle phase of a decades-long process was its beginning. *It wasn't.*

The truly interesting—and easily the least understood—aspect about the initiation of this second phase of urban flight was that it did not necessarily signify any shift down the contributions/needs scale; those who moved in first were just as far up the scale as those they replaced. The new arrivals, of whatever color, could afford to buy good houses in good neighborhoods just like white people, with no more government assistance than was available to white people, and probably less. But they weren't white; that was the only significant difference. But it was enough.

This is where we begin to identify something in the American character prompting a great migration that is rather different from rewarding veterans and restlessly seeking new vistas, as we have discussed so far. I can go so far as to use the words "the American character" due to the widespread nature of what happened, something close to an exchange of population within our urban areas, from great cities to small towns, most prominently in the industrial north and northeast, but by no means confined to those regions.

We will pick up this subject shortly. Until then, let me sum up the fundamental lesson here, applicable to all that follows: Understanding *why* something happened requires an understanding of what is *cause* and what is *effect*. That is tricky enough, as these are closely interrelated. But when you simply reverse the two, as in the belief we are discussing, you perpetuate a myth, at the very least (it depends on your motives). But the very least is harmful enough, for lasting progress toward tomorrow cannot be built on a foundation of myths about yesterday. So, if you want to know what happened to our cities and towns, begin by rejecting the Big Lie.

4/4/14   **#7 in a Series**

A Clash of Two Migrations

The move to the periphery of our traditional urban areas began with the wealthy, before the Second World War. It gathered momentum during the late 1940s for reasons already introduced in this series of posts. Just as it began to be called a migration, quite early in its historical arc, it encountered another migration, one both larger and of longer duration. "Encounter" is not exactly the right word; the two migrations clashed, with results that were both unfortunate and unequal. This clash altered the nature of both migrations, and for the worse. In an example of opposites repelling, the migration to the suburbs consciously strove to exclude these other migrants from joining them, directing it instead to the urban areas the migrants were vacating. We are talking about opposite races, of course, white and black. In the major cities where numbers and density allowed reactions other than flight, those whites who had not joined the migration to the suburbs tried to direct the new black arrivals to some neighborhood other than their own, using a variety of tactics—many of them illegal, and all of them morally and ethically questionable, to say the very least.

This clash was a complex and controversial component of modern American history, and I will spend some time on it. But before I introduce some specifics, about which most people *think* they know a lot, I want to establish the deeper context, about which few know anything at all. There are always levels within reality, and thus it is within history.

This is an important one.

The other migration that would so affect that to the crabgrass frontier had begun earlier, encompassed larger numbers spanning a longer period of time, and produced such fundamental consequences that scholars refer to it as the Great Migration. The phrase describes the movement of over six million African Americans (voluntarily, this time) out of the South, where the vast majority of their ancestors had been taken generations earlier. Historians also divide it into two phases (a third, "reverse" phase is under way), with 1940 as the approximate dividing line.

This migration deserves the appellation "Great" both for its extent and its close-to-countless results. At the dawn of the twentieth century, over 95 percent of African Americans were living a rural existence in the Old South. As the greater industrialization of the northern states produced a greater and still greater need for labor, these areas experienced a labor shortage, even with the enormous numbers of immigrants arriving from southern and eastern Europe at this time. Thus was born an opportunity for the people who had for long been bound to the land, in one way or another. They were technically free to move, but the economic slavery of the sharecropping system had given few the means. The need for labor in the north was so insistent that several of the larger corporations that had already sent representatives into the Southern states to tout the jobs available up north began to making special arrangements to move northward those who could do the work, even if they could not afford the journey. The original arrangement—and its original beneficiary—was the Illinois Central Railroad, which welcomed a passenger influx that did not require much improvement of its services. The railroad brought the new arrivals up from the Mississippi delta. Chicago was the original destination for most, but by no means the final destination for all. The jobs beckoned across the industrial middle and northeast, and these migrants did exactly as America's migrants have always done; they traveled to where the jobs were, settling largely in the cities that hosted industries. The First World War provided a major impetus; with workers leaving for the army, the need for labor became even more pressing. When those soldiers returned, of course, those new African American workers discovered a reality about their industrial jobs: "last hired, first fired." The fact that they were not white did not exactly hurt, either.

The Great Depression effectively stemmed the flow of this migration, but only temporarily. After 1940, rearmament and then war first increased the demands on industry and then removed a great many of the workers needed to meet those demands. The result was a labor shortage of a much greater dimension than in World War I. The response came from African Americans and women; we celebrate the latter as "Rosie the Riveter." Greater demand for industrial labor in the North brought greater migration of African Americans from the South, often along new routes. Some 1.5 million African Americans migrated during the first movement; another five million followed during the second. By the 1970s and 1980s, however, the transformation of the Industrial Belt into the Rust Belt brought the migration to an end.

The result was profound; by the 1960s, almost half of African Americans were living in the northeast and north central regions of the country, and the vast majority of those had settled into the cities. We all know the result;

today, the word "urban" is a euphemism for "black," particularly when followed by such words as "music" or "culture."

This Second Great Migration, occurring as it did during and after the Second World War, neatly overlapped with the migration to the crabgrass frontier. As a result, each had an effect on the other. By the end of the war, the Great Migration had added substantial African American components to the industrial workforce, and therefore to the population of those urban areas where industry was concentrated. They had begun at the lowest levels of work, of course, and had occupied the lowest-quality housing. Many still did, but others had found opportunities and had seized them, gaining job skills sufficient to propel them into America's expanding middle class. Then there were the African American veterans, back from a war where they had suffered discrimination, been forced to join segregated units, and almost uniformly set to performing menial tasks, but where each had made his contribution to the war effort as best he could. This combination of hard-earned opportunities meant that some descendants of the Great Migration attempted to join the migration to the crabgrass frontier. In other words, African Americans began to look for ways to leave behind the pasts that exhibited little good and partake in the new adventure, just as white veterans and those white laborers who had acquired skills and a middle class outlook were doing, *at the same time*. The result was, all too often, not pleasant. The two migrations clashed, fiercely resisting attempts by African Americans to merge them.

We will return to our focus—our urban areas—when I discuss the arrival of African Americans in the better neighborhoods of our cities and towns, and the reaction they provoked. Before that, however, we need to examine the situation out on the crabgrass frontier itself—specifically, why the better-off African Americans did not join that migration until well after it was under way. In other words, when those people I introduced last time—those who would leave because a black family was moving onto their block—did so, why were they so sure that their relocation to the suburbs would be worth the effort? They clearly would move only to those suburbs where they would encounter no African Americans, and they were able to do just that. *Why* will be the subject of the next post in this series.

4/25/14   #8 in a Series

The "Crabgrass Frontier": A Whiter Shade of Pale

In discussing the growth of the suburbs after World War II, I have so far attempted to explain the appeal of leaving urban areas in impressionistic terms, seeking to explain the nature of the general yearning rather than the collection of individual motives actually involved. Thus my use of Professor Kenneth Jackson's term "the crabgrass frontier" and the cultural allusions pedaled by Madison Avenue supposedly drawing on traditional American characteristics. I also mentioned that people's motives for making the move underwent a change during the process. The previous post in this series introduced you to another, larger migration that had been under way much longer than that to the crabgrass frontier, and in fact was in full swing when this new frontier first opened. I used the word "clash, and now we begin to discuss in more detail why I chose that word.

To do so, we must get past postwar yearnings and Madison Avenue slogans and examine how things really went down. First, "frontier" was a buzzword to sell stuff. The reality was quite different, and in considerable contrast to every other frontier in American history. For starters, the crabgrass frontier was neither wild nor ungoverned. No one had to blaze any trail; the roads for reaching it already existed, making the journey both short and comfortable. Drivers had more to fear from law enforcement than from any savages they might encounter along the way (which was good, as this trek was a twice-daily thing). The only ones to stake out any claims were the developers, who purchased the land in large batches, then proceeded to clear it and stake out a number of individual parcels within it, to sell individually. The pioneers of this migration may have lined up a la the rush to the Oklahoma Territory, but the line was in front of the developments' sales offices, not at the land itself, and everybody waited their turn. In other words, plenty of Boomers, but no Sooners.

All this was all done under the (more or less) watchful eye of local governments. They were good at protecting their new residents from those people who, in Woody Guthrie's classic phrase, would "rob you with a six-gun." Unfortunately, they were often in league with those who "rob you with a fountain pen." One result of this was that the developers were largely left to decide which of the many hopefuls queued up outside the front door they were actually going to allow into their new frontier community. And that is where the problem came in.

Those lines were overwhelmingly filled by white people, of course, clutching evidence of their financial qualifications. But from the very beginning, here and there, a darker face appeared among the applicants. African Americans had benefited from the huge demand for labor caused by the war, but as usual they had benefited the least. Still, some had earned and saved enough to allow them to seek this new version of the American dream. They were joined by African American veterans, eligible under the GI Bill, and together they reached for this new interpretation of the American dream. Then came the bitter reality.

A few posts ago I introduced William Levitt, who was to the postwar housing revolution what Henry Ford was to the automobile revolution, for much the same reasons. He introduced mass production to the housing industry, and he reaped massive profits, making him the example whom others followed. Levitt brought affordable housing to the masses, but he was also a racist—and a racist of that most malignant type, the type who fully understood the problem and chooses to profit by it—all the while stoutly claiming that he was no such thing. He also came by his racism in the usual way: he learned it. His parents (ironically, Jewish refugees from discrimination in Russia), resided in Brooklyn until the first black family moved into their neighborhood. They immediately moved to the Long Island suburb of Manhasset. The father in the interloping family was a district attorney, but no matter.

Levitt deflected the many accusations of racism by employing a time-honored tactic: separate and compartmentalize two interlocked issues, then claim that you are only addressing one and simply not involved with the other. Deciding that America had both a race problem and a housing problem, and ignoring their obvious interrelationship, he decided he could solve only one of them, and simply ignored the other. Or so he claimed.

When under fire for his policies, Levitt stoutly maintained that race was just not a factor in what he was doing. For him, it was only an economic issue: when a black family moved into a neighborhood, they would be followed by others, causing the value of nearby white-owned property to go down.

> "I have come to know that if we sell one house to a Negro family, then 90 or 95 percent of our white customers will not buy into the community."[4]

---

4. Tom Lewis, *Divided Highways: Building the Interstate Highways, Transforming American Life* (Ithaca, NY: Cornell University Press, 2013), 78.

Thus it was that a sales prospectus for the first Levittown assured potential buyers that:

> "No dwelling shall be used or occupied except by members of the Caucasian race, but the employment and maintenance of other than Caucasian servants shall be permitted."

Ah, the good old days. Levitt's imitators largely followed his example, because they were allowed to. Local governments joined in, using the same economics-only logic, and together they build a web of interlocking roadblocks for African Americans seeking to join the migration to the crabgrass frontier. African Americans, even veterans, found that such local restrictive covenants and tacit behind-the-scenes agreements virtually shut them out of the new suburbs.

The NAACP and other groups fought to break the several forms of restrictive covenants on the sale of crabgrass frontier properties that developers, local governments, and real estate organizations had jointly established for their mutual economic benefit. In a great oversimplification of a complex historical reality, the federal government declined to intervene. This should not have happened; a 1948 Supreme Court ruling had outlawed precisely such covenants as those Levitt and his imitators inserted into their deeds of sale. The Federal Housing Administration (FHA), however, decided on a tactic that is both still employed and still referred to as "a narrow interpretation of our responsibilities" (the Supreme Court employs it frequently). The FHA decided that its role was only technical; although it would ensure that the accounting was on the up-and-up, it refused to rule against any "social" covenants local authorities employed.

This is, of course, merely a variation of the compartmentalization logic employed by Levitt and the others to establish such restrictions in the first place, but it held, at least for a while. Such restrictive covenants would be overturned after persistent legal effort, but by then Levitt and the others had worked out more subtle means of achieving the same thing, and continued to practice them. To put it simply, those overseeing the migration to the crabgrass frontier simply closed the doors to African Americans (other minorities were affected also, of course, but none to the same degree). The result? With very few exceptions, the new suburbs were white. This is why the city residents I spoke of last time—the ones who left when black people began to appear in their neighborhood—could be sure that their relocation to the suburbs would be worth the effort.

This is also part of what I meant by "clash," but only part. The effect of closing the doors to the new suburbs was to force those African Americans who *had* achieved the so-called American Dream to remain largely within the older urban areas that had been their original destination. As the Second Great Migration brought even more African Americans into these older, established urban areas, they provoked a variety of reactions. One of these was to spur a new wave of migrants to the crabgrass frontier, seeking to hide behind those closed doors. This became the third wave of the urban exodus, and the virtual uniformity of motive quickly gave it a title: White Flight. We will take a closer—and more personal—look at this phenomenon next time.[5]

5/16/14   #9 in a Series

They Call It "White Flight"

Several years ago, while doing research for my book *What Killed Downtown? Norristown, Pennsylvania, from Main Street to the Malls*,[6] I interviewed an elderly man, the son of an Italian immigrant. He related to me his backstory, greatly illuminating what it was to be poor and Italian in Norristown during its heyday. He also, inadvertently, provided me with an equally illuminating insight into how not just our major cities but also much smaller urban communities such as Norristown reacted to the influx of African Americans after World War II.

My interviewee had lived the American experience. Dirt poor in childhood and laboring under ethnic discrimination, he not only survived, he married, raised a family, and served in World War II. He had learned a trade through his GI Bill benefits, and by 1950 he owned a car. Thus empowered, he decided to join those moving to the crabgrass frontier…sort of. He moved just a short distance, to adjoining Plymouth Township. But he did get the lawn and the little bit of distance from his neighbors that he wanted. He also, he admitted, effectively abandoned Norristown, returning only to his church, to which he remained very attached. That in itself is a useful lesson, but what he did during the process of leaving is equally so. By leaving *when* he did, he became (as he remembers it) the first person on his block to sell

---

5. Lewis, *Divided Highways.*

6. Michael E. Tolle, *What Killed Downtown? Norristown, Pennsylvania, from Main Street to the Malls* (North Charleston, SC: CreateSpace, 2012).

his property to an African American family. His specific motives for leaving did not include racism, and thus I would place him in that second phase of the move to the periphery—those veterans enabled by their service in World War II to afford the move. What quickly followed, however, was different. Speaking about his old neighborhood, he admitted, "We all eventually sold to black people." What he also admitted (off the record) was that by the time the last white family left, the price for their house was much lower than what he had received for his.

His act of selling to a black family and what followed offers a microcosm of what we call "white flight," that portion of the post–World War II movement to the periphery that was motivated by the desire to avoid neighbors of a darker hue. This phenomenon came to national attention during the 1950s and 1960s. It struck just about every urban area of any size for which a suburban area was coming into existence, and there were plenty of them, thanks to the followers of William Levitt. The process itself has been studied, with a great many results published, in both scholarly journals and popular magazines. It was complex and remains controversial, and cannot be summed up in a blog post.

I want to make just one point about the first stage of this historical phenomenon, the arrival of the "first black family" into a previously all-white neighborhood. Let's not let any recent history (or myths) distort our understanding of what might have happened—*should* have happened—if our society had actually been as color-blind as many of our elders seem to remember it was. At this time in our history, the new African American arrivals to a previously white, working, middle-class neighborhood weren't clutching any Section 8 housing vouchers, no federal (nor state) programs to assist minorities, no "set-asides," no subsidies, and no other "special benefits" with which you might be familiar. These people bought the property because they could afford to. These were primarily two-parent households in which the husband had a good job and, more often than not, the wife did too. The man may even have been a veteran, exercising his benefits under the GI Bill, just like all the others. The family clearly had upwardly mobile aspirations, just like all the others. Measured on an economic basis (as I suggested earlier), the first African American family to appear in a previously all-white residential neighborhood had at least as strong a claim to home ownership in such a neighborhood as did the family that was leaving. They did not represent decline in any tangible way whatsoever.

So what happened? Did they get the chance to prove that they could fit in? You know, keep the house painted and in repair, shovel the sidewalk, take in the kids' toys at night…that sort of thing? They didn't, of course. They simply triggered one or the other of those most visceral of reactions, fight or flee. So well known is the flee option that it has earned its own niche in US history, as "white flight." Don't let the simplicity of the term fool you. What actually happened varied greatly in detail.

The oft-abused phrase "domino effect" actually seems to apply in this case (rather more than it did to the spread of international Communism, which was allegedly occurring at the same time). That first black family in the neighborhood did not precipitate immediate mass exodus. But it probably did stimulate the exodus of one or two of the most sensitive neighbors, whose departure (and sale to another black family) would in turn discomfit the slightly less intolerant, who would themselves decide to leave as their individual tolerance for diversity was exceeded, and so on, in a descending spiral. I say "descending" because the only ones to profit were those involved in the real estate transactions themselves. The process often accelerated as it progressed, and could devastate a neighborhood's economic value and social cohesion in quite a short time (remember, we are talking *perceptions* here, not reality). The result was a catastrophic decline in the value of many (but by no means all) urban residential properties, brought on by the departure of the very people on which any tax base depends: working and middle-class families enjoying ample employment.

A few managed to profit rather well from all this (they too shall always be with us), but the homeowners who sold, those who bought, and the neighborhoods and towns themselves all lost. This is the point in our urban history when the *irrational* decline began, the one resulting not from dreams or incentives, but from racism. Our urban areas, large and small, deal with its consequences to this day. We can measure the economic loss in an abstract way, but the personal, individual loss and the loss to our urban areas is incalculable. We need to face this truth without flinching, and add it to our list of reasons, making sure to mix thoroughly, as it was in real life.

Please keep in mind that we are simply blending this new factor into an already heady mix of postwar yearning, government subsidies and technology-fueled opportunities. White flight made its contribution to the decline of our urban areas just as surely as did the GI Bill, as both were riding the crest of a transportation revolution and an unprecedented national prosperity, at least for a while. That national prosperity included the transfer of wealth from cities and towns to the new suburbs, so while the net indicators were rising rapidly, those for our older urban areas were not. Once the quickly following collapse of America's urban-concentrated smokestack industries added its hugely negative effects to this already-lethal mix, the condition of our urban areas began a collective descent, differentiated only by the degree, extent, and the specifics of decline.

The largest cities were the most affected by this loss, but the example I began with shows how widespread it was. Of the eight towns in my lower Schuylkill Valley study group, those with the largest populations—Norristown, Pottstown, and Phoenixville—experienced the greatest degree of population replacement, in sharply descending amounts. The smallest—Royersford, Spring City, and West Conshohocken—avoided it almost completely. These preliminary findings require further study.

The visceral options open to racists were to fight or to flee. Don't let the above deceive you for a minute into thinking that white flight was the only reaction of urban residents to the influx of African Americans. There were reactions other than flight, because not all chose to flee. Our larger cities saw neighborhoods resort to violence and intimidation to keep out African Americans. The towns of the Schuylkill Valley saw little of that. The smallest managed to resist the influx of African Americans almost entirely; the larger the town, the greater the influx, and the greater the flight it triggered.

There were, however, other equally disturbing similarities, which collectively reveal that despite the hurt being so widely spread among both large and small urban areas, for specific groups of people, it really was all about the Benjamins, because they knew how to turn a nice profit out of general misery. A brief look at this, perhaps the most sordid portion of a sordid story, and at some other techniques used to determine who moved where within an urban area, will follows.

6/6/14   #10 in a Series

Many Fled, Some Fought, but a Few Profited

My recent posts in this series have offered reasons why residential segregation was the theme of the automobile suburbs, and why it pretty much worked. My previous post introduced the idea that the influx of African Americans into our cities also spurred further residential segregation within the cities themselves, as white flight took its toll. As we turn our attention from how African Americans ended up in our northern cities to what happened to them on arrival, let's pick up from where we left off by understanding that while the phrase white flight describes a reality, it doesn't describe the whole reality. Some whites who felt threatened by the influx did not flee, but defended their neighborhoods with methods ranging from employing the law to ignoring it. Regardless of their tactics, the net result was a loss, not just for those they opposed, but for themselves as well. You can say they have only themselves to blame, but that would be ignoring the existence and importance of a crucial third group, much smaller in size, but huge in influence: those who realized they could profit from the conflict, and profit even more by intensifying it. They succeeded in enriching themselves, and in the process further solidified the racial segregation in our cities while removing the tax base upon which those cities depended. They won because everyone else lost. That's why I focus on them, not those whose desires and fears they exploited.

Keep in mind that I said further solidified because our cities always have been residentially segregated, and I'm not just talking about the ones in the South. African Americans were present in the north from early colonial times. Many of them were servants (or slaves), so they were easily overlooked, and rarely counted accurately. As long as they were few in number, this worked; once there got to be more of them, they were harder to ignore. Southern communities realized this quite early, of course, but while total population growth in the northern cities greatly exceeded that of African Americans, it could be largely ignored. The Great Migration and the opening of the automobile suburbs put an end to that. This is when a great many heretofore settled and content middle class white people actually had to confront the issue of race much too closely.

Some may flee and some may fight, but a few will always profit. An unholy combination of real estate speculators, bankers, and other types that tend to benefit when the general populace suffers saw how racism plus proximity equaled fat profits for them. Some of them resolved that if African Americans could not be kept out entirely, then they were to be directed to specific neighborhoods; others realized how to profit from it. First on the list of neighborhoods in their lens was, of course, were those so unfortunate as to already have African Americans living in them. As proximity was the prime motivator of white flight, those already-integrated neighborhoods tended to expand. This was not left to chance, however.

I have previously introduced you to restrictive covenants as a primary (but not the only) means by which the political/financial power structure ensured that the new automobile suburbs would be white. Now it's time for three new phrases that help to describe the means by which racial segregation was maintained, and even reinforced, in the cities affected by both the Great Migration and white flight. It was an impressive achievement, considering the huge numbers of people involved. Of course, huge numbers of people moving meant equally huge profits for those who subscribed to Ayn Rand's dictum that morality has no place in a market economy, and who were positioned to profit as much from economic crisis as from economic prosperity.

This semialliance that saw profit in population turnover had a huge legal advantage; the National Housing Act of 1934, attempting to manage real estate risk, allowed banks to outline whole neighborhoods as being "insufficiently secure" for investment capital. From this grew the practice of redlining neighborhoods—allowing banks to legally refuse to make loans to certain aspiring businesses or residences within those areas. This quickly caused the flow of that vital ingredient of capitalist enterprise to those neighborhoods to dry up, while spurring the flight to other locations of what capital still remained. Loans to bring in and to sustain industry and commerce—those all-important contributors to the tax base—became virtually unavailable in redlined neighborhoods. This condemned these neighborhoods—as well as all those within them—to decline and decay.

A closely related practice (sometimes so intertwined with redlining as to be inseparable) was mortgage discrimination, specifically on the basis of race or ethnicity. This was also widespread and openly practiced within the financial community, at least until the 1970s. Unlike redlining, which focused on neighborhoods, mortgage discrimination focused on individuals, and thus had to be disguised to a greater extent, for obvious reasons. The two interacted, of course; an African American family applying for a mortgage was much more likely to be denied one, particularly if it was for the wrong neighborhood. This added residential mortgages to the industrial and commercial ones being directed to specific neighborhoods and denied to others, thus completing the trifecta of disinvestment.

It should surprise no one that those neighborhoods most subjected to the combination of discriminatory practices so carefully developed by our financial sector almost always housed not just the poorer populations, which were disproportionately black anyway, but also numerous middle-class neighborhoods that had the "bad luck" to also house African Americans. Luck had nothing to do with it, of course. That is where the real conspiracy came in, and it was all about the Benjamins. The emotional resistance of frightened white people in redlined districts (or those nearby) could turn a profit for the right people in any number of ways.

Block busting is my third phrase, and probably the most well known of the three. It's one of the very best business strategies ever developed, because it is always guaranteed to turn a profit for the middlemen. Both sides in a real estate transaction pay the middlemen regardless, so the key is volume, and nothing drives volume like fear. Please keep in mind that African Americans were by no means the first ones to find themselves playing the villains in this particular melodrama. My book *What Killed Downtown? Norristown, Pennsylvania, from Main Street to the Malls,* describes how a prominent real estate agent, motivated by the ethnic discrimination he had experienced as an Italian, resolved to do exactly what local residents feared most: move Italians into every neighborhood in town. By the by, his idealism, plus the fear of Italians moving into the neighborhood, produced good profits.

These policies and practices effectively divided our cities into those neighborhoods that were protected and those that were not. The story simply gets worse from there. By the 1960s, the effects of this perfect storm of happenstances—government policies, romanticism, and racism, all undergirded by a transportation revolution—were becoming obvious everywhere. The federal government responded by passing new acts designed to combat the ills caused by the postwar acts. I will discuss these in future posts, because many perceive the cures to have been worse than the disease.

It wasn't only the large cities that codified the African American influx, or the effective, if not formal, redlining of its neighborhoods. If you live in a town of any size, aren't there one or more "black" neighborhoods? Size is definitely a factor here; redlining neighborhoods in large cities was commonplace (my use of the past tense doesn't mean it has ended), but much smaller towns the size of Norristown and Pottstown certainly saw it on a substantial scale. The smaller the town, the less opportunity for residential segregation, but it was practiced whenever possible.

So, rather than focus your anger on one side or another of this tragic dispute, how about focusing it on those who simply exploited it for personal gain? They are the ones to blame for the fact that everyone but them lost, with the collective loss to the communities being the greatest of all. Most important, understand that such people are still very much with us. There are still ways to leach wealth and capital from urban areas, and there are still people doing just that. Redlining, mortgage discrimination, and block busting may (or may not) have disappeared, but those who would eat at the vitals of our towns and cities in total disregard of the human consequences are still with us. That's why I periodically remind you of slumlords. The more things change…

CHAPTER TWO

WE'RE ALL IN THIS TOGETHER: SHARED ISSUES

6/13/14

Why So Many Churches in the First Place?

I began this blog in April 2013. In November, I decided that I would post on a weekly basis. I had my articles on urban history pretty much outlined in my mind, but they were only going to be about every third post. I was less confident about the current subjects I would tackle, realizing that I would need recent events to provide relevant topics, and I had no idea what those would be in the future.

I needn't have worried. Day-to-day events in the Schuylkill Valley have provided the subjects for so many posts that I am now stressed about the accumulating backlog. I have added to that stress by bumping those stories for this week's subject from very recent news.

The news? Another closure of Catholic churches in southeastern Pennsylvania. The archdiocese just announced which churches will be closed and have their parishes subsumed into existing ones. The effect was widespread, but the towns along the Schuylkill Valley were hit particularly hard. Bridgeport will lose its only remaining two Catholic churches and become part of Sacred Heart Parish in Swedesburg, Upper Merion. Conshohocken will also lose two churches, and West Conshohocken will lose the only one it has.

The announcement evoked waves of both shock and nostalgia—the latter with good reason. The closings should not come as a surprise to anyone who is aware of the Catholic Church's downward regional membership trend, not to mention the increased secularization of society in general.

As I read through the many comments lamenting the loss and evoking the memories of these churches, I came this one about the situation in Bridgeport, posted on Facebook by an individual (who shall remain nameless) whom I much admire:

> "All of those churches were built by immigrants; why haven't they attracted any of the new immigrants to Bridgeport area? We should always have been a welcoming church and not exclude people because

MICHAEL E. TOLLE

of their ethnic background. There is no reason that a town as small as
Bridgeport should have separate Catholic Churches."

The writer is quite correct about the origins of the churches, and his
remarks exemplify the modern ecumenical approach to religion.
Unfortunately, the existence of the many churches themselves (not to
mention those that have closed already) testifies that religion in American
history has not been quite so accepting of differences as many would
proclaim today.

Not only were the Schuylkill Valley Catholic churches built by immigrants,
but the story behind their construction is a microcosm of American ethnic
and religious history itself. It's an all-American tale, with ethnic prejudice
and nativism (they are not the same thing) playing the lead roles, ably
supported by religious animosity and racism.

Let's put the religious animosity thing in the background first. The earliest
settlers in southeastern Pennsylvania were a diverse lot, but they shared
two things in common: they were from northern or western Europe, and
they were Protestant. Mind you, they were rather fractured themselves
along ethnic and religious lines, and they would endure the decline of their
churches also, but theirs is not our story today.

The Protestant descendants of these early European immigrants had pretty
much settled in and assumed the reins of local control under the new
Republic when they were confronted by the first of what would be
repeated migrations of strange people quite literally coming up the
Schuylkill. The immigrants actually came up the railroad (which came up
the Schuylkill Valley) as far as it had reached, then got off, and went to work
building its route from then on. These people were mostly Irish. They were
considered by the *earlier* immigrants to be close to subhuman—dirty,
brawling alcoholics—which prompted businesses to post signs saying
"dogs and Irishmen need not apply." Worst of all, they were Catholic. The
Irish were consigned to the poorest parts of the towns and exploited in
every conceivable way. As they began to accumulate in the nascent
industrial towns, the Irish Catholics upset the control by the region's
Protestants.

Both unwelcome in Protestant churches and possessing absolutely no
desire to worship there anyway, once enough Irish had accumulated in a
community, they organized and built their own churches. Most of the Irish
settled downriver; they quickly came to dominate the Conshohockens, and

played a large part in the growth of Norristown and Bridgeport, but their numbers and influence were less farther up the river. St. Matthew's Church in Conshohocken was the town's first, organized in 1851 by its Irish residents. West Conshohocken's early residents could also worship at St. Matthew's; it wasn't until 1888 that enough Catholics had settled on the western bank of the river for St. Gertrude's Church to appear. They were Irish. The presence of St. Patrick's in Norristown just across the river also delayed Bridgeport's building a church. St. Augustine's was Bridgeport's first Catholic church, established by its Irish residents in 1892.

Each town on the lower Schuylkill River thus already possessed a Catholic church when the next wave of immigrants began to flood the nation's shores, some of whom also came up the Schuylkill Valley on the railroad. They were greater in number, and they hailed from Europe, but from southern and eastern Europe, not western and northern. Most of them were *also* Catholic. This is a great oversimplification, as this group of immigrants embraced a great variety of religious doctrines and different homelands, but it will suffice to make my point.

Did the Irish, remembering how badly they had been treated, resolve to treat these new fellow religionists better? Of course not; if anything, they treated the new immigrants worse than they had been treated, although the later generations of the Protestant elite contributed their part, just as their ancestors had done to the Irish. Ethnicity trumped religion: an Italian Catholic or a Polish Catholic was not welcome in an Irish Catholic church, period. So, the Italians and the Poles and all the others did the best they could until they accumulated enough of themselves to build their own church. In Conshohocken, Polish Catholics established St. Mary's Church in 1905, and Italians established St. Cosmas and St. Damian in 1926. In Bridgeport, Italians opened Our Lady of Mount Carmel Church in 1926.

See the pattern? An Irish Catholic church is the first to be established, which then offers the back of its hand to later arrivals, because, although they are Catholics, they are "different." Italians, Poles, and the others were routinely not welcomed in Irish churches, and in truth, they also preferred to worship and celebrate with "their own kind.' The new arrivals wasted little time and less effort trying to join existing churches, and set about establishing their own. Ethnic prejudice and nativism are why there were so many churches in these immigrant-built towns.

Amid all of this, keep in the back of your mind that racism thing; as the repeated waves of immigration populated the Schuylkill Valley, regardless of any of their opinions about Catholics or Protestants, or about this or that European ethnicity, they all combined in despising black people the most and treating them the worst. It's an American tradition.

To bring things back to the present, I ask this question: What do the Bridgeport and Conshohocken churches mentioned in the paragraphs above have in common? Answer: They are all being closed by the archdiocese in this current contraction. They have been in the crosshairs of history for some time now, and their demise long foreseen. The flow of immigrants dried up beginning in the 1920s, courtesy of the US government, but the churches still thrived, at least until after the Second World War. Within each municipality, ethnicity continued to be the most-often-employed means of self-identification. However as the era of mass communications and that of mass mobility merged, the local ethnic churches lost their centrality as ethnic identity exerted a lesser pull on each succeeding generation. The young moved away, leaving the borough congregations to age and wither. A yearly festival would bring many back to eat, enjoy, and reminisce, but the sustaining attendance of family groups inexorably decreased, and once in a while wasn't enough.

One final point concerning Bridgeport: the Facebook poster I quoted asked why the Bridgeport area has not been attracting any of the new immigrants. In fact, it has—and, in another fine American tradition, not too many "natives" are happy about it. I am speaking of Latinos, another of the many historical spillovers from Norristown to Bridgeport. As a historian, I find this fascinating, and I'm not even going to make any comments about history repeating itself.

Bridgeport and the Conshohockens find themselves at a turning point in history (I've made this point about Bridgeport before). Their ethnic churches made them the communities they were, and the ethnic churches are all but gone, as is the local focus the churches provided. Current trends differ greatly between Bridgeport and the Conshohockens, but they have this in common: the old community ties that generations developed and could point to with pride—those that defined the communities themselves—are disappearing. What will take their place?

6/27/14

Nativism Is All Around Us; We Just Don't Call It That

My earlier post about the closure of Catholic churches in Conshohocken and Bridgeport offered the unpleasant historical truth that these churches came into existence through a combination of ethnic prejudice and nativism. I made a passing reference to how ethnic prejudice and nativism are actually different things, although they do fit together very well, and always have. I want to follow up on this, beginning with a classic combination of both. I will then argue that while ethnic prejudice has declined substantially in the Schuylkill River towns (although it is making a comeback), nativism still exists, virtually undiminished. In fact, it exists in every town in the region (I won't go any farther than that, although I am tempted)—every one of them. People just don't call it that, because that would upset the nativists, with social ostracism the likely result.

To start, let's consider the following combination of both ethnic prejudice and nativism. More than a decade ago, while I was engaged in research at the Norristown/Montgomery County Public Library for my book *What Killed Downtown? Norristown, Pennsylvania, from Main Street to the Malls*, I happened to read a very recent letter to the editor of the *Times Herald* that I will *never* forget. The subject of the writer's ire was the influx of Latinos into Norristown, but the letter itself was addressed to the "Americans" (his word) already here, who, he contended, were simply allowing the foreigners to come to the community, collect in hovels, work for lower wages, and steal local jobs. He was quite angry that his fellow Americans were letting this happen. When I finished the letter, I saw that the writer had an obviously Italian surname. To a historian, the irony, which appears to have totally escaped him, was blindingly obvious: a century earlier that exact same letter could have appeared in the *Times Herald*—close to word for word—and the immigrants it warned "Americans" against would have been Italian. Incidents like this are why I titled my blog *"The More Things Change…"*

That writer's comments would usually be cited as an example of "nativism." They are, but the letter contains both nativism and ethnic prejudice, and distinguishing between them isn't easy. The ethnic prejudice component of his remarks is obvious, and I doubt any of you need much introduction to ethnic prejudice anyway, so I won't offer any. Nativism needs some clarification, however, because it is much more prevalent than most realize.

It negatively affects communities everywhere, even when issues of ethnicity, or race, are not present.

Nativism actually has multiple meanings, most of them scholarly, but we are focusing on its most well-known variant, the belief system that desires favored status for the established and the known over the new and the different. When discussing examples, the emphasis is usually placed on the *different* part. The influx of Latinos into Norristown motivated that Italian-American letter writer to virtually repeat the slurs hurled at earlier generations of his own people.

But *newness* is a part of it too, and at the very bottom, that's what nativism is actually about. To the writer, Latinos were upsetting the local scene, replacing everything from old familiar stores to older and even more familiar churches. Ethnicity figured into his nativism, but chronology usually trumps even ethnicity. Distaste for and discrimination against the Italians who began to arrive late in the nineteenth century was not limited to Protestants and the Irish; later arrivals discovered that a caste system had developed within the Italian community (in addition to those imported from their homeland), based on native-born versus immigrant. The earliest-arriving Italians, who had suffered such discrimination from fellow Catholics, raised a generation that looked down on and mistreated the newer immigrants, who were not only Catholic and Italian, but may even have come from the same area in Italy. The elderly gentlemen to whom I referred a few posts ago, the man who sold his home to African Americans, also told a most compelling story that supports this. As a youthful Italian immigrant to Norristown in the first decade of the twentieth century, he found that the worst abuse heaped on him came from Italian-Americans of the first generation born in America. That made them "Americans," and they seized every opportunity to express their disdain for people who were of the same religion and ethnicity as they but who were *new*.

This is true nativism—the automatic devaluing of those whose time of arrival in the area is more recent than yours. A preference for the established and the familiar over the new and different is the core of nativism, and provides the most frequent demonstration of its continuing power. Ethnicity or race—even class—need have nothing to do with it. To learn more about nativism and its negative effect on you, regardless of where you live, you can ignore the national discourse as broadcast by your favorite propaganda outlet, and witness it in person. Your best chance of encountering nativism today is to attend a municipal meeting that features a pending issue of controversy that can't be pinned on ethnicity or race. There are lots of these, and they usually center on a proposal to tear something down old, build something new, or both. You can't recognize a nativist physically, although they tend to be older. Nativism isn't a generational thing, however; it's about time in local residence. Nativists are almost invariably the community's mature to senior citizens, because older people will by definition be the longer-term residents while the newer arrivals are more likely to be young.

But once they begin to speak, you'll have no problem recognizing them. They are the ones who invariably preface their remarks by stating how long they have lived in the community. Their meaning is implicit, but obvious: as longtime residents, their opinions *should count for more than those of newcomers*. If you haven't been around as long as they have, you can't possibly have the best interests of the community at heart the way they do; you may actually want to change things for the better, but that means newness, and that's what nativists fear most. They know best what should be done, and rarely does that mean advocating for change. The old voice that supports the new is not so much rare as noticeable by its isolation.

There is, of course, an ironic contradiction in all this. Nativists themselves represent a previous influx of new residents to the area at some time in the past; local reproduction simply does not account for the enormous population increase in southeastern Pennsylvania (or anywhere else, for that matter). But they are oblivious to the fact that *they* were once the newcomers, and that their arrival changed things, upsetting what had been customary before. Now, however, they are the established ones, and all further change must cease; all is to remain they way they set it up because, well…

People tend to arrive in communities in waves, in response to incentives both large and widespread (about which I have written) and small and local, such a new super highway or a new development. Over time, these people can develop a substantial awareness of each other, or at least their common interest in keeping things the way they were when *they* arrived. This is what gives local nativists their power at the ballot box. In our communities, nativism is the reason the same established local political figures remain in office, resisting not just the electoral challenge of newcomers, but the whole concept of a new approach, or just a new idea.

They have lost the distinction between the office and its occupant, and interpret challenges to their personal authority as challenges to the welfare of their community. They do this secure in the knowledge that those who they chronologically represent—in residence more than age—and who have voted for them several times before, are going to turn out at the polls in greater numbers than those vocal, pesky newcomers, keeping them in office, and new ideas for their community on hold. Sound familiar, [fill in name of municipality here]?

7/11/14
Was the "Melting Pot" a Myth in Your Town?

Over the past six months, I have taken several opportunities to excoriate the automobile suburbs (the "crabgrass frontier") for the pernicious effect they have had on both our urban areas and our race relations. It's time I try to balance the books a little. I have encountered a respected scholar who has something very good to say about those very suburbs. I find his take on the subject fascinating, because it also fits quite closely with my current theme, inspired by the continued closing of Catholic churches in Bridgeport and the Conshohockens, of how ethnic and religious discrimination and nativism helped to shape the towns along the lower Schuylkill River. The connection between the two lies, surprisingly enough, in one of our nation's most cherished myths.

There may be no more deeply held claim about the United States than that it is a "melting pot," where ethnicities and races amalgamate into that uniquely blessed person, the American. We retained our hyphenated racial-ethnic-religious identities, but managed to subordinate them and cooperate to build the greatest society the world has ever seen. But was the melting pot truth or just another feel-good myth?

If we actually did as the myth claims, it would have been in the period since World War I. If you have an eastern or southern European lineage, then the great immigration boom that brought most of your ancestors to America around the opening of the twentieth century had been throttled by the mid-1920s. Immigrants continued to arrive in the succeeding decades, but in much smaller numbers. Absent different arrivals, the new ethnic groups largely acclimated to their new land, and even assumed a degree of political power within their communities. This initiated the period our parents taught us to believe was "the good old days," when people were honest, worked hard, and rejected government handouts. This was also when the concept of the melting pot made its appearance, celebrating the work-together attitude of Americans despite their different ethnicities and backgrounds.

A recent claim that the melting pot was a myth arises not from the Left, where one would expect to find it, but from the Right. The Cato Institute's leading Libertarian scholar, Brink Lindsey, has offered a very interesting take on the subject in his book *The Age of Abundance*. Simply put, he says that the melting pot was an American myth for most of our history, and he credits the new post–World War II automobile suburbs as the mechanism that turned myth into reality:

> "Part of suburbia's novelty lay in how it united people across regional, class, ethnic, and religious lines. Blasted by critics for their white-bread homogeneity, suburbs took the myth of the American melting pot and made it a living social reality."[7]

This is quite a claim, but before we examine it through the lens of ethnicity in my subject towns, we must take notice of the one classification Lindsey conspicuously does not mention: race. He slides right over that point on the way to his thesis, and even a cursory knowledge of American history requires us to admit that the melting pot allowed little black input. Lindsey ignores this point, but I have emphasized how the automobile suburbs actually contributed to residential segregation.

But what about Lindsey's claim that it took the postwar suburbs to bring people together across ethnic and religious lines? Region and class have always played a part in our interior isolation from each other, but when we speak of the melting pot, it is the mixing of ethnicity and religion that we are discussing, so that's where we should focus.

Lindsey offers a broad refutation of a widely held belief, so we must be careful in examining such a claim. The first major distinction is to separate the situation in large cities from that in the smaller urban areas. The existence of ethnic enclave neighborhoods in large cities prior to the Second World War is well documented and understood. They had been long established by that time, spanning generations. Their boundaries were unofficial but both recognized and respected. Young men in

---

7. Brink Lindsey, *The Age of Abundance: How Prosperity Transformed America's Politics and Culture* (New York: Collins, 2007), 81.

particular knew which streets were safe to walk, and those where "intruders" were at risk, usually from young men from "the neighborhood." The violence that actually resulted from this pales against what takes place routinely today, but such subdivisions of a large city had a firm foundation in the ethnic and racial divides that existed within our cities at that time.

But what about our small towns—for example, your old hometown? Is Lindsey correct? Was the "melting pot" a myth in your town? Let's pick the admittedly quite arbitrary date of 1950 to examine this question, and focus on the time before that. By then, small-town America still remained largely strong and vibrant, but the automobile suburbs were beginning to drain away longtime urban residents. This was the sunset of the "good old days" that so many people lament, and to which they wish we could all return. It is a good point to divide our analysis of the melting pot into the old—in our traditional urban areas, and the new—in the automobile suburbs.

I can speak with some authority only about the ethnic/religious divisions within Norristown prior to 1950, because I have researched the subject. My research has also produced some insight into Bridgeport's situation at that time. Such knowledge as I have accumulated, I must confess, suggests that Lindsey has a point.

In 1950, Norristown was still one of the more egregious examples of a town riven and divided by ethnic conflict. The first crisis came when the Irish began to arrive. They were "ghettoized," as we term it today, but that was only a rehearsal to what would happen when the Italians began to arrive. That influx was much larger, and Norristown simply directed its Italian immigrants to the east end of town, the least developed area, with the most shanties and shacks. This became an unwritten law, and as late as 1950, it kept all but the most well-off Italians inside the area east of DeKalb Street and south of Fornance Street. This made an ethnic divide into a geographic one. This did produce one unintended result; it forged an Italian political power bloc in the East End, and thus in Norristown Borough Council. You could read about this dispute on a political level, but if you were there at the time, you also lived it on a personal level. Everyone I interviewed about growing up there during the years before 1950 was adamant about the subdivisions within Norristown, and each described them in the same way, only from their individual vantage point. To those growing up during this time, Norristown's internal divisions determined where you could safely go, where you didn't dare go, and even which interethnic dating was "acceptable." The evidence on this is consistent: in the "good old days," Norristown's melting pot did not even heat up.

Here is a fascinating piece of evidence concerning the melting pot in Bridgeport, taken from an editorial in the official publication celebrating the borough's centennial celebration in 1951:

> "The intermingling of people of widely varied cultural and religious backgrounds has not altogether been smooth. One strand frequently sows its dislike of another. Certain elements in the community want to favor people of their extraction in public office. As a result of this racial prejudice, little cliques form in many organizations and do everything to discourage other people from taking part in them…. This is not an Italian town. This is Bridgeport. The celebration of Bridgeport's 100th anniversary shows that it took people from many lands to build the borough. Let not a few try to turn it into sinkhole of bigotry and racial prejudice."

It is clear that the author uses "racial" where we would use "ethnic," as the African American population of Bridgeport was very small at this time, and totally without political influence. The usage also provides insight into the mindset of people in our towns during this era, adding indirectly to the evidence.

What is fascinating is how such a frank statement made its way into an official publication, which normally allows no such thing, regardless of the town or the occasion. Of course, a single statement, even such an authoritative one, is not sufficient to support any conclusions about Bridgeport's political and social fabric prior during its heyday before Second World War. Yet it does suggest that Bridgeport shared yet another issue with its larger neighbor across the river. I would encourage local historians to look into this.

But what about the other river towns on which I focus? My knowledge of how varied the ethnic/religious mix was among these towns is little more than superficial, yet sufficient enough to require an examination of each individual location, because differences among them exist, and were important. I thus address this issue in the form of a request to those of you who grew up in these other towns, or whose parents did, during the ostensibly "good old days." Remember, we are speaking of the period largely before 1950. What stories did your parents tell you about your town in the "good old days"? Were Royersford, Spring City, and West Conshohocken even large enough to demonstrate internal ethnic/religious divisions in the first place? If your parents lived in the larger towns, who were their friends, who could they date, and who couldn't they befriend? Were there places where it was safe for some people to go but not others, and those where the opposite was true? What unwritten rules existed, and were they based on geography or on ethnicity? Could Italian Catholics date Irish Catholics? How about Slovaks and Ukrainians? Or Jews? Ask those who remember; substitute the actual nouns involved in your personal stories, those you learned growing up.

I would very much like to know what your local research into family and community turns up, so feel free to contact me.[8] I repeatedly encourage my readers to look into the way things actually were in their old neighborhoods or towns; only understanding the truth about our problems allows us to craft effective solutions to those problems. But always keep in mind that what is often said of genealogy is also true of local history: don't get into it if you aren't prepared to handle the unpleasant surprises you are sure to encounter, as the myths you so cherish often founder on the rocks of reality. When that happens (and it will), try to remember that the end result—knowledge something closer to the truth—is worth the effort, and even the anguish over lost dreams.

8/8/14

Why So Many Section 8 Vouchers in Norristown and Pottstown?

Let me begin with two statements that seem contradictory, but are not:

1. Housing choice vouchers serve a real need, and more should be funded.
2. There are too many housing choice vouchers in Norristown and Pottstown.

The facts back up both statements. True to my word in a previous post, I'm not going to question the premise behind the Housing Choice Voucher Program, a component of what pretty much everyone refers to as "Section 8." Affordable housing is a major need across the entire nation. The statistics and stories to back this up are readily available. As far as I am concerned, the issues arise from *how well* a government program addresses a problem, not whether it should exist at all, and that's what I'm going to look at.

---

8. For my most current contact information, go to my blog, "The More Things Change…": http://themorethingschange.michaeltolle.com/

As I also promised, I will begin with a look at the way things are now (or at last recently). In an earlier post, I referenced a document on the Norristown municipal website entitled "2012 Analysis of Impediments to Fair Housing Choice for Norristown."[9] I cherry-picked an "Impediment" in order to ridicule both its premise and conclusion, but this week I utilize some of its basic numbers, about which there is no dispute, and certainly not by me. The dispute arises over what the numbers mean.

Section 8 is a more complex set of programs than most people realize, but it's best known for the housing choice vouchers given to low-income individuals to help them afford rental housing. If there is a more controversial federal government program, I don't know what it is. It's also been around for a while; the original Section 8 program was created through an amendment to the US Housing Act of 1937; President Gerald Ford signed the amendment in 1974. The Housing Choice Voucher Program modified the original program, which dates back to the New Deal. And, by the way, it is technically not even called "Section 8" anymore, although many still use the phrase. I would like to avoid the moniker "Section 8" because of the baggage it carries; it long ago became a buzzword for a wider set of problems. So "housing choice vouchers" it is, at least for that component of the "tenant-based" half of the program (I told you it was complicated).

Let's start with the basic facts. There are sixty-two municipalities in Montgomery County, and the holder of a housing choice voucher can theoretically exercise that voucher in any one of them. As of this writing, there are 2,625 vouchers in effect in the county, spread among fifty-five of those municipalities. The boroughs of Athyn, Green Lane, and Jenkintown, plus the townships of Salford, Skippack, Upper Frederick, and Worcester, currently have none.

I extracted information from the "Impediments" document to prepare the table below. It lists the eleven most-populous municipalities in Montgomery County, in descending order. Each name is followed by the percentage of the county population it contains, the number of vouchers being exercised there, and its percentage of the total number of vouchers in the county (the percentages, expressed in hundredths, have been

9. http://www.norristown.org/template/upload_files/
Draft_2012_AI_for_the_Municipality_of_Norristown.pdf

rounded up). I include eleven instead of the usual ten for this type of list because it allows me to include Pottstown, which helps to make my point.

Municipality	Percentage of County Population	Number of Vouchers	Percentage of Vouchers
Lower Merion	7.2	95	3.6
Abington	6.9	78	3.0
Cheltenham	4.6	54	2.1
Norristown	4.3	1,115	42.5
Upper Merion	3.5	19	.7
Horsham	3.3	7	.3
Upper Dublin	3.2	2	.1
Lower Providence	3.2	5	.2
Upper Moreland	3.0	59	2.2
Montgomery	3.1	4	.2
Pottstown	2.8	452	17.2

Do any of the numbers above jump out at you? Those for Norristown and Pottstown sure should.

Norristown is the county's fourth-most-populous municipality, making up 4.3 percent of the total county population, yet it hosts almost 43 percent of the housing choice vouchers *in the entire county*. The three municipalities with larger populations—Lower Merion, Abington, and Cheltenham—together host 227 housing vouchers, barely 20 percent of the number in Norristown alone. To call this a striking disparity is being kind. Also, did you know that Norristown's 1,115 housing vouchers represent almost 16 percent of Norristown's *total occupied rental units*? Such a number of houses inhabited by families that require assistance to pay their rent has a hugely depressive effect on the community.

Now, let's add Pottstown to the mix. It is only the county's eleventh-most-populous municipality, comprising a mere 2.8 percent of the county's population, but it hosts far and away the second-largest number of vouchers, 452. That's 17.2 percent of those *in the entire county*. Consider also that the total number of vouchers in the nine municipalities with greater populations than Pottstown (excluding Norristown) is 323. They *collectively* host but 71 percent of what Pottstown does all by itself.

Norristown and Pottstown together house 1,567 of the county's total of 2,625 vouchers. In other words, two municipalities that together comprise barely 7 percent of the county's population host almost 60 percent of its vouchers. I would call that *prima facie* evidence that something has gone seriously wrong with the housing voucher program, because that's *not* how it's supposed to work.

"Tenant-based" vouchers were part of the move away from Public Housing, one of the most conspicuous failures in the history of urban policy. Instead of locating the poor within a specific area (that's called "segregation"), vouchers were designed to be "portable," and thus to be used to improve a family's condition by allowing it to live in a better neighborhood, not to consign it to a fixed (usually bad) one.

Consider this quote from *Section 8 Tenant-Based Housing Assistance: A Look Back After 30 Years*, issued by the US Department of Housing and Urban Development (HUD) in March 2000:

> "The hallmark of the Section 8 Program is residential choice and mobility. Families may choose to live in any neighborhood they want if they can find a housing unit that is affordable under the rules of the program, that meets Housing Quality Standards, and that has an owner willing to participate in the program. This permits a family to make a housing selection based upon any number of factors including access to employment or transportation; the quality of the schools; the characteristics of the housing or the neighborhood; or nearness to family, friends, church, or other community facilities or services."[10]

Lack of mobility was one of the earliest criticisms of the Federal Housing Program, and housing choice vouchers were created in response. The idea emerged from two federal government acts, passed in 1983 and 1987 (yes, that's right, during the Reagan Administration!). The primary message of the HUD document was to highlight these changes to demonstrate that the program had improved. "Portability" is one of its proudest boasts.

The idea behind housing choice vouchers was to spread their recipients around the county, to *integrate* them into the local communities. The

---

10. United States Department of Housing and Urban Development, *Section 8 Tenant-Based Housing Assistance: A Look Back After 30 Years* (Washington, DC: US Government Printing Office, 2000), 10. Retrieved from http://www.huduser.org/portal//Publications/pdf/look.pdf

above figures suggest it has had almost the opposite effect, at least in Montgomery County, Pennsylvania.

Now that we know how things actually are, and that it's pretty much the exact opposite of what was intended, we can move on to the hard part. The data on housing choice vouchers raise a number of questions, but we will keep things as simple as possible and just ask "Why?" It's a short question, with several long, complex and not necessarily complimentary answers. We will begin to examine them next time.

8/15/14

Public Housing Is Still Around, and Guess Where?

Last week I wrote about housing choice vouchers, and how their current distribution in Montgomery County is obscenely weighted toward Norristown and Pottstown. I promised to begin looking at the question "Why?" but I also mentioned that federal housing assistance is a complex and multifaceted topic, so this time I pile on the evidence about the concentration of housing assistance and extend it to both Royersford and Conshohocken, while simultaneously discussing another well-known form of housing subsidy. Not only is it well known, it's much older. It's called *public housing*.

Public housing a different form of assistance than housing choice vouchers, and these differentiations must be understood. Only you, the residents of these towns, can determine how each variation of assistance affects your community, so you shouldn't just lump them together under some buzzword like "Section 8," but be aware of the nature of each. The public housing program also generates an entirely different subset of the question "Why?" but I'm going to dispose of it rather quickly, because the answer should be considered a minor issue today, and there are more important ones to discuss.

I mentioned last week that housing choice vouchers are part of the shift in emphasis to "tenant-based" programs over the previously emphasized "site-based" ones. The latter have not disappeared, however. In something of an oversimplification, the "site-based" programs fall under two categories: public housing and everything else. The second category really isn't a category, just my lumping together of a number of different programs, administered at different levels of government. They offer subsidies to build or renovate housing with a specified number of units made available to low-income renters. Monthly rent subsidies are a part of some and not a part of others. Some operate under informal names such as "202," "811"; another is formally known as Low-Income Housing Tax Credits (LIHTC). These are not housing choice vouchers; the money passes directly from the monitoring agency to the owner without the residents touching it; it's all by the numbers. These are perhaps the most controversial of the "site-based" subsidies, because new proposals to build subsidized housing show up periodically in the news (can you say "Pennrose," boys and girls?). There is more to be said about these programs, much more, later.

Public housing is the true survivor among housing programs, and still refers to government-owned and -administered housing complexes. The biggest ones in our large cities are long gone, and good riddance. Still, the program remains in existence, as do public housing locations in Montgomery County, administered by the County Housing Authority (MCHA). Public Housing gathers housing aid recipients in one location. This distinguishes it from the other "site-based" subsidy programs, which seek to include some of those under assistance among those who pay the full fare, which makes them somewhat integrative.

There are 614 public housing units directly under the ownership and administration of the MCHA (technically, the federal government owns the properties, but never mind). These are divided among seven public housing complexes. Montgomery County's public housing sites were built between the 1940s and the 1980s. The general occupancy sites are the oldest, built between the 1940s and the 1960s. High-rises (actually mid-rises) for the elderly and disabled are more recent, dating from the 1970s and 1980s. Given my focus on the eight towns on the Schuylkill below Reading, I found it interesting to learn that five of the seven housing complexes are located in the valley, in three of its towns. I suspect that declining property values after World War Two had a lot to do with this.

For those who know how heavily Norristown is laden with housing choice vouchers, the good news is that Norristown does not have any public housing complexes. The bad news is that Pottstown has three, including the largest one of them all. In fact, Pottstown has 361 of the 614 public housing units in Montgomery County, just under 59 percent of the total. This interesting statistic at least adds to the *prima* facie evidence that Pottstown has received a disproportionate share of the MCHA's attention.

There are two categories of public housing complexes: general occupancy and elderly/disabled. Both require the applicant to qualify according to the financial criteria, but the latter groups together those who are additionally not physically capable of living on their own. So let's be careful here, and try to maintain some sort of balance. It only makes sense to group together the elderly and disabled (often the same people, by the way), given the need for special physical accommodations (elevators) and minimum dimensions to allow accessibility and meet their medical needs. This also explains why elderly/disabled complexes tend to be the newer buildings, as retroactively fitting existing ones for accessibility can be prohibitively expensive. Four of the county's seven public housing locations are reserved for the elderly/disabled, and two of Pottstown's three—Pollock House and Smith Towers—fall into this category. It is hard to question money spent on these, and I seriously doubt that their residents contribute greatly to Pottstown's crime problem, at least as perpetrators. The concentration of two out of four such homes in Pottstown does represent a variation of the question "Why?" but the answer will be different from anything about housing choice vouchers.

The other two complexes in the river towns are the Golden Age Manor in Royersford and Lee Towers in Conshohocken, and both are limited to the elderly/disabled. I would be interested in knowing from the residents of these two towns if they have any opinions about these projects, and how well they fit into the town's makeup. There are other examples of housing subsidies in each town, so another question is how these two compare to others as community issues. Are they? I'd like to hear from you.

It should come as no surprise that general occupancy housing complexes are much more likely sources of trouble than their elderly/disabled counterparts. For the record, the two county public housing complexes *not* located in the Schuylkill Valley—North Hills Manor in Upper Dublin and Crest Manor in Willow Grove—are also general occupancy.

The third public housing complex in Pottstown is Bright Hope Community. Bright Hope (not its original name) is located in the borough's west end, and it is the oldest such complex still open in the county. It is by far the largest public housing site in Montgomery County, containing one fewer unit than the other general occupancy complexes in North Hills Manor and Crest Manor combined. It has had an up-and-down history of crime and drugs. No long ago I wrote a post about "gaming the system" and referenced a drug bust at Bright Hope. Pottstown urban activists are well aware of the place.

So, after two posts, it is clear that housing assistance of one sort or another is disproportionately present in both Norristown and Pottstown. We will review possible reasons for this in upcoming posts (hint: it's all about the Benjamins), but until then let's begin by accepting that this is a complex situation. Many factors enter into it, so don't expect to have your simple reason for it all verified by me. On rare occasions, we may encounter something that actually has a simple answer, but only simple minds *insist* on simple answers. The truth is not "out there"; it lies athwart the middle, as it always does, and it contains contradictions.

8/22/14

Housing Choice Vouchers: It's Not *All* About the Benjamins

But a lot of it is, and that's what I will focus on this time. Be warned: the Housing Choice Voucher Program is enormously complicated, and this is no place for a detailed analysis. I will stick to the basics, because understanding why voucher holders seem to end up in one of two locations isn't about corruption or conspiracy (although I accept that corruption is not absent), it's about what the program is designed to do and how the regulations say it *must* be done. These ultimately derive from the funding that is available, so it's the Benjamins that I begin with.

First, I want to clear up an issue of terminology. In my first post on housing assistance I used the term "individual" to describe a voucher holder. While an individual can receive a voucher, the program is structured around the household, and that is the term I will employ from now on. The amount of a voucher is calculated utilizing both household income and household size, (and a few other things, of course).

The 2012 report I have used for my data lists 2,625 vouchers in effect as of that year, and I will continue to use that data. Keep in mind that anything produced in 2012 utilizes data from no later than 2011, and it's now 2015, so don't fixate on the precise numbers. They have probably changed a little, but the reasons for the disparity in voucher locations most certainly have not.

The Montgomery County Housing Authority (MCHA) administers the housing choice voucher program as the jurisdictional public housing authority for the county. At the foundation of everything, of course is the fact that the MCHA has only a fixed—and inadequate—amount of money to distribute on an annual basis. HUD also caps the number of vouchers that MCHA can issue, but the money allotted is not enough to fund all the vouchers it could issue. There is also a waiting list with about nine hundred households on it, but no new names have been added to it since 2007.

Each voucher amount is a separate calculation, but all derive from obedience to the rules and use of the formulas. The formulas aren't basic at all, but we only need to know about them, not the details. I will be just skimming the surface of a hugely complicated program, but will try to outline its fundamental rules.

The foundation of the whole program of housing subsidies is a belief that an American family should have to pay no more than 30 percent of its net income for housing. A lot of research (and no small amount of controversy) went into establishing this baseline number, and a lot of misunderstanding has resulted. Despite all the lip service paid to this number, the program is *not* structured to cover the difference between 30 percent of a voucher-holding household's income and the amount it pays for rent, as we will see. But what makes the 30 percent figure so important is that we are talking about this percentage of the income of the lowest earners on the local wage front. The average annual income of program participants in Montgomery County, Pennsylvania. is $15–16,000. Keep in mind that's an *average* figure, with some lower and some higher. The voucher holder is required to pay 30 percent of its income to the private landlord, and that may not be very much. The MCHA thus ends up paying a substantial amount of the rent (directly to the landlord), but even that will not usually make up the difference between the rent and the tenant's contribution. You'll see why—and how important it is—if you stick with me through this.

Remember, the vouchers are *portable*, so there is theoretically no barrier to a household moving where it wishes to live. But the Benjamins say otherwise. The Housing Choice Voucher Program is *not* designed to make up the difference between 30 percent of a household's income and the prevailing market rent in any particular neighborhood. The actual amount is determined by several bureaucratic calculations, the combination of which reduces how much a voucher is actually worth.

The first is something called the *fair market rent* (FMR). Note the terminology: "fair," not "free." That's important. The term "fair market rent" is borrowed from the real estate industry, although the end product is pretty much the opposite of what the term means in that context. It's not determined by local supply and demand, but by HUD, and it is customized for the huge variation in rental prices in the different jurisdictions all across the country. HUD basically collects rental rates from several locations in a jurisdiction such as Montgomery County, Pennsylvania, from the low to the high. It then processes this information and arrives at a net figure that applies throughout the county, regardless of a housing unit's actual free market rent. This doesn't mean that the FMR is a single number. The amount is based on the number of bedrooms in a unit and how the tenant pays utilities (the FMR includes the cost of utilities in addition to the rent), which makes for an enormous number of variations in the actual amount of each voucher.

There is a second number that figures in here. HUD has different arrangements with each of its jurisdictions about *how much* of the FMR it is actually going to pay. It's called the *percentile*. As the FMR is assumed to be a figure near the middle, the ideal arrangement is when HUD allows a housing authority to spend at the fiftieth percentile. Then—and only then—is the amount the authority can pay for a voucher equal to the FMR. The allowed percentile varies with jurisdictions, and can be lowered. HUD pays Montgomery County at the fiftieth percentile, and thus at the FMR. This becomes the maximum amount the MCHA can offer in a voucher.

This is so important that I will review the point: a public housing authority allocates a specific amount of money to a voucher according to a calculation utilizing bureaucratically processed information. The voucher holder then has to utilize that voucher in the free market world of real estate. That is a major disconnect, because while criticism of the housing choice voucher program derives from real world experience, all housing authority actions—with the Benjamins most definitely included—take place in accordance with a voluminous and detailed collection of regulations. To say that "reality doesn't matter" does not overstate the point by much.

The FMR is an *average* number, and should be somewhere around the middle of the true free market rents available around the county. The actual rents charged are, of course, determined by private landlords. The market rent for a specific bedroom unit in Wynnewood, for example, is considerably more than for the same bedroom unit in Norristown or

Pottstown. So, which landlords are most likely to reject the voucher program? Clearly, those whose rents are so high that the subsidy doesn't make up the difference, and that pretty much means *at least half of all the available rental units in the county.*

Here's the bottom line: the current structure of the Housing Choice Voucher Program, even before considering any other of its many issues, strongly directs the recipients into the less expensive half of the rental units in Montgomery County. Before we continue with a critique of what the program fails to accomplish, we must understand that this is exactly what the voucher program was designed to do: aid low-income families to move into what Wikipedia calls "medium-quality apartments." The MCHA says the actual wording in the act is "modest." Please note that I said "understand," not "accept." I plan to continue educating you about not just the program's shortcomings, but from where they originate, so that blame—and thereby corrective action—can be more efficiently focused.

At a fundamental level, the problem is all about the Benjamins in that, with *a great deal more money*, the other obstructions could be overcome. That's not a real world scenario, however, and adding a smaller amount would have opposite effects on the two goals I set out at the beginning of my first post on this subject. Simply "throwing more money at the problem"— adding to the housing authority's budget but not altering any of the rules under which it is distributed—would at least lessen the number of needy people on the county waiting list, and that's a good thing. But it would also increase the number of housing vouchers in Norristown and Pottstown, and that's not. More money by itself is not the answer. Below, I discuss more about why this is true.

My thanks to Joel Johnson and his staff at the Montgomery County Housing Authority for leading me through the maze of the programs they administer (and some they don't). All errors of fact expressed above—and in future posts—are mine alone.

8/29/14

Housing Subsidies, Housing Vouchers: It's Complicated, People!

In the last post I discussed the unpleasant fact that the Housing Choice Voucher Program is specifically designed to give low-income families access to *somewhat better* housing, whether you describe it as "medium-quality" or "modest." The Benjamins then do their part, as too many better neighborhoods are simply out of reach for a voucher household. Please don't jump to conclusions; this does not begin to excuse the result when that result so concentrates housing vouchers in just a few communities. That is simply unacceptable.

I am proposing the exact opposite of acceptance—the need is for correction. Correction first requires understanding the way things are and why they actually got that way, rather than seeing in a situation what you have already decided you want to see. This has been my mantra from the beginning, and in Section 8, I can see no other subject more in need of this approach. (Okay, "Obamacare" probably ranks higher today, but Section 8 has been around a lot longer.)

That's why I don't like the term Section 8. The phrase long ago became a buzzword, employed only to deliver unspoken judgmental messages to those who hear it. Several completely different programs, administered at different levels of government, comprise the available spectrum of rental housing subsidies. They are lumped together in the public consciousness as Section 8, and the result is predictable: the frequent exchanging of nonsense someone read on the Internet.

I separated out public housing in a previous post because it does not belong in the same conversation as Housing Choice Vouchers or Low Income Tax Credits. Or at least I tried to. A reader then commented on how they seem to be owned by just a few landlords. This is an example of the honest, but all-too-prevalent confusion that results from lumping together very different programs under one buzzword. Public housing is completely free of private landlords; when you see a problem, you know who to call: the MCHA.

Public housing is almost unique in its administration, but vouchers and LITC subsidies do involve private landlords. That's an important shared quality, and we will return to it. The programs themselves, however, are completely different, and there are others that show up from time to time in new development proposals. Any rational attempt to correct the all-too-apparent problems with the programs first requires an understanding of how they are different and what each is actually designed to do.

The various subsidy programs to builders should be discussed by the individual case, whether we are talking about earlier projects—such as the conversion of Rittenhouse School in Norristown—or any new ones that appear (here's where I get to mention Pennrose once more). Their boundaries can be easily identified, and the discussion focused. Housing Choice Subsidies possess no boundaries, at least theoretically. Last week's post should begin to clear up why that doesn't happen, but there is more to examine. The obvious financial boundary I discussed last week does not by itself explain why so many vouchers end up within the boundaries of Norristown and Pottstown. There are additional reasons.

It is time for me to disappoint some of you by rejecting the argument that the concentration of housing choice vouchers in Norristown and Pottstown is the result of some sort of conspiracy. The staff of the Montgomery County Housing Authority is not meeting in secret devising ways to lure certain people to Norristown and Pottstown. At the same time, I am not any more willing to believe that every recipient of a housing choice voucher chose to live in Norristown or Pottstown because that's where they wanted to go than I am that someone simply threw a dart at a map blindfolded to locate public housing. Reality has this annoying way of being complex, despite our best efforts to ignore that basic fact. There are several aspects to the problems of housing choice vouchers, and moral judgments—particularly quick ones—should be avoided. The evidence is incontrovertible, but a conspiracy is not a necessary part of the explanation. Norristown and Pottstown have become "dumping grounds," even if no one has performed any conscious "dumping," and the blame for that can be spread around.

"They" are not in Norristown and Pottstown because of a conspiracy, but they are also not there just through the workings of "market forces" either. They weren't dumped there, they weren't directed there, and they didn't end up there because they need other services, nor for any other reason or even combination of reasons. Why? Because *"they" do not exist.* "They" are a collection of *individuals*, with individual reasons for being in the program. What we must all do is begin by rejecting any explanation that results from viewing Housing Choice Voucher recipients as being any one thing, regardless of what that is. Allusions to homogeneity, regardless of what they focus on, tend to trigger visceral reactions that deliver subtle, often subconscious judgments that are not justified by the collection of individual realities that actually exist. Voucher holders exist across a broad spectrum, from second- or third-generation recipients for whom this condition has become a way of life to those who are on it temporarily because of individual circumstance, often health-related issues. People enter the program and people leave it (just not nearly enough of them; dependency is clearly an issue). The voucher program aids many of those who need it most, and some of them show their gratitude by scamming it. You might perhaps remember that I have previously written about "gaming the system from below," and the principle certainly applies here.

All this exists, and more (Wait until I get to discussing the part landlords play). Recognition doesn't mean acceptance, and is absolutely necessary if you actually want to do something about the problem other than just denounce its results. The point is that *any* and *every* attempt to lump voucher recipients under one classification will produce conclusions that are self-defeating if translated into action.

Next week I take a look at the central player in this complex maze, the Montgomery County Housing Authority, and how we must understand it for what it is if we are to have any positive effect in correcting the evident shortcomings of the Housing Choice Voucher program.

9/5/14
Housing Choice Vouchers: What Can You Expect from a Bureaucracy?

The problems that Housing Choice Vouchers present to Norristown and Pottstown—as well as other towns—need to be addressed. The question is not who is to blame, but who is to blame for what. Our focus is on the central player in this ongoing drama, the Montgomery County Housing Authority (MCHA). The question thus becomes what can we realistically expect from it, and in what areas? The key to that, in turn, lies in understanding just what the MCHA is and does. That's no mystery, it's a government bureaucracy, and that is a beast we need to understand at a very fundamental level. The fact that it is a federal bureaucracy only makes it more dispersed than bureaucracy at any other level, and thus the hardest to target. Bureaucracy is sensitive to only a few, carefully targeted pressures; most of those applied miss the mark or are shed like water off a duck's back, with no discernible effect.

At the root of this is the fundamental disconnect between bureaucracy and the real world. The fiercest critics of the MCHA are those who live in the real world, often near its clients. They view the problems on an individual basis, and at no small risk to themselves. They know something is wrong—not just because of the numbers around them, but in the behavior of all too many of the program's beneficiaries, their neighbors. This viewpoint is widely shared at the municipal level, for all the obvious reasons. If those in closest contact with voucher recipients issued grades for program achievement, the MCHA would probably flunk.

Did you know that the US Department of Housing and Urban Development (HUD) does grade each of its local housing authorities on how they do their jobs? And did you know that the MCHA routinely receives an A grade? How can this be, if local discontent is so rife? This is actually one of those cases where the answer is simple: the MCHA earns its high grade by strict adherence to the regulations that govern its work, not by striving to address the issues that those regulations create when they interact with the real world. It's not that the people don't care; they do. They are professionally trained in a field that does not pay all that well and that offers little emotional job satisfaction, but they do it anyway and would like to be allowed to continue doing it. That means they do it strictly according to the regulations, and to them alone.

I cannot emphasize this too strongly. There is nothing strange at all about this; every organization does it. Policies and adherence to them are rigidly enforced in fields that range from finance to football. Government bureaucracies alone, however, are not required to win, to offer the best price or service, or to beat the competition. There is usually no competition, because no one has figured out a way to make money doing it. In such a structure, job security and career advancement begin with—and depend on—rigid adherence to the rules. That's the core of the disconnect, because bureaucracies undertake the activities that require dealing with a great many people, who thus present a great many difficulties interpreting just how they fit into the regulations. And they must fit into the established niches; a bureaucracy has no choice but to assign them to one if they are to do anything for them at all. This holds true in all fields, at all levels. Few of you deal with HUD, but each of you deals with the DMV, right? Need I say more? Rigidity does tend to increase as you go up the government food chain, but it is evident everywhere.

Bureaucracies are the worst in insisting on fitting a complex reality into a rigidly arranged structure, but let's be fair here. How many of you work for a company that allows you to deviate from its policies? Or lets you allocate money in different amounts or to different people than the rules specify? Thought so. So why expect it from a bureaucracy? Remember, it's spending *your* tax money. Don't you want every precaution taken to avoid waste and graft? Do you really want a federal agency to be able to just experiment with your money?

In the interest of full disclosure, I must reveal that after my graduation from college, I worked in a federal bureaucracy. I spent my time playing a very small role in what in what I believe to be a contender for the title of "most colossal and corrupt bureaucratic waste of money ever." I also know a little something about trying to help those most in need with entirely inadequate resources while adhering strictly to rules written by the type of bureaucracy whose office has no windows to the real world. I loved my work, but I quickly established an adversary relationship with the federal bureaucracy itself; hence, my tenure was brief. The fundamental lesson, however, has stayed with me, and has remained relevant in my later professional studies. It provides a clarifying filter through which to understand what you can get a bureaucracy to do, and what you can't.

While conducting an interview at the MCHA, and despite my hard-earned underlying assumption about what the answer would be, I asked Joel Johnson and his assembled staff what plans they had to address the problem of too many housing vouchers in specific locations. Their answer was prompt and delivered without hesitation. They plan to do nothing further than the one thing they already do. They do it because it's the only thing HUD allows them to do, and even that's optional. They wouldn't lose any grade points if they didn't do it.

Real, fundamental change in the several HUD programs we lump together as "Section 8" will require careful, reasoned action by Congress, and we all know that's not going to happen anytime soon. So if we actually want to do some good, let's look at what can be accomplished under the existing regulations. In a previous post, I argued that we can only discuss public housing or any of the various Low-Income Housing Tax Credit (LIHTC) programs on an individual basis. Last week I made the too-often-overlooked point that vouchers are not held by any *they*. That means that issues with housing choice vouchers also need to be addressed on an *individual* basis. Recipients are individuals, and they deserve that. The MCHA only administers regulations, but it interacts individually with each recipient household and each landlord to ensure that relevant portions of its regulations are enforced. Or at least it is supposed to. These are the areas where public pressure, properly applied, has a chance of being effective. So, let's focus on actually making things better, and save your venting for Facebook.

This week's post was about what you *can't* get a bureaucracy to do. Next week we get more detailed and discuss what the MCHA is actually supposed to do. That's where you, the readers, get to chime in, because you know the reality in your neighborhoods. I will work on getting that message passed along and together we will monitor what happens, or doesn't. This is a long-term endeavor, and very tiresome, but it's worth it.

9/12/14

Housing Choice Vouchers: Here's What's *Supposed* to Happen

In Bureaucracy World, the Housing Choice Voucher Program works precisely like this: A household seeking a voucher applies to the MCHA. He/she fills out several forms, wherein he/she lists each person in the household and all sources of income, among other things. The MCHA conducts background checks, including a criminal one, to make sure that all voucher recipients are of good character and honest. It totals the household income and determines the critical 30 percent figure that the household can afford to pay for rent. It then calculates how much assistance will be given—that is, the difference between the 30 percent figure and the *fair market rent*. With everything in place, the household then seeks out housing for which it has qualified (that pretty much means number of bedrooms). Once the household has found housing of the right size whose landlord is willing to submit to the rigorous standards that will be imposed, the MCHA again enters the picture. Every potential housing unit is first inspected by the MCHA, thus ensuring that it meets all current code standards. If any deficiencies are found, the landlord must make improvements until the MCHA is satisfied. The potential landlord then signs a "Housing Assistance Payments Contract" with the MCHA, devoutly promising to follow the rules. Once everyone is satisfied and all standards have been fully met, the landlord and the tenant execute a standard lease, and the household moves into its new home. They faithfully pay their share of the rent—and dutifully report all future changes in either household income or composition—while the landlord ensures that they continue to live in a safe and healthy environment; the MCHA, meanwhile, punches another ticket toward its A grade, and everyone lives happily afterward. "God bless America."

"What a wonderful world this would be...." Of course, that phrase comes from the song about the guy who "don't know nothin' 'bout history," so be advised.

Let's examine the basic structure of this all-American fantasy for its weak spots, because they are where the Benjamins leak out. We will climb our way up the leakage scale, because more leakage means more expense to you, the taxpayer. Let's follow the money, continuously asking the same question: who stands to profit by not following the rules?

The voucher program is a tri-party arrangement involving the housing authority, the income-eligible household, and the private sector landlord. If each fulfills its end of the bargain, then harm is mitigated, and the larger good may actually surpass the local damage done. Maybe. If any party fails in its obligations, however, it only encourages one or both of the others to do so also. An increasing scale of harm results.

If the failure is on the part of the tenant, it is in the interests of both the landlord and the housing authority to either correct the failure or expel the tenant. Money is usually involved somehow, but neither the landlord nor the housing authority stands to profit. (Yes, the landlord may be "in on it," but let's keep a reasonable balance here.)

If the landlord fails to keep his or her part of the bargain, things get complicated, because the profit motive enters into it—at least for the landlord, who has a very personal understanding of the concept. Correcting the problem is in the interests of both the tenant and the housing authority, but ratting out one's landlord is rarely in the interests of the tenant, so the housing authority may not even be informed of it.

If, however, the housing authority fails to do what it is supposed to do—properly monitor the reality of what the other two components are doing—then both the other components have the opportunity for illicit profit. Both are also prime candidates for seizing such an opportunity, so trouble is pretty much guaranteed.

That's why we will conclude this financial ascent focusing on the MCHA. Ironically, that's where you will find by far the least actual malfeasance; MCHA errors are usually related to the agency's level of diligence and oversight. Their actions or inactions can either open or close loopholes that mean the different between everyone following the rules and the one or both of the two non-MCHA parties profiting improperly.

That's why I begin with malfeasance by the tenant. It is frequently the most obvious, and it is usually the most castigated: most people hare seeing other people cheat the government. I'm going to disagree with that assessment based solely on my adherence to the Benjamins as my guiding criteria, not by comparing the heinousness of various crimes. Tenant malfeasance in the Housing Choice Voucher Program is yet another example of "gaming the system from the bottom." I don't ignore it, I don't mitigate it, I encourage relentless pursuit and elimination of all examples of it, but I contend that "gaming the system from the top" costs us all a lot more. Top-down malfeasance is nowhere near as obvious, and easier to overlook. But if you follow the money, it's not where you start that counts, it's where you end up. That is the route we will follow, and the next post moves up the scamming ladder, because we will add the possibility of profit that is legal, although ethically dubious.

The real cost of tenant malfeasance is very locally focused, in the immediate neighborhood, and the Benjamins are only one method of measuring it. That real cost to a neighborhood and its people is the reason I'm going to wrap up this post with some nonadvice about what to do. There is not necessarily any actual difference between malfeasance and crime, so it's best you stay as far as possible from both. I don't want to ignore this enormously important aspect of the problem, but neither am I qualified to make any valuable contribution to those who find themselves involved in it. I would never offer any fatuous, from-a-distance advice to *anyone* about how to deal with a situation in your neighborhood. There are several things more important than the Benjamins; always put them first.

Let me finish with a question. Why, given what "everybody knows about housing voucher holders," would a potential landlord even *consider* entering the program when they could easily—and legally—avoid it and all the obvious hassle? Gee, what do you think?

9/19/14

Surprise! For Landlords, It *Is* All about the Benjamins

Last week I closed with the question of why a potential landlord even consider entering the Housing Choice Voucher (HCV) Program. Why get involved in a program that essentially encourages its beneficiaries to lie, cheat, and steal?

If you doubt this, look at it from the voucher holders' point of view: the program punishes you for being honest. If you report an increase in income—even if it's legal—your voucher amount stands to go down. Need to take in an extra family member, even temporarily? Don't tell the MCHA: that's changing your "household composition," and it could cause problems. Unhappy about how your landlord is treating you? Better keep your mouth shut if you don't have the time or the resources it will take to interface with the bureaucracy, because your landlord probably does—at least enough to deal with the likes of you. All things considered, what's the reason for being honest, outside of being caught for being dishonest?

That might be your potential tenant's point of view. Why rent to the type of people who would cheat the very program that benefits them? If they would do that, they would cheat you, right? This is not exactly a formula for a smooth landlord/tenant relationship.

And then there's the federal bureaucracy to deal with, forms to fill out, the additional inspections of your property, and all that. Why then would landlords want to be in the program, if they have to deal with both low-income tenants and the federal bureaucracy?

Okay, let's acknowledge the reliability factor. A substantial portion of the rent is paid not by the tenant, but by the MCHA directly to the landlord. The tenant may have more excuses than cash on the rental due date, but the check from the MCHA is going to arrive unless there is a postal strike.

But you know the real reason, of course. It's all about the Benjamins. The HCV Program is a financial boon to those who, in my humble opinion, deserve it the least—the landlords who own and rent out the cheapest half of the housing in our towns and cities. That's because the HCV Program financially benefits the bottom feeders in the urban real estate market. Housing choice vouchers are a guaranteed source of *additional* income to these landlords, allowing them to get paid much more than they would if they were not part of the program.

This wasn't part of the plan, but it is a major part of the result. These low-rent landlords (I mean that as much figuratively as literally) purchase the cheapest houses they can find, all too often in Norristown and Pottstown. If they were just rented out, these housing units would not command even the local community's median rent, let alone that of the county. If a voucher holder is about to move in a cheap apartment, or if an existing tenant receives a voucher, the landlord can raise the rent, quite legally it seems, as long as it does not exceed the fair market rent. Profit is rent minus expenses, and they know that if they accept HCV recipients, a higher rent is basically forced on them, courtesy of the taxpayers. Who would refuse such a deal? Besides, bottom-feeder landlords are not overly concerned with building maintenance, because that eats into the profit. You don't think they purchased those old houses to help preserve our irreplaceable stock of existing urban housing, did you? As I pointed out above, renting to HCV tenants greatly lowers the chance that those tenants are going to complain about substandard conditions. Unrepentant exploitation of the HCV Program thus fattens such a landlord's profit from both ends.

This is where the true evil of concentrated housing choice vouchers in specific communities becomes more apparent. Towns like Norristown and Pottstown suffer from having so many voucher households end up there, some of which are not exactly a benefit to the community. On top of that, the concentration of imposes a financial penalty on the nonvoucher households in the same community. That's because the HCV Program artificially maintains *a higher local rent than the neighborhood and the housing units would otherwise warrant*. The HCV Program's commitment to the fair market rate artificially raises the average rent across an entire neighborhood, affecting everyone. The MCHA pays the extra for the voucher households, but all other renters in the neighborhood have to pay the difference out of their own pocket. If you are not in the program and live in the neighborhood, you pay a higher rent because of the program. All this, of course, in neighborhoods where conditions are already at the lower end of the scale, because that's where the money is in such a skewed real estate market. Any landlord with an apartment that is good enough (and located in a good enough neighborhood) to command a rental fee above the fair market rent simply has no economic incentive to enter the program. The neighbors might not be too happy about it either. This last can be important in a community that has few (or no) housing choice vouchers. When the local municipality joins in the exclusion effort (unofficially, of course), the resulting peer pressure helps to keep vouchers out. Those towns already swamped with vouchers end up getting more; it's a vicious, self-reinforcing circle, lowering the condition of a community while keeping rental costs artificially high. When disgusted homeowners leave, the low-rent landlords swoop in, pick up the property for a depressed amount, and look for equally low-rent tenants. That's why I bet all such slumlords would sanctimoniously support a funding increase for the HCV Program; much of it will end up in their pockets.

Yes, the HCV Program encourages its recipients to cheat, but it encourages landlords to cheat more, because they stand to make more. Recipients cheat to keep a roof over their heads for a smaller percentage of their income; they don't get any money from MCHA. Landlords cheat for profit, pure and simple. If landlords properly maintained their properties and exercised care in their rentals, the biggest money leaks in the system would close, and it would make tenant cheating both more difficult and less rewarding. Of course, if wishes were horses, even beggars would ride, so we will have to take a more difficult approach if we want to actually see results.

Next week we will simultaneously narrow and broaden our focus, and ask: What's the *real* problem here?

9/26/14
"Section 8" Is a Myth. What's the REAL Problem Here?

I was going to conclude my series on subsidized housing with some thoughts on the questions you should be asking your public housing authority about why the Housing Choice Voucher Program operates so differently in your real world than it does in Bureaucracy World. Disturbing news out of Norristown, Pennsylvania—and part of the reaction to it—suggests yet again that many of you have the right understanding of the core issue, but direct way too much of your anger at the wrong target. So I will instead write about how the news from Norristown helps to put Section 8 in a better context. But the questions will be included.

The Norristown case involves those old favorite bureaucratic bugaboos, cronyism and favoritism (it can be difficult to distinguish between them), and how useful it is to know people in the right places. It appears that the Norristown's housing inspector allowed a district justice to rent out an apartment without a license, and, presumably, without inspections. He has been relieved of his job, and everyone eagerly awaits further revelations, or at least news.

Part (and only part, I am pleased to say) of the reaction has been to reflexively lump this case under Section 8. That's where my problem comes in. The tenant in this case did not hold such a voucher. She is a woman who has worked hard all her life, is now elderly, and still pays the entire rent (I spoke with her). Section 8 simply doesn't apply in this case, but it certainly helps to make my point about how people see a housing issue in their community and *automatically* blame it on Section 8.

What has happened in Norristown cuts to the very core of the housing issues in many towns. The Norristown case—and the response to it—offer a microcosm of what takes place in the minds of a great many all over this country. Some of you have focused from the beginning on the real issue, the (alleged) corruption, but there are those who require little incentive to damn a welfare program before establishing the facts. The result is no action, exactly when action is warranted.

Myths are accepted, not fought, and "Section 8" is a myth—not the program itself, but what putting the term in quotation marks signifies; so many layers of spin and misinformation have been lathered onto the reality that they hide its actual shape. There is truth at the core of every myth, but once people have coated it again and again with their personal/political agendas, the truth is obscured beneath, and by accepting the myth, people believe what the spin doctors want them to believe, not the truth.

The most pernicious aspect of the Section 8 myth is how it discourages people from actually doing something about the housing problems they see all around them. When people drive by a depressed neighborhood, past dilapidated residences and trash-strewn yards where residents seem to have nothing better to do but hang out all day, how many do you suppose quickly think Section 8? Once they do that, the battle is lost. After all, *"It's Section 8; it's a federal giveaway. We can't do anything about it."*

There are two misstatements contained here. First, it's probably not Section 8, and second, you *can* do something about it. You can call your local public housing authority and complain. Here's where those questions I was going to focus on come into play. Don't just call and complain; know *what* violations are taking place and ask the right questions to find out why. Remember, in the absence of you pointing out a failure to comply with a regulation, a government bureaucracy isn't going to do anything. Here are just a few of the basic questions; you can take it from here.

Does the authority's have its own employees perform required inspections, or does it contract them out? What do they look for? There is pretty much a standard building code in place across this area; are its standards the same as those of the municipality? Do reinspections take place? If so, how often and for what reasons? I suggest you obtain copies of the Housing Assistance Payments Contract mentioned previously to find out what landlords should be doing. Anyone interested in doing something about HCV problems in their neighborhood should start by obtaining a copy of that contract. Armed with that and your own eyes, locate a *specific problem* and report it to the housing authority. Remember my earlier point about attacking each case on an individual basis? Have the basic facts—dates, addresses, etc.—available when you call. Wait for follow-up, then repeat as required until results are achieved. Notice that I did not use the word "names." It's actually best to avoid using names; the safeguards for personal privacy are many and unforgiving. I'll bet we never learn exactly what the Norristown codes inspector actually did, because that comes under "personnel matters" and will be kept private.

If it's not Section 8, you can call and complain anyway; just call the phone number for the code enforcement department of your local municipality. In fact, *always* call that number first. After all, shouldn't the supervision you want to see in the HCV Program also be taking place next door, where no voucher exists? Can you tell the difference between a house not properly monitored by the MCHA and one not properly monitored by your municipality? And besides, aren't *all* houses supposed to be subject to municipal standards, whether inhabited by a HCV recipient or not?

What's the real problem here? Aren't we really talking about slipshod work, overlooked violations, and cronyism and favoritism in the administration of our towns themselves? Does it really matter whether the house is "Section 8" or not? Shouldn't *all* housing be held to the same standards of codes and regulations?

If all you really want to do is bitch, then by all means complain about "Section 8" program. You're right, actually, to think that the federal government is not going to do anything about the program—at least not until the next major shakeup in Congress—and it is certainly not going to do anything based on your request (or mine). Thus, you get to do what you really want to do—complain—secure in the knowledge that the target of your ire will be unaffected, and therefore available to you in the future.

But if your goal is to actually make thing better, stop obsessing on "Section 8," housing choice vouchers, public housing, or any of that. Events in

Norristown offer an opportunity to focus on what I less-than-humbly suggest is the much bigger problem. The emerging—but already smelly—story in Norristown is right on point about conditions in too many of our municipalities today, and it says a lot more about money, connections, and the corruption that results from their intersection than any individual Section 8 abuse story ever could. It's a bigger issue, because it can encompass many Section 8 components and still rank them rather low on any cost-to-our-communities scale. Communities the size of Norristown and Pottstown, Pennsylvania—not to mention larger ones—face housing issues with many facets, and all the Section 8 programs lumped together are actually just a component of them. Abuse in these programs exists alongside abuse that has nothing to do with it. Let's stop using a buzzword to explain away a problem and instead learn more about the real world before we point fingers at the villains and demand reforms.

The root of the *correctable* problems in both Norristown and Pottstown—and, I submit, elsewhere—lies in the porous collection of inspections, corrections, and follow-up that is supposed to see that the rules are actually being followed, regardless of whose rules they are. That's why you pay taxes to your municipality as well as to the federal government; we expect them to not just to write laws and regulations but to enforce them, too. Complain about taxation—and what it is being spent on—all you want, and see what it gets you. But if you unite and offer specific positive suggestions, your voice in your community can actually change things for the better. It's up to you.

5/9/14

Perception Trumps Reality, Just about Every Time

I always began the first meeting of one of my history classes with an explanation of how I approach the subject of history itself. My goal was to make clear how little attention I was going to pay to the so-called "facts" of history, the who, what, where, and when. I was going to emphasize *how* and *why*. You can always look up the facts, but understanding what they mean is an entirely different thing.

I would always, at the right moment, tell my students, "The facts of history really aren't all that important anyway," and then observe the looks on their faces. My point was that, throughout history, people who didn't know the facts made decisions and acted regardless, thus creating history. My point about historical "facts" and my point about today's history in the making are pretty much the same, unfortunately. Facts are all well and good, but *perception* is much more important. For those who doubt this, I offer the current so-called "debate" over the Affordable Care Act as proof. The decisions about the ACA to come are not going to be based on the facts—not if organized factions of our populace have anything to say about it. (Please do not take the foregoing statement as evidence that I know the facts; I'm just as confused as everyone.)

Recent evidence that perception trumps reality pretty much all the time was offered on Wednesday, April 30, 2014, at Norristown Municipal Hall. Against that imposing backdrop, several Norristown municipal officials were joined by an impressive array of county officials—among them all three commissioners—for a press conference. The presence of District Attorney Risa Ferman and high-ranking law enforcement personnel seemed to telegraph a theme of public safety in Norristown. It did, sort of.

They were all gathered to announce the activation of the "Norristown Quality-of-Life Policing Task Force." Such a title is intriguing enough, but I found its stated goals to be downright fascinating: "To decrease fear of crime, increase the visibility of multifaceted community policing, and establish a more effective collaboration around policing priorities in the municipality."

Notice the rhetorical sleight of hand here. They were not announcing the formation of a top-level group that will be working together to improve the quality of life in Norristown, but a top-level group working together to convince the public that the quality of life in Norristown *is already good*. The problem is not the reality, it's the *perception* of that reality. Council President Bill Caldwell's opening statement revealed the underlying assumption about the real problem with which Norristown must contend: "Urban communities often get a bum rap for being places where random crime happens, and we're here to tell you today that that is not what happens in Norristown."

Their answer to this problem (the problem of *perception*, not reality, remember) continued in the same vein. "The chiefs will present a new approach that we're going to take to make people feel comfortable…to live, work, and play in Norristown." The new Norristown police chief, Mark Talbott, followed with his own valiant effort to bridge the reality/perception gap, proclaiming "a public commitment to do more," then staunchly defending the "reality" [my quotes this time] that "crime is down significantly.… The objective data supports this" [his quotes]. In other words, they were proudly announcing an unprecedented joint effort to pool the resources of many agencies to get people to realize that what everybody thinks is a problem not only isn't as much of a problem as everybody thinks, but has already become a lot better recently. We should all accept the data, not the perception, but they are all going to do a lot more anyway. Got that?

The message may have been muddy, but the basic problem is not just fundamental but widespread: there exists, it is claimed, a gap between the public's perception and the objective data about a situation. But why is this a problem at all? Shouldn't we all just accept the objective data and change our perceptions, if required? Back in the "good old days," getting any information at all about a situation before you had to make a decision was often chancy, let alone seeing any objective data. But, please, tell me how, in this information age, when we are past mere data into something called "big data," when we have access to multiple twenty-four-hour streams of information and even more relational databases, can there exist such a gap between perception and reality?

Okay, that's a rhetorical question. We all know of this reality gap, because it is all around us. *Doonesbury's* "myFacts" parody ("myFacts, privatizing the truth since 2003") is entirely too close to reality. In one of the great contradictions of our time, the more information we have available to draw upon in reaching a balanced, rational conclusion, the more insistent we seem to become on believing only those "facts" that support our preconceived viewpoint on the subject. Objective, critical thinking has an annoying tendency to upset those cherished viewpoints, and is thus to be avoided at all costs. Why concern ourselves that what the other side is saying might be true when we can instead just return serve with some truth of our own? Somewhere during this serve-and-volley, the net truth disappears. It's always "net," by the way, because no person, no idea, no cause, no law, no ideology, no *nothing* is either all right or all wrong, all good or all bad. There will be both winners and losers, regardless. On the ground (or in Congress), the fight isn't about ideals (let alone truth), but about who emerges financially better off when the deal is done.

I digress, but not much. I'm focusing on a specific perception vs. reality situation—but one that is, I would argue, not only consistent with but also deeply rooted in several national issues bedeviling us today. Some people are going to continue to believe the bad perception of Norristown's situation because it fits so neatly into their closely arranged universe of race, ethnicity, and welfare; others will have more legitimate reasons, and I am willing to bet that there exists a spectrum of motives for holding tightly to one's perception, even to the point of consciously excluding any intruding reality.

But in this specific case, how much difference is there, really, between perception and reality? That's an unpleasant thought to air, but I know several quite rational, informed people who have judged Norristown to be a less safe place to live than they wish on the basis of their personal experience with that very reality. This rather complicates the issue, even in the presence of objective data. Changing these more-informed perceptions is going to take a lot more than just making law enforcement more visible on the streets.

There was a noticeable lack of specifics to back up the claims that, in the words of County Commissioners Chairman Josh Shapiro, "Great days lie ahead for Norristown." This was pointed out in the reports of the press to whom this little event was delivered. Margaret Gibbons, who must have long ago lost track of how many similar performances she has witnessed, termed it "grandstanding." As a critique of the first episode of this little show, she was correct.

It also took no time at all for those congenitally so disposed to decry the press conference and its message as a scam, and dismiss it. I'm not going to join them, despite having had my admittedly low tolerance for grandstanding exceeded in this case. Such a judgment may be correct in the long run, but not immediately. I've made this point before, and I do not hesitate to make it again: to simply *assume* that something is hype, disinformation, or even mendacity not only does not help, it is counterproductive, and that makes it stupid.

The joint press conference was totally a media event (scheduled as it was for 1:00 p.m. on a workday), and that provides a clue as to how we should receive it. As with the pilot episode of any show that we find promising, we should exercise "temporary suspension of disbelief." The first-rate cast stuck tightly to the script and delivered the lines with the necessary panache, producing an uplifting message, as intended. Even ye who are without sin should not stone this cast; first let them actually *act*, and judge the result by how it plays out before your eyes. Will the show deliver on the promise of its pilot? You really need to stay tuned for this one.

The most realistic and informed statements of the day came after the conference was over, and were made by members of Norristown Council, those who are really on the spot over this issue. Their message was "don't prejudge; give us a chance to make this work, and then hold us accountable." They are the ones taking a rational, unadorned approach, and will ultimately be the ones responsible for bringing perceptions into alignment with reality, if such a thing is ever possible. Even if you don't think they actually mean it, try to remember the words of the man many of you hold to have been a great president: "trust, but verify." If Ronald Reagan could apply that approach to dealing with Communists, surely you can apply it to your own local municipal government.

The best thing to do at this point is to suspend judgment (as it often must be at many points). Give Norristown's municipal officials, the county officials, and all those law enforcement personnel the benefit of the doubt. Then give them some time. The press conference was conspicuously short on specifics about what they are all going to do collectively, and thus close monitoring is called for in the future. The most important thing to remember, however, after the warm and fuzzy feeling generated by this "new initiative" has worn off, is this: once you have given them a reasonable amount of time and learned more about just how complex the problem really is, *hold them accountable*. It's not just your right, it's your duty. Don't prejudge, but once you have determined the actual facts of the matter, don't hesitate or let up.

12/12/14

Perception Versus Reality, Revisited

Back on May 9, 2014, I published a post that discussed the activation of the "Norristown Quality-of-Life Policing Task Force," an effort launched with some fanfare and the presence of all three county commissioners. What I found fascinating about the program was that its goal was not to improve the quality of life in Norristown, but to convince the public that the quality of life in Norristown was *already good*. Council President Bill Caldwell set the tone by proclaiming that "urban communities often get a bum rap for being places where random crime happens, and we're here to tell you today that that is not what happens in Norristown." Thus spake the authorities, both of Norristown and of Montgomery County.

I tried to throw the Wet Blanket of Reality on all this by observing that I knew several rational, informed people who judged Norristown to be a less safe place to live than they wish on the basis of some personal experience. In other words, they live there. I predicted that changing these more informed perceptions would take a lot more than just making law enforcement more visible.

At the press conference, the principals asked the public to give them a year before making a judgment, and that was a fair request. It has now been seven months since that new initiative was launched, so it's not too early to check in for a preliminary survey. So, residents of Norristown, Pennsylvania, I have two questions:

First, "Do local events in the last six months suggest that Norristown's 'Quality of Life' initiative is contributing to making the streets safer?" If so, kudos, but remember that such a change of mind was not what the initiative sought; it was designed to help you believe that you *were already* living in a safe, secure community. That was the "reality," remember?

So, here's my second question: "Have you realized the error you have been making all this time, and now accept as reality that Norristown is a safe community in which to live, work, and play?" If so, then the Norristown Quality-of-Life initiative has truly been a success. Quite frankly, a majority "yes" to the first question would be achievement enough, but I don't want to rule anything out.

While I wait for responses to these admittedly loaded questions, I want to return to the basic perception vs. reality dichotomy issue as it concerns urban safety. Norristown authorities claim that the town suffers from a bad perception/good reality problem. As it turns out (not altogether surprisingly), so do the authorities in Pottstown. As with Norristown, the Pottstown authorities are upset with all the "negative publicity" about public safety in the borough. Various elected leaders have voiced this opinion, on more than one occasion. I believe I have been included among those detractors so identified, if only in a minor way. I take pride in that.

Strangely, the *Pottstown Mercury* seems to have joined the chorus that people just don't know how good they have it in their urban world. A recent editorial cast "THORNS to those who vent their frustrations about crime in Pottstown on social media and in conversation rather than trying to do something about it." It then proceeded to make several dubious statements that speak to the perception/reality issue.

Before I proceed, let me go on record as agreeing with the basic truth behind that initial statement. Pottstown residents have been noticeably reticent to get active in the cause of civic betterment. The number voicing their concerns online is larger than those who get involved—no question. This is the truth, but a truth that extends to a great many more municipalities as well. No one deplores this more than I do, but it is a fact that cannot be denied.

Now for what I didn't like about the *Mercury*'s editorial. A correct—but narrow—view of its phraseology says it condemns only those who speak but do not act. But what if speaking is part of the action? A number of residents are concerned enough about the situation on Pottstown's streets to establish Facebook pages and websites to publicize the borough's issues. In my view, these people *are* trying to "do something" about it. Allowing others to vent frustrations is only a byproduct of their efforts.

The editorial rightly points out that those who complain far outnumber even those who take even that basic first step, attending meetings of the Borough Council. Those who do attend, however, and who keep trying to organize ways to make things better, are the same ones who administer the Facebook pages and even websites. They spread the word about what is happening around town, rather better than the municipal website. These pages and websites, in turn, continually implore their neighbors to get involved, beginning with attendance at meetings. At the risk of repeating myself, these vocal residents of Pottstown *are* the ones trying to "do something" about it.

If the *Mercury* was trying to improve people's perception of Pottstown, its next comments did not exactly help: "To date, the crime victims have been people who were associating with those committing the violence. The incidents of violent crimes being committed against innocent victims is not any higher in Pottstown than anywhere else." I don't exactly find that reassuring, and certainly not something to post on "Positives in Pottstown." The same thing might have been said of Chicago in the Twenties; the gangsters were pretty much killing each other, right? If I don't think much of this, what about the "innocent" people who actually live in Pottstown? Many would dispute whether such a claim has any reality behind it; is this just their *perception*?

But my favorite is this conclusion: "Pottstown needs a plan to improve the perception and reality of crime here; it doesn't need more detractors. Sound familiar? Does anyone besides me find it disturbing that "perception" takes precedence over "reality" in that sentence? If perception is the big problem, then Pottstown need only look to Norristown, which is implementing a plan to improve people's perception; perhaps Pottstown can get a copy.

A municipality can generate its objective reality from statistics, and call them facts. But the question of one's personal safety on the streets and at home is definitely an example of what I meant in my original post when I wrote that the facts are all well and good, but *perception* is much more important. Statistics are cold comfort when one's reality says something different, particularly if that reality is predominately fear. And, I would suggest, *the best way to improve the public's perception of the situation is to improve the situation itself.* Remove the fear, and people's perception of reality will improve.

Municipal governments have more than enough problems confronting them; they ought not to consider the most concerned of their citizens as part of that number. It's a natural enough tendency, to blame those who publicize an area's problems to the world for making the problems seem to be worse than they actually are. Those of us of sufficient years recall when an entire section of the country employed such a tactic, arguing that if "troublemakers" would only cease their outcries, then the rest of us would see the "reality," and wouldn't be as concerned. That was then; in today's information age, attempts to impose a gag rule are not only hopeless, they are quickly proven to be, in reality, counterproductive.

We celebrate the child who is honest enough to point out that the emperor wears no clothes, but only because it's a fairy tale. We show rather less tolerance to adults who make the same observation. Some (like me) can be dismissed as "outsiders," but by far the greater number are those who actually live in places like Pottstown and Norristown, and experience the reality of their streets. People who just bitch just bitch; those who go to the trouble to set up and administer Facebook pages and websites, attend borough meetings, and continuously implore others to get involved are among any community's most valuable citizens, and should not be placed in the same group as the bitchers. Communities need more of these people, particularly communities like Pottstown and Norristown. They should not be demonized, because their perception *is* of the reality in their towns. Because of that, they must not be ignored.

When It Comes to the River, Forget History and Start Anew

They say people who ignore history are doomed to repeat it. We need to be very careful about that, however. It's not about *remembering* history, it's about learning the lessons that history offers. In Pennsylvania's lower Schuylkill Valley, one of those lessons is that history provides almost no guide for the present or the future. Not only have things changed, they have virtually reversed themselves.

The most fundamental change has been that of the Schuylkill River itself. A result of that change (and only one of them) is a complete reversal in the historic relationship between the river and the towns that occupy portions of its floodplain. The most obvious evidence of this change is seen in the Conshohockens, but that is the result of outside economic forces, not the leadership or the populations of either town. I will focus on that part of the change later. Here I discuss the broader change itself.

Every one of the Schuylkill River towns, as it grew, developed the same relationship with the river. That relationship had two aspects: the towns drew drinking water from it and dumped sewage and industrial wastes into it. Those activities were, in turn, largely undertaken by private enterprise, with only occasional and loose supervision by any municipal authority. Back then, no one even thought of limiting the options of "job creators." It did not take long for the basic incompatibility of these two uses to become evident, and because it was much cheaper to filter water drawn from the river than to ban dumping into it, that course was followed.

The result was that the Schuylkill River, during the glory days of the towns along it, was avoided by all who could do so. The river was little more than an open sewer, particularly in the periods of warm weather and low flow. The riverbanks hosted the railroad and the industries it serviced, with the shopping streets very close by. The floodplain itself, the site of both factories and railroads, was a scene out of Dante's *Inferno*—fiery hot, noisy, and shrouded in a noxious atmosphere. This was true in every town; only the names of the contributors differed.

This meant that of all the possible uses of the river during the glory days of the towns along its course, residence and recreation were at the bottom of the list. In "the good old days" of the Schuylkill River towns, the only people who lived at the river's edge were the economic and social dregs of the community, the day laborers, bums, and alcoholics—those who for one reason or another could not afford to live anywhere else. The river flooded often in these lowest parts, and it stank all the time. In those days, a family's relative wealth could be determined by how far *away* it lived from the river. The better off the family, the farther up the hill it lived. As for recreation, well, there were brave attempts, some of which actually became locally popular for a brief time. These efforts, whether by private clubs or businesses, all utilized the water's surface, of course. If you immersed yourself in the river, the coal culm left you more grimy than when you entered, and there was not telling what other objects or organisms might have attached themselves to you. Even the boaters had to contend with the smell, not to mention the steady stream of unpleasant objects floating ever so slowly downriver. In "the good old days," people sought their leisure on higher ground.

Since then, industry has largely departed—the biggest ones in particular—and the old, decrepit buildings it left behind have been almost all torn down. The railroad is a mere shadow of itself, a commuter line for the Conshohockens and Norristown, and stretches that are still used—infrequently—for product transportation. All use electric or diesel power, so smoke and some noise have also disappeared. The departure of the industrial and transportation polluters, together with government mandates for municipal sewage systems, have combined to make enormous strides in cleaning up the river. The Schuylkill now is hugely different from back in the day. That fact deserves its place as one of the proudest achievements of the Pennsylvania Scenic River System Program.

The result of all this is that today, the relationship between the river and the towns along it has exactly reversed itself. Residence and recreation now top the list of popular activities along the Schuylkill River. Today, people pay more—sometimes much more—to live along the river. This would have been incomprehensible to everyone who lived in the Schuylkill basin prior to World War II. As for recreation, well, I could spend an entire post just listing the many ideas for enjoying the river that are making the news today, and could employ several posts to talk about them. Some are traditional, such as rowing, a Pennsylvania tradition. But history is not the point—not when it comes to the river. Dragon boat racing does not have much of a history on the Schuylkill River (you can take my word for it; I'm a historian), but the club in Norristown symbolizes just how little you need feel bound by what they did way back when, and how you can start your own traditions, from just about any source. (It also reminds all potential new users of the river what we of longtime residence along the river already know: if you don't secure it, it will float away.)

The need to actually ignore history is true not just for private groups, but for the river towns themselves, at least most of them. As history no longer serves as a guide, those towns whose riverfronts are not in much demand, Norristown and Bridgeport, to name just two, can pretty much start from scratch. No so for the Conshohockens. I've already mentioned the reason for this, but it cannot be overemphasized, because it has brought big money to the area. That's crucial, because a major difference between residence and recreation is that the former requires a great deal more upfront expenditure of capital. New single-family houses along the river would be quite expensive, and no one is building those. Not enough profit in it. What we are seeing are largely condominium or rental complexes of considerable size. They occupy former industrial sites, because rehabilitation projects for such sites ("brownfields") get lucrative financial subsidies and because, in the right location, they can be very profitable. There is one in West Norriton, and even a proposal pending for Bridgeport (although I am not sure of its current status).

Right now, however, the hot location for residences is the Conshohockens. The new residences—and the new office buildings, also—are evidence that the two boroughs will experience a very different future from the towns upriver with which both have always been grouped. There is a very fundamental—and very ancient—historical scenario playing out there, one that really does repeat itself, if you view it broadly enough. The reason is the same as it has always been: there is big money to be made. That money is bringing about big changes, which at this point may have actually only begun. Pottstown and Norristown would love to have even a small part of it happening in their towns. But something's lost when something's gained, and the size of what is being gained suggests that the Conshohockens could lose a lot. Last week, I inquired about what West Conshohocken might be losing. Next week I shift my gaze across the river, but my focus remains on what is fundamentally happening to both communities. I do so because it is all one happening, and all for the same reason. That makes it worth understanding.

2/13/15

Rebirth of *Part* of the Past

For a great many years, I routinely drove along Ridge Pike between Conshohocken and my home in West Norriton, and thus through Norristown. Just west of the SEPTA rail crossing was a large mural, visible to those driving west, out of town. The painting was of the old Valley Forge Hotel, with an appropriately 1920s-era automobile parked in front. Below it was the slogan, "Rebirth of the Past." (I never did learn the circumstances of its painting, so if anyone remembers, please let me know). What struck me every time I saw the mural was how wrong it was; the slogan, I mean. There will be no "rebirth of the past." That past that the Valley Forge Hotel symbolized is as dead and gone as the Valley Forge Hotel itself. The evidence is overwhelming. Industry, in the numbers and size worthy of capitalizing it, is not coming back to the Schuylkill River. Neither is the railroad network around which each town was built. In other words, the basic reasons for each river town coming into existence, growing, and prospering, *no longer exist*. But the towns still do; the question is: *as what*?

If the past is not coming back, then a rebirth of the river towns requires reinvention and reuse. Here is where the Phoenixville example is useful. Its revival is internally generated, and thus can be replicated. Phoenixville also demonstrates how a part of the past can be reborn, if it is also repurposed. That part is the old downtown, the core of which in Phoenixville is Bridge Street. The downtowns in the other river towns range from empty to underutilized, but Bridge Street is alive with shops, restaurants, and drinking establishments. A sure sign of prosperity is that parking is once again hard to find. A prosperous Bridge Street is the core around which literally every other component of Phoenixville's revival is built.

This is not exactly a secret, and that is why the larger towns—Norristown and Pottstown—do their best to promote their downtowns. The surviving downtowns are key to the rebirth of most, if not all, of the river towns, regardless of their size. Only West Conshohocken appears to be the exception, through no fault of its own. Whether Conshohocken will, at the end of the current building frenzy, actually have a downtown is yet uncertain. The future of the downtowns of Royersford and Spring City is equally uncertain—Spring City's due to its small size, and Royersford's due to the fact that much of its old downtown has been removed but not replaced. Whether there is a future for a Bridgeport downtown is the most open question, a fact of which its residents are well aware.

It would not be too far from the mark today to label the river towns—excepting Phoenixville—as examples of what we term "bedroom communities." That is a recent condition, however. For most of their history, each river town was a largely self-contained entity; the residents lived, worked, shopped, and worshipped all within the town boundaries. But that has changed. Living in one location, working in another one, and shopping in yet another one is pretty much the common theme today. The clearest examples are the automobile suburbs. Their residents live in housing developments, but they work elsewhere. They also shop and worship elsewhere, and require cars to get back and forth between these activities and their homes. The result is not a community in the true sense, because there are few opportunities for residents to relate to each other and to the condition of their common area of residence.

The automobile suburbs can never be more than bedroom communities because of how they were planned. Zoning ensures a separation between residences and businesses providing services to their occupants. The businesses that provide such services are gathered into artificial groupings designed (and located) to expedite the arrival and departure of automobiles, not walkers. Any real sense of community has been rendered close to physically impossible.

Our old towns are different. For those who want to avoid living in a bedroom community, the old river towns in particular can be ideal places to relocate. They are physically well suited to host a revival of community spirit, because of the closeness of everything. Their biggest advantage is their existing old (and therefore charming) downtowns. Phoenixville has an advantage here, but not a major one. It has the best preserved of the old downtowns, but Pottstown is not far behind, and Norristown possesses a small one that may be the best kept secret around.

To properly appreciate how much of an asset an old downtown can be, we must first understand how much has changed since our ancestors shopped in these old downtowns. The post–World War II prosperity, unprecedented in both its amount and its spread, has fundamentally revised the concept of shopping. The old downtowns had always offered everything, but that approach proved to be inadequate to compete with the new shopping centers and malls. Today, the bulk of our shopping for the essentials is still being done in those shopping centers and malls. But there is another kind of shopping, funded by that recent prosperity. Today, people spend more time shopping for the extras they can afford than for the necessities they need. Shopping has become recreation and, as with every form of recreation, the physical environment makes all the difference. People with cash to spend prefer to spend it not just on items they want, but to do so in locations they find entertaining. A number of customer surveys tell us that charming old downtowns are excellent locations for such "boutique" shopping centers.

The commercial cores of each river town used to be the place where the largest number of people interacted the most. They can be again, and you need look no further than Phoenixville to appreciate that, and what an asset an existing downtown can be. Want more proof? Get to Norristown— not to its famous old Main Street, but to its much less well known other shopping center on West Marshall Street. The old buildings not only remain but are almost fully occupied by both stores and restaurants. Walk down the great wide sidewalks and you can see the spirit of enterprise that is filling the shops, smell the food and hear music in the air. That is what I call hope for the future.

Want to live in a real community? By all means, visit Phoenixville and see for yourself how an old downtown has been reborn. Then check out West Marshall Street in Norristown to see one in the process. So why not Pottstown?

CHAPTER THREE

WHAT'S HAPPENING (OR NOT HAPPENING) IN . . .

Norristown

11/15/13   **#1 in a Series**

Logan Square: What It Was, and What It Wasn't Quite

News broke this past May that a mortgage foreclosure will probably send Logan Square up for sheriff's sale. For most of you, even in the Delaware Valley, the name Logan Square probably means nothing. Those who are aware of it—mostly people in the Norristown area—probably associate Logan Square with a recent financial debacle involving a proposed hotel and movie studio that will end up costing the county taxpayers a bundle.

A few, however, particularly the Norristown area's older residents (and some farther afield who also heard the news), remember Logan Square as a shopping center, what it was designed and built to be. The key here is "designed," and that's what makes the history of Logan Square relevant. I would, in fact, make the following argument: "The creation of Logan Square was a seminal event in the commercial history of southeastern Pennsylvania, a piece of local history that deserves to be better understood, and more widely appreciated."

Today, shopping centers proliferate in southeastern Pennsylvania (and elsewhere, I am told). They range in size from strip malls and local road intersection centers to the King of Prussia Mall, shortly to be the biggest of them all. Yet it wasn't too long ago that the first one appeared somewhere other than the Main Line, and that somewhere was the north end of Norristown. It was called Logan Square.

What makes Logan Square's history significant is that it was the first local shopping center *planned solely for the automobile*. There is some dispute over where and when the actual "first shopping center" appeared in the United States, but Suburban Square in Ardmore has the honor of being the first planned shopping center in the Philadelphia area. Its design inspired the design of Logan Square. But while Suburban Square, which appeared before the war, was designed to accommodate the automobile, it was deliberately built adjacent to the heavily used Main Line rail tracks. Logan Square, by contrast, was a very early example of what would soon become common—a shopping center accessed solely by automobile. A trolley line ran nearby, but it was clearly on its last legs by the end of the war, and was not counted on to deliver customers.

Well into the twentieth century, shopping centers outside Philadelphia were located where they always had been: in the towns and boroughs, and usually along a Main Street. We called these "downtowns." Most had not been planned; they had evolved and, in the process, grew rather like Topsy (it's a generational reference; if you don't get it, ask someone older than you). Unfortunately, they grew in the horse-and-buggy days, when no one had yet heard of the automobile, let alone the concept of parking. The automobile began to proliferate after the First World War, and by the eve of the Second, the downtowns of southeastern Pennsylvania were already feeling the resulting crunch. Afterward, things got worse, much worse.

In the late 1940s, a few forward-thinking entrepreneurs, recognizing early how the automobile would render virtually every urban downtown unsuitable for future shopping, thought of designing a new kind of shopping center, one built around the automobile. In other words, one with ample, free parking. Our downtowns could not be adapted; they had to be replaced. One such entrepreneur was Joseph Butera, who, advised by his uncle Harry, then the dean of local real estate agents, decided to locate his new idea at the very north end of Norristown, at the intersection of Swede Street and Johnson Highway.

Logan Square opened in 1954, after a construction phase that lasted only a little longer than the struggle to get the project approved in the first place. Norristown's downtown merchants fought it bitterly. History has shown that their fears were justified. Logan Square was a full frontal challenge to the shopping tradition that downtown Norristown represented. It quickly stole Sears from Main Street, where it had been since 1934, and continued to accommodate other stores that left downtown.

Logan Square prospered, for a brief period of time. Then the other neighborhood malls began to appear. They tended to be smaller than Logan Square, but they were more convenient to the residents in the new developments around Norristown. The King of Prussia and Plymouth Meeting Malls did not exactly help.

The story of Logan Square's decline is a complex one, and such things as the local economy and management decisions certainly played their part. Nothing is inevitable, but hindsight allows us to see clearly both what Logan Square was, and was it wasn't quite. As a historian, and leaving aside the complex local specifics, I see the story of Logan Square as something close to a tragedy, a pioneering idea that began a movement, and then fell victim to the movement it heralded.

That movement was to the periphery, away from downtown. That movement has taken place, leaving our traditional downtowns barren and crumbling. Logan Square began the movement; it just didn't move far enough. It was doomed at birth by a decision that seemed bold and progressive at the time: to locate an entirely new shopping center where it did. The actual municipality is not the point; had Logan Square been located just across the street (Johnson Highway) in East Norriton Township, it would probably have suffered the same fate. The fatal flaw was in the center's access roads. Don't let the term "Johnson Highway" fool you. It was a two-lane asphalt street when Logan Square opened; it lacked traffic lights, and it did not connect to any major local highway. It also came to a dead end one block east of the center. Swede Street south led down through Norristown, and thus to a desired market. Unfortunately, it also led out of town, where it intersected with the much larger and much more heavily trafficked Germantown Pike. Outside of town was where the new residents were appearing, and in short order, a whole array of mini-malls sprang up at the intersections of not only Germantown Pike and Swede Street, but also at the intersections of Ridge Pike, Butler Pike, and…well, the list goes on. These new residents needed many things to make their new suburban houses into homes, and it was just too difficult to get to Logan Square, given the other alternatives. As long as Sears remained, hope remained, but Sears finally left, long after it should have, and joined the crowd at King of Prussia Mall.

Had Logan Square been located out in a surrounding township (other than Upper Merion, of course), it might have survived. If the center itself did not survive, its buildings would most likely still be in use, however modified. The shopping centers of comparable size, or even smaller, located at the intersections of major local roads, have had a checkered history, but are still sites of commerce, and some are still shopping centers. Ground at the intersection of the local highways around Norristown still has commercial value; whether Logan Square's site within Norristown still does will be decided at auction. The urge to see the contrasting fates of Logan Square and its surrounding malls as a metaphor for post–World War II urban history is irresistible. How many of you were part of it?

4/11/14   **#2 in a Series**

Norristown Missing Financial Records? The "Good Old Days" Were Worse

People in Norristown—and elsewhere, I'll bet—are talking about the town's finances, spurred by two rather unusual events, probably related. In November of 2013, police escorted the finance director, Richard Zawisza, out of his office; he has been variously described since as being "on leave," or "on vacation." Then, in March 2014 came the news that the municipality of Norristown had not received its annual audit reports (required by law) for five years in a row, from 2008 through 2012. This was discovered by the new municipal administrator, Crandall Jones, shortly after he was hired in August 2013. There is reason to suspect that the two events are connected, because the municipal council is now paying more to the audit firms that did not complete their reports the first time. Why? Because, as Jones admitted, "They never completed those audit reports, through no fault of their own."

This is disturbing, and has given ammunition to those critical of Norristown municipal administration, particularly because the law surrounding "personnel matters" allows—no, *mandates*—little release of details to the public. Municipal critics are right to be concerned; we are talking about the public tax dollars here. There may be much more to this, or there may not.

What this event should *not* do is add to the already-pervasive attitudes of suspicion and worst assumptions that permeate the social media today, at least about such small municipalities as Norristown. This is an all-too-common problem, particularly when it is frequently fed horror stories, such as the one about that little town in Florida that seems to have not just practiced corruption, but institutionalized it. I've attacked this concept before as the "wrong attitude," arguing that it's simply not justified to believe that things are worse now than they used to be back in the "good old days." People carry around this myth that back then ("then" being some unspecified date in the past), honest administration kept employment up, taxes low, and crime down because we "didn't need no welfare state;

everybody pulled his weight,"[11] and all the rest of that nostalgic nonsense. If you think that it's only present-day Norristown that has incompetent administrators and council, let's return to those "good old days" for a lesson in historical context.

Back in 1975 (not so very old, but before both Section 8 and deinstitutionalization, remember?), Norristown's financial condition was far worse than just some missing audit reports. Norristown Borough Council, caught between a collapsing tax base and a political refusal to raise taxes, had failed to pass a 1975 budget by January 1 of that year, as required by law. At the March 1975 meeting, Councilman William Lessig, who had been appointed chairman of the finance committee the previous year, shared with his colleagues some of the singularly unpleasant things he had discovered during his brief tenure. Running a municipality requires complex and reliable financial records, and Lessig summarized the state of things in Norristown quite succinctly:

> "In a very short period of time, it became apparent to me that the record-keeping procedures employed by the borough fell into one or more of three classifications. They were either inaccurate, inadequate, or nonexistent."

Mind you, the borough council had every reason to see the crisis coming long before it arrived. Back in April 1974, the council realized that no tax collector's report had so far been submitted to it for that year, and resolved to write a letter asking the borough's tax collector to please do his job and prepare a report for each monthly meeting. The May meeting arrived, but the tax collector's report didn't. Council girded itself and wrote another letter asking for a report by the June meeting. The June meeting convened, but again, no tax collector's report. When pressed, Borough Manager James Coyle stated that he had talked to the tax collector by phone, and would send him another letter immediately. The July meeting convened, only to reveal that…wait for it…no report had been prepared. There is no mention in the council's meeting records whether anyone went so far as to speak to the tax collector in person, or to take other such drastic measures in later months, but to wrap up this part of the story, the Norristown Borough tax collector did not file a single report for the entire year of 1974.

Councilman Lessig also offered evidence that the tax collector's report was

---

11. Lee Adams (lyrics) and Charles Strouse (music), "Those Were The Days," 1971.

by no means the only problem, and that the problems were anything but new. Such things should have been reported during the annual audit and, as it turned out, the auditors had done exactly that. Lessig produced a series of statements by previous auditors that had pointed out the borough's lack of even the most basic elements of financial oversight. In other words, the auditors weren't at fault this time, either. Here is a brief selection of those statements, going back to 1969 (the even better years, right?):

> 1969: "We are signing this report under protest." The borough had no official competent in the field of finance, the treasurer had signed blank checks, and the petty cash account was "impossible to audit, figures were written over, erased or illegible."

> 1973: The borough kept no books at all for its secondary funds, bank statements were missing, and there were no controls on investments.

> 1975: "The general fund, receipts and disbursements, has not been reconciled with the cash in the bank. In other words, the books are not in balance." And "there isn't any list of delinquent real estate tax receivables for all prior years up to and including 1974."

I'm not even tempted to make the obvious "the more things change…" reference about this matter, because I believe it would be a rhetorical cheap shot, and unjustified. The full story behind the missing audit reports and the dismissal of the finance director has yet to come out, and given the strict controls over "personnel issues," it might never. But unless someone uncovers something more substantially wrong than uncompleted audits, there's really no comparing Norristown government today to Norristown government then, in financial matters or on any other subject. The borough structure of members elected from different wards had long since reduced both the council and administration to competing miniempires utterly unable to even visualize what was good for the entire town, let alone act on it. The mayor had little real power, and the borough manager had none (the office was a revolving door for years, as optimistic managers arrived and frustrated ones left). The problem was not one of individuals (although many certainly contributed); it was systemic. In other words, when it comes to lack of vision or lack of several other characteristics desirable in municipal leaders, those of Norristown today cannot hold a candle to those of Norristown yesterday. People who look back with nostalgia on the "good old days of Norristown," and include local government in that rosy remembrance, don't know what they're talking about.

So, whatever you may feel regarding how today is worse than when you were growing up, try to accept that this "things have been going to hell since [insert your own favorite here]" is part of the human condition; every generation feels it. It is not history, and we really must understand and deal with this tendency if we want to know the truth, not some collection of self-serving myths. Many things really have changed, and this one, at least, for the better.

7/25/14   **#3 in a Series**

The History of a Volunteer Fire Department: Preserved in Alcohol?

The loss of a volunteer fire company is a grievous blow to any community, a loss that cuts much deeper than just that of fire protection. Norristown's Humane Fire Company officially closed its building at #129 East Main Street in early 2012, a site it had occupied since 1852, the year of its formation. The reason was an all-too-common one these days: the dwindling number of people willing to be volunteer firefighters. The company merged with the Norristown Hose Fire Company, and moved its equipment.

The Humane Fire Company is gone, but its building—and more important, its history—are not being lost. Two partners have purchased the building, and obtained the necessary financing to renovate it and open a microdistillery called "Five Saints." This could be an outstanding addition to Main Street when it opens in January 2016. The project has the full support of Norristown Municipal Council, as it should.

It's good news that the building will be saved, and a micro-distillery might be just the type of trendy new spot that will bring people to Norristown for recreation, which is the best news of all. But there is one more reason to celebrate, and it's the one I want to highlight.

The building's new owners have pledged to preserve the old firehouse's memory, and make it the central component of their local identity. Norristown residents, regardless of whether they even drink or not, should be pleased about that. Such a pledge could mean many things, and only time will tell. I am all in favor of preserving an old firehouse, but I hope that the new occupant's commitment to telling the story of the building it calls home will go beyond displaying curious hats, items of brass, and yellowed photographs. That's nostalgia, not history, and the Humane Fire Company was an important part of the real history of Norristown. That makes it a potentially rich source of badly needed knowledge about the way things really were "back in the day," and we can all use more of that.

Volunteer fire companies used to exist everywhere, but they were of particular significance to our smaller towns. A town's volunteer fire companies are, together with its ethnic churches, the best windows into its past. Even the obvious things about these companies have meaning. The fact that Norristown's different fire companies have different color schemes was not accidental; they symbolize the ethnic affiliations of their founders. When you look below the surface, you find even more meaning woven into their very existence.

Volunteer fire companies came into existence because fire was the omnipresent danger in those towns during their period of growth, but they were social organizations first and foremost. They may not actually have been all that effective at their primary task until well into the twentieth century—the history of the Schuylkill River towns is rife with accounts of devastating fires—but ultimately their most important function was as symbols of civic organization and individual belonging. This went way beyond parades, the social function for which they are best known.

Their influence overlapped with that of the ethnic religious congregations in each town, because they were reflections of those groups. These ethnic populations set the tone within each town (largely in their order of arrival), and the fire companies reflect that history. Geography played a part, of course, because each company was established to serve a specific physical area. Still, ethnic discrimination shaped who lived where in a town of any size, making geography largely an expression of ethnicity. Who could join what department and who couldn't was universally understood, if not openly expressed. In the larger towns on the Schuylkill River, size allowed repetition, which meant that the different volunteer companies could divide along ethnic lines. In the smallest ones, this was much more problematic.

Another reason fire companies could discriminate was that they had a large pool of applicants to draw from. The nineteenth century (and well into the twentieth) was also a time that membership in local organizations was absolutely central to the social life of both individuals and families. No mass media meant no mass culture; very few people focused much attention beyond their narrowly defined communities. Community organizations—civic, service, religious, and commemorative—flourished.

Volunteer fire companies were prestigious organizations, and membership in them was highly desired. Ethnicity and location determined what company a man might join, but the underlying reason was that in those days men lived and worked in the same town, and thus had a vested interest in protecting it from fires.

But that was then. This is now, and things have changed. We no longer live in a locally centered culture; we have much more free time than in the old days, but also a great many more calls on it. Perhaps the most important change for firefighters is the fact that today very few people live and work in the same town; the availability of volunteers can be chancy. Thus, fire companies have come to depend on paid firefighters to staff the houses, but still face the prospect of consolidation and closure. Their loss means that rich sources of local history are disappearing.

There is so much that the history of a volunteer company can teach us about the history of our towns, and how much has changed since the glory days of both. The fact that ethnic discrimination lies at the foundation of that history has been almost ignored in the telling of their history. They are the subjects of such veneration, and the reality of their time is so distant from us that they have become myths themselves, each with a carefully shaped and polished appearance designed to obscure the truth that lies within.

Norristown's Humane Fire Company was no exception. John George's partner in this effort, Louis "Jay" Rachelli, might have a personal reason to promote an understanding of its central—if unpleasant—truth. The Company's location on East Main Street made it the only company located in the east end, and the population of the east end was overwhelmingly Italian. Yet as late as 1950, the Humane Fire Company had never admitted an Italian member. That little fact should serve up some interesting questions, of course. Did this policy change and, if so, when? What about Norristown's other companies? How long did they retain their original complexion? Do they have any remaining traditions about membership?

I have been writing frequently of the need to know the truth about our past if we want to make our future better. That's why words and phrases like "racism" and "ethnic discrimination" pepper my blog posts. In this post, I have simply added one more component to the picture and, I hope, thereby opened one more door to that better future. This isn't about uncovering dark secrets; fire companies and what each represented are part of the history of our towns. The fact that they did not display the attitudes of today should surprise no one, nor should anyone try to sugarcoat history out of some misplaced sense of shame. This was a time when overt discrimination against any number of "others" could be openly practiced, so ethnic divisions among fire companies must be understood in context. Our volunteer fire companies played a role in shaping our communities that was both vital and multifaceted. The fact that one or more of those facets are displeasing to the modern eye is not a reason to obscure them. It is, rather a reason to highlight them, because only the truth will set you free.

8/1/14   #4 in a Series

Deinstitutionalization Déjà Vu in Norristown?

This is actually my first post on that ever-controversial subject of housing—fair, affordable, subsidized, call it what you will. It won't seem that way, because the immediate subject is a specious "threat" to housing in Norristown. I begin with it because that allows me to dismiss the threat as nonexistent, freeing me in later posts to focus on the relevant issues. Doing it this way also allows me to demonstrate that even "authoritative" sources should be viewed with a skeptical eye, and I never miss a chance to make that point.

Deinstitutionalization is the word used to describe a period when society concluded that treatment of needy individuals is better accomplished in a community setting than by incarcerating them in institutions. It is considered to be an outgrowth of the Civil Rights movement. Until 1963, standard policy had been to send the mentally ill or the mentally retarded away, to "institutionalize" them, due to the cultural stigma surrounding both conditions. In 1963, President Kennedy signed the Community Mental Health Centers Act, which initiated a new national policy to serve people in the community, in "the least restrictive environment," and not isolated in hospitals. The Commonwealth of Pennsylvania followed in 1966 with the Mental Health/Mental Retardation Act. The state's plan was to grow the community-based services that the patients being released would need.

At least, that was the way it was supposed to go. The release of people judged capable of living in a community environment with varying levels of assistance proceeded apace; by the late 1960s, Norristown State Hospital (NSH) was releasing people in accordance with the directive. This is not well understood locally; most date deinstitutionalization as after "the Broderick Decision" in *Halderman v. Pennhurst*, which was issued in 1977. The Pennhurst case contributed to the local wave of deinstitutionalization, but Pennhurst was a state hospital that housed only persons suffering from mental retardation. Norristown State Hospital housed only patients with mental illness. There were many court decisions involved in the overall process, but they became subsumed into a national advocacy movement for several groups of people.

Unlike Pennhurst, Norristown State Hospital was not closed down, but it did discharge many patients judged capable of living in the community with assistance. The subsequent experience of both the individuals themselves and the Norristown community into which they were inserted provides a microcosm of what happened nationally. Neither the federal government nor the Commonwealth of Pennsylvania (nor any other state, for that matter) ever provided the funds necessary to properly establish, let alone grow, the community services that both the mentally ill and the mentally retarded needed so desperately. The level of support some of these people needed was underestimated, as was their economic situation. These people were not only poor, but most had little or no experience in holding down a job or even living in a nonmedical community.

Deinstitutionalization was yet another example of a good idea that suffered greatly in its execution. It was a national disaster, pretty much all the way around. Although it improved the conditions of some of its intended beneficiaries, it consigned far too many to homelessness and life on the streets. Locally, it removed NSH as a community asset it had always been, one of Norristown's largest employers. The exact number of how many people moved into some form of assisted living—as well as where they were moved to—is lacking, although an attempt was made to reintroduce as many as possible back into the communities from where they had come. Even if the numbers could be pinned down, they would not convey the perception that arose about the damage being done to Norristown. The chapter about Norristown in *Montgomery County: The Second Hundred Years*, the county's official bicentennial publication in 1984, contains a telling quote (on page 470) about the effects of deinstitutionalization on the community:

> "Quite a few residents, still on government assistance, were once under treatment at Norristown State Hospital, Eagleville Hospital and Rehabilitation Center, or some other nearby institution. In 1980, about

sixty-five halfway houses were scattered about the borough to the dismay and annoyance of many a citizen."

The quote is twice unfortunate; it's unclear on actual numbers and confusing in its use of terminology. How many constituted "quite a few"? This would have been useful to know, because sixty-five halfway houses is a large number, particularly as halfway house sounds suspiciously like "group home." The phraseology certainly leads you to believe that rather more than sixty-five individuals were causing "dismay and annoyance" in Norristown that year.

Even greater confusion arises from incorrect terminology. A "halfway house" is one housing alcohol or drug patients on a temporary basis. They do not house those with extensive mental illness or mental retardation extensive enough to have hospitalized them in the first place. Besides, the assistance needed by such people is permanent; there is no "halfway" involved. "Halfway house" had already assumed the status of all-inclusive buzzword, and its use only serves to confuse, not enlighten.

This conflation of separate subjects has assumed the status of conventional wisdom among those who lived in Norristown during that era, and left a residual fear that it could happen all over again. This is why the numbers do not matter; the perception does.

A document entitled "2012 Analysis of Impediments to Fair Housing Choice for Norristown, " prepared by Urban Design Ventures, of Homestead, Pennsylvania, stokes that fear. It is the kind of official document one sees frequently these days, a combination of American bureaucracy and Maoist "self-criticism," wherein municipalities or programs sum up what they have failed to accomplish and lay out how they are going to correct their shortcomings in the future. It was prompted, I suspect, by the mounting complaints about how housing choice vouchers are being distributed in Montgomery County. It can be found on Norristown's website. I will reference it again, on the subject of fair housing choice itself, but the document also addresses the possibility that mental patients might be released into Norristown once again, perhaps even replicating the town's previous experience with deinstitutionalization. This must be disposed of before we move to actual problems.

Impediment Nine (there are more) is "Deinstitutionalization of Norristown State Hospital Patients." This is what follows that title:

> "With the reduction in the number of inpatients that will be housed in the state mental health care facility in Norristown, there is a possibility that the dispersal will be into the surrounding neighborhoods, where there are more rental units than single family homes, and the area is already impacted."

There are two problems with this statement. First, it appears to assume that a reduction in the number of mental patients at NSH is actually being planned. There is no—repeat no—evidence that such a move has even crossed anyone's mind. Norristown State Hospital is a mere shadow of its former self, but it remained open when several other state hospitals were closed, and is now an integral part of a regional program of health services.

Second, the sentence's tone seems to indicate that there are many mental patients still in NSH, enough for their release to impact the municipality's housing market. This is also not true. Although NSH now serves the entire eastern half of Pennsylvania, its mental population is capped at eighty-six beds, with each county allotted a specific number. There are actually one hundred thirty people housed there at present, the result of other counties exceeding their caps, as ordered by different courts. These are actually patients from the criminal section, which is a cause for concern. Of these one hundred thirty however, only twenty-two beds are allotted to residents of Montgomery County. Even if some court were to order NSH closed (a more than farfetched proposition), only those twenty-two people would be released into Montgomery County, and not all into Norristown. The remainder would be sent to their home counties. But that is not going to happen anyway. Deinstitutionalization in Norristown is over, and it's not coming back. It is long past time to focus on *real* issues.[12]

Pottstown

2/14/14   #1 in a Series

What's in a Number? The Route of US Route 422

Back in 1985, the US Department of Transportation changed the route one of its "shield" highways, US 422. Actually, it changed only a portion of one

---

12. My thanks to Nancy Wieman, Montgomery County deputy administrator for Mental Health Services, for the information contained above.

section of the route, at its eastern terminus. This was by no means the first such change; US Route 422 had seen changes in designation several times before. People took notice, adjusted, and then went on about their business. The opening of the final segment of the "Pottstown Expressway" occasioned the change, and in turn became part of the new route of Route 422. The opening of this long-anticipated highway was a most welcome event, but almost totally overlooked in the celebration was the enormous symbolism behind this simple act.

An early historian of the Philadelphia area named John Faris described the main roads out of the city as being "fan-shaped." They exited the city and spread out along the compass points from north to south (except east, of course). Two of the earliest roads to fan out from Philadelphia to its northwest were Germantown Pike and Ridge Pike; their origins date back to the eighteenth century. Germantown Pike first connected a much smaller Philadelphia to Germantown, and then gradually added points beyond. Ridge Pike extended out from Philadelphia following, roughly, the "ridge" of the Schuylkill River's left bank, also in fits and starts.

As settlement spread to the northwest, so did these two roads, until they came together to cross the Perkiomen Creek at Collegeville. From there, one road continued on as Germantown Pike to Pottstown, gradually extending the area of southeast Pennsylvania that could access Philadelphia. The railroads would do the heavy lifting, but the lifeblood of local commerce flowed between Philadelphia and its northwestern environs along Germantown Pike and Ridge Pike. They remained the main roads in southeastern Pennsylvania for people to access Philadelphia until the 1960s. The opening of the Schuylkill Expressway would begin their demise as the area's main roads, and hasten the decline of Philadelphia itself. The culmination of this process was the rerouting of US Route 422.

Both the Germantown and Ridge Pikes never needed any validation of their importance in southeastern Pennsylvania, but the US government provided one anyway when it established the first national highway system in 1926–27. In every region of the country, engineers (and politicians) examined the local roads, and selected from them the main ones—the ones that connected major towns and carried the most traffic. These were awarded the "shield" designation as a US highway, according to an overall numbering system. The road connection between Philadelphia and its northwest was designated US Route 422 in 1927. (The history of plain old

Route 422 is actually much longer, but a very complicated story.)

Over the succeeding decades, substantial changes in the highway's actual route took place. To greatly simplify, the shield designation was applied to both Germantown Pike and Ridge Pike for the section between Collegeville and Philadelphia at different times, while largely continuing on Germantown Pike from there. These changes included the highway's terminus in Philadelphia itself, which moved eastward in stages to the Delaware River.

The designation of these local highways as a US Route was more than symbolic. They became broader lines on local road maps, further encouraging their use for travel, commercial development, and residential construction. All spread population and commerce along them prior to World War II. This meant that by war's end, while both pikes continued to be primary access roads to Philadelphia, local traffic on them had also greatly increased.

The explosive population growth outside of Philadelphia after the war was initially dependent on these pikes and their counterparts along other points of the compass, with a predictable result: traffic congestion. Strip shopping centers appeared along their paths, and their intersections with the more significant local roads across their paths sprouted small to medium-size shopping centers.

Then came the era of limited-access highways. Such a highway made its first appearance northwest of Philadelphia in 1950, when the Pennsylvania Turnpike's Eastern Extension arrived in the quiet farmland of Upper Merion Township, known (only locally, then) as King of Prussia. It stopped there only briefly before proceeding to the Delaware River. Not long afterward came the start of a Northeast Extension. Philadelphia reached out to this new highway via the Schuylkill Expressway; a fundamental motivation (although by no means the only one) for the road's construction was to lure traffic from the turnpike to the city. Roads work their will in both directions, however, and it wasn't too long before people realized that the net value was heading out of Philadelphia, not into it.

An entirely new US Route 422 between Philadelphia and Pottstown was a late entry in the road-building sweepstakes of the period. That, to a degree, accounts for its prolonged, section-by-section construction over a period of twenty years. The first flush of interstate road building had passed, while opposition to these highways had risen—as had their costs. The story of this route is a fascinating one, and I shall continue on with it in my next post. For now, however, I will jump ahead to the date of its conclusion: 1985. This new section of highway, built to interstate highways standards, became the new route of US Route 422.

Remember how I mentioned above that the terminus of US Route 422 had changed over the years? It did so again in 1985, in a big way. Its previous relocations had moved it steadily eastward within Philadelphia, until it reached the New Jersey border. This time, however, the terminus of US Route 422 was not only moved to the west, it was removed from Philadelphia altogether. Since 1985, it has ended at its intersection with US Route 202, in King of Prussia. You can still get to Philadelphia, but you have to take two additional roads (at least) to actually get there.

By 1985, what had happened to Germantown Pike and Ridge Pike had happened to the other main roads that had always connected Philadelphia to its environs. US Routes 1 and 30 still entered the city, but they had become local roads, despite considerable upgrading. The new main roads were the Interstate highways, and of them, only I-95 actually entered Philadelphia; by that date, a bypass, I-476, was well under way. Not an designated an Interstate highway, but built to Interstate standards, US Route 422 was merely joining the new main roads that direct traffic to the new regional economic and social hub of southeastern Pennsylvania: King of Prussia.

The symbolism is obvious, for it describes not just changes in a region's main roads, but of the region itself. For fifty-nine years, US Route 422 had connected Philadelphia to the wide swath of land—and its people—to its northwest. The actual roads that bore the "US Route" designation had served that same purpose for over two centuries. A numerical change in 1985 symbolized the much greater change that had taken place: for some two hundred fifty years, from the early Colonial period to 1985, the main roads in southeastern Pennsylvania converged on Philadelphia. Now they converge on King of Prussia.

For southeastern Pennsylvania, that pretty much sums up the last half of the twentieth century, doesn't it?

Why Did They Build the "Pottstown Expressway"?

Earlier I talked about how the completion of a limited-access highway between the Schuylkill River and Pottstown symbolized the shift in wealth and power from Philadelphia to the suburbs. While this was not quite the last link in the bypassing of Philadelphia (the final section of I-476, the "Blue Route," had not yet opened), the rerouting of US Route 422 to King of Prussia would contribute further to the decline of the city. Its story also provides insight into the process by which our super highways were designed and built.

Hopes for a modern highway to connect King of Prussia and Pottstown date back a long way; the thought had probably occurred to everyone who had traveled along Germantown Pike the entire distance, from town to town and stoplight to stoplight, for the several decades it provided the best route available. The real push began, however, after the Schuylkill Expressway appeared on the scene. Not just Pottstown, but the communities between it and King of Prussia began to express official hope that the Expressway could be "extended" to the northwest. That didn't happen, and no concrete plan (pun intended) emerged before the public backlash against Interstate construction gathered force. Financing became tighter, and construction of the system largely ground to a halt before the last portions of the grand plan had been implemented. The lower section of what was to become US Route 422 got caught up in the extremely complicated maneuvering that followed.

Thus was born the pitch to build the Pottstown Expressway. The construction of a limited-access highway to replace Germantown Pike was sold to the public largely for its benefit to the long-distressed borough of Pottstown, with the new US Route 422 cast in the role of lifeline. Of course, connecting anyone or anything to Pottstown was not the road's true purpose, although that would have been an appreciated side benefit. This substantial stretch of highway was constructed to foster development in what was then still largely rural land west of the then-existing Route 422 on Germantown Pike. This was undeveloped land, with a few ancient roads crossing it. The intersections of these roads and the new highway would create prime commercial space, while the rolling fields close to those intersections would be perfect locations for housing developments. Thus, in obedience to the real estate dictum about location, location, and location, the exact route where the new highway would be built became quite important.

Mind you, none of this was new, in any way. There is always a web of influence, both financial and political, around selecting the exact path of a road, and there always has been. A thorough study of the influences contending over this project would produce some interesting revelations, and not just about how the prime commercial locations came to be. Close to the road's southern end, for example, it takes a very roundabout—and thus expensive—path to avoid an estate known as "Fatland" that has been around since colonial times. Whether this was due to concern for historic preservation or because the estate's owner was Peter J. Camiel, who was chairman of both the Pennsylvania Turnpike Commission and the Philadelphia Democratic Party at the time, is officially uncertain.

By the way, the Pottstown Expressway does not actually connect to Pottstown itself, but to another limited-access highway, the Pottstown Bypass, that is technically part of the same highway, Route 422. This bypass at the highway's northern end and the high bridge over the Schuylkill at its southern end were built first, both being completed by 1967 (a portion of the Schuylkill bridge opened earlier, due to a local traffic crisis). The short-term effect was to give drivers an easy way to avoid Pottstown altogether, while teasing drivers in King of Prussia with the vista of a promised future while they were being shuttled onto a distinctly local road, Pennsylvania Route 363. The thirteen-mile gap between the two was subject to numerous delays, for a multitude of reasons. An intermediate section opened in 1978, but the Pottstown Expressway did not open from end to end until 1985. The total cost of the highway by that time had reached $102 million.

The twenty-year delay in the road's construction made all the difference. Some investors had speculated early, but after the exact route of the road was known (not to be confused with "publicly known"), the jockeying for property and financing really began. The spasmodic appearance of the road's sections then proceeded to play hell with even those calculations, reminding all involved that while location, location, and location are important, timing is everything. Thus, while the eventual profit from development along the new route was basically guaranteed, the vagaries of the financial and real estate sectors served to enrich some but not others, largely according to the timing.

Once the new highway was fully opened between King of Prussia, and christened US Route 422, development did indeed take off. It has included pharmaceutical laboratories, churches, and schools, in addition to the guaranteed housing developments and shopping centers. Development extends along service roads parallel to US Route 422, and for short distances along each of the roads that intersect it, as everyone could have predicted.

But what about Pottstown? What has been the road's effect on it? The most obvious physical result has been the Hanover Square Townhomes, at the foot of the old industrial district. One hopes that its residents contribute to downtown Pottstown (an easy walking distance) in their off-hours, because few probably work there. The company's sales pitch on its website features this statement: "Hanover Square lies just off Route 422 and the Route 202 corridor [this last is something of a stretch], offering easy access to Philadelphia, thirty-five miles to the southeast, and Reading, twenty miles to the northwest." Clearly, the marketing emphasis is not local. That doesn't mean it isn't a step forward for the borough, which could use an influx of people who can afford such housing.

Has US Route 422 brought other measurable benefits to Pottstown? I'd like to hear more from local residents on this point.

While how much benefit the new US Route 422 has been to Pottstown is debatable, there is no question as to its effect on all that undeveloped land along its path. In the final analysis, the new road did what it was intended to do: earn a great deal of money for those investors whose good political connections allowed them to purchase land in the right place at the right time, as well as for those politicians with good business connections (meaning *only* as political contributions, of course).

4/3/15   #3 in a Series

The "Pottstown Expressway": Opposite Ends, Opposite Fates

A development proposal presented to West Norriton Township, Pennsylvania, my home of long residence, that allows me to revisit the subject of a previous post. The fact that this new tidbit provides additional evidence that I was right the first time probably influenced my decision.

Picture, if you will, a road—a rather new and modern superhighway, lanes separated by a median, accessible only by grade-separated cloverleafs, pretty much the whole nine yards. It is very heavily traveled in both directions. At each end is a housing development. They are by no means mirror images of one another, but both were built to take advantage of the new highway and the traffic it would bring. That traffic has materialized— more than had been planned for. (Surprise, surprise!) The development at the road's eastern end not only prospers, it has recently offered plans for a dramatic increase in the number of units. The one at the western end? Opinions differ, but only in varying degrees of disappointment. Why should this be? For starters, because one development is adjacent to King of Prussia, while the other is in Pottstown.

The fate of these two projects, one at each end of a new road, is testimony to how the construction of a road can be sold to the general public as one thing, when it is actually something quite different. The road about which I write is US Route 422, and I have written about it before, in my post on February 20, 2014 (*Why Did They Build the "Pottstown Expressway"?*). That post contains what you should know about the project, but here is a brief summary: The road was sold to the public (who would pay for it) as a benefit to a needy community at one end. Its true purpose, however, was to open for development the land along the road itself, to the benefit of a very different group of people.

The success of the road's real purpose is beyond obvious, whether you live in the area or just have to drive through it. This post is essentially just piling on, but the contrast between the two ends of the road has many facets, none of them good for Pottstown. That deserves to be better known.

The two housing developments in question were built to take advantage of the same two things: a scenic river along which people would want to live, and a new, modern road to connect the new residents to their workplaces some distance away. That very same combination—with a much stronger road component—is what drives the current building frenzy in the Conshohocken area, but it attracts the roving eye of entrepreneurs wherever it occurs.

It did so at each end of the "Pottstown Expressway," and two entrepreneurs chose to build housing developments at those points. Pottstown Borough Council approved the Hanover Square Townhomes project in 2005. The site had earlier hosted Mrs. Smith's Pies, and great hopes were entertained for this repurposing of abandoned land. Ownership changes and the economy postponed groundbreaking until 2009, after which the construction site was sold again, this time to Cornell Homes Inc. It initially offered townhouses for sale, but the lack of response led to offering some for rent. This has had decidedly mixed results. Hanover Square currently advertises itself as "the lowest-priced new home community in the Philadelphia area," which I guess tells you something. As for amenities, a former spokesperson offered the following: "There are a lot of amenities; for this community we are looking at the Schuylkill River and the Schuylkill River Trail. It's also only twenty minutes from King of Prussia." As local amenities go, that is pretty thin. Many might also question the "twenty minutes from King of Prussia."

The eastern site is also an old industrial one, repurposed. The area is known as Betzwood, after an early industrialist, and has hosted several occupants, but its brief early twentieth-century turn as a movie studio for a silent film production company, Lubin Manufacturing Company, is its chief claim to fame. It sits at the foot of the high bridge over the Schuylkill at that point, not quite at the end of US Route 422, which is just a short distance away after crossing the river. Brian O'Neill, who specializes in converting former brownfield industrial sites (and is a major player downriver in Conshohocken), won approval for what became The Lofts at Valley Forge.[13] Additional units were later built on the same site, just downriver from The Lofts, and named Riverview Landing. Its website inexplicably identifies Eagleville its location, but it is really in West Norriton.

While Hanover Square emphasizes affordability, The Lofts and Riverview Landing aim rather more upscale. The Lofts pitches itself as "luxury waterfront homes for the Philadelphia and King of Prussia area." True, it is a considerably more picturesque location than that of Hanover Square, although marred by the huge bridge virtually overhead. The bridge, of course, is what quickly connects their residents to King of Prussia, so its looming presence be damned. Without it, there would be no Lofts at Valley Forge or Riverview Landing in the first place. Want more evidence of success at this end of the road? The Lofts and Riverview Landing are about to be joined by an additional 1,330 more apartments in four large

---

13. In the interest of full disclosure, I confess that I, upon discovering that the original plans for The Lofts called for the destruction of the only two remaining buildings from the Lubin area, contacted the late Dr. Joseph Eckhardt, the leading authority on the Lubin studios. Together, we successfully lobbied for their retention. I must also note that the developers have written a request to West Norriton Township to allow the conversion of these two buildings into residences, in addition to all the others.

buildings, somehow squeezed into the same site. West Norriton has received the "conditional use" request, and unless the township commissioners somehow grow a backbone and insist on more than one entrance for all these people and their cars, we can expect construction to start in due course.

So, it's location, location, and location, right? King of Prussia is "happening" (and for those who crave something different, Phoenixville is nearby), and Pottstown isn't, despite the lifeline road having been in place for some years now. No one calls it the Pottstown Expressway any more; that was just a campaign slogan. It's just Route 422 now. You can read a great deal about US Route 422, and about its traffic nightmares and proposed solutions, but you won't read anything about how it has energized Pottstown, because it hasn't. Then again, that wasn't its real purpose in the first place, remember? That was just the party line, and if you control the terms of the discourse, you determine the result.

Phoenixville

1/2/15   #1 in a Series

Why Phoenixville?

Historians ask a lot of questions, but all of them are designed to eventually provide an answer to the Only Real Question: "Why?" That's why we amass facts and dispute their significance. Who, what, where, and when are necessary, but ultimately only why matters. So here's a fact: Phoenixville, Pennsylvania, is the only town on the lower Schuylkill River undergoing a locally generated community revival. I employ the phrases "locally generated" and "community" to distinguish what is happening there from what is happening to the Conshohockens. As I have written, both the Conshohockens are essentially being overwhelmed by outside forces. Phoenixville, by contrast, is not only retaining its community-centered identity, it is strengthening it.

So why Phoenixville?

In 1980, Phoenixville stood in company with the other towns on the lower Schuylkill; its industrial backbone had virtually disintegrated, and its once-prosperous commercial section was suffering, just as those of all the other towns. Thirty years later, only Phoenixville has crafted a revival on its own terms. Pottstown, Spring City, Royersford, Norristown, and Bridgeport remain in stagnation, still seeking what Phoenixville has found.

I don't know "why Phoenixville," but I am very interested in finding out. I am asking this question, and putting it out not just to borough residents themselves, but to every reader who can contribute something. An understanding of the underlying (that is, the "real") reasons will help to sustain Phoenixville's upward momentum, and could be very useful to those towns on the river that still stagnate. That makes such an understanding a goal worth seeking.

That's why I am not going to discuss (at least not initially), Phoenixville's current "trendiness." Such an appellation had to follow revival, although as with the other subjects just below, success can be reinvested, and what begins as results can contribute to future success.

I'm also going to quickly discuss and dispense with the two other things for which Phoenixville is most widely known. Neither of these are reasons for revival; they represent only opportunities, but Phoenixville has taken both and literally run—or paraded—with them. That has made them continuing contributors to community revival. The first is the Firebird Festival, which builds on the fact that Phoenixville possesses the perfect name for a reviving town. The myth of the phoenix is that of a new, vibrant creature reborn from the ashes of a previous existence. It's the perfect metaphor, and in Phoenixville's case one that is literally appropriate. Phoenixville has also received a big break from a most unlikely source: a "B movie" (at best) called *The Blob*, which has become a national cult favorite. Here we must also credit Phoenixville's penchant for historic preservation, for if the Colonial Theatre—the site at which the "people flee in panic" scene was originally filmed—had fallen to the wrecking ball, there probably wouldn't be any *Blob*fest.

All public events are about having fun, and the *Blob*fest is a pretty good example—fun that is both growing and expanding in concept. The Firebird Festival is certainly about having fun, but it is about rather more than that, and provides a more promising avenue of exploration about the phenomenon that is Phoenixville. The Firebird Festival exploits both Phoenixville's name and its industrial history, but it is a community event that is increasingly all about creativity, a concept more easily connected to the myth of the phoenix than a sci-fi movie, even one that has achieved cult status. Its organizers seem to be deliberately creating an East Coast version of Burning Man, employing its "use up and promise to do again, only better" approach to stimulate newer, broader, and even more committed festivals each year. There is, unfortunately, a downside to betting everything on the gradual buildup to a climactic act of consuming by fire. The Firebird Festival discovered this last year, as Burning Man did a few years ago. This approach seems to tempt those who would preempt a community festival with a little personal vandalism. Still, it didn't deter Burning Man, and it won't deter the Firebird Festival.

Phoenixville's name, and its connections to pop history (and even more significant, to industrial history), are gifts that other river towns greatly envy. These unique assets must be acknowledged, but the point is that they have been exploited properly, and have become woven into Phoenixville's image as a reviving town. The same is true for the many other events that populate the calendar in Phoenixville. The borough boasts a great many community festivals and celebrations, including rather more organized runs than *Blob*fest. There are more than can be listed here, let alone described. Yet these, even together with the big ones, are not causes for revival; they are results that have been reinvested and now contribute also. But results of what?

As regards these events, one thing is certain: while Phoenixville can give thanks to those gifts history has bestowed upon it, those gifts have been very well employed. The popularity and usefulness of all these efforts did not just magically appear. Their success derives from the vision and hard work of the people who seized these opportunities and made them contributors to a strong community. Yes, Phoenixville possesses the raw materials, but these elements' contribution to the revival was by no means automatic; the right people had to be in place. Phoenixville seems to possess such people in the private sector, and they are numerous.

So, continuing on the subject of people, we can list people in the private sector for sure. But how about the quality of leadership from elected municipal officials? This has to be a community decision, because the evidence up and down the river is ambiguous. Some Conshohocken residents claim that the boroughs' breakthrough required an infusion of "fresh blood" into municipal government. Pottstown activists tend to agree that such an infusion is sorely overdue in their town, and focus on the council chairman, who has been in office for fifteen years. Yet Phoenixville recently saw the retirement of the man who had been its mayor for thirteen years, and everyone applauded his achievements, not his departure. Both are Conshohocken and Phoenixville are boroughs, but of different variations. Norristown was a borough, too, but changed its municipal structure…then changed it again. It has no mayor. "New blood" sits on Norristown Council, but the town continues to stagnate. Clearly, no conclusions can be drawn from this small sample, except perhaps that it depends on the people, not the structure. I look forward to hearing from readers on that subject, because that's where the real differences come in.

I'm sure there is more to be said about people (and not just to explain why there are people I plan to mention), and I want to hear about this from readers. But not just about people, because while a community revival must have the right people, there is much more to it than personalities. There are more fundamental reasons for Phoenixville's resurgence, and it will take some time before enough evidence is in for conclusions. At this point, I am still in search of theses, and that's where you come in. This "Why Phoenixville?" query is a long-term project, and I will be holding forth again, but what I am really trying to do is stimulate discussion. Together, let's amass the facts, so we can seek the answer.

1/16/15   **#2 in a Series**
"Walkable Streets, a Downtown to Go to…"

The response to my opening post in this series has been excellent, and I thank everyone who took the time to comment. I am very encouraged, and I hope that this exchange of information continues. Several of you took some time to offer detailed observations, and I will be getting to at least some of them, because they make good points. But I want to begin with a more general comment I received, because it echoes the basic theme of my whole approach to urban revival. It reflects just what Phoenixville's revival is all about, and the great contrast with what is happening to Conshohocken.

A lady wrote to tell me "Why Phoenixville?" for her and her husband, who are not from Pennsylvania, but who moved there after checking it out. She didn't offer a historical explanation but a cultural one. In Phoenixville, she says, "We walk our dog down to Bridge Street and the Farmers' Market [and] greet/meet neighbors along the way…"

To me, that pretty much says it all, especially the walking part; a livable town is a walkable town. (Automobiles only pit residents against one another over everything from safety to "owning" shoveled parking spaces.) It also points out that Phoenixville possesses a downtown to go to. How many other towns on the Schuylkill River can make that statement? Okay, Norristown has West Marshall Street, but isn't that pretty much about it? And Phoenixville's downtown isn't just Starbucks or wine bars; the Phoenixville Farmers' Market is a community destination, as is the Colonial Theatre, and there are more. Finally, the opportunity to "greet/meet neighbors along the way" may be the most important component of all. That comes from walking, of course, but it also speaks to the type of people who live there—those who experience the community and are part of it, not isolated, indifferent observers in some new high-rise apartment.

This reader's comment excellently summed up how Phoenixville is conducting its ascent, and the type of people it attracts as new residents. This couple came, liked what they saw, and decided to not just stay, but contribute to what was happening, even if just by walking downtown (and actually talking to people!). But why was what they liked there at all?

As a historian, I believe we must begin by giving credit to where credit is due, and some of that goes back a long way. Phoenixville has the best-preserved "Main Street"—it's Bridge Street in Phoenixville—of all the towns on the lower Schuylkill River. Many great buildings in the borough were lost, but others have survived, enough to anchor a modern revival of an old-time downtown. The importance of historic preservation cannot be overstated. A Phoenixville that had to rebuild all of Bridge Street would not have become the Phoenixville of today. Those old buildings represent a legacy that far exceeds their property value. Thus, when we are apportioning credit, we must make sure to look far enough back to acknowledge those who contributed to this preservation. I suspect there are many names, both of individuals and of companies.

Still, a town's revival isn't just a matter of having old buildings on an even older street. The physical components were present in Phoenixville, but the purposes they were put to made all the difference. Phoenixville's nightlife gets most of the ink, and those old buildings are great settings for just that, but I suspect that the writer of the comment I am referencing and her husband are not in the age demographic that is found in those places on Friday and Saturday evenings. People who come into town to party make a town "trendy," stimulate business, and certainly make a contribution. But it is the people who live in the town, pay taxes, and vote who are the backbone of the sense of community that has arisen.

People are attracted to small towns for different reasons, of course. In my blog series on what is happening to the Conshohockens, I predicted that a great many of the people who will move there will do so primarily because the location offers quick access to two Interstate highways. They may choose Conshohocken over similar locations because of the area's great natural beauty, but that will be the clincher, not the motivation. I also questioned how many will actually take a sufficient interest in their new home town to get involved, and whether their primary interests might conflict with those of the existing residents uphill. My concern is about Conshohocken's future as a *community*, not just valuable real estate.

Nobody is moving to Phoenixville for its great access to Interstate highways. The highways aren't very far away, but rush-hour traffic on the local roads from Phoenixville to them makes the journey take rather long. People who move to Phoenixville are attracted by what the town itself has to offer. Of course, location counts; Phoenixville's surroundings are rich in history and culture, and there is no point in making a distinction between the borough and its adjacent townships in that regard.

I would argue strongly that what Phoenixville has to offer begins with walkable streets and a downtown to go to. Without those two, a town's revival may be measured in economic terms, but not in those things that really go into making a town a community. That's the beginning, the basic requirements. But they aren't enough by themselves, and piecing together the story behind Phoenixville's revival will require the addition of several more components. That's why I repeat my call for contributions, because there is a lot more to be said. I plan to say more, but as always, I take my inspiration from what people in the Schuylkill Valley say and do, and the many people responsible for Phoenixville's revival know more than I do. A historian cannot make bricks without straw, and that straw must come from the knowledgeable, as many of them as possible.

Several of the comments I have received speak of Phoenixville's "air," its "DNA," and its sense of "tolerance and inclusion." Some attribute this to religion or spirituality, but more often to traditions left from when Phoenixville was a "company town." These are subjects I want to address, so if you have thoughts on this, let me know soon. I would like to consider them before I write about the subjects themselves.

1/30/15   #3 in a Series

"Community Spirit"?

Several of the replies to my question "Why Phoenixville?" referenced the town's "community spirit"; some used the phrase itself, others pointed to manifestations of it. A few actually attempted to identify its roots, and I am grateful for these, because roots are what I am all about. The problem comes with trying to come to grips with the concept itself. Evidence of it can be seen, and it can be expressed, but just exactly what is it?

Community spirit is a very local example of an "ideology," a belief system that people hold about themselves and others. The role of ideology in historical causation is extraordinarily difficult to grapple with, because it cannot be quantified, and therefore compared easily with those things that can be quantified. I am, however, very sympathetic to the attempt, because I believe that how people perceive things is ultimately more important than the facts of the things themselves. People view reality through filters, they make decisions on those filtered perceptions, and those decisions make history. Still, history is a profession based on facts, so perceptions tend to get short shrift.

Except by me. You know that already if you have been following this blog, but if not, be advised that I have an intense interest that the facts be correct, but I don't give them primary place in my analysis. So, I am glad of the opportunity to discuss community spirit, one of the most important, yet most elusive, forms of ideology.

So what is community spirit? You can see it, you can hear it, you know it exists, you know it's important, but how do you measure it in ways that you can compare to other contributions to revival and assess its relative value? That's a rhetorical question, by the way. I don't expect an answer, because there can't be one. That's the problem with employing "ideology" in anything more than the most general way in historical discourse. But don't we all know in our hearts how important "community spirit" is?

I would venture that Phoenixville has more "community spirit" than any other town on the lower Schuylkill. You can count festivals and the like and pretend to measure it, but it's really something you just feel. Besides, when we ask the question "why?" we are not talking about the Phoenixville of today; its revival has achieved critical mass and reproduces itself. It attracts the type of people who embody "community spirit." To point out that

Phoenixville has more "community spirit" today than, say, Norristown (to pick the most obvious example) does not say anything of value about either town. Their conditions differ too much to make such a comparison. Phoenixville was never Norristown, but it did suffer its share of dark days. *That* is the period we must look at to even begin to answer the "Why Phoenixville?" question.

Or maybe earlier? Can a town posses "DNA," as one respondent put it? And if so, as a result of what? I'm open to suggestions on this point, but I would nominate Phoenixville's history as a "company town." This is primarily what distinguishes it from the other towns along the lower Schuylkill River. All the towns had a manufacturing base, the core of which was metals and metal fabrication. Conshohocken and Pottstown also made iron and then steel, and both can point to early settlers leading the way. Pottstown's steel industry was eventually consolidated under an outsider, Bethlehem Steel. Conshohocken retained a close connection to Alan Wood Steel, even though it moved outside the borough itself (Alan Wood had been a Conshohocken resident), but Phoenixville's connection to the Phoenix Iron (later Steel) Works is on an entirely different level.

To say that the Phoenix Iron Works had a massive physical imprint on its namesake town is to understate the obvious. It's a mixed legacy, to be sure. The company eventually owned almost all of the land around lower French Creek, and what wasn't suitable for production had "workers housing" built on it, which made the company the borough's biggest landlord, in addition to being the biggest of pretty much everything else. Much of Bridge Street was its creation, from office buildings to hotels. Its leaders built their mansions on the best ground.

Bridge Street and the mansions were lasting gifts, but the company's initial legacy upon its death was a substantial brownfield around lower French Creek. Nobody cared much about pollution in the "good old days." A brownfield can be cleansed, and the remaining structures (let's not forget the Foundry and the Phoenix Column Bridge) repurposed, so that mixed legacy tends toward the positive. If no one is counting money spent ameliorating pollution, even more so.

Then there's the question of an ideological legacy, and that's where things get tricky. In American history, the phrase "company town," has had several different examples, and few of them were good for their workers. People claim that Phoenix Iron Works was different; they speak of its "inclusivity," and see the company's legacy as a positive one in ideological terms.

There is less question about another legacy, one that the borough's history of unionism has bequeathed. Unionism is an ideology, and one that promotes a spirit of community among its workers. When we are talking legacies, however, this creates a problem. In American industrial history, company and union were antagonistic, and never more so than in a "company town." In theory, two such opposing forces should have bred two equally separate—and contending—ideologies. It is difficult to see how they could have blended to jointly underpin a spirit that embraces the whole community.

Yet there is evidence that this happened; in Phoenixville, the steelworkers union was more agreeable than in many towns, although whether that was a positive thing or not is debatable. The last "heat" of steel at the plant took place in 1976, but the final closing did not happen until 1987. By that date, the president of the steelworkers union declared his workers (those few who had held onto their jobs amid repeated layoffs) to be "the lowest paid steelworkers union in the country." They had demonstrated a greater willingness to sacrifice, accepting both wage and benefit reductions. All to no avail, of course.

Are we talking separate legacies here? Perhaps the focus of company ideology is on its proud place in US industrial history, rather than its actual local actions. Or is the company's legacy largely physical, while that of the workers is the ideological taproot of the community and its "spirit"? Could these two usually opposed factors have somehow combined in their legacy to Phoenixville? Perhaps enough time has passed that the beautiful physical legacies have become so integral to the image—and the reality— of Phoenixville as to replace the memory of a profit-driven company that held a community in the palm of its hand. What is the population's general opinion of the town's industrial history? Speaking of which, is there a difference on the subject between the attitudes of the longer-term residents versus those who have recently moved there?

I ask a lot of questions, but even more about Phoenixville, for the causes of success are harder to evaluate than those of failure. The borough displays abundant community spirit, but is that a recent thing, since its revival took hold? How important was this spirit, compared to the great physical remains, or the input of money, or of other potential causes, to the revival that has taken place?

I seek some answers, hoping not only that Phoenixville benefits still further, but also to see these same efforts successfully applied to other towns on the Schuylkill, which could certainly use them. That's why I seek the deeper answers, the historical ones. Phoenixville is unique today, but that is a very recent development; the borough began to revive before it became "trendy." So I continue to ask why, and I continue to need your help in finding some answers.

The Conshohockens

10/3/14   **#1 in a Series**

From an *Instrument* to an *Institution*: Why Do They Still Exist?

Many of my posts have focused on the disconnect between Bureaucracy World and the real world—particularly the bureaucracy of the US Department of Housing and Urban Development (HUD), and its local extensions, the local public housing authorities. My take on them has been critical, but not compared to what else is circulating on the Internet. A quick look at Facebook alone will reveal how much national discontent with HUD exists, and how far it has spread. (Check out the Occupy HUD page, as just one example.)

At the core of the disconnect is the lamentable fact that HUD has ceased to be an *instrument*, and has become an *institution*. Understanding the difference between the two, and why the latter seems to be the inevitable fate of the former, will help to clarify what has gone wrong not only with HUD, but the rest of the "War on Poverty," and why we have situations like the concentration of housing choice vouchers in poorer communities. Such an understanding will also help with the analysis of just about any group or organization. So much so, in fact, that I will use it to address the situation in the Conshohockens, where a very different reality is under way.

I was blessed during my undergraduate years to study under a history professor who impressed several lessons upon me, all ultimately about the difference between knowing something and actually understanding it. These lessons were already old when I first encountered them in the mid-1960s, but they have stood the test of time. One of them is the distinction between an *instrument* and an *institution*.

An *instrument* is designed to fulfill a function, and when it's first organized, its focus is on doing just that. With the passage of time, however, the purpose for an instrument's continuation diffuses, morphing into a focus on maintaining the physical structure—size, personnel, and, most of all, its budget—more than on actually accomplishing the task for which it was formed. The instrument becomes an *institution*. This slow, almost-imperceptible transformation seems to be the fate of all instruments, and certainly those that arise from good intentions. The organization survives, and it likely grows, but it increasingly solidifies its right to continued existence by the fact—and duration—of its existence itself.

The rule of an instrument's inevitable deterioration into an institution applies to virtually all creations of man, but I will take a very narrow perspective, and offer the following thesis: American history has taught us that government-created instruments are more liable to suffer this transformation, and are much more resistant to course correction. The general impossibility of the formal goal such instruments are charged with, from winning the "War on Poverty" to protecting America's "national interests," is tacitly accepted, and keeping things from getting worse is considered success. So, the instrument enters the fray, slowly but surely recognizes the impossibility of victory, and turns the inevitable disillusionment into individual methods of balancing continued commitment with career advancement and eventual retirement. Those who labor within an institution must accept their obvious inadequacy and the ultimate futility of what they are trying to accomplish. How they work through that dilemma determines whether they are on the instrument or institution side of the bureaucracy's internal struggle. Staying on the instrument side is difficult to sustain, and those who manage to do so should be celebrated, not cast into the same rhetorical pit with those bureaucrats we all love to castigate.

Let's not forget the military in all of this; the Pentagon has pretty much defined How to Succeed at Bureaucracy, but then again, America's "national interests" is a very elastic phrase, and one that trumps "help the poor" just about every time. But I digress. The US Department of Housing and Urban Development (HUD), which administers the housing subsidy programs, is excellent an example of this unfortunate evolutionary process. It is also a sad commentary on how even a failed approach must be continued to avoid making things even worse.

I'll bet that each and every one of you can quickly name another program—or even an entire department—of the federal government that you believe fits this description, one that has ceased to serve the purpose for which it was created, and now exists largely to perpetuate its own existence. Like shooting fish in a barrel, right?

But how about closer to home? Let's start with the Commonwealth of Pennsylvania itself. In searching for such instruments-become-institutions at the state level, we need look no further than how alcohol is sold in Pennsylvania. Few examples of my subject—at any level of government— stand out more blatantly than the Pennsylvania State Liquor Control Board. Does the reason for which it was created even still exist? If not, shouldn't the whole thing be eliminated? Anything further I might add to that subject would be just piling on, but those two questions should be asked of each and every institution, particularly those of government. Tune in next week for that.

Okay, that was easy. Dare I come still closer to home? I know full well the passion that can arise when certain local sacred cows are questioned, as I have sat through a number of such confrontations (and, in truth, contributed to a few). Local police forces are one. For a very long time, separate township and municipal police forces were necessary. These were the days of slow travel and even slower communications; crime was overwhelmingly local, and best combatted by locals who knew the territory. But that was then, and this is now, and things have changed. Criminals routinely use the highways to range over the territory of several municipalities, and their information- gathering systems range much farther than that. Still, periodic trial balloons floated about combining local municipal police departments into more regional ones go down in flames before the impassioned opposition of local residents. Paradoxically, these traditionalists are sustained by the information revolution, which greatly facilitates local law enforcement while keeping the payroll down.

But I propose to offer next time an example on an even more fundamental level, that of a municipality itself. I do so at considerable risk, because I know from experience that when my take on recent urban history gores someone's sacred cow, their anger and astonishment will be blind them to any further appreciation of what I am trying to do, however well they understood my point when it was aimed at someone else. I know better, but I can't resist: Does West Conshohocken still have a reason to exist?

10/10/14   #2 in a Series

Does West Conshohocken Still Have a Reason To Exist?

Across the entire scope of human history, there may be nothing more constantly present, regardless of time or locale, than this defense of the *status quo*: "Why do we do it this way? Because we have *always* done it this way!" Our very human love of predictability, and perhaps even more of ritual, has set among us a great many structures that easily fit into that process I introduced last week, *instruments* that have become *institutions*. Some, like federal welfare departments, are under sufficient duress from enough people that the ideal of actually eliminating them seems close to possible. Others, like the Pennsylvania Liquor Control Board (PLCB), are understood to be pointless relics by just about everyone, but remain somehow resistant to being dismantled.

Then there are those institutions so deeply ingrained into our everyday lives that we literally never think of changing them, unless something major comes along, and often not even then. Religions are the most obvious example, but secular governments are not far behind. Just about every American wants to change something about the United States, but few want to eliminate it (even Clive Bundy was just blowing smoke, to cover his legal debts). The occasional western county tries to secede from its state because it believes in democracy right up to the point where its conservative ways no longer hold sway over the rest of the state, then not so much. Nothing comes of this, of course. Any US territorial subdivision that has survived thus far can be the focus of much controversy, but can also pretty much count on no one questioning whether or not it should exist at all.

Except me. I am going to offer the most fundamental question of all about a very small municipality on the lower Schuylkill River in Southeastern Pennsylvania: Does the Borough of West Conshohocken still have a reason to exist? Mind you, I do not ask if West Conshohocken *should* continue to exist. Such a question must arise from within the borough itself, and be tested in public discourse. I, as a historian and as someone focused on the future of our region's small towns, confine myself to asking of West Conshohocken the very same two questions I applied to the PLCB:

1. Does the reason for which the borough of West Conshohocken was created still exist?
2. If not, shouldn't the whole thing be eliminated?

Previously I said that these two questions had wide applicability, and I meant it. I recognize no sacred cows as exempt from the basic scrutiny that we should apply to all institutions, particularly those that have an automatic call on our money. If the answer to the first question is "no," then the second question is legitimate. Everybody seemed to agree when the subject was the Liquor Control Board. Now I'm going to briefly point out why the same answer of "no" applies to West Conshohocken.

This is not about what most people would point to, which is West Conshohocken's declining population. The borough has always had the smallest population of any town on the lower Schuylkill; those numbers peaked in 1930 at 2,579, and have declined since. As of the 2010 Census, only 1,320 people still call West Conshohocken home. For a sense of perspective, consider that at any given daylight hour, there are more than five times as many people employed by the King of Prussia Mall. But numbers alone are an insufficient reason to question the any town's continued existence. A great many towns with smaller numbers exist all across the country. Of course, these tend to be surrounded by large swaths of farmland, not big-city suburbs with a population density close to—or perhaps greater than—their own. That presents a fundamentally different situation, because those great many towns still continue to be different from their surroundings and continue function differently within them. West Conshohocken does neither.

If we remain at a general level, the story of West Conshohocken is simple. The borough came into existence for the very same reason as the seven other towns on the lower Schuylkill and, I expect, a great many more towns all across the country. Only the specifics differ. This particular locale had seen people gather for the same combination of reasons as that of other towns along the Schuylkill: a fording location to cross the river and nearby creeks capable of powering the small manufacturing of the times. For a great many years, the area was simply a collection of people, an unincorporated village within the Township of Upper Merion.

At some point, however, the area's "leading citizens" concluded that their location had become significantly different from that of the rest of the governmental subdivision to which they belonged. For all eight locations along the Schuylkill between Reading and Philadelphia that evolved into towns, West Conshohocken most definitely included, this meant they had become focused on manufacturing and commerce, not agriculture. Their leading citizens were active in those occupations and saw the opportunity to add politics to their sphere of influence. Equally important was the fact that the residents of these river locations lived very closely together, and thus were consumers, not producers, of food. As their numbers increased and remained crowded together, these small, unique areas began.

The townships that surrounded these locations, however, were rural, meaning that their residents lived far apart, working their farms, consuming much of their own agricultural produce, and often shipping the remainder no farther than the more-densely populated river locations. Within each township, these people had the numbers and the traditional influence that went with working the land. They held the political power, such as it was, and their self-contained lifestyle saw little reason for public expenditures (meaning taxes) on general principles, let alone taxes that would aid just one part of their township. Those leading citizens of manufacturing and commerce at each river location knew that the taxes necessary to construct the necessary public improvements would not be forthcoming from an agricultural tax base. And so they acted, petitioning the Commonwealth to create a new municipality—small, but busy and prosperous.

It used to be a lot easier to secede from one locality and form your own, and it was done often (although not often enough, as some devotees of Pottstown history would proclaim). That's how the other Schuylkill River towns came into being, even Norristown. The Montgomery County seat had been an unincorporated village for twenty-eight years before Norristown incorporated as a borough in 1812. Its status as the county seat did not matter; Norristown's reasons for incorporation were the same as everyone else's.

West Conshohocken stands out in this regard only because of its late appearance; it did not become a borough until 1874, taking land from both Upper and Lower Merion because, as the West Conshohocken chapter of *The Second Hundred Years* put it, "Residents wanted a separate government suited to the community's industrial character, which was totally unlike the other parts of the two townships." Conshohocken, by contrast, had taken this step in 1850. That gave it a major head start, which it has never relinquished.

West Conshohocken, despite remaining by far the smallest town on the lower Schuylkill River, managed to carve out its own little niche in

Pennsylvania history. As small as it was, its transportation connections—local roads that led to Matson's Ford, and the railroad along the river itself—sustained an industrial base, and thus a closely grouped population. Its earlier and much larger neighbor across the river largely prevented West Conshohocken from ever developing much of a commercial district, however. So the borough lived out its life as a miniature version of an American mill town—hard-working, locally focused, and proud of itself. At least, it did until about a decade or so after World War II and the 1950s—the sunset period of a golden era of growth, work, and prosperity. Then several things began to change simultaneously, and every town on the Schuylkill suffered largely the same fate.

By 1980, however, investment money had begun to flow into the area once more. Within a few years, it was clear that the Conshohockens had embarked on a very different historical arc from that of the other towns upriver. What was not clear was the price that would be paid, and that West Conshohocken would have to pay by far the heavier one. That price has become much clearer to everyone in recent years, and I focus on that part of the story next week.

10/17/14   **#3 in a Series**

Does West Conshohocken Still Have a Reason to Exist? (Revisited)

Previously I began the story of West Conshohocken, Pennsylvania, by pointing out that it although its history, up until about 1980, was virtually the same as for each of the eight towns on the lower Schuylkill, after that it was clear that the two Conshohockens were going to experience a very different future from those towns upriver. That future would be, by comparison, very much better, but there would be a price to pay, and West Conshohocken's share would be the greater one.

In the Schuylkill Valley, not only have things changed, most of them have changed a full 180 degrees. This hold true for the Conshohockens, but their change—and theirs alone—also invokes my mantra, "The more things change…" (You know the rest.) The Conshohockens came into existence because of the intersection of two travel routes, originally the township line roads, meeting the river at Matson's Ford. This time both are being recreated by the intersection of two roads (one of which does follow the path of the river, by the way). These are not just any roads, mind you, but two Interstate highways. The Conshohockens now lie at an intersection that can be reached easily from a great distance (yes, I am ignoring traffic jams here, but so are the developers and buyers/renters). Upriver, only Pottstown might make this claim, but both its highways and the region they access are not in as good a shape.

The intersection of these two major highways had to go somewhere, and West Conshohocken was that somewhere. The intersection arrived incrementally, as the second of the two highways—what would eventually become the Mid-County Expressway, Interstate 476 (the "Blue Route")— was built in segments. The Conshohocken off-ramp, an auxiliary route connecting to I-76, dates back to the early fifties. Conshohocken got the name, but West Conshohocken got the ramp, and lost ground, residences, and borough revenue in the process. By the time the whole process was completed almost forty years later, West Conshohocken had been gutted—drawn and quartered, as it were.

West Conshohocken's total area is still listed as .9 square miles. Its livable area is much smaller than that. The highways took what they needed, and left the rest. The result has been unkind to any sense of community. The new, widened, and realigned roads necessary to service the much greater number of vehicles that now passes through the borough have, in turn, divided its remaining land into pieces, each effectively cut off from one another. The absolute prioritization of vehicle traffic passing through has rendered it challenging to even walk from one section of the small borough to another.

That is just looking at things from a purely physical point of view. But what about West Conshohocken's historic sense of community identity, of its reason for being? What was once a typical locally focused Schuylkill Valley community, where people lived, worked, and worshipped in the same town, has been rent asunder—much eliminated, with parts isolated and everything local de-emphasized. Can the fragments that remain even see themselves as members of a community at all? Those who descend from the old days and live in the older residential sections very likely do, but as residents of what…today's reality, or just a memory? West Conshohocken's historic self-image is that of a gritty mill town, overshadowed by its much larger, and even more gritty, neighbor across the river. Both are no longer mill towns, but is West Conshohocken a town at all these days?

For a long time, the Borough of West Conshohocken served a purpose for both its residents and those in nearby areas. It no longer does. The money flowing into the Conshohocken area respects no political boundaries, and has come close to eliminating any difference between West Conshohocken and its surroundings. The basic components of what makes a grouping of people into an actual community once existed, but no longer.

Much has changed along this bend in the Schuylkill River, and the pace, as this is written, actually appears to be picking up. New office buildings and residences have physically replaced the old industries. What that means is that with a minute number of exceptions, the new residents work elsewhere while the new workers live elsewhere. That is a fundamental, 180-degree change from why the Schuylkill River towns came into existence in the first place. These days, we don't expect a town's temporary daylight occupants to show much interest in the community, but what about the new residents, and those who will inhabit the developments currently pending? Will these new people consider themselves residents of West Conshohocken, or will it be just a mailing address for them? They will pay their taxes, but how many of them will vote in local elections? Will they support the George Clay Fire Company? How will they view the community in which they technically live? As anything at all?

Let's put it another way: do the people moving in now have any reason to feel of sense of community about today's West Conshohocken? What does the borough—and being a part of it—contribute to their lives? The core of West Conshohocken has always been its ethnic churches, just as with every other town on the lower Schuylkill. St. Gertrude's, the borough's first Catholic church, founded in 1888, is now closed. Does Sunday still promote a sense of community as it used to, and, if not, has anything taken its place? A community's youth is the medium in which traditions are passed along, with the new generations accepting some of those traditions, changing others, and then passing the new mix along their children. But what happens when the new "generations" aren't former residents but new ones? The borough no longer has an elementary, middle, or high school. The ties between the two Conshohockens were not strong enough to keep their children together. West Conshohocken students attend the Upper Merion School District, while those in Conshohocken are part of the Plymouth-Whitemarsh School District.

The answer to my first question ("Does the reason for which the borough of West Conshohocken was created still exist?") is clearly "no." What about the second question? ("If not, shouldn't the whole thing be eliminated?") It's up to the residents of West Conshohocken to decide whether to even ask, let alone vote on the answer. It's clear that the reasons for West Conshohocken's birth no longer exist, and the reasons it sustained itself so long for so well no longer exist, either. Both of these facts are true for the other towns on the lower Schuylkill as well, which is why their futures remain uncertain. The difference is that the Conshohockens are having that future forced on them. Conshohocken's crisis lies in which path it will follow, but at least it has a choice, albeit a limited one. The problem surrounding West Conshohocken lies in the strong possibility that it has no choice at all. The forces arrayed against its continuation as a coherent community arise from the exercise of the free-market economy, and they are hugely more powerful than those that can be marshaled to protect the borough's traditional community identity. The name may remain the same, but what else will, really?

10/31/14   **#1 in a Series**

Is Conshohocken Coming Back…or Just Being Taken Over?—"The Old"

I try to ask fundamental questions. I believe that in the context of what Conshohocken in undergoing, the question I ask is the most fundamental of all. I don't live in Conshohocken, and never have, and I have no legal say in the specific issues that are confronting the borough…this project or that one. I am, however, trained to take the long view and to identify historical patterns evident amid the details, and for that reason what is happening in the Conshohockens fascinates me. We live in exciting times: a major turning point in the history of both boroughs is well under way. The past is past and over with; the future will not only be different from the past, but that future will be different from that of the other six towns on the lower Schuylkill River, for the very first time in their collective history.

I do not remember the old Conshohocken—the self-centered industrial community with a crowded downtown. I began to visit Conshohocken only in the middle 1980s, when I twice a week delivered first one son and then another to DeStolfo's School of Tae Kwon Do, then located in the Patriotic Sons of America building on Fayette Street. My route took me past the old Alan Wood Iron and Steel Company to the core of downtown before I turned left up the hill, and then reversed itself for our return. It was a depressing experience. Years of brief, repetitive views caused me to arrange what I saw as a series of historical vignettes, as is my wont. As I drove along Conshohocken State Road past the remnants of Alan Wood, the site showed but flickering signs of life. I tried to imagine what that stretch would have looked, sounded, and smelled like in earlier times, with its furnaces in operation and its many workers passing each other between shifts, but it was difficult. I'm old, but not that old.

Next came a passage down western Elm Street, a stretch of simple, unadorned row housing built for the workers at the then-nearby plants before the days of the automobile. Their original occupants didn't have cars, and didn't need them. Their successors did, because they had to; they could no longer walk to work. This bit of historical timing meant that the current residents had to deal with both the lack of parking spaces for *their* cars and the speed with which other people's cars drove past their front doors. Signs implored drivers to obey a resident-friendly speed limit, which, if memory serves, was routinely ignored.

My memories of downtown are simple: fences, just fences. In the early 1980s, downtown Conshohocken did not exist; it had been removed under the Federal Urban Renewal Program. Therein lies a tale, for at the time the conventional wisdom was that a huge mistake had been made, and not just because of all the old buildings that had been demolished. The critics had a point. Conshohocken's urban renewal effort was the last one the federal government ever contracted for. In fact, by the time Conshohocken jumped on board, the Urban Renewal Program was already being judged a national failure. Locally, the condition of an urban renewal project just up the river in Royersford should have been a sobering reality check. Be that as it may, the contract was signed and old downtown Conshohocken proceeded to fall under the wrecker's ball. As with Royersford, the removal and teardown was easy to accomplish; the revival of new buildings, new businesses, and new residents…not so much.

In the mid-1980s, to passersby like me, it seemed that nothing was happening, but appearances were deceiving. Things were happening, but urban renewal had nothing to do with it. The only project in the long record of new developments that can properly be considered as part of the urban renewal effort was the first one, the Pleasant Valley Apartments. This was a Section 8 project, and one I first wrote about in May 2013 because it was being pitched on a website as the first of the successes that would follow. While the same developer was hired, what followed wasn't a federally funded urban renewal effort but a much older and much more fundamental process. The process that gathered steam and began to reshape Conshohocken during the 1980s was a very traditional American one: developers transform a large property, letting private enterprises and investors develop portions of it at a time, for their own reasons and according to their own schedule. For these developers, Conshohocken's empty downtown was a gift. It saved them the cost of doing the same thing, which was what they had in mind anyway.

By the time I began to view Conshohocken on a regular schedule, the transformation of both boroughs was already well under way, but largely just in the sketches of developers. Only the first steps had begun in terms of establishing a physical presence, and the developers had taken a long time to do that. The process had actually began in the late 1940s, when work on the Schuylkill Expressway got under way. A small portion in West Conshohocken was one of the first segments to open, but was of little use. The full expressway did not open until 1960. This certainly helped, but for several years Conshohocken was just an off-ramp of a single road—one actually located in West Conshohocken—that received no mention.

This is where the long and tangled tale of what is now known as I-476 enters the picture. There may have been more controversial sections of the Interstate System, but few have been opposed by people with such deep pockets. The construction of the whole road gives new meaning to the term "spasmodic." Delaware County was the site of my first visits to southeastern Pennsylvania, back in the late 1960s. I would periodically drive down Bryn Mawr Avenue, underneath a section of road upon which I never saw any traffic. My curiosity aroused, I learned that it was an early portion of what is known locally as the "Blue Route." It carried no traffic because it connected nothing to nothing. Years passed and portions were built, and the promise of the future began to be glimpsed from the Conshohockens. The connection to Norristown was welcome, with its wide new bridge, but the real northward goal was the Pennsylvania Turnpike, including its Northeast Extension, and that took a long time to achieve. The southward connection was opened from I-95, and with the final link to the turnpike completed at long last, the Conshohockens found themselves at the intersection of two heavily traveled highways, the new I-476 and the much-updated Schuylkill Expressway, which had earlier become I-76.

With that, the fate of both towns was sealed. Make no mistake about it: what has happened, and what will happen, to both Conshohockens has been and will be the direct result of that intersection of Interstate highways. Private enterprise is succeeding where a government program failed, but its success is due to timing and, of course, two government-financed roads. What has been happening to both the Conshohockens has nothing to do with either of the boroughs themselves; they just happened to be there when the connections were completed.

As were a few people, who by now should feel just as ignored, if not more so, than the boroughs. Let's call them the "Old." These are those residents who experienced this multidecade process, or their children ("Old" here is more related to duration than to chronological age). Often descendants of earlier residents, they are the ones who did not leave when so many others did. The Old are proud of their community history and remain locally focused, as the residents of both towns historically have been. Few now alive can remember the "good old days," but the Old recognize their place in a long tradition, a place that may even include residence in the old family home. Their local focus makes them the backbone of the community, as it always has. They are also the most aware that the people who occupy the new buildings—whether during the day or the night—do not share that focus.

The implications for Conshohocken from the influx of the New are potentially more significant than those that will arise from the buildings they will occupy. The New may be a heterogeneous lot, but they will all share one fundamental difference from the Old. That difference may well determine what kind of community the new Conshohocken becomes.

11/7/14   **#2 in a Series**

Is Conshohocken Coming Back…or Just Being Taken Over?—"The New"

My previous post was history-focused, but introduced the idea that in today's Conshohockens, "old" doesn't mean *that* old. For both towns, the 1980s marked the transition from the old to the new. If you are old enough to remember that, or even heard it from your parents, then you are part of those people I termed the Old. This is not about chronological age, but length of residence. And place of residence, as I pointed out at the beginning of this series, because very few of the Old live along the riverfront. Most live up the hill, in the time-honored tradition. Most of my Conshohocken readers are also the Old, and they didn't need me to belabor something they already knew.

The New are different. Recent arrival and location close to the riverfront identify them. They fall into two quite distinct groups, but the significant characteristic that they have in common poses the greatest threat to Conshohocken's future as a community. While the Old retain their local focus on the community of Conshohocken itself, for the New, it's the exact opposite. They are arriving because it is physically convenient to work or live near an intersection of Interstate highways. They are quite aware that they live in "The Conshohockens," and prioritize its connections to the rest of the world over the condition of their local community. They are likely to feel little connection to the municipality; it is just the place where they reside or work. Whether they live in the new condo or apartment complexes or work in the new office buildings, their interest in the community may be limited to how quickly they can drive from their home to the Intersection.

This will hold true despite the fact that there is a second reason for people to settle in Conshohocken, one we must not lose sight of. The waterfront is a beautiful location along a scenic river. We should never allow my focus on what changes money can bring to obscure this important fact. There are, after all, other locations available to live and work in that are perhaps just as convenient to these highways, or even more so. For some, this second (and still secondary) consideration will be the one to actually tip the scales. It's a beautiful location because its previous inhabitants—coal-powered industries and railroads—exist no more. Opinions on the new buildings vary, with most agreeing only that they are preferable to what was there before. Whatever else Conshohocken was—and it was many things, to many people—it was not beautiful. People came, and stayed, for the jobs. Some have come for the jobs, and some have come to live in this now-beautiful bend of a scenic river, but they are not the same people.

Regardless of who comes to occupy the new buildings, we can expect them to adhere to a well-known rule about today's residential communities and workplaces. Those who will work in the new office buildings will not live in the Conshohockens. Those who will reside in the new condos and apartments will not work in the Conshohockens. The very few exceptions to this rule (there will be some; there always are) will, by their uniqueness, demonstrate the validity of the rule itself. This rule has important consequences for both towns, but sheer numbers means greater consequences for the larger town.

The municipal leaders of every town, Conshohocken most definitely included, are quite receptive to development proposals for new office buildings (or laboratories, or whatever). Such projects generate taxes for the municipality, and sit vacant during the night hours, often with their own security. Simply put, their financial contribution to the community is greater than their cost. Residences are different. They are a twenty-four-hour responsibility; less so when new, but as they age, that changes, along with the income level of their occupants. In the long run, every residential development begins to cost more in services than it brings in through taxes. It's a basic rule, and well understood.

The new office buildings are already having a considerable impact, which can only increase. Still, the new residences will have the greatest impact of all. One of my early observations in this series was that residences in this case meant large condominium or apartment complexes, not single-family homes. Economic calculation—that is, profit potential—has everything to do with this. Each residential development project will accommodate the need of its residents to get to the Intersection quickly and conveniently, to the maximum extent purchasable by law. The inclusion of community-focused connections is less certain. The effect of these new projects on the soon-to-be-host community receives little attention beyond that which the zoning codes call for.

You can, unfortunately, be certain that the occupants of the new offices will largely disregard the municipality in which they find themselves. The indifference of workers to the local community in which their workplace resides is understandable in today's world, and accepted. Conshohocken grew first during the era when people lived, worked, worshipped, and shopped in the same community. That era is over, and now even those Conshohocken residents I am calling the Old largely work (and shop) elsewhere. Do they give much thought to the municipality in which they work, other than how easy it is to get into and out of?

But what about the New residents? If they came for easy accessibility to an Interstate or for a beautiful river view, are they really going to care about what happens up the hill? They are not going to either work or shop in Conshohocken. Their children will attend different school systems depending on which Conshohocken they live in. What local issues will they care about, and what will their positions be? It's worth some thought.

The bottom line is that the influx of new investment is increasingly dividing both of its host municipalities into the New and the Old. These titles belong not just to physical structures of both towns, but also to the people who inhabit them, whether during the day or the night. Each municipality physically incorporates both, but their respective reasons for being there are fundamentally different, and that makes all the difference. The Old live in either Conshohocken or West Conshohocken; the New live in "The Conshohockens." Call it *attitude apartheid*.

The inevitable tension between the Old and the New is beginning to be felt, and can only increase as the New steadily increase in numbers and influence. Next time I'll address what I consider to be the most important issue facing Conshohocken, to illustrate how the fundamental difference between the Old and the New will significantly affect how the new Conshohocken develops, even before most of the New actually arrive. Here's a hint: cars figure into it. I'll bet you can think of others.

11/14/14   **#3 in a Series**

Is Conshohocken Coming Back…or Just Being Taken Over?—"The Old, the New, and the New Old"

Last time I closed with a promise to review a significant issue that is pitting the New versus the Old in Conshohocken. But let's first establish a common goal for Conshohocken's future. How about this: "A Community, Not An Exit." With that goal in mind, I will proceed to examine what I believe to a fundamental issue, one that will largely determine which of these two futures will prevail. Not only is this important, but it's also being currently being decided. There is no time to waste.

I want my underlying viewpoint to be clear from the outset. I contend that there is a fundamental contradiction between the urban grid and the automobile. The automobile is by far the least efficient means of getting people into and out of such a grid, and then there is the question of what to do with all those automobiles while their drivers are within the grid doing the various things that they do. It's the central theme of my book about Norristown,[14] and I believe it applies to Conshohocken, because it applies everywhere.

My contention has a corollary that says when the number of tall buildings

---

14. Tolle, *What Killed Downtown?*

in an urban grid increases arithmetically, the contradiction increases exponentially. This corollary is clearly going to apply to Conshohocken also.

Conshohocken, like every town on the lower Schuylkill, today faces its specific version of what I term the "Transportation Conundrum." It's a multifaceted subject, and the first half of this book[15] discusses it more comprehensively, but here I will sum it up in two words: traffic and parking. They are not just interrelated; they are two halves of the same walnut. They also stem from the same source: America's current fascination with—and dependency on—the automobile.

The automobile played a significant part in the decline of the old Conshohocken, because the town could not adapt to a changing culture where the automobile represented the future. Decisions taken now may once again place Conshohocken one step behind a changing culture. The irony lies in the fact that this time the automobile represents the past. Let me explain.

The automobile—or, rather, our embrace of it—played a greater part in the decline of Conshohocken than is generally understood. Both the Conshohockens came into being and grew during the nineteenth century without regard to the automobile, because it didn't exist. Their residents either walked or took what we today call "alternative transportation" to get to work or shopping. The result was a compact urban layout, with the industrial, commercial, and lower-income residences placed as close to each other as possible. As the twentieth century progressed, the increasing number of automobiles made this more and more of a problem, and downtowns everywhere began to suffer. Streets that had been perfectly adequate during the age of walking and public transportation could not handle even the fewer numbers who were going downtown in automobiles. Those new drivers didn't like the traffic congestion, and found parking difficult. Downtown could not deliver sufficient improvements for either problem, so shoppers began to drive their cars to the malls instead. The roads to these shopping areas were bigger, and the malls and plazas had not only parking, but ample, *free* parking.

The tightly packed homes in Conshohocken, also built for people who did not own cars, began to have their own automobile-related problems.

---

15. Michael E. Tolle, *They've Been Down So Long...* (North Charleston, SC: CreateSpace, 2015).

Parking was chief among them, and it remains so, but at least twice a day, traffic has become a problem, and one that is getting worse. Downtown's parking problem disappeared with downtown, but that of residential Conshohocken did not. In response, what had been originally designed and built as public spaces—local streets—came to be conceived as the private property of two groups of people. Local homeowners claimed the lanes closest to the curbs in front of their homes for parking their automobile(s) when they were not in use, leaving only the two middle two for moving vehicles. In those lanes reserved for people operating their automobiles, many of whom are only using them to either get

Today, Conshohocken is experiencing the highly unusual opportunity to build anew almost its entire lower floodplain, the core of that compact, urban layout. Proposals for residences, office buildings, and even a hotel are pending, and there seems to be no end to the trend. This is important because decisions made *right now* will go a long way toward determining whether the Old and the New ever have a chance of uniting in the new Conshohocken. These decisions involve the physical requirements for two separate priorities, and those requirements are antithetical. The issue is whether to prioritize the internal connections necessary for any sense of true community to arise, or the physical requirements for getting automobiles through town to one of the Interstates. In other words, what gets priority, the community or the automobile?

Once these priorities are set in concrete, steel, asphalt, and traffic-control systems, they will be next to impossible to change. The old Conshohocken, built before the automobile, could not be adapted for many reasons, but key among them was the simple fact that it could not substantially change its layout, particularly the width of its streets, nor could it supply parking without removing the very businesses for which the parking was needed.

New construction allows the parking half of the issue to be substantially dealt with, by simply including parking within the lots, if not the building itself. This is not true for the issue's other half, traffic congestion. Here is where the difference between remembering history and understanding it comes in. Today we know that no matter what changes are made, no matter how much space is allotted to roads or ramps, it will never be enough. The United States has spent untold billions of dollars attempting to reconcile the urban grid and the automobile, and they have all failed. Priority allotted to roads separates and isolates communities, but always fails to deal adequately with the number of automobiles that will use them. It's a lose-lose proposition. Conshohocken will experience increasing traffic congestion regardless of how much deference is given to streets, ramps, and signals, while that deference will detract from its livability. In 2012, the Facebook page "Conshohocken Business Development Commission" posted an interesting claim about what it perceived to be happening:

> "A once thought nearly impossible mission is quickly becoming a reality: the fusion of upper and lower Fayette Street is helping to achieve the goal of a walkable small-town Main Street."

I want to ask my Conshohocken readers if the past few years have proved this to be true. I have my suspicions, not least because that two-year-old post is also the last one ever to appear on the group's Facebook page. The article itself was borrowed from another Facebook page, that of the "Conshohocken Revitalization Alliance." That page is still active, and may have perhaps changed its positions. A recent post in "Conshohocken Real" says traffic is bad, and getting worse. I have also heard from one reader that the Conshohocken Elementary School's Halloween parade was relocated from Fayette Street to Harry Street due to parents' concerns over safety. There's a message emerging here.

Here's the irony of it all: today, many urban areas are reorienting themselves away from the automobile, and are, by this action, transforming themselves into more vibrant communities. The basic theme behind this movement is a "walkable city is a livable city," and it applies to towns as well. For communities looking to the future, an automobile-oriented town is the New Old. Been there, tried to do that, failed. Yet Conshohocken, blessed with an almost unique opportunity to make its new version virtually anew, seems to be building it around what is now the old, discredited approach, giving priority to the automobile. The Conshohocken that results from such decisions will make the borough just an exit off the Interstate, not a community.

11/21/14   **#4 in a Series**

Is Conshohocken Coming Back…or Just Being Taken Over? —"How to Be More of an Exit AND More of a Community"

I have been sounding the alarm lately about the downside to what is happening near the Conshohocken exit of the Interstates in southeastern Pennsylvania. I have suggested that the Borough faces—*right now*—

decisions that will determine its future, and have phrased that future as a choice: either a community, or just an exit off the Interstates.

Nothing is quite so simple, of course, and to give an example, I am going to clarify my stance on the all-important issue of transportation by making the apparently counterintuitive argument that Conshohocken can be more of a community if it becomes more of an exit. This does not apply to the automobile; the choice it presents is both stark and clear, and is as I have expressed it. The more that Conshohocken structures itself to accommodate the automobile, the more it mortgages its future as a community. It most definitely applies to what we today call "alternative transportation." Conshohocken is doubly blessed in this regard, and should work to take greater advantage of that fortuitous fact. The borough as a community can only benefit.

I have previously made the point that a "walkable town is a livable town." Today, walking counts as alternative transportation, along with bicycling and public transit. This is but one of the many 180-degree turns that history has made along the Schuylkill River. What had been the primary means of transportation during the glory days of the Schuylkill River towns has all but disappeared, but its remnants constitute the core of what we today call "alternative."

In the old days, the railroad delivered everything, from raw materials into the towns and factories to finished products from them to the world. Its lighter cousins, in turn, knit Conshohocken into a regional network. They delivered the better off to their jobs during the week and all classes of workers to the countryside for recreation on the weekends. The bicycle fad preceded the automobile fad. Still, when all is said and done, walking was the primary means of transportation for the vast majority of Conshohocken residents. They walked to work, they walked to shop, and they walked to visit friends in the neighborhood. The result? The proud, tightly knit, community-centered population of Conshohocken, Pennsylvania.

But that was then, this is now, and things have changed. The rail era is over. Light rail is gone, and isn't coming back anytime soon. But a survivor, the Norristown Regional Rail Line—I still want to call it the R6—still delivers people to and from the borough. This is a means of transportation for which Conshohocken should want to be even *more* of an exit than it is today. Every new rider is one fewer driver congesting the roads. I would like to think that a portion of the New coming to the Conshohockens to either live or to work will arrive and leave on it. It's a limited connection, but only Norristown has anything better, and it's just upriver on the same Regional Rail Line that passes through Conshohocken.

The railroad has also delivered to Conshohocken two other forms of alternative transportation, albeit rather indirectly: walking and bicycling. Back in the old days, two railroads ran through Conshohocken. The track bed of the Reading is now the Norristown line, but that of the long-gone Pennsylvania Railroad now hosts a rail trail, the Schuylkill River Trail. Conshohocken was an early beneficiary, and as the trail has been extended, improved, and connected, the number of people employing "alternative transportation" through town has steadily increased. Businesses that cater to trail users are beginning to find Conshohocken a potentially profitable location. The current campaign to bring a bicycle shop to the borough is an early sign of what will happen.

The New who will reside along the riverbank will find the Schuylkill Valley Trail to be convenient, perhaps even enticing, as they are expected to be a younger demographic. Few will likely use it to commute to and from work, but weekend use will be another story. Those who reside elsewhere and use the trail (walkers and bicyclists) will likely find Conshohocken attractive, if just as a brief refreshment stop. The borough's scenic location will draw a great many people who will not arrive in motor vehicles. That's all good—for them and for the town.

In marked contrast to my previous comments about the borough becoming no more than an exit for automobiles, Conshohocken's future as an exit for alternative transportation should actually be encouraged, for the general good of all. Whether you are riding on the train or moving yourself along the rail trail, you are not contributing to traffic congestion, oil consumption (and rising prices), or environmental degradation, to name but three of many bad things. The latter two may be somewhat ephemeral for Conshohocken residents, but the first is emphatically real, and getting worse. Thus, the more people who employ alternative transportation (this phrase sounds so strange to a historian) to or from their residences on weekdays or weekends, the better.

But there is much more to the story, and additional reasons for promoting these old-but-back-to-being-popular means of getting around. Alternative transportation is also closely associated with improving urban livability. If anything should be obvious from a study of American history, this should be. Communities actually existed back when today's *alternative* means of getting around was the primary one. It follows that while becoming more of an exit for alternative transportation will be a good thing, promoting alternative transportation within the borough will be even better. It will be great to have riverfront businesses and residents benefiting from those who come and go, but it will be even better if borough residents find it easy to get around town, and the riverfront benefits are shared.

Let's be realistic, of course. Old railroad track beds are perfect sites for bikes and walking paths because trains could only surmount low grades. Much the same is true of the New users. Much of Conshohocken, in considerable contrast, sits on a steep hillside. Still, a great deal can be done for the area in which a considerable portion of the population is coming to reside, and decisions concerning roads in that area should take into account the transit needs of the residents of the whole town. This is where transportation becomes subsumed into a larger issue, that of community access to the riverfront. That issue most definitely needs to be addressed, and I will do so in the next post.

But for now, let's accept two concepts: first, it will be a good thing if the new Conshohocken becomes as much an exit off the Schuylkill River Trail as it is off two Interstate highways; second, it will be an even better thing if the new Conshohocken is structured to allow some old-fashioned ideas to demonstrate their current relevance. The first is going to happen regardless. The second will require action by the Borough Council, supported by the population, because *it will be opposed by the developers*. That makes it much less likely to happen.

Conshohocken can only benefit by becoming friendlier to its readily available means of alternative transportation. It would be not just ironic but tragic if the community-building aspects of alternative transportation are shortchanged. If it only becomes much easier to leave or enter Conshohocken on foot or by bicycle than to get to other parts of town, then the full benefits of alternative transportation will not be realized. The age of the automobile and the Internet works against the human instinct for community. An emphasis on alternative transportation is a proven antidote to these decentralizing forces because it promotes both interpersonal and intracommunity connections. Building both is essential if the New Conshohocken wants to call itself what the Old Conshohocken certainly could: a *community*.

Is Conshohocken Coming Back…or Just Being Taken Over?—"Residence and Recreation…for the Favored Few?"

I introduced this series of blog posts about Conshohocken on by pointing out one of the 180-degree changes time has wrought on the lower Schuylkill Valley. I was talking about how what had historically been the lowest priorities for the riverbanks of every town—residence and recreation—were now the highest. All should be happy to hear that the new development is producing open space and recreation opportunities along Conshohocken's riverbank, where they have never been before. I am all about alternative transportation, open space, and community recreation, and so I applaud these aspects of what seems to be emerging in Conshohocken. Unfortunately, I also have my suspicions that all three may prove to be less significant builders of community than is everywhere else the case.

I have already written about alternative transportation that connects Conshohocken along the river and would help to connect it as a community. The questions involving open space and recreation are much broader, and require stepping back to review a basic issue first. This issue tends to get lost among the news about *this* building, *that* property, and a whole lot of money arriving. Fortunately, it isn't necessary for an outsider such as me to introduce it. A post from the Facebook page "Conshohocken Real" has already laid it out:

> "Are we okay with taking the river away from the people?"

The specific subject was O'Neill's proposed almost-six-hundred-unit apartment complex, but the question is appropriate for the entire waterfront. The old, dirty vestiges of an industrial past are almost gone. Conshohocken's riverfront is seeing—and will soon see more—new buildings, either residences or workplaces. As virtually the entire riverfront is being redeveloped, isn't it at least theoretically possible for Borough Council to foster that development with the whole community in mind? This would have been unthinkable in the "good old days," but isn't this a rare—almost unique—opportunity to visualize the new Conshohocken as an integrated, vibrant community, and to take actions to ensure development proceeds along that route?

Time for a reality check. First, "Conshohocken Real" phrased the issue in a rather populist manner, but as a historian, I'm compelled to point out that you can't take something away from those who never possessed it in the first place, and the "people" of Conshohocken never possessed the riverfront. Yes, a few did, due to our private property/free enterprise system, but they didn't purchase it for either their own residences or for the recreation of others. By the time they installed their railroads, furnaces, foundries, and power looms, no one with any money wanted to either live or recreate along the river anyway, so the issue never really came up.

Second, Conshohocken has already had the opportunity to design and build a planned, integrated development on just a portion of the land being affected now, and it didn't happen, largely (but not entirely) because of timing. The borough is now doing it the old-fashioned way, parcel by parcel, with purpose and implementation under the control of individual applicants who own each parcel. What is built where will have nothing to do with community needs, but will be strictly a function of the most profitable use of a particular piece of property. Writ large, it's the "American Way," in an interpretation recently demonstrating political strength. It's produced results in Conshohocken where community planning failed, and it will continue to dictate both the product and the pace.

Thus, the riverfront is again being carved up as private property because, in truth, it never ceased to be that. Still, developers know that inclusion of terms like "open space," "recreation," and the like help to smooth the application process, so expressions of these terms are sprinkled among the buildings that appear in the conceptual drawings. That's why O'Neill's current proposal for not quite six hundred new apartments comes with a "boardwalk" and a dock. I suspect that the details of both these concepts are still somewhat hazy. A boardwalk could mean anything, and as a longtime resident along the river, I can assure you that a public dock without a nearby public boat ramp is pretty much just a site to fish from.

The larger question is not about the nature of the benefits themselves, but in who will have access to them. A beautiful riverside view must be purchased (or rented), and individual companies will determine who gets the best view from their new office buildings. As for recreation, the story is more complex. Access will vary according to the activity, at least to some extent. Consider that time-honored Pennsylvania sport, rowing. A borough-owned strip of riverfront land will house the Conshohocken Rowing Center. The building itself is financed by the two schools whose rowing programs it will house, Malvern Prep and the Haverford School. Those are pretty upscale, not to mention private, programs (okay, rowing *is* a pretty upscale sport), but it's supposed to include a community rowing program. Sounds good…for a limited number of people. But how about more common, less specialized use of open space and recreational areas? What other, more broadly based recreational opportunities could be made available along the river, and what will it take to bring them about?

Then there is the question of broad community access to these benefits. They will all be located in the lower valley. How easy will it be for the residents up the hill to use them, and to actually get to them? How many wide, busy streets will they have to cross? Will the new recreational benefits help to unite the New and the Old, or will they give the New a privilege by location, further dividing them? The Conshohocken Rowing Center is a good idea, but it is also evidence that even outsiders can obtain access to the river by paying money. Is money to be the operative factor?

Questions are easy to ask, particularly semi-rhetorical ones like those above. When we begin to get into the issue of responsibility for actually achieving what we want—or failing to—we must simultaneously examine the restraints those in positions of responsibility must operate within. That means the second point of my reality check above deserves greater scrutiny. It will be all too easy to place blame incorrectly for what is probably going to happen. So, I will conclude this blog series on Conshohocken next time by throwing the wet blanket of reality over the chances of obtaining the utopia I have spent the previous weeks promoting. It's my way of balancing the books.

12/5/14   **#6 in a Series**

Is Conshohocken Coming Back…or Just Being Taken Over?—"The Credit, the Blame, and the Responsibility"

As I promised last time, I'm going to close out this blog series on Conshohocken's past and future by assigning the credit, the blame, and the responsibility for what is happening and what will happen. The credit and the blame are easy to place; it's the responsibility that will be tricky. That's where the Wet Blanket of Reality comes in.

First, the easy part. There is no argument about *what* has brought this all about; the only argument there is whether you assign to it the credit or the blame, and that pretty much depends on your point of view. The intersection of two Interstate highways in West Conshohocken is the reason for all that is happening around it. As I pointed out, the development of the area around an intersection of two major travel routes is a process that is both global and much older than capitalism, so the Conshohocken experience is nothing unusual at all (at least from a historian's point of view).

How it's happening is a function of our capitalist economic system. Industrial capitalism has moved on, but the modern "services" version is producing the details for the development of the "Conshohocken Exit." This new version recognizes no political boundaries. What is happening in Conshohocken is exactly the same as what is happening in West Conshohocken, minus the actual intersection. It can't be stopped, and the influence of local municipalities is largely limited to trimming its physical manifestations around the edges. That unpleasant truth must be recognized when we try to assign the responsibility for what we don't like.

I'm going to use O'Neill's new apartment complex proposal as an example of what happens when well-funded developers come to town, and to illustrate why "responsibility" is a difficult thing to properly assess. I have not looked at the details (or researched the specific facts) of the project, but I am trained to detect patterns, and what is happening hews closely to one of the basic patterns seen in communities, over and over again. Here's how it works:

Step 1: A municipal council, alarmed by size/nature of a developer's proposal, rejects it.

Step 2: Negotiations ensue, and a *slightly* modified proposal is offered to the council.

Step 3: The council approves the "new" proposal, as quietly as possible.

Step 4: Public reacts with "WTF?"

That's pretty much the way it went down for O'Neill's latest proposal for apartments along the riverfront. The Conshohocken Borough Council, justifiably alarmed at the scale of what is happening to Conshohocken, found sufficient objections to the zoning relief being desired to deny the project when it was first presented in September 2014. Negotiations nonetheless ensued, and less than a month later a "special meeting" was called to reconsider a modified proposal (in other words, they didn't even wait for the next regularly scheduled meeting). The changes were minimal, but they were sufficient; two council members switched their votes, and the new version passed.

Then came the public reaction. It largely held to the pattern, holding members of council responsible. The meeting was described as "questionable, off-schedule, and even as 'secret,'" and the council members who changed their votes were identified. Subsequent publicity has accused the two of "leading the way to the demise of Conshohocken." There has been an upsurge of resident awareness (which is all to the good), and even an attempt to establish how "developer friendly" each member of council is. One post summed the reactions up by saying, "We are scratching our heads. When are local elections already?"

I am late in offering to be the Wet Blanket of Reality to all this, because *Morethanthecurve.com* has already done the job, offering by far the most rational assessment of the affair. The site reminded its readers that the project was a "by right" development: the zoning code allows apartments to be built there. It also pointed out that looming over everything was the matter of O'Brien's lawsuit against Conshohocken, and "Concern that an existing legal action over the project could receive a favorable ruling from a judge, and then Borough Council would have no influence over what would be built. Through the settlement they were able to negotiate and get some concessions." Unfortunately, that site's subsequent dialogue—I use the term advisedly—with a reader demonstrated that even reality does not influence the opinions of some readers, but kudos to *Morethanthecurve.com* for trying.

My assessment of the O'Neill affair to date is largely the same, from painful experience. I have seen this pattern happen in my township upriver, and in several other places. Large developers employ packs of legal eagles that feast on the ordinances and zoning codes of each locality on which they descend. They examine each word, sentence, and paragraph, looking for any flaw, weakness, or opening into which a legal wedge can be inserted. Once they find one, the developer acts, and the locality is pretty much screwed, faced with an unpleasant choice: either fight the proposal and probably lose, or "negotiate," while a very large sword dangles over its head. If the community chooses the former course and loses, they have no control over what happens. If they "negotiate," they can at least get a fig leaf or two to help conceal the surrender.

The two council members who switched their votes may have been motivated by some version of this. If so, and the facts sustain this assessment, then it was a defensible choice, albeit an unpleasant one. You don't spend the taxpayers' money on legal fights you are pretty sure you are going to lose, so you hold your nose and cut the best deal you can. The pattern is unfortunately all too common, and illustrates the tilted playing field between government and private enterprise. After all, the sanctity of private property is the "American Way."

Morethanthecurve.com's most salient observation was this, however:

> "So, if this approval concerns you, your issue isn't with the developers, but the zoning code for the Borough.… If you are concerned about the health of the riverfront, traffic, etc., your efforts should be focused on changing the zoning code."

I am pleased to second that thought. O'Neill's proposed development—and, in fact, most of what is being proposed along the riverfront—lies within two "special zoning districts" established in 2001 and amended in 2005. These two districts were an attempt to provide for "orderly development" of the riverfront by "a mix of uses, including residential." There was never any question about O'Neill's right to build; the council could only trim around the margins. That zoning code, by the way, was changed as recently as 2013, when the allowable height of buildings on the riverfront was lowered from 250 feet to 75, among other things. The zoning code can be changed again, but only if borough residents realize how important it actually is, and push their elected representatives to change it.

So, residents of Conshohocken, where does the responsibility actually lie? The zoning code was rewritten to promote riverfront development, and that is exactly what is happening. It is easy (and occasionally justified) to blame politicians, but you should understand the legal restraints under which your elected representatives operate, and the potentially financially catastrophic results of having them follow their hearts instead of the recommendations of their legal counsel. We proclaim rather too strongly that the "people rule," when it's much more complicated than that.

I close this series of posts that might appear to be throwing a wet blanket on the rebirth of the Borough of Conshohocken, Pennsylvania, by offering one final consoling thought: too much money pouring into a small community will create problems, but it is better than too little money, or no money at all. Just ask the towns upriver. I am reminded of the popular saying: "Money can't buy happiness, but crying in a Mercedes beats crying on a bus." Even if you're stuck in traffic.

Bridgeport

3/28/14

Poor Bridgeport, So Close to...?

The people of Mexico have long had a saying that encapsulates their country's history: "Poor Mexico, so far from God, and so close to the United States." I would borrow that approach when speaking of the history of Bridgeport, Pennsylvania. I have no idea as to any theological distance for either Mexico or Bridgeport, but just as Mexico's history has been heavily influenced by its proximity to the United States, so has Bridgeport's history been influenced by its proximity to Norristown. Such geographic closeness has not served Bridgeport well.

Bridgeport became a self-governing borough in 1851; by that date, Norristown had been a borough for thirty-nine years, and the seat of Montgomery County for sixty-eight years. That gave it not only a head start, but also an insurmountable edge over its neighbor across the Schuylkill. Norristown spurned the Schuylkill Navigation Company's request to build on its bank of the river, so the company built a canal section along the floodplain of what would become the borough of Bridgeport. Schuylkill Navigation would contribute half of Bridgeport's name, but little else. By considerable contrast, the Philadelphia, Germantown & Norristown Railroad's (PG&N) arrival in 1835 would begin Norristown's rapid ascent as a community.

Bridgeport was not very far behind in establishing its own railroad connection, but the chronological comparison does not reflect the reality of the situation. The Reading Railroad built its line down the Schuylkill's right bank, and opened service between Reading and Philadelphia—and thus Bridgeport—in 1839. Unfortunately for Bridgeport, however, the Reading's sole focus was on moving coal, not people. The PG&N to Norristown was a general cargo line, and that cargo included people from the very beginning. Even after the Reading leased the line in 1870, it largely continued the general cargo practice. On the Reading's own line, people were hardly even considered at first, and servicing them was initially subcontracted. Transporting people never assumed any degree of priority along this line; many Bridgeport residents desiring to travel found that a walk across the DeKalb Street Bridge brought them a much more congenial treatment.

The most serious problems from the nearby presence of Norristown fell on the fundamental institutions any growing community must establish. Those of both self-government and policing could be underwritten by even a slowly growing population, given the low expectations of the time. Bridgeport was thus able to establish and maintain the modest level of local government characteristic of the times. Those private institutions around which an actual community arises and shapes itself, however, proved more difficult to establish. The local volunteer fire companies are an excellent example. Bridgeport experienced in full perhaps the most common event to strike the Schuylkill River towns during their industrial heyday: fire. Pretty much lacking revenue from commerce and, unlike Norristown, obtaining none from the presence of government, Bridgeport lagged badly in establishing a volunteer fire department. The borough depended on Norristown fire companies for the first forty years of its existence—and beyond that, in truth. This arrangement pleased no one. Norristown companies rotated the responsibility for calls from Bridgeport, which caused no little ill will, and occasional claims of failure to respond. Bridgeport's first volunteer fire company came into formal existence in 1891. The volunteer spirit was there from the beginning, but several years passed before it obtained enough equipment to be an effective presence, thus requiring continued assistance from Norristown. The Good Will Fire Company, Bridgeport's second, came into formal existence in 1915, and it, too, required some years to achieve usefulness.

No newspaper that established itself in Bridgeport ever survived for more than a few years. Bridgeport's only trolley line was a spur of the Norristown Passenger Railway Company until the Philadelphia and Western Railway built the high bridge across the Schuylkill. The P&W's goal was Norristown; Bridgeport received only a stop on the line, which was later closed.

Perhaps the heaviest, and easily the most obvious, of the many baneful effects Norristown's presence inflicted on Bridgeport was that imposed on the borough's commercial district. Bridgeport never caught up to Norristown's head start; Norristown's commercial sector had become the shopping location of choice for a wide swath of Montgomery County by the time Bridgeport came into existence, by which time the residents of the new borough had already been longtime customers of Main Street, Norristown, for anything more than the necessities of daily life. The major economic reason to establish a business in Bridgeport was the toll charged for crossing the DeKalb Street Bridge; that encouraged the establishment of small businesses that could provide items a family needed on a daily basis. After bridge travel was made free in 1884, even those businesses were threatened.

A business directory published jointly for Norristown and Bridgeport in 1912 (the year of Norristown's centennial as a borough) demonstrates the commercial dominance that the larger borough exercised during the "golden years" of both communities. Every category listed stores in Norristown, but few listed any in Bridgeport. Among the facts the directory revealed was that while Norristown possessed thirteen stores selling "dry and fancy goods," Bridgeport possessed none. Norristown boasted twelve furniture stores, but there were none in Bridgeport. And the list goes on: category after category lists stores in Norristown, but none in Bridgeport. The only category that comes as no surprise is that of lawyers; none had hung out their shingles in Bridgeport, but sixty-nine had done so in Norristown. It was the county seat, after all.

Any numerical summation comparing the respective business centers of the two towns would also not reflect how many Bridgeport commercial firms were actually branches of the original Norristown store. Two prominent examples were Spillane's Five and Ten Cent Store and Daub Hardware. Both locations of both stores would close, as commercial collapse enveloped both boroughs.

But that was then, this is now, and things have changed. Simply put, it is doubtful that Norristown still exerts sway of *any* sort over Bridgeport. It still possesses the superior transit connections it always has, although considerably diminished in both number and variety, but little else in Norristown would deter Bridgeport from establishing anything that could be supported by a population of its size.

But what should those things be, in this time of stagnation for most of the towns along the Schuylkill River? Industry has pretty much gone, and it's not coming back, at least in a size sufficient to employ more than a fraction of the borough's residents. A commercial resurgence is even more unlikely, because for Bridgeport, the burden of nearness to a larger, more prosperous neighbor has merely shifted from north of the borough to south of it. Bridgeport is now "so close to King of Prussia" that any plans for commercial resurgence should be given a very close reading.

Let's examine Bridgeport's situation through a broad historical lens. In the early twenty-first century, Bridgeport is enduring, as are countless small, traditional urban areas, the complete reversal of the conditions that led to its birth, growth and prosperity in the nineteenth century. The residents of Bridgeport, as with each Schuylkill River town, found work, religion, information, and entertainment—the whole package excepting big-ticket items—within the boundaries of their respective communities. As a result, each town along the Schuylkill River has historically been inwardly focused. The vast majority of residents not only worked within their own borough, but they walked to work, to church, and to the store. Bridgeport's residents were no doubt patrons of commercial entertainment across the river, as Norristown possessed several such venues, but as with every river town, Bridgeport's entertainment centered on the community's churches.

Not only have those things changed, most of them have changed a full 180 degrees. At the dawn of the twenty-first century, what percentage of Bridgeport residents work in the borough? How many walk to work, to shop, or even to church? In this information age, do they even socialize in large groups at all? Most significantly, the looming presence of Norristown is no longer a factor, because Norristown no longer looms. Bridgeport is now, for the first time in its existence, free to pursue its future without significant reference to Norristown, and certainly no deference. Bridgeport has a past as a quiet, unassuming, modestly sized and locally oriented community, but that past is no longer a guide for the future.

For Bridgeport, the fundamental physical facts remain: it's a small, urban area on a hillside with decent, if not exactly adjacent, transportation connections. The housing stock is old, but there are several vacant lots and even areas. The railroad remains a presence, but not a stimulus, and the western end of town will probably remain under the shadow of the SEPTA Route 100 trolley for some time. Little else about the past need direct Bridgeport's future. The borough's population, and pretty much that alone, holds Bridgeport's fate in its hands. They should take advantage of the opportunity.

Royersford and Spring City

5/30/14

The Discreet Charm of the Twin Boroughs

Many adjectives are being employed to describe the state of the towns along the lower Schuylkill River; I have yet to encounter "charming." That's a shame, but quite understandable. Norristown and Pottstown, the larger towns—with the larger problems—get the most attention—mostly negative, the kind that makes news. Phoenixville, by considerable contrast, is a "happening" town, as are "the Conshohockens," although what is happening there is fundamentally different. The smaller towns assume a sort of invisibility; they don't enter into the discussion.

So I hereby nominate two Schuylkill River towns. Of the eight towns along the Schuylkill River between Reading and Philadelphia, Royersford and Spring City are the only two that deserve the appellation "charming," because they *are* charming, in the old-fashioned sense of the term.

Note that I said charming, not "bustling," and certainly not "happening." Their attraction is simply their atmosphere. They are lifestyle gems lying along the riverbank, waiting to be rediscovered. Both are little versions of the norm for Schuylkill towns, built along the road that approaches the river and that which parallels the river, and out from their intersection near the riverbank itself. Royersford's Main Street descends to the river, while Spring City's Main Street parallels it. The downtowns that spread out from those intersections are largely empty now. Royersford's last remaining large downtown commercial business, the LeBow Furniture Store, a Main Street fixture since the 1940s and family owned, just closed in 2014. Spring City clings even more precariously to its hillside than does Royersford. Its Main Street offers the contrasting view of buildings along the riverside that are built out on foundations over the incline, while those on the opposite site are cut into the hillside itself. Spring City's downtown retains more of its old, graceful buildings, including the Spring City Hotel, which dates back to 1896, at the center.

But it is the area between downtown and the river of both boroughs that has changed the most. The industries that used to line the banks of both boroughs are virtually gone. Buckwalter Stove Company was Royersford's largest employer, with a payroll at its height of about twelve hundred workers. It was located just upriver from the bridge. Little remains save one building, preserved and repurposed with a grant. Across the river, the Spring City Foundry Company, which sits on the site of the original 1840 stove factory, still makes cast iron products. Today, they make lampposts. The new ones being installed in both Royersford and Spring City were made here, but so were all the lampposts in all Disney locations. That's pretty much it.

This is the important change, the one that has made both Royersford and Spring City quaint and, to me at least, charming places to live. For those of us who don't remember the industrial heyday of the Schuylkill River towns, it is difficult to imagine how utterly un-charming their riversides were. Descending to the river from either side would have been akin to entering Dante's *Inferno*. Right up close to both downtowns—within one block at the most—were the very fires of hell that rendered iron and steel into usable items. The factories were bunched closely together, and the cumulative heat and smoke literally hung over the area, sometimes obscuring the sun. The riverside was a cacophony of noise; the ground itself shook and the air stank from the factories, augmented frequently by the sound and smoke of the railroad trains that delivered the raw materials and carried away the finished products. The din was awful, as hammers pounded metal, and metal shrieked in protest. The fewer but still numerous textile factories did not belch as much heat or flame, but the air inside them, filled with small bits of thread, must have been at least as unhealthy for the women crowded at their spindles. Those industries all dumped their wastes into the river indiscriminately, rendering it little more than a fetid sewer in warm weather. No one used it for anything if they could avoid it.

Ah, the good old days.

During the industrial heyday of the Schuylkill River towns, the objective of virtually all their residents was to live *as far away from* the river as their incomes allowed. Only the poorest—the day laborers, the unskilled, the feeble—lived close to the river, and then only because that's where the cheapest shacks were. Those with steadier working class lives moved as far up the hillsides of both towns as they could and still be able to walk to work. The emerging management, white-collar class could afford to move farther away, particularly once local trolleys began operating. The earliest local tycoons built homes in downtown, the better to demonstrate their wealth, but later generations would construct their mansions farther and farther away, usually up the hill. They had private carriages, and then automobiles, to transport them.

But that was then, this is now, and things have changed. In fact, they have changed a full 180 degrees. The old realities that gave birth to and shaped the river towns are gone. Industry is one of them. Businesses, even factories, remain, but the riverbanks have undergone and are still undergoing fundamental changes. Now, as you descend into either Royersford or Spring City, the air is not just clean, it's cooler, not to mention quieter. The area near Main Street and 1st Avenue in Royersford was ground zero for noise in the good old days; now it has a small riverfront park, featuring lampposts made just across the river. A few trains belonging to Norfolk Southern Railroad still pass through, but they carry no passengers. The old Reading track bed now hosts bikers and walkers on the Schuylkill River Trail, along what is now a scenic river.

The future of the old riverside industrial sectors in each Schuylkill River town lies in residence and recreation. Yet the "twin boroughs" demonstrate by their differing paths in this direction that the specific future still depends on the ancient past, the geography of the land itself. Royersford possesses the larger riverside floodplain. Empty buildings littered the area until after the turn of the new century, but that is changing. South of the bridge is Riverwalk at Royersford, a planned residential development. The proposed plan had been more transformative, but the bad economic times of recent years have diminished those hopes. Not all the old buildings have been torn down; one nearby sports a mural that evokes Royersford's industrial past. It should be judged as art, not history (in the mural, the Reading locomotive should have been green). The recent bad economic times also explain the riverfront park. A six-floor apartment building was planned for the site, but a developer could not be found. The borough bought the ground and made it into a recreation area instead.

Spring City has taken a different path. It has also refurbished and repurposed old factories for housing—not condominiums for young couples but residence communities for seniors. There are no fewer than four such centers in the community. One of them is in the center of town, the former Flag Factory, renovated and converted into housing. Another is located in the old Gruber Mill farther along Main Street. All four are for seniors with limited incomes.

Even less may be "happening" in Spring City than in Royersford, but that—

and the beautiful old buildings—are exactly why I would, if forced, rate Spring City as the more "charming" of the two. But there's another reason I like it: Spring City is actually about to open a new library. I feel like that statement should be boldfaced, or at least capitalized, and the news spread far and wide. What town opens a new library today? Ten years ago, a hundred-year old former Spring City librarian died without heirs, and left $500,000 each to the library and to her church. The library struggled for ten years to fulfill her wish for a new building. Opposition arose, from some on borough council, who believed that libraries are a thing of the past in this digital era, but, more sadly, some from the church that was the beneficiary of her will. They placed every possible obstacle in the way, but when I drove by this past spring, the parking lot had just been paved. Any town that makes such a stake in the future deserves a good one.

In the final analysis, what makes the twin boroughs charming places to live is that they have managed to retain much of what was good about the old days—the closeness of everything, beautiful old buildings—while having shed what was bad: the grime, pollution, noise, smoke, and smell. They are quiet, scenic places to live, and those are hard to find these days. And who knows? Your arrival might be the spark that allows them to be "discovered." The old storefronts virtually cry out for new, trendy niche businesses, and the several vacant ones suggest that the rent will be cheap. Why couldn't Royersford and Spring City become miniature versions of Phoenixville?

CHAPTER FOUR
SOME ADVICE ON TACTICS

8/13/13

The Wrong Attitude

I actively solicit—and truly welcome—reader comments on my blog posts. I make it a point to focus on controversial subjects, and the subjects themselves originate from what I learn from you. One reader of this blog responded to my question, "When were the Good Old Days?" with an opinion that I consider significant, although I do not agree with it. This gives me the opportunity to make a point long planned, except for its time of insertion in this blog. That time is now.

The writer begins his reply to my question with an observation about the closing of Norristown State Hospital. He is on solid ground with this, on a subject I have discussed and will discuss further. He next shifts to national politics and to his main point. His phraseology reveals him as an extreme example of a type whose numbers give every appearance of being substantial. People may not be comfortable with the totality of his claim, but what he says strikes a responsive and sympathetic emotional chord among many.

I reprint the fundamental point of his letter here in full:

> "We must remember it's not about Dems vs. Reps. It's about We the people vs. the Government. It's about an illegitimate government, and that is Federal and LOCAL. It's about government that has lost it's rightful purpose, to serve and protect, and now is the enemy of free spirit."

To hear such rhetoric about the federal government is rather common these days, and that aspect of it shall not concern us here. The writer did, however, go out of his way to capitalize LOCAL, so he clearly meant our municipal and township governments, both the elected and those who occupy the many boards, authorities, and committees at the local and county level. I can at least agree with the writer that in our municipalities, it's rarely about "Dems. vs. Reps.," or at least it shouldn't be. From that point on, however, we part ways.

While it is unlikely that too many people would agree totally with his opinion (I hope), his blanket condemnation of those in government resonates with many of those are move vocal lately. I have attended a considerable number of local government public meetings over the decades, and the sight of residents angrily asking why the council/authority/board/committee is not working "for the people" has been commonplace.

This blanket assumption that government is inherently oppressive, and that those in it are engaged in a behind-the-scenes plot to enrich themselves and fritter away everyone's hard-earned tax money, fatally skews the viewpoint of those who allow it to dominate. Such an assumption processes life's experiences through a very dark lens—one that predisposes far too many toward easy, soul-satisfying judgments about people and issues that deserve a more nuanced and balanced examination. Those afflicted with this syndrome tend to be grouped among a community's "apathetic" citizens, but they deserve a category all their own, for they exert an influence that is quite different from that of true apathy. In fact, it's much worse; whereas a characteristic of the apathetic is that they don't care enough to comment, let alone act, nihilists of this persuasion care too much to realize the negative effect of either.

I term this "The Wrong Attitude" for two reasons: One, it's not true, two, it's counterproductive.

I shouldn't have to produce facts to substantiate my first point (remember, we are talking about *local* government here). These people really are your neighbors; they are much more like you than any bureaucrats at the state or federal level. Why would they join in this alleged massive conspiracy in our boroughs and townships? What's in it for them? It certainly isn't money. We are, after all, talking about governments caught between the rising costs of providing the services you all expect and the political death that results from raising taxes. Where is the opportunity for self-enrichment? Not all that many years ago, the combination of better economic times, a more trusting public, and a much less intrusive press did occasionally allow such activities, but those conditions have virtually disappeared.

Not only is it ridiculous to *assume* that local officials are both venal and incompetent, it is counterproductive to let them know you think along those lines. Once you develop such a reputation, they will smile and politely give you your say, but they will no longer actually listen. That can be unfortunate if you really do have a solid point to make.

Please do not read the above as a blanket endorsement of any, let alone all, local elected or appointed government officials, but only as a denial of any claim that they are *ipso facto* venal and/or oppressive—that they are "out to get you" or "out to get rich." They may be lazy, they may have the wrong vision for your community, and they may actually be incompetent. However, each one deserves careful scrutiny on a regular basis, and should be called to account if the facts so warrant. Distrust can be healthy, but beware of reflexive disbelief. Blanket condemnation of and disassociation from your local governments can only lead to them being allowed to operate without the necessary scrutiny. That, in turn will only help those assumptions about lack of accountability and purpose become self-fulfilling.

While you are exercising the due diligence that your are allowed under today's laws governing lawmakers, you should begin by giving them the benefit of the doubt about why they sought election or appointment. Then, as you examine their actions, recognize that they are very liable to see situations in different terms than you do, often because of the requirements of their offices or positions. They may be wrong, but they didn't just suddenly go over to the dark side. It is your right as a citizen to judge, but do so according to the facts, as unfiltered as possible by some underlying assumption.

As a final point, let me further distance myself from those with "the wrong attitude" by encouraging any of you across the region who are dissatisfied with local conditions to actually *run* for office, or volunteer to serve on a board. You, and your attitude of working toward community improvement, are greatly needed. Just don't be surprised if, having achieved your goal, some people begin to view you in a different way, perhaps even those who know you well. It's part of the price you pay, and part of why that so-common attitude is wrong: those who serve in local government are not takers, they are givers.

11/1/13

It's Municipal Election Time: Get Out and Vote!

Every November, and occasionally at other times, each of you has an opportunity to make a statement about how you view your local community. It's municipal election time. If you don't read this post soon, it might be pretty much academic, and that would be a real shame.

Let's be realistic. You probably won't have a wide variety of opportunities, and you may be unhappy with the opportunities you do have. That doesn't mean you shouldn't make the best of them this time, and see what you can do to make next time better.

Perhaps the saddest thing about the electoral process in our country is the low turnout; municipal elections see the lowest turnout, making them the saddest of all. To my academic mind, this seems strange. Local government is responsible, directly or indirectly, for community safety, street repair and plowing, code enforcement, and a host of things of direct, personal interest to voters. It is also the smallest body politic in which we cast votes, meaning it takes fewer people to have a real effect. This is the only redeeming corollary to the problem of low turnout: if the total number of votes cast is small, the number needed to win is even smaller. That makes the local odds the best anyone who ventures into politics will ever have to face. Thus, the occasional independent candidate does enter the lists, and the success rate in local elections is much higher than at any other level.

For all that, the task of making an impact for good on the local level remains huge. The numbers a candidate needs to win appear small, until you actually go out and try to find voters on your side. A major part of the reason is apathy. There is absolutely nothing new about this, of course, and apathy remains the real enemy, just as it always has been. Some people just can't be reached, but you keep on trying anyway. I hope. If local history suggested any differently, I would say so, but it doesn't. The more things change…

Apathy may be the community activist's primary enemy, but it is by no means the only one. Another problem stems from what I have called in these posts "the wrong attitude." That particular post produced the most negative comments of any (so far), but I stand by what I said. Many of you may be tempted to "throw *all* the bums out," and vote accordingly. That is an attitude toward which I have greater sympathy these days, in view of recent events in Washington. Still, I don't recommend you apply it even on the national level, and *absolutely not* on the municipal level. Your vote counts too much.

What is coming up shortly is an election, your constitutional opportunity to replace those who need replacing. You make (or you should make) that decision after becoming acquainted with the local issues, on an individual basis. An informed, selective "no" is always justified, and an across-the-board "no" may on occasion be justified when it is based on accumulated facts; however, an *uninformed, reflexive* "no" is *never* justified.

That's why I find the efforts of the local community activist groups so encouraging. They know full well the problems of apathy and attitude, and get involved anyway. Each group is taking its own approach, because different communities present different conditions and require different approaches. Each group of the Facebook Alliance, from the Schuylkill Valley to Bellevue in western Pennsylvania and from Norristown to Allentown, is active in making people aware of the election, what the issues are, and who is running. Some are endorsing or at least promoting specific candidates. Others are not. All, however, post appeals to vote on Facebook, and continue to inform their residents of the conditions the existing officials tolerate and the new voices that want change.

Most important of all is how so many local groups are trying to educate people, making them not just voters but *informed* voters. They post election information, organize events, and invite municipal officials, representatives and candidates to participate. A most encouraging sign is that the different activist groups are doing this good work *jointly*, in addition to keeping each other informed. I can't mention each event in each town, but want to offer major kudos to Norristown Men of Excellence[16] and Norristown Nudge[17] for jointly organizing a candidates' forum, as just one example. There are many others.

While I want to commend the usual groups for their more-than-usual efforts, I also want to place a spotlight on those who have emerged from other groups to lead these information crusades. The Facebook page Bridgeport, PA,[18] is a general discussion group, not primarily an activist one. A few members of the group joined together to generate resident interest in the upcoming election (not to mention the appointment of a new chief of police). This was not an attempt to take sides, but to inform borough residents of who the candidates were and where they stood on local issues. They went about this the right way—openly discussing the process, seeking input from other members of the discussion group. They first asked other residents for the issues they want raised and the questions they want

---

16. Norristown Men of Excellence: https://www.facebook.com/nmoe19401?fref=ts
17. Norristown Nudge: https://www.facebook.com/NorristownNudge?fref=ts
18. Bridgeport, PA: https://www.facebook.com/groups/bridgeportpa/

put to borough candidates. They assembled the responses and cast them into ten questions. They put the questions to the candidates for council, then posted the questions and the responses one by one. The fact that each candidate answered each question is a tribute to just how open and fair the process was. This judgment is reinforced by the fact that one current council member responded, despite his not running for office again. The online discussion was the important thing, of course, and Bridgeport residents were the beneficiaries. There are also signs that resident activism might continue after the elections, a very encouraging development.

So, once again, dear friends, into the breach, even though this democracy thing can be really annoying. Winston Churchill, who knew a little about the subject, once said, "Democracy is the worst form of government ever conceived by the mind of man, except for all the others." Win or lose, we should keep that in mind.

11/29/13

Lessons from the Pennrose Affair

Some years ago a mentor of mine, a veteran of many local government skirmishes, observed rather bitterly to me, "You know that old saying, 'You can't fight city hall?' Well, it's wrong. You can fight city hall; you just can't win." I'm sure he wasn't the first to make that observation, nor the last, because it is, lamentably, very close to true. But not always.

News broke this past July that may herald a rare win for a group of organized local residents over a development project that gave every appearance of being "wired" and on its way to approval. The project, referred to by the name of its developer, Pennrose, was to build a retail/apartment complex at the corner of DeKalb and Airy Streets in Norristown. The news that Pennrose Inc. had failed to meet a deadline for a portion of the financing called the project's future into serious question. The residents who led the opposition appear to have won a victory in their effort to keep a subsidized housing complex out of Norristown's core. This deserves to be celebrated. It also deserves to be studied.

Now that some time has passed, we can examine the Pennrose affair within a larger context. There are lessons to be learned—lessons that urban community activists would do well to heed, regardless of the nature of their communities or where they happen to be located. The specifics of this case apply to Norristown alone, but the rules of the game are the same everywhere. You may ignore the specific facts, if you wish, but I would submit to you that the lessons apply to *you*, and *you*, and *you* too.

In the interests of full disclosure, let me declare that the following opinions are mine alone, and derive solely from my reading of the publications available to everyone. I have not communicated in any way with any of the participants as to motives, plans, tactics or anything else.

A Bit of Background

The Pennrose project was to construct a ninety-six-unit apartment building, with five thousand square feet of retail space on its ground floor. Twenty-two of the rental units would also be located on the ground floor. This was a point of contention, and I will return to that in a future post. A much bigger issue was that sixty of the ninety-six rental units would offer "affordable" rents subsidized by a tax credit program. In other words, Pennrose was "subsidized housing."

About the location: today the site is a sporadically used parking lot, owned by Montgomery County (this is important), useful mostly to churchgoers on Sundays. Years ago, however, it was the site of Norristown Borough Hall (a building always referred to as "city hall," for unknown reasons), and lies directly adjacent to the old, long-closed, county prison. In short, it's in the core of old Norristown.

The two issues coalesced to offer both municipal officials and residents this basic question: is such a combined-use, subsidized-rent building a suitable occupant for this core location? The project's progress through the approval thicket seemed to indicate that Norristown's municipal government believed it was. The project required a number of variances from zoning requirements, which it received, but which proved to be the source of its undoing. A citizen's group arose out of nowhere christened itself "Norristown Nudge," and began to agitate against the project. The project's funding came undone back in July, and no word of its future has surfaced as of the date this was written.

The best way I can pay tribute to the "Pennrose Affair" is to extract from it the lessons that I believe are applicable elsewhere. There are three lessons, and each will be the subject of a separate post.

Lesson #1: It's Not Over; It Never Is

Everyone concerned should believe that reports of the project's death are greatly exaggerated. Assume instead that it is merely on hold, and keep your ear to the ground.

Pennrose lost a portion of its financing, and the delay imposed by the lawsuit (more about this in a later post) may cause other components of that financial structure to exit, which they may have already done. Or they may not. More likely, another financial structure for the same or a similar project is being planned for the future. Pennrose is in the business of constructing such government-supported housing structures; it's what they do, and they are good at it, particularly the financing part. The same news of their failure to qualify for funding for their Norristown project contained news of their success in another project in another location. Funding cycles mean just that; they will come around again. The July date was cycle two of the finance agency's calendar. You should assume that the cycle process will continue. Companies like Pennrose don't take rejection personally; they are not going to get offended and walk away. Exactly what they might do is not yet known, but you can be sure Pennrose is exploring all possibilities, with walking away from something that was so close to approval not very high on their priority list.

Keep in mind also that Pennrose has no financial "carrying costs" on the property while the legal issue is resolved. They don't own it, didn't take an option on it, or (as far as we know) commit any money that would be due regardless. On that score, at least, Pennrose can essentially afford to wait. Such costs are often critical in a fish-or-cut-bait decision on whether to advance a project, but not in this case. Also, do not lose sight of the fact that if the property's owner, Montgomery County, was willing to sell it for this project, they would probably be amenable if approached again, by Pennrose or some other developer.

A company that specializes in such projects should not be counted out after the first round—and that's just what it was, not the end of the fight. I might be wrong, but both research and personal experience tell me otherwise.

Lesson #2: A Lawsuit is Worth a Thousand Petitions

As I observed in my previous post, the Pennrose project in Norristown was "wired." Municipal leaders (a majority, at least) and planners were expeditiously removing all obstacles to its final approval. Then everything came to a sudden halt.

Why?

At the risk of offending some dear souls in Norristown Nudge, the Pennrose project was not stopped by the petition against it, nor by the public pleas of outraged residents. The municipal council might have been swayed by this expression of popular opinion had the issue ever actually gotten to it, but I seriously doubt it. This tactic, exercised alone, had two chances of success: slim and none. Many of you in other towns might have your own evidence that this is true.

Don't get the wrong idea here. I hold that there are few rights in a democracy more precious that the ability to petition for redress of grievances. That right was exercised during the Pennrose Affair, in its modern, digital, form. For that, I offer kudos all around. At this point in my life, I have long ago forgotten how many petitions I have carried, let alone how many I have signed. I have not kept careful track, but it is entirely possible that not one of them was successful. Maybe I am just the patron saint of lost causes, but I think there is more to it.

A petition has two fundamental weaknesses. First, it is virtually impossible to get an absolute majority of any body politic to sign a particular petition. You always get far fewer than that, and in this day of urban community apathy the percentage of signatures you get is hugely smaller. Thus anyone can dispute your claim to be voicing "the will of the people."

The second weakness is more fundamental, and ultimately unanswerable: a body of elected officials may choose to heed your petition…or it may choose not to. The job description allows this kind of judgment call, albeit with the attendant electoral risks down the road. It's part of our republican form of government (that's small "r," by the way), as is the deliberate inclusion of "down the road," via scheduled elections, to keep the people's representatives from being removed at the people's whim.

Please understand: I am in *no way* denigrating the importance of petitions, only suggesting that people should have a realistic understanding of how, where, and why petitions are important. Everyone who initiates or carries one believes in its cause; this naturally leads you to believe that once its obvious rightness is brought to the attention of your leaders, they will recognize the justice of your cause and take remedial action. When this doesn't happen, the resulting hurt and anger too often lead to a rejection of further efforts: "They didn't listen! They never do! It's hopeless! The game is rigged!" Been there, done that.

You should treat a petition, first and foremost, as an organizing tool. Keep track of who signed. You should not only contact those people the *next* time something similar appears on the horizon, but also keep them informed of the current actions in the interim. A series of *ad hoc* unconnected campaigns that have to repeat the organize-and-build-enthusiasm part each time is a waste of energy and resources that could be better applied to achieving your goal. Nevertheless, a petition is still a virtual requirement to obtain the needed publicity for your cause; the fourth estate (even in digital disguise) always pays attention when the word "petition" is mentioned.

It is important to understand, however, that the petition opposing Pennrose did not bring the project to a halt—a lawsuit did. Opponents of the lawsuit filed a lawsuit appealing the variances the project had been granted. That lawsuit is still pending. The simple existence of the suit, pending though it is, was sufficient. The lawsuit meant that Pennrose was not in position to "build by right" when a deadline approached, a necessary precondition for construction loans, regardless of their source.

That's the difference between any number of petitions and one lawsuit: confronted by petitions, a representative governmental authority has the right to say yes or no; confronted by a lawsuit, it has no choice but to respond, in the legal arena, not the political one. In that arena, political skills and connections count for a lot less; the citizen and his government are a lot more equal.

Unsure about how the lawsuit will turn out? Worried that you might lose? Don't be. A lawsuit is not about winning or losing; it's about delay and expense. You file a lawsuit to inflict both on the other side. In our legal system, few lawsuits are judged without merit and dismissed. "Everybody deserves their day in court." That day will take some time to arrive, and attorneys charge by the hour. The goal of a lawsuit is usually to force the other side to the point where it no longer makes financial sense to continue the struggle. The problem here is that the developers utilize the law on a more or less continuous basis; they have deep pockets and the names of attorneys on speed dial. Civic organizations do not. That's all the more reason to keep your ear to the ground and your people (the ones who signed your previous petition) on standby. You never know when or where the next one is coming from.

Lesson #3: It's All About the Benjamins; It Always Is

Lesson #3 is actually an old expression, long popular with historians. Okay, so I updated the words a little; the principle hasn't changed. A generation ago, my cultural reference might have been, "follow the money"; that means the same thing. It always has been, is now, and ever shall be the best road to understanding *how* and *why* something happened the way it did. It also explains why Norristown municipal government wanted the Pennrose project to go through.

Other motives were advanced, of course. One member of council claimed that subsidized apartments on the location were consistent with the community effort to develop an "Arts Hill," as it would provide low-cost housing for low-income artists. This is patent sophistry, of course, but even sophistry has a cause to support, however deceptively.

It was actually all about the Benjamins or, put more properly, *revenue*. Norristown needs more revenue, and the project would have provided some, in the form of property tax revenue at the very least. Norristown residents are always pointing out how few services they receive for the taxes they pay (sound familiar, anyone?). They are right (as are you in other towns), but the unpleasant fact is that *every* municipality is in a constant struggle for more revenue. Many face a declining tax base, but even for those that don't, the cost of municipal services rises at a greater rate than the tax base grows. Everyone is aware that over the past few decades municipal governments have been shedding what have been traditional services financed by the general fund, instead transforming each, one by one, into a specific service financed by a specific tax (excuse me, I meant "fee," of course). Municipal services from trash collection to emergency response have been subjected to this, all for the same reason: revenue.

As I mentioned earlier, the fact that the project was subsidized housing led a group of residents (who are otherwise among those who clamor for greater municipal services) to oppose the project despite the revenue it would generate. They had a very valid point (remember, I celebrated their accomplishment), but we should at least recognize that this wasn't a one-sided issue. I have no problem believing that the municipal council would rather have had a more appropriate use for the site, but they were willing to accept the Pennrose offer. Why? Because they need revenue badly, and probably believed that *this was the best offer they were going to get.* That's a harsh judgment, but I suspect it hews all too closely to the financial facts of life today. Recognition of the realities facing municipal governments should, I believe, serve to mitigate the moral judgments that too often follow their unpopular decisions.

Speaking of harsh realities, let's focus on the figure at the heart of the unpleasant choice that the council faced. That figure is five thousand. That is the square footage of the building's ground floor allotted to commercial space. It's smaller than the project's footprint, and the reason why the plan included apartments on the ground floor. The variance granted for this departure from the zoning code led to the project's demise, because it was why the lawsuit against the project was filed. Pennrose was quite clear as to why they sought the variance. Here's how the *Times Herald* article phrased it:

> "Pennrose alleged that it cannot construct more commercial space on the ground floor because 5,000 square feet of commercial space is what Pennrose is comfortable with, that constructing more than 5,000 square feet of commercial space would present a leasing risk to Pennrose, and that it would effect [sic] the development budget making the development infeasible."

That conclusion was not the result of any corporate animosity toward Norristown, or a desire to stick the municipality with yet another Section 8 housing project. It derived from a dispassionate analysis of the condition of Norristown today, expressed in strictly financial terms. It was all about the Benjamins, and how much risk Pennrose was willing to take to make some. At no time did Pennrose even consider whether Norristown "needed" what it planned to build. It follows that all arguments about what Norristown needs or doesn't need expressed in opposition to these projects are irrelevant—soul-satisfying to utter, yet inadmissible in the court of capitalism (that was Lesson #2).

As difficult as it may be to admit, no individual, board, or corporation involved in this affair meant to do harm. Those who fight for their communities must never forget that, to your opposition (to borrow an expression from another milieu), "it's nothing personal; it's just business." The result to Norristown from this common and legal application of that belief, however, may have been just as dangerous. That makes it very personal on the receiving end.

Therein lies the challenge. Your opposition looks upon all this as strictly business, and the percentage of their victories should indicate how important such an attitude is, whether in the midst of the fight or during the interval between the last one and the next one (remember Lesson #1). The most important thing is to maintain a constant—yet dispassionate—vigilance. Every community activist knows, however, that this most important thing is also the most difficult task you face, to retain that spirit which fueled and animated the effort you take pride in. I would add to this truth my belief that retaining the structure (i.e., communication) you developed during your effort is as important—and as difficult. Your opposition, whose very business it is to retain both structure and spirit, expect—with considerable reason—that you will not be able to retain either. Thus they go about their business, and if the ever-shifting arrangement of funding sources presents another opportunity for such a project, they will seize it. It's what they do; it's why they exist and operate under the more-than-full protection of the law in a market economy. After all, giving those with money the advantage is the American way.

12/19/14

Parochialism Might Be Your Town's Biggest Weakness

This post deals with a question that has appeared frequently in response to my series of posts on the Conshohockens, and that addresses an important issue: "How can you understand what [fill in the name of your town here] is like if you didn't live there?" My readers don't phrase it that way, of course; they just assume it can't be done. This is an example of parochialism, an attitude that is not only wrong but also counterproductive.

It is, unfortunately, very commonly held. One of my greatest pleasures during my years working for the Historical Society of Montgomery County (HSMC) was getting to know a woman named Florence Young, known to everybody as "Johnny." She was a grand lady—witty, gracious, and a volunteer at the HSMC for decades. She contributed greatly to preserving the HSMC's collections during a period of leadership and funding stagnation. She possessed an extraordinary mind, still razor-sharp when I met her, with an encyclopedic knowledge of Norristown social history. She knew who was descended from and related to whom, and I was never around her but that I wished I had a tape recorder with me. When I began to research *What Killed Downtown?*[19] she was one of the first people I contacted. I began a recorded interview by assuring her that I was going to write a history of downtown Norristown, not of Norristown itself. She gave me that sweet smile and paused (telling me what was coming), then replied, "No offense, but you couldn't." I disagreed, but silently, and I did not take offense.

I have since expanded my study and writing to encompass the eight towns along the Schuylkill River below Reading, and have often encountered the same response (usually expressed less politely). One reader took great exception (two exclamation points' worth!) to a recent Facebook post about Norristown because, "Further more you don't live anywhere near Norristown!!" My two posts about West Conshohocken have also aroused some anger, including from a reader who expressed the reason for her anger: "I just do not like it when someone who has never lived here tries to sum things up simply when our history is diverse and complex." She is correct about the nature of her town, but not about who is qualified to write about its history. I have been professionally trained to do just that.

Another reader struck at the heart of the matter when, responding to my question about whether West Conshohocken still possessed a reason to exist, she wrote: "Who would ever ask a question like that? Oh yea, someone who's never lived/experienced West Conshy." She has a valid point; it is unlikely that such a question could be asked by anyone who grew up and still lived in that place. That's where a professionally installed sense of perspective is required. One of the foundations of graduate study in history is the understanding that one should never attempt to write about a subject he/she has personally experienced, precisely because of that loss of perspective. I attempted to ignore this wisdom during my PhD studies, only to learn just how correct it is.

I am pleased by the sense of community pride that these comments to my posts evidence, but considerably less so by the belief that I could not possibly know anything about a particular town because I did not ever reside there. I have attacked this belief before, because it cripples community efforts to make things better. It's an example of parochialism— that is, narrowness of interests, opinions, or views. I believe, on the contrary, that it is quite possible to be both interested in and helpful to a

---

19. Tolle, *What Killed Downtown?*

local community's efforts to better itself without being a resident of that community. The only issue should be, do I possesses useful knowledge? You can judge that by what I write, whether a specific post applies to your town or not. There is a consistency to my approach, based on research. I have studied the history of the lower Schuylkill Valley, within the broader context of my study of urban history, which, in turn, lies within the context of American history itself.

Please understand that a great deal of my training was in how to find and analyze local sources of information. That usually means information written by people who actually *did* live in the community, and includes such sources as newspapers and diaries. A historian such as I who renders his/her work in broad strokes and primary colors depends on such sources for their close, immediate perspective. I am a voracious reader of local accounts *of all the locations I am researching*. As regards the Conshohockens, I have previously acknowledged reading everything Jack Coll writes, and cheerfully do so again. I have cultivated relationships with the sources of local history in the other Schuylkill River towns as well, whose assistance I also openly acknowledge. The writing of history is a collegial effort; it cannot properly be done alone.

For the record, I make no pretense at being an "expert" (whatever that is) on any of the towns about which I write, with the partial exception of Norristown, which I have studied at some length. I have, however, done considerable research on the eight towns on the lower Schuylkill River, and believe myself generally knowledgeable about their broad historical arcs.

The pattern is clear. All eight towns have commonalities that are much more important than their differences. They all came into existence for the same reason and they all assumed a common shape, again for the same reason. None varied much from the regional pattern of a riverside mill town, although Norristown, as the county seat, added a new dimension. They all grew into locally focused communities, whose residents largely lived, worked, and worshipped within the municipal boundaries. That work was in the "smokestack" industries, and these provided the jobs for the successive waves of immigrants that would populate each town. They all prospered, subject to the vagaries of the national economy (e.g., the Great Depression), until they all fell on hard times after the 1950s.

I am a historian, but if you have been reading my posts, you have encountered my favorite expression: "That was then, this is now, and things have changed." The fundamental realities of life along the river have changed, and thus the once-common condition and histories of the river towns have begun to diverge. I offer the Conshohockens, Phoenixville, and Pottstown as examples of that divergence. The Schuylkill River towns are no longer all alike, but neither do they exist in their individual vacuums. The force besieging the Conshohockens is the same, and I would like to think that both municipal governments and residents realize that, and that their response should thus be as united as possible. Earlier, I pointed out yet another similarity between Pottstown and Norristown, one of many. Bridgeport's ethnic issues reflect its closeness to Norristown, and their resolution will also. Royersford and Spring City have always been "the twin boroughs," and still share a great deal, despite occupying different counties. The list goes on, except for Phoenixville. This means that all those truly interested in the improvement of their community should stay abreast of what is happening in other communities like theirs.

Sheer accumulation of knowledge about the past is fascinating and to be encouraged, but for those whose focus is the future, it is irrelevant. Knowing what has changed is necessary if one desires to improve his/her present and future. I try to put urban history in the service of urban activism, because activists will continue to make mistakes as long as they continue to believe in myths about why things are the way they are. The odds are stacked heavily against them as it is, and parochialism only makes things worse. This is not about listening to me; it is about listening to all those who can aid you, regardless of their physical location.

The experience of your town is not unique, and ideas for a better future need not come from within your town alone. What has worked elsewhere in towns similar to yours is worth considering, and what hasn't should just be rejected without wasting your time. Your knowledge of what might work, what probably won't—and of the distinction between them—is crucial for the future of your community. The problems that each community faces are much larger than the community itself, and no community by itself can be a match for them. Those who are united in understanding this, who realize that they are truly "all in this together," and who are willing to accept the help of knowledgeable "outsiders" will fare better in this unequal contest. Shared knowledge can only improve the otherwise very bad odds that our older urban centers still face. That's why I do what I do.

2/27/15

Crime and Section 8: You *Can* Make a Difference

During August and September of 2014, I published a series of posts on the Housing Choice Voucher Program, the most infamous component of what is known as "Section 8." I focused on the Montgomery County Housing Authority (MCHA), and on the disconnect between Bureaucracy World and the real world, and pointed this out:

> "The fiercest critics of the MCHA are those who live in the real world, often near its clients. They view the problems on an individual basis, and at no small risk to themselves. They know something is wrong, not just because of the numbers around them, but in the behavior of all too many of the program's beneficiaries, *their neighbors*."

I'm pleased to tell you about a few neighbors in Pottstown, Pennsylvania, who, after realizing what was wrong, decided to do something about it. It's a story of a small victory achieved after much effort. That's why Pottstown should be pleased that it has such citizens.

On April 15, 2013, *Goldencockroach.com* posted the first of several articles about a woman named Tracey Accor, a single parent and, it would appear, a serial criminal, with drugs being a recurrent theme. She had just moved from one house in Pottstown—after trashing it—to another. She brought her Housing Choice Voucher with her. She had somehow managed to retain it, despite having been the frequent target of the Pottstown police and the subject of a complaint filed with the Montgomery County Housing Authority by her previous landlord. The change of address did not alter her habits, but it brought her close to residents who care about their neighborhood, and were willing to step forward and do something.

These people saw their neighborhood being damaged by a "family" (of differing numbers) living in squalor and in defiance of pretty much every law and standard of human conduct, including that of proper child care. They contacted the police, and then they went further. That's because they learned that Tracey Accor's residence next to them was being substantially subsidized by the MCHA. They began to pursue the matter, at no small risk to themselves. I say that because they lived near to the residence in question, and had every reason to fear retaliation. One of these individuals emailed Joel Johnson, director of the MCHA, on May 30, 2014. He informed Johnson of the many violations of the law that were ongoing, and asked for an investigation. Johnson replied on August 27. He apologized for the delay, informed the writer that the investigation was "ongoing and active," and thanked him for his "new information."

If the May 30 inquiry was "new information," then the MCHA was already well aware of the situation by that date. That made the delayed reply both hopeful and worrisome at the same time. A matter already under way in May might actually be close to resolution by the end of August, right?

Wrong.

The writer was not deterred by bureaucratic delay. He kept sending emails, to keep up the pressure. They make for depressing reading, particularly when you factor in the passage of time. The resident faithfully reported a consistent pattern of misconduct that certainly included violations of MCHA regulations. In one reply, the MCHA reminded the resident that even if the voucher was revoked, any eviction was solely up to the landlord, not the MCHA. Not a good sign, but the writer would not give up.

Finally, an email dated December 31 from the MCHA informed the writer that as of January 1, 2015, Tracey Accor would no longer possess a housing choice voucher. Remember that back in 2013, the landlord at her previous residence had filed a complaint, and that Joel Johnson had termed our writer's email as "new information" in May 2014? *Goldencockroach.com* estimates that it required 2.5 years for Tracey Accor to lose her voucher, and she would know. The complaint that I was able to track required seven months, despite periodic stimulation by email.

That is clearly too long. Unfortunately, I am willing to believe that it is probably the norm for such actions, even the ones that are aggressively pursued by the citizen complainers. I'm also not going to make it personal and suggest that Joel Johnson or any of his staff were deliberately dogging it. The wheels of government, as powered by federal regulations, grind exceedingly slowly. That's not a defense, by the way. I do not approve; I merely understand, and part of what I understand is that venting on Facebook doesn't speed things up.

And what about the owner of the building during all this time? Didn't he know what was going on? Didn't he care? The answer to the last two questions appear to be "yes," and "no." In the interest of full disclosure— and because I hold slumlords in even lower regard than I hold poverty scammers—the landlord's name is Sam Essam Shedid (the spelling seems to vary). He bears a responsibility for what happened, but more for the fact that things continued to happen, which he did nothing about. I want to contrast his (non)reaction to what was happening on his property to the response of the owner of Tracey Accor's previous residence, who filed a complaint with the MCHA. His name is Chris Dailey, and if I am going to publish the names of landlords who do wrong or do nothing, then it is only fair that I mention landlords like Dailey, who try to do right. So, if you're looking for a rental property in Pottstown, you know someone to avoid and someone worth a look.

This is the very definition of a "small victory." Tracey Accor lost her voucher, which hopefully can now go to someone more honest, and these are two points to the good. On the other hand, it is unlikely that the loss has spurred her to more responsible behavior, so the problem hasn't been solved. In fact, it's just been relocated. In a final indignity, it is reported that Accor has just moved to another address, whose renter is also reputedly a voucher holder.

A great many people would say that the effort wasn't worth it. They are wrong. They are also the ones who would rather rail against the darkness than light a candle, and that is worse than being wrong. They are also the ones who have helped to render Section 8 into the myth that it has become. So I will conclude this post with a tribute to those who are willing to make the effort for a better neighborhood. Pottstown is the better for those I have been writing about, and I continue to believe that its sister towns on the Schuylkill River that face the same problems possess such residents also. This subject can't wait for my current every-two-weeks publication schedule, so next week I'll take it up again, and talk about that title of "myth" I apply to Section 8, and why that is the real problem.

3/6/15

Crime and Section 8: Blaming a Victim?

Last week I related the tale of a few Pottstown residents who decided to fight back against crime and drugs in their community. They hounded the Montgomery County Housing Authority (MCHA) to remove a housing choice voucher from a woman who was blatantly violating the rules. It took many months, but was eventually successful; in fact, these citizens were rather more successful than the Pottstown police in dealing with this woman. I commended this last week, and I shall continue to do so. But I have a question about the affair, one that attempts to introduce some perspective into the issue, which I believe is sorely needed. This is why I often refer to myself as the "Wet Blanket of Reality," and why I am never radical enough for those who see the world through the lens of their ideology. I know better, but here goes.

It's time to ask the question that has been nagging at me as I read the continuing Facebook and blog posts about this story. Section 8 is the featured topic, but isn't this story really more about crime than Section 8? Tracey Accor continued to have the MCHA (that means you, the taxpayers) pay a portion of her rent for much too long a period of time, but the abuse of Section 8 may have been the least of the offenses committed by her and the various residents of 377 North Charlotte Street.

Why did her neighbors place the greater focus on one targets—the voucher program—than on the perpetrator and her crimes? Aren't we, in a sense, blaming a victim? Yes, the way the Housing Choice Voucher Program was written and is administered virtually invites abuse, but that excuse does not fly with people, so why apply it to government programs? Isn't abuse *abuse*, regardless?

There is definitely a very relevant factor here, not so much rational (read: financial) as visceral, but no less real or important for that fact. To see daily evidence of criminal activity is certainly cause enough for anger, but to know that a neighborhood criminal is living on *your* dollar, partially subsidized by a program designed to help the needy but otherwise law-abiding, really sticks in the craw. Facebook's "Pottstown Homeowner at Large" put this feeling quite succinctly: "Here we are, working, paying our taxes and contributing to society, but by us doing the right thing we are enabling others to do 'nothing'." The writer was being kind; taxpayers are enabling such people to do positive harm to their communities, and that is much worse than nothing.

The results of this quite legitimate feeling, multiplied by the many who experience something like it somewhere else, produce a tragedy no one intended, and visits it on those who don't deserve it. The voucher program's weaknesses and glacially slow procedures turn people not just against the criminals who abuse them, but the program itself. The law-abiding neighbors of its abusers are victims, and have collected a multitude of very personal—and thus quite valid—reasons to hate the program. The greater numbers of victims here, unfortunately, are those voucher holders who *do* obey the law and the program regulations, because they don't have to live anywhere near the violator to be hurt. It is this last group of people that scammers like Tracey Accor truly victimize, because amid the almost-daily evidence of a criminal mentality, the thing people tend to remember is the Section 8 Voucher part.

We simply must establish a sense of perspective, and see the problem for what it is—a crime problem, not a Section 8 problem. Section 8 is most certainly part of the problem, and in its present form cannot be the solution. But to conflate Section 8 with crime is to do a great disservice to the complexity of the reality that is the Housing Choice Voucher Program.

So, keeping with my reality thing, what does the future hold for the program, and thus for the innocent victims of its shortcomings? There are—in theory—three broad options regarding the future of housing choice vouchers. In truth, however, two of those are not options, because they require government action. Only the third is possible, because it can be undertaken by private citizens.

First, the government could simply eliminate the program. To those who recommend this, I ask only, "as opposed to what?" If you think your neighborhood and your community's streets are unsafe now, just try to imagine them after enormous numbers of people who cannot afford a place to live on what they earn are cast into the streets. Calls to simply eliminate the program are many things, beginning with un-Christian. They are also pure posturing, designed to score visceral points without having to actually be serious about the issue. Simply eliminating "welfare" programs solves nothing, and only makes things worse. It won't happen.

Second, Congress could undertake a wholesale, thoughtful rewrite of the program, addressing the flaws that everyone knows about by now. If anyone thinks that a Republican-led Congress will undertake such an effort any time in the near future, please contact me. I have a bridge to sell you. And please, don't write to me about how a Democrat-led Congress wouldn't do this either; that's not relevant to reality, and therefore another example of pure posturing. When either political party comes up with an improvement, then my attitude will change. I'm not holding my breath, and neither should you.

What this means is that we all must continue to live with (and perhaps next to) the results of a horribly flawed program, because our government is not going to do anything. In the face of this unfortunate truth, that leaves only the third option: people, within each of our communities, should not attack the voucher program, but should focus on those who violate it—landlords and residents alike. That's the only real option, if your goal is to make things better, and not just bitch. Let's not just give thanks for those citizens willing to undertake such a thankless, repetitious task as prodding a federal agency, but emulate their example. Citizens must get involved, report housing choice voucher violations to the authority, and then keep on hounding it relentlessly. That's what the citizens in Pottstown who I wrote about earlier did. The story demonstrates what can be done, but fully acknowledges the time and effort required. To call something time-consuming, difficult, and productive of, at best, a "small victory" is pretty much the definition of a "wet blanket," but that is the reality.

If you ask the people who hounded the MCHA for a long time just to remove one voucher from its holder, I'm not sure they would say things are really any better. North Charlotte Street in Pottstown has much greater problems than abuse of the voucher system; witness recent headlines about drug and weapons seizures a few blocks up from our subject building. But it also still has those citizens I wrote about, and others who keep the public's focus on the problem, so there is hope. We must remember that for them, the problem is not only real, it's real close. That makes what they do not only a thankless task, but also a downright risky one. Perspective must tell us that also.

Perspective also says that the people I wrote about last week only lit one candle in the struggle against urban crime, so the view is not much improved. But what if many others, in other communities, undertook such actions? Even a wet blanket couldn't put out the fires they would kindle.

ABOUT THE AUTHOR

Michael E. Tolle has lived a variety of experiences that have influenced both his selection of a late-in-life career and how he pursues it. The author of *What Killed Downtown? Norristown, Pennsylvania, from Main Street to the Malls*, he blogs regularly in support of urban revival in America's small towns, using the eight towns on the lower Schuylkill River as his examples.[20]

Michael was born in Kansas but raised on Long Island, New York. As a college student, he spent a summer in Vietnam as a volunteer for the World Relief Commission, delivering commodities to refugees. In 1969, after receiving a bachelor of science in foreign service (BSFS) from Georgetown University, he began a year-long study program in the Vietnamese language at Roslyn, Virginia, before returning to Vietnam as an assistant relief and rehabilitation advisor for the US Agency for International Development (USAID). He spent two years in Vietnam, first in a province resettling refugees, and then in Saigon. As the deputy chief of the Refugee Division, he was responsible for the day-to-day operations in support of refugees throughout the country.

After returning to the United States, Michael started a business that specialized in home remodeling, energy conservation, and alternative energy projects. In 1983, in support of his wife's career, Michael became the primary caregiver for their two sons. Once the boys were in school, Michael began graduate studies at Villanova University, earning a master's degree in history, and then attended Temple University to pursue a PhD, completing all requirements except the dissertation.

Michael taught history at Delaware County Community College and Montgomery County Community College until early 2006, when his wife's career sent them to San Francisco, where they reside today. Michael continues his research, focusing on the history and future of our nation's small towns.

---

20. For Michael Tolle's blog, *The More Things Change…*, visit http://themorethingschange.michaeltolle.com/

Made in the USA
Middletown, DE
29 October 2015